A Distant Prospect of Wessex: Archaeology and the Past in the Life and Works of Thomas Hardy

Martin J. P. Davies

Illustrated with photographs taken by the author

Archaeopress

Gordon House
276 Banbury Road
Oxford OX2 7ED

www.archaeopress.com

ISBN 978 1 905739 41 7

© Archaeopress and Martin J. P. Davies

All rights reserved. No part of this book may be reproduced, stored in retrieval system,
or transmitted, in any form or by any means, electronic, mechanical, photocopying or otherwise,
without the prior written permission of the copyright owners.

Printed in England by Information Press, Oxford

Cover images
A view of Stonehenge from *English Pictures Drawn with Pen and Pencil* by S. Manning and S.G. Green
published by The Religious Tract Society, London *c.* 1880
Statue of Thomas Hardy by William Barnes, adjacent to the Dorset County Museum, Dorchester

Map of Wessex, page viii
After the Macmillan edition of 'Under the Greenwood Tree', London 1929,
courtesy of The Thomas Hardy Association

*For my parents,
and all those who have taught me, including those I have taught*

Deo Gratias

Contents

Acknowledgements	iv
Preface	vi
Chapter One Introduction: Perspectives on the Past	1

Chapter Two
    Ancient Inspiration from the Science of the Imagination:
    Hardy, Archaeology, and Wessex (a Name Revived)
	10

Chapter Three Novelist and 'Born Archaeologist': Hardy's Personal Writings	36
Chapter Four Hardy's Roman Town: The Setting for *The Mayor of Casterbridge*	62
Chapter Five Ancient and Modern Collide: *Tess of the d'Urbervilles* and Stonehenge	90
Chapter Six Barrows and Beyond: Landscapes of the Past	126
Chapter Seven Personal Memories and Ancient Remains: The Poetry	157
Chapter Eight Beyond Wessex: Architecture and Ideas in Oxford and Cornwall	188
Bibliography	206
Index of People and Places	211

Acknowledgements

This book has its origin in my doctoral thesis submitted to the University of Leicester in 2002 (awarded 2003). In this connection, first and foremost, I must express my gratitude to Professor Vince Newey for allowing me to pursue my very personal quest under his expert and patient supervision. He is a fine teacher, a sure guide, and a real friend – in short, the ideal complement to renewing my learning at the University of Leicester after a gap of two dozen years.

I acknowledge most warmly their welcome, and the very generous and extensive help given to me, both on my two research visits and by correspondence in the interim, by the Curator and Secretary of the Dorset County Museum, Mr Richard de Peyer and his staff. I should like to thank especially Mrs Lilian Swindall, Honorary Curator of the Thomas Hardy Memorial Collection who has patiently answered my many awkward queries.

Mrs Josephine Pentney most generously allowed me to use her 1980 lecture 'Archaeology and Thomas Hardy', providing me with a photocopy of her complete text with a slide and notes.

Graeme Barker, Head of the School of Archaeology at the University of Leicester at the time of my research (and now Disney Professor of Archaeology in the University of Cambridge) kindly gave of his expertise, books, and advice in two extensive interviews.

I much enjoyed the hospitality of Mrs Doris Haggett of Vartrees House, her home built by Hardy's friend Hermann Lea and named by Hardy, who kindly loaned me books and talked to me of her Hardy associations.

Thank you to the staff of the National Trust both at Hardy's Cottage for their courteous welcome and at Max Gate, whose Custodian, Mr Andrew Leah, kindly answered my questions by the 'Druid Stone' while showing me round the property; he also gave me the map that enabled me to visit Rainbarrows.

I express my renewed and heartfelt thanks to my friends Julian and Irene Piper who provided me with a second home during my many visits to Leicester, and patiently solved innumerable tricky and potentially disastrous problems with my computer.

Several other friends have given me help and encouragement of various kinds, recommending, lending, and giving me books, in particular Brian Simmons, and Sue Phyall; also Philip Neville and Janet Mackenzie. Arthur Durrant and my late friend Malcolm Blackwell gave valuable help with the computer. David Marsden, Hardy enthusiast, late friend and neighbour, lent me two invaluable books, and sadly died just before I finished my first revisions to the text.

My late friend Richard Gosling very kindly undertook the onerous task of proof reading the original draft of the whole thesis, and loaned me both books and expert knowledge. Special thanks are due to Donald Drew for his persistent encouragement to undertake and complete this project.

The present study emerged from the inspirational MA course 'Language, the Arts, and Education' run by Dr Peter Abbs at Sussex University; his support helped me take my first steps on the road back to Leicester. Peter Braggins encouraged these further studies and subsequently suggested a return to Leicester for this project.

Warm thanks to Nadia Durrani of *Current World Archaeology* who put me in touch with Archaeopress after fruitless years of trying to interest the literary world in this research.

Last, and far from least, I record the debt I owe to Alf Sinfield, the doyen of English teachers, who first taught me to write about Literature.

Many thanks to Andrew Corbett for checking the proofs.

M.J.P.D.

Preface

'... some ruin bibber, randy for antique ...' (Philip Larkin, 'Church Going') – and rather
keen on a literary legend as well?

My interest in archaeology dates back to an almost accidental first visit to Greece in 1982, a revelatory experience that I recounted in a magazine article. I returned from Athens determined not only to visit Greece as often as possible, but also to learn as much as I could about archaeology and visit as many sites in Britain as opportunity would allow. Being an English teacher of thirty-five years' experience, I suppose I should claim that an interest in Thomas Hardy's work dates back to studying *The Mayor of Casterbridge* at 'A' Level, but, in common with my students of that book, I admit that the opposite is the case; in fact it was only on being offered the opportunity to teach the book in 1994 that I returned to 'give Hardy a second chance'. That same year I began Dr (later Professor) Peter Abbs's two-year MA course at the University of Sussex, 'Language, the Arts, and Education', which allowed me in the second year to write, with boundless enthusiasm and inevitable superficiality, a dissertation on the influence of archaeology on the arts. To pursue this theme further, there could be no better literary subject than Thomas Hardy.

Both of these disparate topics – Hardy and archaeology – enjoy a wide and enduring following of long standing. Among the sciences (though, as many archaeologists would argue, their chosen discipline is one of the humanities), perhaps only archaeology has the inherent ability to arouse popular, imaginative interest to match the technical specialisation necessary for its professional pursuit. In 2010, for example, no fewer than 500 books were published – in English – on ancient Egypt alone. Thomas Hardy seems to attract a comparable level of interest, again, among general readership as well as in the realms of academe: all his works remain in print, and all eight of Hardy's most celebrated novels, plus the early *A Pair of Blue Eyes*, and the complete poems, are available in one or more of the budget-priced series of paperbacks; one academic web-site, moreover, lists over seventy biographical and critical books about the author.

But why try to put these two topics together? In a television programme some years ago, I heard Lucinda Lambton give one of the best definitions of education that I have come across: the ability to make connections; and it is in a spirit of liberal, educational exploration that I bring together Thomas Hardy and archaeology.

When I re-read *The Mayor of Casterbridge*, with twelve years accumulated knowledge of archaeological sites, artefacts, and ideas behind me, the small collection of allusions in the book to actual Roman and prehistoric features in and around Dorchester automatically gained resonance, giving an extra, unanticipated, dimension to a visit to the town while I was part-way through my re-reading of the novel.

Perhaps this was a purely subjective coincidence of interests; yet, here was a famous author who grew up in one of the world's most significant archaeological regions, whose eclectic interests included archaeology, whose life-span of almost eighty-eight years embraced the transformation of archaeology from the realm of the dilettante collector to that of a complex scientific discipline, and whose works made limited but frequent references to the subject. My interest was aroused. How much was Hardy concerned with archaeology *per se* amongst his plethora of interests? How much did he actually know about it? Did his Classical education, architectural training, and visit to Italy impinge on his perception of the mysterious traces of British prehistory and the Roman occupation with which he had grown up? How does reference to archaeology fit in with his overall narrative, aesthetic, and philosophical scheme? Such was the range of questions which arose in my mind once the conjunction of subjects had been made.

This study was never conceived as one of literary criticism only and the proportion of such material in particular chapters is dependent on the nature of the works dealt with. Two disparate topics, an author and a subject in which he was interested, will be unified in this examination. The two run along parallel lines, but the unifying factor in the dichotomy is always the man Thomas Hardy. My reading of Hardy is thus only one part of the discussion: often, I will digress, and Hardy will appear to be set aside, for part of the aim of the research is to discover, gather, and synthesise all the archaeological materials that are employed in his works. He is nonetheless implicitly present, since these are the very materials he selected to fashion into this significant and hitherto neglected aspect of his art. In this I am following, in a specialised way, in the footsteps of Herman Lea and his successors who identified and catalogued the settings in Hardy's works. Much of this knowledge is not otherwise readily available to Hardy's readers; conversely, archaeological texts usually make only the most fleeting reference – if any – to the appearance of archaeological sites and artefacts in fiction. The evident imbalance in the Bibliography between books on Hardy and related topics and those about archaeology is more apparent than real: most of those on the latter have provided only brief references.

****

In examining Hardy's novels, I have referred to the Penguin Classics edition as being reliable and readily available to both scholars and general readers. The editors are listed in the Bibliography along with details of the texts of the short stories and poems.

The presentation of footnotes and the Bibliography is in accordance with the MLA Handbook[1] throughout, with the exception that I have preferred to include initial 'p.' or 'pp.' for page numbers as being clearer in meaning, and book titles are italicised rather than underlined. To prevent confusion, in poems I have used line number(s) (l./ll.) for short poems or referred to stanzas (st.) or couplets (coup.) in longer works.

---

[1] Joseph Gibaldi, *MLA Handbook for Writers of Research Papers*, 4th ed. (New York: The Modern Language Association of America, 1995).

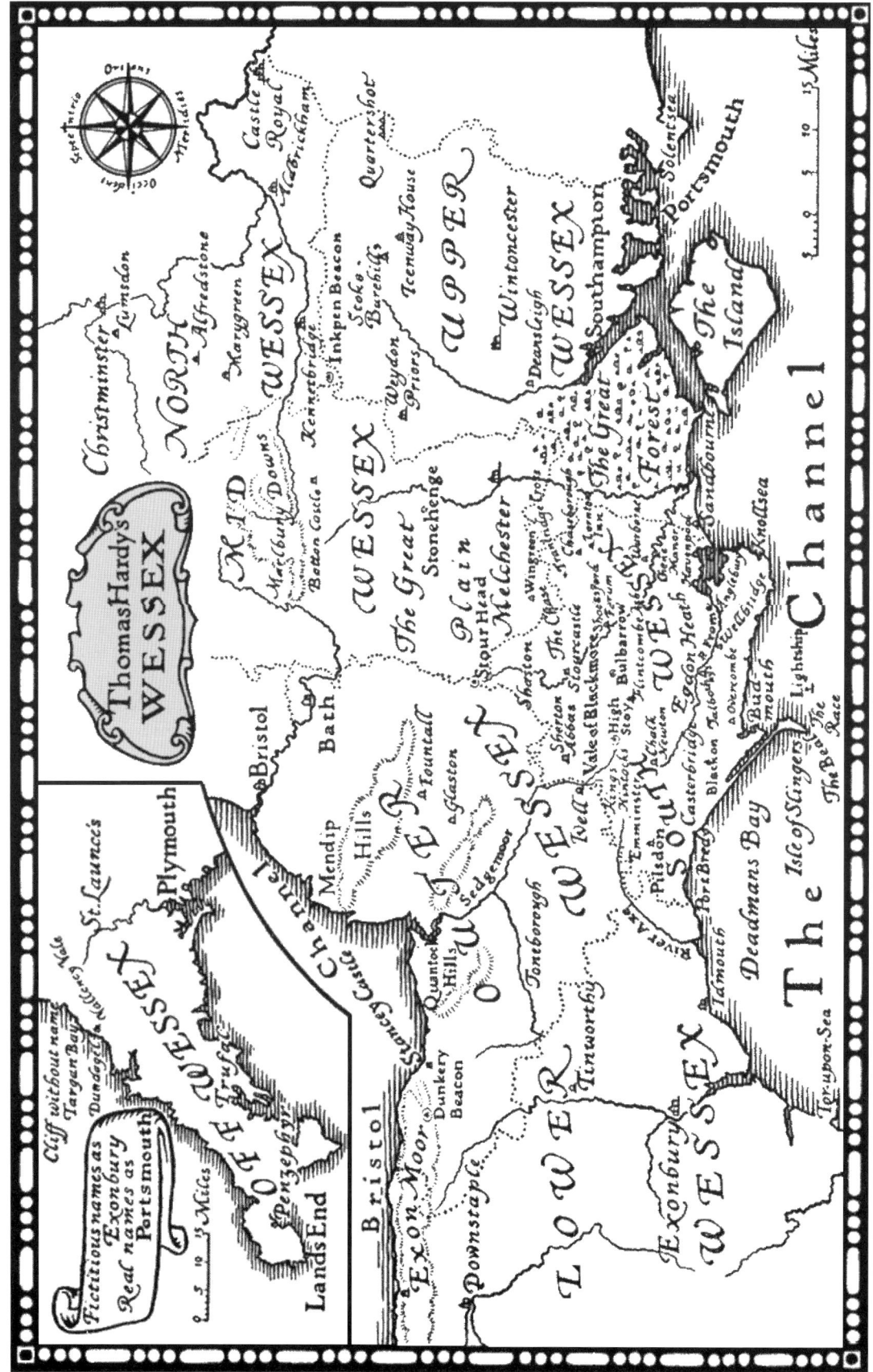

Chapter One

INTRODUCTION: PERSPECTIVES ON THE PAST

> 'Time present and Time past
> Are both perhaps present in Time future
> And Time future contained in Time past.'
>
> T.S. Eliot, Four Quartets – 'Burnt Norton.'

Many would regard *Tess of the d'Urbervilles* as Thomas Hardy's greatest novel, and surely a prime candidate for its most memorable scene must be the climactic events at Stonehenge, one of the few universally recognisable archaeological sites in the world. Few readers of *The Mayor of Casterbridge* can fail to notice the constant references to archaeological remains, and another of the finest Wessex novels, *The Return of the Native*, uses an ancient barrow as an almost magnetic focus for its narrative. Less obvious is the occurrence of archaeological references in many other of Hardy's writings, including poems and short stories; and even his attempt at a society novel, *The Hand of Ethelberta*, includes reference to the ubiquitous barrows of the Wessex landscape, and to the pursuits of an archaeological society (the 'Imperial Archaeological Association'). Yet, as even a cursory reading of his widely allusive works will show, Hardy's interests were catholic and his reading voracious, encouraged from young childhood by his mother's aspirations for her frail son. The combination of the imaginative and the scientific were evident from this early stage: at the age of nine, he was reading scientific books and mathematics as well as the Classics. The mix of interests is significant in his first professional career, for before becoming an author, he qualified as an architect and won prizes for his work. Throughout his long life, he continued to enjoy all the arts, especially painting, as well as practising his own art of literature. He made himself expert in the history of the Napoleonic period, and was an authority on rural Dorset. As he grew older, he became acquainted with many of the leading contemporary minds with whom he corresponded about current affairs, and developed an enthusiasm for many other disciplines including astronomy and the developing sciences such as geology and biology.

Can archaeology be regarded as any more than just one example of all his many interests, and is Hardy's use of matters archaeological more than simply local colouring, part of the distinctive scenery and old world Wessexness which made the writer legendary in his own lifetime? Archaeology cannot be said to be the *subject* of more than isolated examples of Hardy's work: apart from a scattering of journalistic and non-fiction pieces, only the minor and relatively unsatisfactory story *A Tryst at an Ancient Earthwork* is actually *about* archaeology; all the other references are apparently incidental to Hardy's main themes.

Few writers before Hardy used archaeological sites and material in fiction, though twentieth-century readers have become accustomed to a plethora of fiction which involves the discipline, an adjunct to the increasing popularity of archaeology among a non-specialist readership. J.B. Priestley's wife Jacquetta Hawkes was an archaeologist and writer, but her husband found no inspiration in the subject. Agatha Christie, however, whose second husband was the archaeologist Max Mallowan, set three novels in archaeological contexts: *Death on the Nile*, and two actually set at archaeological excavations, viz *Murder in Mesopotamia* and *Appointment with Death*. She is the only notable novelist apart from Hardy who actually engaged directly in archaeological excavation, and, to an extent like Hardy, she came to it by chance. On Mallowan's dig in Syria, his new wife became involved in cleaning and recording finds, and her experiences there are recorded in the delightful *Come, Tell Me How You Live – an archaeological memoir*, written under the name Agatha Christie-Mallowan. Mary Renault's fine series of novels covers the whole story of ancient Greece from the mythical age of Theseus to the dawn of the Hellenistic period after the death of Alexander and weaves much well-known extant archaeology in a quite seamless way into her fictional tapestry which recreates the ancient world. Rosemary Sutcliff's classic 1954 children's adventure *The Eagle of the Ninth*, subject of a 2010 film, similarly brings together an artefact and a historical event, the loss of the Ninth Legion in the land of the Picts – though lifelong fans of the book are inevitably disappointed to learn that the Eagle (now at Reading Museum) is definitely not from a legionary standard and the mysterious disappearance of the Legion did not occur in Britain! More recently, Penelope Lively's *Treasures of Time*, Peter Ackroyd's *First Light*, and Adam Thorpe's *Ulverton* are each set at a prehistoric burial mound (Ackroyd's in Dorset), while Penelope Fitzgerald's *The Golden Child* is a comedy thriller in a fictionalised British Museum about the eponymous artefact from an invented African culture. In Iris Murdoch's most extraordinary novel, *The Philosopher's Pupil*, the fictional Ennistone Ring is restored, Seamus Heaney's poems include reference to the prehistoric past including 'bog bodies', and indeed through the twentieth century, a host of novels and poems show increasingly a fascination with archaeology as the discipline has become part of mainstream culture.

Any reader who might expect a similarity between the use of archaeological reference in Hardy's fiction and works such as Mary Renault's would, however, be disappointed; but Hardy's use of archaeology does have something in common with both *Treasures of Time* and *First Light* in that they deal with sites from British prehistory. Any work that uses a Biblical or Homeric setting is automatically constrained by centuries and millennia of cultural accretion. In contrast, the symbolic or aesthetic use of material from a pre-literate environment allows not only imaginative scope, but predisposes the artist to a more diffuse and philosophical approach, freed from the specifics of deeply ingrained myth or historical interpretation.

Aside from the frequent archaeological allusion in Hardy's works, we find strong evidence of his interest in archaeology from his contemporaries. Edmund Blunden noted that, in 1927, the year before Hardy's death: 'One of his lifelong enthusiasms found a new occasion … when a beautiful Roman pavement was unearthed at the Dorchester Foundry. With Mrs Hardy he paid more than one visit to the site. In old days this would have meant a fine page or two in a new Wessex tale.'[1] (This mosaic floor was lifted and re-laid in the Dorchester County Museum just before Hardy's death.) A letter from the Reverend T. Perkins, dated 23/8/1906, requesting an article from Hardy on the archaeology of Dorset, includes: 'I am sure you know a lot more about archaeology than most people, and at any rate, anything you write would be sure to be most charming reading. I don't want dry-as-dust archaeology and extracts from old deeds or pedigrees ... I want something that will interest people at large, not deadly dull archives ... the growing popularity of Dorset is surely due to your novels.'[2] An interview with Hardy, about a proposed sale of Stonehenge, by the literary editor of *The Daily Chronicle*, James Milne, was published on 24th August 1899. It refers to the site as 'a national relic, and now a literary monument', and to the author of *Tess of the Durbervilles* as 'the one-time architect and born archaeologist'.[3]

In one of the earlier literary biographies, Evelyn Hardy notes, while writing of *The Mayor of Casterbridge*, that 'Hardy was not merely interested in ancient remains as an archaeologist; he could penetrate the past imaginatively and clothe these hoary hulks of antiquity with vanished magnificence.'[4] More recently, Claire Tomalin's best-selling biography fortuitously describes Hardy the poet as, 'like an archaeologist uncovering objects that have not been seen for many decades ... some curious bones and broken bits, and some shining treasures.'[5] What is interesting in all these diverse sources – particularly his contemporaries who took it as a given – is not only that the authors know that Hardy was an enthusiast (and one with expertise in the subject), but that all recognise that archaeology provides imaginative material that the great writer had proved he was well qualified to exploit. It is notable that in regard to science and imagination, Hardy proved to be the very opposite of Heinrich Schliemann, the passionate Homerist whose methods and approach were the antithesis of the modern scientific methodology that Hardy so admired. William Borlase, in a damning critique of Schliemann in *Fraser's Review* in 1878, wrote: 'Imagination is a very important qualification for an archaeologist to possess ... but in proportion to the strength of this power, a counterpoise of judgement is necessary ... Dr Schliemann ... must be credited with a vast amount of this sort of unbalanced imagination ... '.[6] It is as if Schliemann muddled science and imagination, whereas Hardy – in both his interests and his practical activity – distinguished the two precisely.

More direct evidence of his precise knowledge is tantalisingly limited. Much of archival importance in all areas of Hardy studies was destroyed at Max Gate not long before the author's death, and the *Life* (defensively attributed to Florence, but largely dictated by Hardy himself) omits much that a researcher would like to know. A primary source is Hardy's eclectic notebooks, but William Greenslade notes that, although twelve notebooks were preserved, 'Many others ... from the 1870s ... would not survive the later Max Gate bonfires.'[7] Hardy himself, his literary executor Sydney Cockerell, and Florence all had a hand in the depredations; indeed the true extent of these notebooks, and other material, can only be guessed at. What

---

[1] Edmund Blunden, *Thomas Hardy* (London: Macmillan, 1951), p.175.
[2] Dorset County Museum Hardy Archives. Manuscript letter no. 1162.
[3] James Gibson, ed., *Thomas Hardy – Interviews and Recollections* (London: Macmillan, 1999), quoted p.58.
[4] Evelyn Hardy, *Thomas Hardy: A Critical Biography* (London: Hogarth Press, 1954), p.196.
[5] Tomalin, Claire, *Thomas Hardy- The Time-Torn Man* (London: Viking, 2006), p.xxiii.
[6] Michael Wood, *In Search of the Trojan War* (London: BBC 1985), p.47, quoted.
[7] William Greenslade, ed., *Thomas Hardy's Facts Notebooks: A Critical Edition* (Aldershot: Ashgate, 2004), p.xv.

we do know is that Hardy's reading, experience, acquaintance, and observations all added up to Andrew D. Radford's observation of 'Hardy's promiscuous discovery of time'.[8]

What *precisely*, I wonder, did Hardy learn from his friend and fellow-Dorsetman General Pitt-Rivers, the founder of modern archaeology and 'greatest of all archaeological excavators' according to Mortimer Wheeler,[9] besides the lifestyle of the very rich? The influence on Hardy of such a signally important figure in the history of scientific archaeology cannot be underestimated. And what did Hardy talk about, apart from *Jude*, when on holiday with the great archaeologist Flinders Petrie or when visited by him at Max Gate in July 1915? Petrie, who, like Hardy, continued in his professional career into his eighties, was the first Edwards Professor of Archaeology at London University and one of his early important projects was to survey

Hardy's grave in Stinsford churchyard

Stonehenge in 1874–1877. It is difficult to imagine that the climactic scene at Stonehenge in *Tess of the d'Urbervilles* did not figure in their conversations. Near the end of Hardy's life, one of a new circle of young friends was T.E. Lawrence, 'Lawrence of Arabia', by that time living in self-imposed obscurity under an alias; he paid weekly visits to the old author from his curious house Clouds Hill near Moreton and he must have found the company of the equally very private and celebrated Hardy very congenial. Lawrence's first contact with the Middle East was as an archaeologist. Having read History at Jesus College Oxford, and writing a thesis on the Crusader castles, he worked as a junior member of the British Museum expedition on the

---

[8] Andrew D. Radford, *Thomas Hardy and the Survivals of Time* (Aldershot: Ashgate, 2003), p.21.
[9] Sir Mortimer Wheeler, *Archaeology from the Earth* (1954; London: Penguin Books, 1956), p.13.

Introduction: Perspectives on the Past

Euphrates at Carchemish under the famous archaeologists D.G. Hogarth and his successor Leonard Woolley during 1911–1914. Immediately prior to the Great War, Lawrence surveyed Sinai for British intelligence under the guise of further archaeological work and visited sites such as Petra. It is surely unlikely that the two men's frequent conversations did not touch on a shared fascination with the past and with archaeology in particular. Another charismatic member of this circle of regular visitors was Siegfried Sassoon whose time at Clare College Cambridge inspired a comic poem, 'Early Chronology', about students' attentions drifting far away during a tutorial on history and archaeology. Again, it is entirely possible that he and Hardy talked about archaeology as well as poetry as they sat within sight of the ancient remains around Max Gate.

Hardy's reference to antiquities in his creative works is almost always couched in the terminology of the antiquarian, and he rarely uses the word archaeology in his limited writings on specifically archaeological subject matter; yet these display the precision and circumspection of the experts he knew, as well as the imaginative insights of the poet, including his reports on the excavations at Max Gate – for Hardy designed and built his home not merely in a true archaeological landscape, but on an archaeological site, and, as Blunden tells us, nearly named the house Conquer Barrow after one of the local features.[10]

***

Now, time is an inevitable function of narrative and most narrative, whether fiction or non-fiction, in verse or prose, is concerned with past time; even a good deal of lyric poetry has a chronological basis. It is a truism, therefore, to state that Thomas Hardy, unusual in being celebrated as poet, novelist, and short story writer, is concerned with the passage and effects of time. What is noteworthy, however, is Hardy's almost obsessive interest in the phenomenon of past time; Andrew D. Radford states that 'the essence of Hardy's art [is] to conjure up the relics of time.'[11] Michael Millgate writes: 'The stimulation of his deepest creative instincts – in fiction, poetry, and drama – seems to have been inseparable from a profound brooding upon the past and upon the practical and philosophical implications of time's passage. That consciousness of mortality ... also informs ... all of Hardy's best work ... '.[12] Hardy's concern with archaeology is one facet of this preoccupation. Indeed, if Hardy's life and career may be said to be a series of enigmas and ambiguities, then his obsession with the past may be viewed as a large jigsaw puzzle of which a large 'archaeology-shaped' piece is missing: the size and outline are very evident, but the precise contents are uncertain and incomplete. The object of this study is to create a picture by giving colour and form to that significant missing piece.

***

As I have indicated in the Preface, this study will have two parallel focuses in exploring the whole gamut of Thomas Hardy's involvement with archaeology. Hardy's life saw the transformation of the dilettante pursuit of the antiquarian into the popular scientifically-based discipline of archaeology, and I shall examine how Hardy became interested in this developing subject in the context of his overall fascination with the past and with the sciences in general.

---
[10] Blunden, p.51.
[11] Radford, p.29.
[12] Michael Millgate, *Thomas Hardy – His Career as a Novelist* (London, Macmillan, 1971), pp.247/248.

Equally, I shall discuss how he responded imaginatively to the physical remains of the ancient past, identifying the sites and objects as they appear in his fiction and poetry, and exploring what use he made of them in the context of each work.

∗∗∗

Our human preoccupation with the past is clearly evidenced by the numerous ways in which we attempt to delineate it: autobiography, researching the family tree, history, archaeology, palaeontology, geology – all are attempts, in personal or academic spheres, to unravel the enigma of what has preceded the present.

The most remote perspective on the past that is possible must surely be that of the inconceivable distances suggested by astronomy; in terms of the Earth, however, geology seeks to reveal the earliest – and very lengthy – chapters in the story of the planet. Both of these disciplines are, *ipso facto*, devoid of humanity. Palaeontology ('the study of old existence') examines extinct and fossilised animals and plants, and, because this includes the remains of the earliest human beings, overlaps with archaeology. Anthropology is, literally, 'the study of man', especially of human society and customs. Chronologically, it is through archaeology that we gain our knowledge of, amongst others, the embryonic phases of civilisation. Archaeology, then, provided a fruitful source of material for Hardy the humane novelist, surrounded as he was from boyhood by the physical remains of the ancient past.

Before proceeding further, it is important to clarify the relationship of archaeology with history. As cognate but discrete disciplines, archaeology ('the study of the ancient') is the study of the human past from objects alone: history is the study of the past primarily from written records alone. The two disciplines overlap in the sense that ancient written materials are often of intrinsic archaeological and artistic merit and are frequently the fruits of archaeological excavation. Protohistory ('primitive' or 'first' history) concerns periods where written accounts are at a rudimentary level of development (and by implication, where archaeology may provide more factual information). Glyn Daniel, writing in 1951, suggests a further nice distinction of a hierarchical kind:

> Archaeology has at the present day two meanings: the study of the material remains of man's past, and the study of the material remains of man's prehistoric past. The first meaning, which for convenience we may refer to as general archaeology, comprises both prehistoric archaeology and historic archaeology ...
>
> There is this very important difference between the prehistoric and the historic archaeologist. In the later periods of man's development *the archaeologist is the handmaiden of history* [my italics] and supplements the story provided by written records. But in the earlier periods the archaeologist is not merely the handmaiden: he is the prime source for writing early history. Prehistory is written from many sources - the material remains of the past, deductions from language, physical anthropology, place names and comparative ethnology. All these are sources which in historical times are auxiliary to the written sources. But in prehistory they are the main sources and archaeology is by far the most important of them.[13]

---

[13] Glyn Daniel, *A Hundred Years of Archaeology* (London: Duckworth, 1950), p.9.

Introduction: Perspectives on the Past

Ancient History, one leg of the Classical Tripos, is more accurately the history of ancient Greece and Rome as drawn from their historians. Beyond such nice distinctions, 'history' in common parlance is the generic term for all study of the past, thus embracing archaeology for practical purposes.

In this study, archaeology will be used in its discrete sense, but also with the cluster of nuances that the term embraces. These need to be explained. Firstly, archaeology is the name of a scientific discipline, though practitioners are very much divided about the extent to which (if any) it is really part of the humanities (the link with history is both inevitable and complicating here). Secondly, the word may be used in a verbal sense to imply the activity involved, especially excavation. Thirdly, as a noun distinct from the embracing name of the discipline, the word is used in two rather different ways: either in the sense of the stratum or strata of archaeological remains found beneath the present-day ground level ('the excavators came upon a mass of archaeology three feet below the ground'); or in the more general sense of the archaeological remains (features and artefacts) of a particular area or country (such as the Archaeology of Wiltshire or the Archaeology of Greece) – in which case it becomes a proper noun. In this study, as I have already indicated, both of the principal uses of the word (academic discipline, and objects or places) will be engaged, for Hardy's knowledge and interest was in the subject generally (including its practical application); whereas in examining the topic in Hardy's works, I intend to discuss both the way he uses archaeological objects and places (the final nuance above), and the way his understanding of them is revealed (the academic discipline).

***

Why, even though I have given clues in the Preface, should archaeology be a legitimate focus at all in a study of Thomas Hardy's fascination with the past? His catholic interests and eclectic reading might surely make geology, astronomy, or history an equally apt choice. I shall certainly draw on these subjects in my study, but their use by the author is far more limited than archaeology, and Hardy's contact with them was either peripheral (geology was just one facet of the whole Victorian discovery of the age of the Earth) or learned for a purpose: astronomy, though a long-standing interest, he studied in depth specifically in preparation for *Two on a Tower*; his interest in the Napoleonic period was pursued in the British Museum and elsewhere like the Royal Hospital, Chelsea where he met veterans of Wellington's army. History was certainly a more substantial interest for Hardy, especially in his abiding enthusiasm for the Napoleonic period because of its family significance and its importance in the recent folk-memory of Dorset. The intention of writing a monumental work set in this period is mentioned in virtually every chapter of the *Life* and eventually came to fruition in *The Dynasts* and its precursors *The Trumpet-Major, A Tradition of Eighteen Hundred and Four, The Melancholy Hussar of the German Legion,* and various poems. However, this obsession is with a particular period rather than with history as a discipline, and the mass of other allusions to past events does not amount to an interest in the subject of history *per se*, but rather in the past generally.

With archaeology it is otherwise. The historian R.J. White opens his *Hardy and History* with: 'The climax of Hardy's lifelong fascination with history came with the publication of *The Dynasts* ... '.[14] Nonetheless, he continues shortly thereafter:

---

[14] R. J. White, edited James Gibson, *Hardy and History* (London: Macmillan, 1974), p.1.

> Hardy's archaeological endeavours are borne out at the Dorchester Museum and in a number of contributions to archaeological journals [an overstatement, but an allowable one] … If he had not become a working novelist he could well have lived his life as a professional architect, just as he might have become a classical scholar or an archaeologist. … The one art that may safely be declared outside his scope, however, is that of the historian.[15]

Archaeology, then, is pivotal to our understanding of Hardy as a man, and as an artist, both in illuminating his use of materials and in revealing his conception of the past.

> Before he was able to read, let alone embark on researching his family history or the Napoleonic period, Hardy was growing up in a landscape dotted with prehistoric remains and replete with evidences of the Roman occupation; later he engaged in excavation and wrote and spoke about the subject; he knew archaeologists and admired them in contradiction to the outmoded pre-scientific dilettantism of the antiquarians. In a mass of Hardy's works, the archaeological past is as naturally occurring and inevitable as are the ancient remains pervasive and inescapable in the landscape of his native county: as such, archaeology demands to receive specialised attention.

Notwithstanding Hardy's lifelong interest in archaeology, Michael Millgate, in examining the author's perception of the past, confirms the importance of the Napoleonic period in Hardy's thinking. He notes that Elliott Felkin kept a record of some conversations with Hardy in 1919:

> Talking about time, he said that he always saw it stretch away in a long blue line like a railway line on the left (the past) and disappearing just round the crossing on his right. 'It's like a railway line covered with a blue haze, and it goes uphill till 1900 and then goes over the hill and disappears to about the middle of the century, and then it rises again up to about 1800, and then it disappears altogether.
>
> Hardy's historical imagination was apparently distinguished by elements of discontinuity and by a peculiar intensity of focus on the early years of the nineteenth century. Not only had the events of the Napoleonic era been of extraordinary magnitude, but the survival of witnesses of those events into Hardy's own lifetime had given him a special sense of the part played by history in shaping both his own region and the nation at large. Dorset / Wessex as he knew it was the product not only of its geography and its climate but of its past.[16]

How like a notable Victorian to envisage time as a railway line! But the seventy-nine-year-old Hardy was surely being more than a little selective in that exchange, for the churches and occasionally the castles of the Middle Ages are very much in view in the backward gaze of many works, and the Roman past seems a very significant hump in the further distance; the prehistoric past, however dim in the blue haze of the far distance, is deeply suggestive in its omnipresent solidity in the landscape. The Dorset / Wessex that Hardy created in his oeuvre is

---

[15] White, pp.9/10.
[16] Millgate, *Career*, pp.162/163.

indeed the product of its past. This observation also obscures the paradox that, though Hardy set most of his works in the past and one senses strongly a sense of loss for a simpler, if harder and more 'primitive', way of life, in his attitudes and interests he was very up-to-date and could be markedly forward-looking in his approach to social and moral issues. Claire Tomalin's title *Thomas Hardy – The Time-Torn Man*[17] is no mere *jeu d'esprit*.

Another question needs to be answered: if archaeology was indeed of such interest to Hardy, and if it can justifiably provide a focus for this study, then why does he use the word only rarely, even in his 'scientific' or journalistic writings on the subject? One answer must be that even experts in a particular field only need to use the name of their specialism sparingly within their work on the discipline, and so it must be chance that Hardy did not need to use the word archaeology either. Archaeology was not a new subject that needed to be named specifically, but a modernised, systematised development of a pre-scientific interest that went back millennia and which we can see from a modern perspective as formerly a component of antiquarianism. Another point is that Hardy's works are largely set in the decades before and around his own birth, before the word archaeology came to be narrowly applied to a newly developed scientific discipline.

Finally, if the word archaeology was inapplicable in Hardy's works, if he rarely even needed to use the word in writing about the subject, and if it was not in common usage for at least the early part of the author's adult life, then why do I use it in the title? I use the word in two of the senses already explained: objectively to refer, from a modern standpoint, to material evidence of the human past that is significant in Hardy's works; and to a field of study that had existed in an inchoate, pre-scientific form for many centuries before its methodology and thinking transformed it into a true scientific discipline with a new name to match. Hardy the writer used archaeological places and objects in his works and Hardy the man of modern interests and sensibility was a supporter of the forward-looking scientific approach to studying the past: only the word archaeology with its wide semantic embrace could satisfy the titular demands of this study.

Thomas Hardy's life and personality embody a mass of contradiction and ambivalence: the nineteenth-century novelist who became a twentieth-century poet, the humble countryman who was lionised in London society, the man fascinated by the past who was in the vanguard of progressive thinking and ideas in everything from theology to animal welfare. The list could be extended almost indefinitely. In archaeology, Hardy found a sympathetically ambivalent endeavour: an up-to-the-minute, scientific discipline newly developing in the wake of Darwin which nonetheless revealed and examined humanity's early traces in an inevitably imaginative manner and with decidedly affective consequences. Such a discipline might, we may suppose, provide Hardy vicariously with an emotional and intellectual synthesis or resolution which was to elude him as a person throughout the whole of his long and complex life.

---

[17] Tomalin.

Chapter Two

Ancient Inspiration from the Science of the Imagination:
Hardy, Archaeology, and Wessex
(A Name Revived)

'So we beat on, boats against the current, borne back ceaselessly into the past.'

F. Scott Fitzgerald, *The Great Gatsby*.

The purpose of this chapter is to place Hardy into the historical context of the gradual development of human understanding of past time, partly by examining how the author was affected by the specifically Victorian 'discovery' of the remote past, and partly by discussing in general terms how various facets of this new knowledge, especially archaeology, in which he had a special interest, impinged on his work as a creative artist. Later chapters will expand on both of these by looking in depth at the way that Hardy used the past as an integral element of his art. This broad subject area will also provide the opportunity to explore – or at least comment on – some of the surprising gaps and absences in Hardy's involvement with the study of the past, and with archaeology in particular, during his mature years – and to examine Hardy's well-known creation of a fictionalised region of the past for which he employed the long-defunct name of Wessex. Direct references to Hardy will be necessarily limited in the early pages of this chapter which will trace the distant and complex origins of what we now call archaeology; the year of Hardy's birth will be shown to be a nodal point in that story, however. His personal involvement, including his writings on the subject, will receive more detailed scrutiny in Chapter Three.

One essential source for this chapter and the next is Harold Orel's article 'Hardy and the Developing Science of Archaeology'.[1] Also of particular interest here is a lecture, 'Archaeology and Thomas Hardy', given at Salisbury Museum by Mrs Josephine Pentney (when Miss Dool)

---

[1] Harold Orel, 'Thomas Hardy and the Developing Science of Archaeology', Hardy Annual no. 4, ed. Norman Page (London: Macmillan, 1986).

in 1980, a copy of which was kindly supplied by the author.² Harold Orel's article is the work of a Hardy scholar, impressed by the amount of archaeological allusion in the author's works, who, concisely but in impressively cogent detail, outlines the development of the intellectual climate in which Hardy was born and grew up, and recounts the ways in which his interest in archaeology was expressed in his life and works. Miss Dool's lecture was, as she explains, the fruit of an archaeology enthusiast who became interested in Hardy's writings because of the very fact that he makes such frequent reference to archaeological remains (her material is for the specialist to the extent of quoting RCHM (Royal Commission on Historic Monuments)

Hardy's Cottage, his birthplace in Higher Bockhampton

inventory numbers for the sites mentioned). The combination of these two sources makes for a fascinating comparison of overlapping material, and their geneses mirror the origins of the present study; in fact, Harold Orel's mention of Miss Dool's lecture led to the present writer's contacting her.

***

Archaeology is perhaps unique among those fields of endeavour called sciences in its appeal to the imagination, both general and artistic; indeed, its nature often places it among the humanities as a discipline cognate with history. The subject is richly endowed – surely as a result of its innate character – with articulate advocates. Mortimer Wheeler, whose beautifully

---

² Josephine Dool, 'Thomas Hardy and Archaeology', Salisbury and South Wiltshire Museum, 9/12/1980. Acknowledged in Orel, p.35 (see footnote 1).

written books are worth reading for their wit and wisdom alone, asserts that 'archaeology is a science that must be lived, must be 'seasoned with humanity'.'[3] Though it is 'primarily a fact-finding discipline' ... [the archaeologist] is also ... a humanist and his secondary task is that of revivifying or humanizing his materials with a controlled imagination that inevitably partakes of the qualities of art and even of philosophy.' He then quotes the archaeologist O.G.S. Crawford, that 'archaeology is an art which employs a scientific technique.'[4] Going still further in his championing of the discipline as a humanity, Glyn Daniel states in his *A Short History of Archaeology*, 'The scientific revolution in archaeology has taken, and is still taking, place and archaeology is now a new discipline. But this does not mean, as some have easily slipped into thinking, that archaeology is now a science.'[5] This same bias in the thinking of archaeologists persists right up to the beginning of the twenty-first century, after the heyday of 'the new archaeology' of post-processualism (an equivalent to post-modernism). Francis Pryor in a recent article writes: 'I do not believe that archaeology is a science. It is a humanity but also a very personal business ... it is customary to think that archaeologists view the past in an objective, unbiased manner. We do not. We find the past that is appropriate to our personal present and we interpret it in the same way.'[6] Such sentiments, even the very wording, might be exactly those of Thomas Hardy had he commented directly for posterity on his use of archaeology in his literary works. The ambivalence to their subject evident in archaeologists' classification of the discipline is mirrored in Hardy's attitude to archaeological places and things, on the one hand finding a source of irony and pathos, on the other, a modern, objective attempt to understand the past. To take some words of Michael Millgate on 'the Dorsetshire Labourer' out of context, 'The conflict is partly one between intellectual progressivism and emotional conservatism'.[7] If Hardy is in any sense 'nostalgic' for times past in his works, then perhaps there is a nostalgia for a pre-scientific time when archaeological sites and artefacts retained their enigma, their aura of the mythic, undiminished by the prosaic objectivity of the archaeologist, or even the rapacious spade of the antiquarian-collector.

It is small wonder, then, that a creative artist like Hardy, who was also interested in the developing sciences, should find archaeology so especially congenial and fascinating. The pretty woman – a descendant of the Doges, he was told – who, very typically, captivated Hardy in Venice (*Life* p.195) might almost be a simulacrum of any of the ancient human remains, graves, or artefacts Hardy saw dug up or excavated himself, for he declares: 'the chief effect ... was to carry him back at one spring to those behind the centuries ... '. In this same way, a powerful imaginative and affective potential was provided for Hardy by ancient remains and by the new discipline of archaeology, but particularly by its *human* character, more so than by the colder, more factual sciences like geology and astronomy – and there is a distinct difference in the use Hardy makes of these in his works, with their frightening, belittling and dehumanising power, compared with his treatment of archaeology. Archaeology provides both a sense of the immense stretches of time but with, paradoxically, a human perspective; Gillian Beer states: 'Though the individual may be of small consequence in the long sequence of suc-

---

[3] Wheeler, Earth, p.13.
[4] Wheeler, Earth, pp.228-230.
[5] Glyn Daniel, A Short History of Archaeology (London: Thames and Hudson, 1981), p.187.
[6] Francis Pryor, 'The 'Seahenge' Phenomenon', Minerva 12-5 (2001), p.46.
[7] Millgate, Career, p.210.

cession and generation, yet Hardy in his emplotment opposes this perception and does so by adopting the single life span as his scale.'[8] History, with its weighing of evidence and viewpoint could not provide the cold, hard symbol, the unremarked irony of an archaeological site or object as background or symbol (what Roger Robinson called the 'instant ironic reduction'[9] provided by the ancient); the historian R.J. White declares: '[Hardy] was too much under the dominion of the … historian's greatest enemies: passion and philosophy.'[10]

One measure of the widespread imaginative appeal of archaeology is indeed the number of books on the subject, including numerous historical accounts of the discipline, both academic and popular. One of the standard histories of archaeology is Glyn Daniel's earlier *A Hundred Years of Archaeology*.[11] The first and second parts of this classic book include the word 'antiquarian' in their titles: the third part is headed 'The Birth of Archaeology, 1840–1870', thus assigning the notional start of true archaeology to the very year of Thomas Hardy's birth. The first local amateur archaeological society was founded in 1840 and the British Archaeological Association in 1843, 'The Archaeological Journal' Volume One appeared in 1844, and chiming with Daniels' choice of date, David Wetherall notes: 'Like other disciplines in this period, archaeology aspired to the status of an exact science.'[12] (We must note, however, that Wetherall's title is retrospective; the use of the word 'archaeology' will be discussed in Chapter Three). By the end of the decade, there existed a wide variety of clubs interested in the past, and – of coincidental relevance to Hardy – architectural societies were being formed, four in 1841 alone. Wetherall also notes that the '1840s saw the beginning of a new era , in which public money would be made available for expeditions to acquire Greek and Roman antiquities on a large scale from sites in the Aegean.'[13] 1840 was also, incidentally, the year that Roland Hill's Penny Post was introduced, a sudden development of more rapid

Poet, Revd William Barnes, one of Hardy's mentors

---

[8] Gillian Beer, Darwin's Plots (London: Routledge and Kegan Paul, 1983), p.239.
[9] Roger Robinson, 'Hardy and Darwin', Thomas Hardy: The Writer and his Background, ed. Norman Page (London: Bell and Hyman, 1980), p.129.
[10] White, p.10.
[11] Glyn Daniel, A Hundred Years of Archaeology (London: Duckworth, 1950).
[12] David Wetherall, 'The Growth of Archaeological Societies', The Study of the Past in the Victorian Age, Oxbow Monograph 73, ed. Vanessa Brand (Oxford: Oxbow, 1998), p.32.
[13] Brand, pp.139–140.

communication as important as the gradual building of railways which play almost as significant a symbolic role in Hardy's novels as in Dickens'.

The arrival of the railway in Dorchester in 1845, when Hardy was five years old, was an event he later alluded to in *The Mayor of Casterbridge*. Railways betray the Victorians' extreme ambivalence to the past, on the one hand discovering the extent of prehistory and reverencing objects found in ancient graves, while on the other hand destroying anything that got in the way of new industries or railways; the complete destruction of Tonbridge Priory in Kent is but one example. Hardy's later mentor William Barnes gave a new twist to this ambivalence: for all his scholarly retrospection, he 'took the opportunity it gave to expose his pupils to both subjects [geology and archaeology] and help found the Dorset County Museum, designed to save mutually relevant objects from the depredations of railway diggers.'[14]

In 1852, E. Oldfield wrote: 'Within no very distant period, the study of antiquities has passed in popular esteem, from contempt to comparative honour.'[15] By the time of Hardy's death, the new science of archaeology had become a rigorously codified university subject.

The visual arts (another of Hardy the architect-poet's enthusiasms) underwent a parallel revolution: in their depiction of the past during the mid- and late Victorian era, the period of Hardy's maturity and that of the development of archaeology, archaeology itself encouraged painters away from fanciful scenes of heroic myth to an increasing reliance on an accurate depiction of real discoveries from the ancient world. This cultural shift is explored in a fascinating article by W. Vaughan.[16]

***

Hardy was born at the start of 'the hungry forties', the decade of hardship that so exercised Dickens and which cannot fail to have affected the sensibility of the rural child growing up in Higher Bockhampton. The repeal of the 1815 Corn Laws in 1846 marked a decisive shift of influence from country to city and led to exclusively agricultural areas like Dorset slowly becoming backwaters. If there is an inevitable melancholy associated with archaeology in Hardy's works, then not the least reason may be the close conjunction of traces of the ancient dead and the impoverished dying in the author's infant environment.

Born in 1840, Hardy was just eleven in 1851, the year of the Great Exhibition which David Newsome notes[17] was the year that the term 'Victorian' was first coined: no surprise, then, that Hardy was counted among a new generation of post-Romantic novelists by his contemporaries,[18] and as a key Victorian novelist by our own. As a poet, however, Hardy is firmly placed among the moderns, a twentieth-century poet admired by others much younger than himself. Such is the dichotomous nature of the man, his attitudes, and his work.

Hardy's long life spanned eras of immense historical change and Peter Widdowson places his literary career in this broad context thus: 'It is difficult to imagine how a period so long and eventful – beginning some 14 years before the Charge of the Light Brigade, when Tennyson and Dickens were in their prime, and ending ten years after World War I, when Hardy's literary

---

[14] H.S. Torrens, 'Geology and the Natural Sciences: Some Contributions to Archaeology in Britain 1780 – 1850', ed. Brand, p.58.
[15] Wheeler, Earth, pp. 20-21, quoted.
[16] W. Vaughan, 'Picturing the Past: Art and Architecture in Victorian England', ed. Brand.
[17] David Newsome, The Victorian World Picture (London: John Murray, 1997), p.1.
[18] Newsome, p.7.

contemporaries included Eliot, Joyce and Woolf – could be anything but transitional.'[19] This perspective can be paralleled with many of the great archaeological discoveries and with the gradual rise of the subject itself. Austen Henry Layard was among the pioneers of Mesopotamian archaeology in his excavation of Nimrud in 1845–1847 during Hardy's early childhood; the spectacular finds of Tutankhamun's tomb by Howard Carter in 1922 and of the royal tombs of Ur by Leonard Woolley in 1926 occurred just before the author's death. Two major developments marked the coming of age of archaeology during Hardy's early adulthood and middle years. The former was the discovery and gradual acceptance of the great antiquity of the Earth and of Man. Secondly, the development of excavation, an activity virtually synonymous with archaeology, into a truly disciplined practice, was the principal landmark in archaeology during Hardy's middle age, an achievement in its scientific form largely effected by his friend General Pitt-Rivers, though with its origins in Schliemann's rapacious digs. In 1880, when Hardy reached forty, R. Dawkins could write in *Early Man* that 'The archaeologists have raised the study of antiquities to the rank of a science.'[20] In Hardy's old age, the methodology and organisation of modern archaeology – and its popular appeal – became fully established.

Hardy's most personal acknowledgement of the importance of his own past was that he never lost his affection for the cottage at Higher Bockhampton where he spent his early years. Here, he was not only introduced to the human and literary past by his mother's assiduous and careful development of her son's reading, but to his family past, not least by his paternal grandmother whose vivid retelling of past times is recorded in his first poem, 'Domicilium'. Hardy's lifelong interest in the Napoleonic period was engendered at this time, for this was a recent and heroic past for all the old people of the vicinity, and memories of the King's visit to Weymouth, the stationing of troops to counter an expected invasion, and apprehension about the French assault were as fresh to Hardy's elderly neighbours as was the Battle of Britain to those who relived it for a younger generation in the nineteen seventies. Hardy's sharing the name of the Captain of HMS *Victory* only fuelled his fascination and led to his later research at the British Museum, visits to the Chelsea Hospital to meet elderly veterans of Waterloo, and ultimately to the important clutch of works in several genres with a Napoleonic setting. R.J. White writes that 'Thomas Hardy was born and grew up in 'The Age of History' ... the nineteenth century (and especially the Victorian Age) ... [he] belonged to a time and place which ... thought everything was to be understood in historical terms. Not only understood but explained ... History was not only explanation but justification.'[21] Hardy's home could only emphasise the importance of the past, for it was built by his great-grandfather in 1800, at the height of the Napoleonic era, and a physical embodiment of both family and general history. Close by are the well-preserved Roman road and the Bronze Age Rainbarrows. Hardy's education inevitably emphasised the Classical, underpinned by his mentor the Classical scholar Horace Moule, and possibly more importantly (and widely) by the senior influence, William Barnes; Millgate notes Hardy's 'admiration for the old poet's many-sided achievement, especially in verse, philology, archaeology, and the study of folklore, and his gratitude for the opportunity of frequent intercourse with a mind 'naturally imbued' with 'now obso-

---

[19] Peter Widdowson, On Thomas Hardy: Late Essays and Earlier (London: Macmillan, 1998), p.10.
[20] Michael Wood, In Search of the Trojan War (London: BBC, 1985), p.50, quoted.
[21] R.J. White, p.131.

lete customs and beliefs', with 'forgotten manners, words, and sentiments'.[22] All the concentric circles of influence on the young Hardy's mind, then – familial, environmental, local, regional, historical – combined to stress the importance of time and of the past in particular. The result can readily be seen; Gillian Beer notes that 'In Hardy's novels, all scales are absolute, but multiple. So he includes many time-scales, from the geological time of Egdon Heath to the world of the ephemerons.'[23]

The famous aphorism of Sir Mortimer Wheeler in his *Archaeology from the Earth* that 'the archaeologist is digging up not *things*, but *people*'[24] no doubt helps to explain the peculiar appeal of this science to everyman, and, equally, further emphasises its inspirational power for a creative artist like Hardy. Gilbert Charles-Pickard in *The Larousse Encyclopedia of Archaeology* states that 'today's public does not know the true nature of this science for which it shows an almost instinctive affection.'[25] The proliferation of material, not least on television, about archaeology probably makes this assertion less true than it was when written or in Hardy's latter years, but the involvement of the emotional ('affection') with the objective realm ('science') is particularly apt in relation to this one discipline, and to Hardy's interest in it.

Interest in antiquities goes back much further, however; in fact, the distant origins of archaeology – and the beginnings of the complex story of its development – are in times and places that have themselves long been of archaeological interest. The first record of archaeological activity is of the last two kings of Babylon, Nebuchadnezzar and Nabonidus in the sixth century BC, who dug and restored Ur of the Chaldees, the latter discovering inscriptions of ancient kings. His daughter, the princess En-nigaldi-Nannar, spent years digging the temple of Agade at Ur and collected local antiquities – an activity taken up by Sir Leonard Woolley, as already mentioned, during the final years of Hardy's life, starting in 1922 and continuing for twelve seasons. One of Alexander's first acts on arriving in Asia Minor in 334 BC was to find the presumed site of Troy and pay homage at the grave of his 'ancestor', Achilles, a motivational attitude not far removed from Hardy's famous near-contemporary, Heinrich Schliemann. The next important figure to investigate the past was the Emperor Hadrian (AD 76–138), the forerunner of the Renaissance or the Enlightenment collector of antiquities.

Hardy had few antecedents in the literary use of archaeological relics, but the most important were those whose works he read (and noted from) with his usual thoroughness: Sir Thomas Browne (1605–1682) and the English Romantic poets. Browne lived in the earlier phase of antiquarianism and was the doyen of philosophic musers on the past. Hardy's '1867' notebook records a few gruesome medical details and other items on the transience of man, taken, perhaps (despite the notebook date), from the 1886 edition of *Religio Medici* ('Letter to a Friend' section, *c*.1635).[26] Hardy's jottings, typically, include: (note 230) 'this deliberate and creeping progress unto the grave' and (note 233) 'since every age makes a step unto the end of all things'. As a doctor, Browne had regular contact with human mortality, but his consideration of the transience of life was also specifically inspired by the discovery of prehistoric

---

[22] Millgate, *Career*, p.126.
[23] Beer, p.240.
[24] Wheeler, *Earth*, p.13.
[25] Gilbert-Charles Pickard, editor, *The Larousse Encyclopedia of Archaeology*, (English edition, London: Hamlyn, 1972), p.6.
[26] Lenart A. Bjork, editor, *The Literary Notebooks of Thomas Hardy*, Appendix, 'The '1867' Notebook' (Gothenburg University, 1974).

burial urns. There is no reason to believe that Hardy's omnivorous reading did not also include the equally important *Hydriotaphia, Urne Buriall* of 1658, and possibly also *Concerning some Urnes found in Brampton-Field, Norfolk, Anno 1667*. These latter two inevitably remind us of the digging up of urns in *The Return of the Native*, but Browne's avowal of Christian faith in these highly-wrought products of pondering the traces of the human past, whatever the coincidences of approach, is very different from Hardy's agnostic fatalism. Browne's consideration of the burial urns leads him not only to ponder the brevity of life and the ephemeral nature of civilisations, but also to a respect for those who honoured their dead, and with no thought that any later generation would remark their remains. Hardy's attention as a novelist is more particularly on the transience of the individual, such as Tess, and the wider context even here is comparatively incidental. Although both authors examine the link between the archaeological vestiges of the past with mortality, importantly, Hardy's approach is generally implicit, without authorial comment, for instance in his many mentions of burial tumuli as part of the landscape.

The urns that fascinated Browne and attracted Hardy's attention, together with Hardy's frequent allusion to tumuli and Roman burials, are a fortuitous reminder of the nature of much Northern archaeology which is distinct from that of the Mediterranean world in two key respects: firstly, that the former is more enigmatic because it is unconnected with written records or even mythology (both before and even into the Roman period and beyond), and secondly, because a significantly higher proportion of its sites and artefacts is directly concerned with death rather than being in balance with material concerned with other spheres of human activity (hill-forts being a notable exception). This fact clearly suits Hardy's artistic purposes as well as his nature as a man, but I believe it is secondary to his main reason for the use of Wessex archaeology, and that is simply that it *is* Wessex archaeology. Hardy's deep engagement with his home area, symbolised by his re-creation of its ancient name and personal creation of its identity, meant that it was not archaeology *per se* that recommended itself to Hardy, but the archaeology of his home area, along with its folklore, history, topography, and so on. Thus, the particular point that seems strikingly obvious when we parallel the development of archaeology with Hardy's life – the scant engagement which this 'born archaeologist' had with the main focus of nineteenth century archaeology, that is the Classical and Biblical world – becomes unsurprising. Nonetheless, the powerful orthodoxy of Classical learning influenced Hardy not only in his early reading and his further education at school, under the kindly and eclectic tutelage of William Barnes, and powerful influence of the Classical scholar Horace Moule – but also in his study of architecture of which the Classical orders were a mainstay. Classical archaeology may have been present in Hardy's works only in as marginal a way as Dorset was on the margins of the Roman Empire, but his Classical allusion and imagery are ubiquitous and pervasive.

The Emperor Hadrian's foreshadowing of the early development of archaeology had resonance in its course through later periods and into most of Hardy's lifetime. The Emperor's travels round the Empire resembled the Grandest of Tours, and his enthusiasm, though antiquarian in his collecting of ancient artefacts (an old Roman vice), was primarily philhellene-dilettantish in its selection, and characteristic of the assumption of Classical superiority which marked – or perhaps blighted – the smooth development of true archaeology until almost the twentieth century. The Renaissance fixed the superiority of the Classical in the Western psyche, and during the Enlightenment, the discovery of Pompeii and Herculaneum in 1738 created a vogue for the Classical translated to Britain by artists like Robert Adam and 'Capability' Brown, and by collectors of Classical *objets d'art* like Sir William Hamilton. Johann Winckelmann acted as guide to numerous foreign visitors in his capacity as Chief Supervisor of Antiquities in Rome and became an important catalyst in the apotheosis of Classical art with his *The History of Ancient Art among the Greeks* (1764). Serious scholarship reinforced the fashionable popularity of Classicism that had been stirred in the Grand Tourists: James Stuart and Nicholas Revett's *The Antiquities of Athens* (1762-1812), Nicholas Revett, Richard Chandler, and William Parr's *The Antiquities of Ionia* (1769-1797), Robert Wood's *The Ruins of Palmyra* (1753), and *The Ruins of Baalbec* (1757) being the most important. Hardy, lacking the inculcation of such attitudes by Victorian public school or university, untravelled much beyond his native Wessex until his maturity, and despite his extensive knowledge of the Classics born of assiduous study and the guidance of Horace Moule, never felt that Classical archaeological remains or artefacts were inherently more interesting, inspirational, or affective than those of his native environment: rather than the embrace of Oxford's neo-Classical environment reverberating with daily Latin ritual, the nineteen-year-old Hardy walked every day into a countryside marked by the vast and mysterious earthworks of prehistory accompanied by the sounds of nature. It is tempting to suggest that his concentration on native archaeology is as much a conscious rebuff to the ideal of 'Classical superiority' as a by-product of his local settings – or perhaps an unconscious rebuttal to the system that found its fullest expression in *Jude the Obscure*. The Victorians adulated the Classical despite their re-invention of the Gothic – indeed, Hardy knew Sir Lawrence Alma-Tadema, that conjuror in paint of Classical scenes – but there gradually developed in the later nineteenth century a broader interest in the past that paralleled the excitement generated by the development of geological and archaeological recovery of 'things hidden in the ground'. A more 'democratic', less exclusive interest in the new sciences found expression in field archaeology channelled by such bodies as the Field Club that Hardy and others of the middle class could join.

Hardy's one visit to the Classical world, in Italy, led him inevitably to turn his artistic attention to its past, including its archaeology, as I shall discuss in a chapter on his poetry. His wide reading led him to a particular admiration for the Romantic poets (as is evidenced by his poems written in Italy) historically, a generation before his own birth, and whose era immediately preceded the setting of the Wessex of the novels. Hardy's response to the ancient world was very different from that of his hero Shelley, or Keats, or Byron. Apart from the poems written in Italy, two of which are about the poets who died there, Hardy's engagement is with Rome as it impinged upon Wessex as part of its Empire, and not in the phenomenon of Rome. Further, Keats's 'Ode on a Grecian Urn' and Shelley's 'Ozymandias', for instance, take archaeological objects and shine a personal, philosophical spotlight on them; whereas for Hardy, even in the poems, the archaeology is not something to be separated and examined as if an isolate, nor of innate interest (despite his expertise in and enthusiasm for the visual arts), but an inevitable and ingrained aspect of the whole human and temporal context. The significance of Hardy's visit to Italy is in the negative, that it produced so few poems and that, even as a wealthy and famous author, the journey remained an isolated instance which did not even extend so far as the buried cities of Vesuvius. Hardy (albeit in truncated form) and his Romantic predecessors were continuing that quintessential Enlightenment tradition, the Grand Tour.

Before any such inherently archaeological activity as excavation was thought of, ancient myth-systems sought to explain the past through a pattern of descent from a 'Golden Age', rather the opposite to the evolutionary theme which is the hallmark of thinkers in Hardy's time. Interestingly, both the Roman and Chinese traditions posit a decline from a golden age, from stone to bronze to iron, exactly the scheme – but supporting the reverse notion of regression rather than progress – which was to prove a turning point in applying the evolutionary model to archaeology. The 'Darwinian' idea that stone preceded bronze which was replaced by iron was postulated in Scandinavia in the late eighteenth century and fully realised in the schematic layout of the Old Nordic Museum in Copenhagen by Christian Thomsen in 1816 and his successor as director Jens Worsaae - a revolutionary concept originating in the years immediately preceding Hardy's birth which gained wide acceptance by the time of his early maturity, and which survives, with modification, through the whole story of archaeology to the present day. Hardy's work, insofar as he regrets the passing of the ancient and purely agricultural basis of his region's life and economy in which time-honoured customs survive, also looks back to a golden age, albeit a tarnished one that has already suffered banishment from Eden. Further, his characters, such as the unrepentant, recidivistic pagans of Egdon Heath or conjuror Trendle, are atavistic survivals of a time which did not even seek to explore its past, and whose obscurity is only marginally pierced by the amateurish efforts of an antiquary like Parson Tringham. These characters will receive further attention in the chapters on the relevant books.

Between the ancient world, with its isolated examples of an interest in the physical remains of the past, and Hardy's own time, progress in understanding the past was remarkably limited. The Three Age system took decades to be recognised as the quantum leap in understanding that it was; Kevin Greene points out that the difference between Geoffrey de Monmouth (died *c*.1155) and the eighteenth-century Enlightenment was merely in the quantity of mythology that was accepted as explanation of the past; further, sites and ancient peoples were understood solely through their connection with documents right into the nineteenth century because there was no way of going back in time before the existence of such records. This meant that 'Most conspicuously lacking was a concept of the depth of time'. Hardy was born, therefore, into a world of learning where 'most historians found no difficulty in compressing the period before written records into a biblical time scale involving only six to seven thousand years. Interpretations of geology or evolution that demanded an unimaginable length of time were fiercely contested.' [27] There is no doubt that Hardy regarded the discovery and acceptance of the time-scale of prehistory as a watershed in human knowledge. In his only attempt to write for a young audience, *Our Exploits at West Poley*, written in 1883 at the start of the 'archaeological period' of his fiction, Hardy's youthful narrator comments of the Mendip cave that the boys are exploring: 'Skeletons of great extinct beasts and the remains of prehistoric men have been found thereabouts since that time; but at the date of which I write science was not so ardent as she is now, in the pursuit of the unknown; … '.[28]

---

[27] Kevin Greene, Archaeology: An Introduction (London: Routledge, 1983), p.13.
[28] Thomas Hardy, Our Exploits at West Poley (Oxford: OUP, 1952), p.9.

As one can infer from Glyn Daniel's books, the progress towards true archaeology is the story of the development of the antiquary (Hardy's preferred word), but also given without discrimination in texts as 'antiquarian'. As so often, Mortimer Wheeler seems to be Hardy's descendent soul-mate in sundry archaeological matters, calling the latter usage 'that hideous and unnecessary pseudo-noun 'antiquarian''.[29] Stuart Piggott's incisive study of the development of antiquarianism, *Ancient Britons and the Antiquarian Imagination* (subtitled 'Ideas from the Renaissance to the Regency', so dealing with the topic almost right up to Hardy's time) describes the long story of the development of archaeology as far from a smooth and natural progression but as 'this long record of irregular achievement and failure.'[30] His other main point is that antiquaries were not merely opposed by philosophers as being primitive in the Enlightenment age of Sir Isaac Newton's Royal Society, but they were figures of popular ridicule on the stage and in print. Moreover, the field of antiquarianism, as Hardy shows through his latter day object of (in context, rather bleak) satire, Parson Tringham in *Tess*, is only slightly interested in what we nowadays call archaeology, being mostly concerned with old documents, inscriptions, genealogies, and the like which Piggott calls 'an amorphous antiquarianism'.[31] Piggott explains that the new empiricism engendered by the founding of the Royal Society in 1660 (but not lasting long into the eighteenth century and the lionising of mathematics) did, however, give one branch of antiquarianism the opportunity to 'break away and grope towards a new discipline that was eventually, but not before the late nineteenth century, to become archaeology rather than antiquarianism.'[32] This estimation therefore means that only in Hardy's maturity as a writer – in his 'archaeological phase' of the 1880s and his friendship with General Pitt-Rivers – did true archaeology come into being. Piggott quotes a rare counter-note (and an interesting instance of 'archaeology' in its modern sense) from Alexander Gordon in 1726: '... Antiquity claims a great share, particularly Archaiology [sic], which consists of Monuments, or rather Inscriptions, still subsisting.'[33] Millgate, correctly in view of Hardy's polymath/ 'renaissance man' inclinations, comments on Hardy's 'antiquarian enthusiasm',[34] and later notes: 'much of the Victorian antiquary there was in Hardy – delver into the back files of local newspapers, amateur archaeologist and dialectologist ... ',[35] thus marking Hardy as one who pursued the breadth of antiquarianism in its original sense, but who simultaneously observed the rigour of the new scientific discipline.

Those antiquaries who operated in Hardy's earlier years and in the generations immediately preceding his life, were the heirs to a quasi-academic dynasty that, at least in British histories of archaeology, dates back to Henry VIII's reign when John Leland (*c*.1503–1552) as King's Antiquary visited poorly documented and little-understood sites like Hadrian's Wall and Offa's Dyke. Actually to *visit* sites is a necessary prelude to the digging and collecting which typified the antiquaries of Hardy's period. But it is three of Leland's successors who directly impinge on the present study, for all of them are not only crucial to the development of archaeology, particularly in the more Anglo-centric studies of the subject, but each was con-

---

[29] Wheeler, Earth, p.230.
[30] Stuart Piggott, Ancient Britons and the Antiquarian Imagination (London: Thames and Hudson, 1989), p.10.
[31] Piggott, Antiquarian, p.8.
[32] Piggott, Antiquarian, p.25.
[33] Piggott, Antiquarian, p.20.
[34] Millgate, Career, p.204.
[35] Millgate, Career, p.244.

cerned to a greater or lesser degree with Wessex; indeed Andrew D. Radford notes that Dorset was 'a major focus for antiquarian research ... '.[36] William Camden (1551–1623) published his *Britannia*, the first comprehensive guide to British antiquities, in 1585. Unsurprisingly for a Renaissance figure, Camden, for all his objectivity of detailed description of ancient sites, liked to link Britain with Europe through its Roman inheritance – and three centuries later, the tradition of this norm of Classical superiority meant that Hardy would report some public disappointment in his 1908 article 'Maumbury Ring' when it became apparent that this site being excavated in Dorchester had its origins in pre-Roman pre-history. This piece will receive detailed consideration later in the next chapter.

The widely-travelled antiquary and polymath Edward Lhwyd (or Lhuyd or Llwyd, 1660-1708), who took the key step of making deductions from material remains rather than Classical texts, was a friend of John Aubrey (1626–1697), the second of this trio of 'Wessex' antiquaries. A member of the Royal Society, Aubrey was firmly of the Enlightenment, and in this Age of Reason, it was facts and things that were of interest as he recorded ancient sites in his (unpublished) tripartite *Monumenta Britannica*, whose first part included Stonehenge, Avebury, and Silbury. He avidly pursued classification, but by that limitation which survived well into Hardy's lifetime, the Romans were 'civilised' but not the Celts. William Stukeley (1687-1765) is the third of the important triumvirate of antiquaries. As an Enlightenment scholar in the earlier part of his career, he pursued extensive fieldwork in Wessex, reading Aubrey and producing accurate and thorough surveys of Avebury, Stonehenge, and Silbury.

Camden's and Aubrey's works are in the Dorset County Museum and were there from the early years of its existence. It is more than likely, with his appetite for reading and strong inclination to study the past, that Hardy examined these volumes in his formative, often autodidactic, years. This institution was founded as the County Museum and Library at a meeting in 1845 after a number of interested parties had saved the important local archaeological sites of Maumbury Rings (the modern usage is in the plural) and Poundbury Camp (which both feature in *The Mayor of Casterbridge*) from the course of Brunel's proposed G.W.R. Chippenham – Weymouth line. The Museum's original building in a back street location at 3, Trinity Street is alluded to with wry humour about its eclectic collections in *The Mayor of Casterbridge* chapter XXII. It is a happy chance that such a significant event in the archaeological and cultural life of Dorset should have happened so nearly coincidentally with Hardy's birth. Hardy joined – and became an active member of – the Dorset Natural History and Antiquarian Field Club in about 1882 while living in Wimborne. The new (and present) Museum building was opened on January 7th 1884 with an address by General Pitt-Rivers, who had such an important influence on Hardy, by now a well-known writer and one of the guests. These two important elements in the author's involvement in the past of his home county, the Club and the Museum, amalgamated to form the Dorset Natural History and Archaeological Society in 1928, the year of Hardy's death.

A book of more immediate interest to Hardy in his artistic creations than those just mentioned was by the historian and antiquary of Dorset, John Hutchins (1698–1773). Hardy owned and studied in depth the four-volume third edition *History and Antiquities of the*

---

[36] Radford, p.7.

County of Dorset,[37] first published posthumously in 1774, in which he made copious notes; the venerable volumes in the County Museum were doubtless studied by Hardy before he acquired his own which are now in the reconstruction of his study in the Museum. Charles Warne's *Celtic Tumuli of Dorset* (1866) and William Greenwell's *British Barrows* (1877), both of which are in the Museum Library, must surely also have formed part of Hardy's reading in view of the prominence of barrows in his works. Michael Millgate emphasises the importance of the Museum (and other libraries) to Hardy: '... it is clear that most of the entries in the notebooks were taken precisely from books and periodicals that were not on Hardy's own shelves but had been consulted in such places as the British Museum, the Athenaeum, and the Dorset County Museum ... '.[38] However, Edmund Blunden notes that 'The Max Gate library [by the time of its sale] naturally contained a selection of books splendid or modest on Dorset antiquities, genealogies and topography, including the eighteenth-century historian Hutchins, who played a part in giving Hardy's imagination some points of departure.'[39] Millgate cautions, however, that 'we know remarkably little, either in general or specific terms, about the accumulation of the substantial library that Hardy left behind him at his death.'[40] Millgate in his biography notes that 'when the Dorset County Museum re-opened ... on 1st January 1884, [Hardy] immediately became a frequent visitor.' In late 1883 and during 1884, Hardy 'was living meanwhile [at Shire-Hall Place] in the centre of town within three minutes' walk of the new Museum and its handsome reading room, well stocked with works on the history, natural history, geology, and archaeology of the locality, and regularly supplied with the latest issues of the leading newspapers and magazines.'[41] Millgate notes that among the latter was *The Illustrated London News*, which, as I shall explain later, was an important populariser of archaeology and a valuable source of the latest news on the subject from both Britain and abroad. It is worth pondering just what Hardy must have read about but of which no trace is evident in either his creative or personal writings.

Another Wessex antiquarian with a distant Hardy connection was William Cunnington (1754–1810), who, with Sir Richard Colt Hoare (1758–1838) and Dean John Mereweather (1797–1850), were excavating and recording antiquities in researching a wide range of sites on Salisbury Plain. Their more objective approach desired knowledge rather than romantic conjecture, and they form part of the final phase of antiquarianism in Glyn Daniel's analysis occupying the four decades before Hardy's birth. A descendant of William Cunnington was Edward Cunnington, the Dorchester antiquarian who was satirised by Hardy in *A Tryst at an Ancient Earthwork*, a story crucially revealing of Hardy's attitude to archaeology as a scientific discipline, and equally illuminating of the influence of Pitt-Rivers on the author; this work will be discussed in detail in the next chapter. Despite the strides towards scientific method and knowledge made by the antiquarians, their motivation as Classically-educated men was

---

[37] Hardy's, and the Museum's own, sets are of The History and Antiquities of the County of Dorset by John Hutchins, MA. The Third Edition, Corrected, Augmented, and Improved, by William Shipp and James Whitworth Hodson. Westminster. Printed by Bowyer Nichols and Sons, 25 Parliament Street, 1861. [four volumes, 1861, 1863, 1868, (1870) 1873].
[38] Michael Millgate, 'The Max Gate Library', A Spacious Vision: Essays on Hardy, ed. Phillip P. Mallett and Ronald P. Draper (Penzance: the Patten Press, 1994), p.139.
[39] Blunden, p.183.
[40] Millgate, 'Library', Mallett and Draper, p.139.
[41] Millgate, Biography, pp.244/245.

not yet that of the (ideally) disinterested researcher of today. Harold Orel in his article in *Hardy Annual No.4* mentions that they 'were patriots, seeking to demonstrate to their neighbours and the world that the antiquities of the British past were worthy of attention, and in some respects rivalled the antiquities of the Mediterranean Basin.'[42] Interestingly, Colt Hoare commissioned Josiah Wedgwood, no less, to make reproductions of some of the pottery they found in their digs, some of which are now displayed alongside the originals in Devizes Museum. Perhaps this was an attempt to see their mysterious makers as on a par with the universally admired Classical potters, but it was to be a long time before any parity of interest, let alone esteem, could be accorded to prehistoric artefacts in the popular mind. Another of Orel's observations about these antiquaries is particularly applicable to Sir Thomas Browne, to Byron, Keats, and Shelley – and very much to Hardy, since for them, 'every dig seemed to confirm a melancholy reading of the meaning of existence … '.[43]

That same article immediately distinguishes Hardy's interest in archaeology from antiquarianism, so placing him firmly in the van of modern thinking:

> It may be that Hardy's concern with the pagan and Roman past of England has been treated somewhat cavalierly, even dismissed by the all-embracing term 'antiquarianism', as if Hardy's investigations of that past required no more than an intermittent focusing of attention on his part. Hardy's concern was far more than that of an antiquarian.[44]

Later, the author comments that Hardy 'knew more than a little something about the behaviour of diggers', usefully distinguishing antiquarians from mere barrow-diggers, who 'violated good sense no less than the site they were excavating' and of whom a 'surprising number behaved like pirates.' Such rapacious and totally unscientific collecting – for either souvenirs, like the heath-folk in *The Return of the Native*, or for 'treasure' like the nefarious 'friend' in *A Tryst at an Ancient Earthwork*, was anathema to Hardy. Later, Orel's terminology is less carefully chosen, William Stukeley being dubbed 'the first important English field archaeologist', while William Cunnington and Richard Colt-Hoare fall within the pejorative category of 'diggers'. This, I feel, is unfortunate because the correct application of these terms is crucial to our understanding both of the development of archaeology and of Hardy's interest in it.

The *annus mirabilis* of the nineteenth century's discovery of the past was 1859, during which Hardy celebrated his nineteenth birthday. Hardy's basic education and his lifelong habit of energetic and wide reading, encouraged by his mother and further consolidated at school, had ended, and the young man was maturing at the exact midpoint of his articled time with John Hicks the architect in Dorchester. This year marked the coming of age of archaeology and the symbolic end of antiquarianism as the means of investigating and understanding the human past – though full acceptance of some precepts of these and cognate disciplines took longer to become orthodox. One term which came to prominence at this time is of immense importance to archaeologists, and that is 'prehistoric'. The distinction between prehistoric and historic archaeology is crucial because the latter is often a process of inter-corroboration be-

---

[42] Orel, 'Archaeology', p.27.
[43] Orel, 'Archaeology', p.27.
[44] Orel, 'Archaeology', p.19.

tween objects and documents. Documentary evidence is dominant, of course, in studies of the Classical (including Biblical) civilisations, and still dominates much of the popular appeal of archaeology. The former is a 'purer' form of archaeology in the sense that all the knowledge is deduced from objects and their context. This form of archaeology was held to be impossible before the mid-nineteenth century simply because the Bible was held to be a literal account of the whole history of the earth, and therefore all excavations could be considered as revealing the history given in the Bible and other ancient texts. Daniel Wilson coined the word in 1851 for his book *Prehistoric Annals of Scotland* and shortly afterwards, in 1865, Sir John Lubbock brought the term into general use with his *Prehistoric Times*; Lubbock also coined the term 'Palaeolithic' in the same work. A revolution in ideas and terminology therefore took place during Hardy's adolescent years.

1859 is important because three milestones were passed. First, the Three Age system of archaeological classification (referred to earlier) began to attain universal acceptance (the system was not adopted by the British Museum until 1871, however, but some years before the maturing of Hardy's interest in archaeology).

Second, Joseph Prestwich and John Evans (father of Sir Arthur Evans, excavator of Knossos and discoverer of the Minoan civilisation of Crete) visited the Somme gravels and noted flint axes and implements in the same stratum as that containing remains of fossilised animals, thus confirming by observation Jacques Boucher de Perthes' claim that early man had far more ancient origins than had ever been previously known; indeed, the human origin of stone tools had first been claimed in the seventeenth century, and John Frere had written a letter to *Archaeologia* in London in 1800 – the year Daniel assigns to the beginning of the end of antiquarianism – about his discovery in Hoxne in Suffolk of flint tools below the level of extinct animal bones. Coincidentally with this, William Pengelly's excavations at Windmill Hill Cave, Brixham, in 1858–1859 also found man-made tools in slowly deposited strata below the level of long-extinct animals. These discoveries also marked the beginning of the end of the catastrophist theory of the Earth's past and its replacement by the fluvialist idea and uniformitarianism, though, as with all these revolutionary concepts, it was very slow to be accepted. It is interesting to note that Boucher de Perthes and other pioneers of prehistory first started to notice and investigate strata that indicated the antiquity of man in the new railway cuttings. Hardy was probably unconscious of the paradox that the monstrous icon of the industrial age – one that Hardy was to become so fond of using as a symbol of disruption – was the means by which such an important phenomenon came to light. This was linked to the key development in geology that the earth is much older than the traditional age of 4004 BC as published by Archbishop Ussher (or Usher) in 1658, which more or less confirmed the age deduced by Jerome from Biblical genealogies and, in corrected form, was accepted by Luther as 4000 BC then corrected by Kepler – the date found in a marginal note in the King James Authorised Version of the Bible of 1611. This dogma was already on the wane before Hardy's birth as a result of such works as Charles Lyell's *The Principles of Geology* (1830–1833).

The third and most celebrated event of 1859 was the publication of Charles Darwin's *On the Origin of Species* which had such a profound effect on all intellectual ideas, not least on archaeology. Harold Orel states that Hardy was 'a very early 'acclaimer' of *The Origin of Species*' and 'alluded often and approvingly to the doctrine of evolution in his short stories and novels ... '.⁴⁵ Geology and palaeontology, the temporally vaster and frighteningly non-human cousins of archaeology, find their place in Hardy's scheme as contextualisers which make the human scale of archaeology all the more significant: of Henry Knight on the cliff in *A Pair of Blue Eyes*, Gillian Beer declares: 'Man here still feels himself at the summit of creation – the *incongruity* of companionship with minute fossil life thwarts him. Yet kinship is acknowledged ... '.⁴⁶ Hardy attended Darwin's funeral on 26th April 1882, such was his admiration for Darwinian ideas and sympathy for the modern thinking of which it was such an important catalyst; the Victorian crisis of faith, which was largely a result of Darwin, finds a strong counterpart in Hardy's agnosticism, though it cannot be adduced as the sole cause. Beer finds not only a philosophical link, but also a source of the typical Hardyesque melancholy in Darwin, that 'Hardy always acknowledged Darwin as a major intellectual influence in his work and his way of seeing ... in terms of pessimism, a sense that the laws of life are themselves flawed. That Hardy did feel this is undeniable.'⁴⁷ Beer stresses the crucial effect of Darwinism on Hardy's work, asserting: 'The two major emotional and creative problems which evolutionary theory forced on Hardy were to find a scale for the human and a place for the human within the natural order.'⁴⁸ Archaeology provided both a temporal scale and a physical, topographical context for Hardy's characters.

The word 'archaeologist' slowly, imperceptibly, replaced 'antiquarian' during the second half of the nineteenth century as the former became more closely defined and the latter was rendered obsolete by both its connotations and its eclecticism. In chapter L of *Tess of the d'Urbervilles*, which is set in the 1870s, Jack Durbeyfield's casual comment about 'antiqueerians'' activities incidentally shows that, in this age of Schliemann, the notion of antiquarianism has already shifted its focus onto specifically archaeological activity and away from wider pursuits – despite the overwhelming effects of Parson Tringham's genealogical researches. He remarks that '[antiquaries] spend lots o' money in keeping up old ruins, and finding the bones o' things, and such like; and living remains must be more interesting to 'em still, if only they knowed of me.'

The OED currently can give no help in tracing the increasing use of the word archaeology as the name of a science (its earlier, more general meaning given from 1607 is 'Ancient history generally; systematic description or study of antiquities') other than pointing to the development of the science itself.⁴⁹ The first university department devoted to archaeology was the Institute of Archaeology at London University, founded by Mortimer Wheeler in 1948, so formalised academic acceptance *per se* postdates the application of the word to a discrete discipline by some time. A notional, but helpful indicator, however, is to look at the pages of the *Illustrated London News*. This periodical, published from 1842, gave special emphasis to archaeological discoveries, and so, with that particular life span, coinciding with Daniel's proposed

---

⁴⁵ Orel, 'Archaeology', p.30.
⁴⁶ Beer, p.253.
⁴⁷ Beer, p.238.
⁴⁸ Beer, p.252.
⁴⁹ The reply to an enquiry to OWLS (Oxford English Dictionary Word and Language Service) (received 28/2/2000) states: 'It is unfortunate for your researches that the entry for archaeology in the Oxford English Dictionary belongs, as one might say, to the lowest, undisturbed stratum of Murray's lexicography. The entry has remained unchanged since its first publication in 1885, and though we are now engaged on a complete revision of the dictionary, we have not yet done the work in A which might answer your question.'

start of modern archaeology, it embraced the development of archaeology as a science from its antiquarian beginnings right up to the introduction of some of the most sophisticated techniques – and incidentally including almost the whole of Thomas Hardy's life. A useful selection of the most important archaeological discoveries reported in the magazine is reproduced in *The Great Archaeologists* edited by Edward Bacon.[50] This must be only an approximate guide to the relative usage of the two terms, but a perusal reveals the first use of 'archaeologist' in the edition of 9th March, 1861. Generally, 'antiquary' is gradually replaced by 'archaeologist', though they are found mixed with no apparent discrimination for most of the nineteenth century. It may be significant that 1861 is only two years after the annus mirabilis of the century's discovery of the remote past. Interestingly, an early and rare use of 'archaeological' occurs in Hardy's first published novel, *Desperate Remedies* (1871), a book set in the present-day which glories early on in the revelatory experience of rail travel and the popular treat of a steamboat excursion: the incidental use of this term is fortuitously indicative of a modern outlook by the young writer as well as a hint of his nascent interest in the subject of archaeology:

> ... Graye recollected that a mile or two inland from this spot was an interesting medi-aeval ruin. He was already familiar with its characteristics through the medium of an archaeological work ... (*Desperate Remedies* p.29)

Ironically, Carl J. Weber's book on Hardy, published sixty-nine years later, notes that 'Hardy's service as an *antiquarian* [my italics] and historian came in time to be recognised.'[51]

***

With Hardy, person, place, and past are inseparable. Around the time of his first stirrings of intense interest in the past, as focused through the lens of the developing sciences – especially archaeology – Hardy began to develop the feature of his work that later became the most well-known and immediate indicator of his interest in the past: his rediscovery, or perhaps re-invention, of 'Wessex'. Tom Paulin writes that a 'sense of place was a most important part of personal identity for Hardy,'[52] though Wessex was dismissed by one contemporary reviewer in the witticism, 'Of all forms of sex-mania ... the most unpleasant [is] the Wessex-mania of Mr Thomas Hardy.'[53] And so closely did Hardy become associated with his regional name that one of the earliest biographical studies of the author is entitled *Hardy of Wessex – His Life and Literary Career*.[54] In this same work, Weber notes that as early as 1889, J. M. Barrie wrote one of the first articles on Hardy, for the *Contemporary Review*, entitled 'The Historian of Wessex', praising, *inter alia*, Hardy's historical research.[55] David Newsome comments on 'the rustic world of Thomas Hardy's Wessex, the popularity of which caused its author some surprise.'[56] Though his characterising of this popularity as a 'nostalgic appeal'[57] may accurately reflect the

---

[50] Edward Bacon, ed., The Great Archaeologists – and their discoveries as originally reported in the pages of The Illustrated London News (London: Martin Secker and Warburg, 1976).
[51] Carl J. Weber, Hardy of Wessex: His Life and Literary Career (Rev Ed: New York: Columbia UP, 1965), p.109.
[52] Tom Paulin, Thomas Hardy: The Poetry of Perception (London: Macmillan, 1975), p.118.
[53] Millgate, Career, p.295.
[54] Weber.
[55] Weber, p.109.
[56] Newsome, p.125.
[57] Newsome, p.126.

affection of the novels' early urban readers, it is an error engendered by highly selective reading and ignorance of the historical facts. Louis Macneice's 1955 poem 'Wessex Guidebook' associates the region with its long and dense past, tacitly acknowledging Hardy in using the name, and paying homage to the man in periphrasis as 'one who chronicled a fading world'.

A Pair of Blue Eyes, with its questions about the destruction and preservation of ancient buildings and the famous scene on the cliff with the geological strata, appeared in 1873; *The Return of the Native*, the first work in which things archaeological play a significant role, was published in 1878. Between these two, *Far from the Madding Crowd* began the creation of a region of the literary imagination. Malcolm Bradbury's unusual and useful *Atlas of Literature* opens and concludes the article on the region thus:

> Thomas Hardy's creation of his fictional Wessex is a supreme instance of the systematic imposition of literary imagination upon an existing geographical location. ... that profoundly imagined world he so indelibly projected onto the landscape of an entire region.[58]

In his *Regional History of England – Wessex to AD 1000*, Barry Cunliffe begins his general preface [to the series] by declaring:

> England cannot be divided satisfactorily into regions based on former kingdoms or principalities in the manner of France, Germany or Italy ... English regional identities are imprecise and no firm boundaries can be drawn.[59]

He elaborates the point, regarding this volume in the book's Introduction:

> The Wessex of this book is not a natural geographical entity nor is it the legally defined territory ruled by the kings of the West Saxons. 'Wessex' is a more diffuse concept – it is all things to all men. Thomas Hardy, responsible for re-introducing the word into everyday use, used it with delightful vagueness though to him the Dorset focus was all-important. 'Wessex' has an undoubted charm about it due in no small part to Hardy's lively imagination.[60]

Cunliffe seems to forget the depth of Hardy's scholarship, not to mention his local knowledge, for he never uses the name 'with delightful vagueness' – and the well-known maps of Wessex in the standard editions define the region and its constituent counties precisely. Hardy's knowledge led him to use the name of Alfred the Great's kingdom in *Far from the Madding Crowd*, the first major popular success for Hardy's bucolic world. However incidental might have been the name's introduction, it was not used whimsically, in ignorance, as Cunliffe implies. In the *Life,* Hardy comments:

> A peculiarity in the local descriptions running through all Hardy's writings may be instanced here – that he never uses the word 'Dorset', never names the county at all (except possibly in an explanatory footnote), but obliterates the names of the six

---

[58] Malcolm Bradbury, ed., The Atlas of Literature (London: De Agostini, 1996), p.133.
[59] Bradbury, p.136.
[60] Barry Cunliffe, A Regional History of England – Wessex to AD 1000 (London: Longman, 1993), pp.xii, 1.

counties, whose areas he traverses in his scenes, under the general appellation of 'Wessex' – an old word that became quite popular after the date of *Far from the Madding Crowd*, where he first introduced it. So far did he carry this idea of the unity of Wessex that he used to say he had grown to forget the crossing of county boundaries within the ancient kingdom … .[61]

No vagueness here in Hardy's knowledge, nor in his application of the name. The six counties are: Devon, Dorset, Somerset, Wiltshire, Hampshire, and Berkshire, the boundaries of which remain today more or less as Alfred would have recognised them during his reign. Though Hardy may have forgotten the crossing of county boundaries, they are certainly there in the novels, exactly, according to the author's own map, matching the equivalent 'real' counties they represent: Dorset is South Wessex; Devon, Lower Wessex; Somerset, Outer Wessex; Wiltshire, Mid Wessex; Berkshire, North Wessex; Hampshire, Upper Wessex. Celtic Cornwall is involved, being allocated the name Off Wessex, though Hardy shows that he is aware of that county's anomalous identity within England, and also acknowledges the indeterminacy of the borders of Wessex in the preface to the 1895 edition of *A Pair of Blue Eyes*, the one novel set almost entirely outside the home region that he had circumscribed. Here (p.389) he reminds us that Wessex is as much (if not more) a country of the author's mind, as a geographical entity with fixed political borders:

> The spot is, I may add, the furthest westward of all the convenient corners wherein I have ventured to erect my theatre for these little dramas of country life and passions; and it lies near to, or no great way beyond, the vague border of the Wessex kingdom on that side, which, like the westering verge of modern American settlements, was progressive and uncertain.

Michael Millgate notes the inextricable link between the geography of the region and the pastness of the region: 'Hardy's Wessex was located somewhere in a vague, unspecifiable past' and as such it 'is sufficiently the stuff of imagination to meet all of Hardy's creative needs'[62] but always, 'Wessex *is* fictional … an autonomous world essentially outside of time and space.'[63] For Richard H. Taylor, Wessex is 'a psychic entity, the objective correlative of the author's imagination. … The real Hardy country is off the map and in the mind'[64] - a comment that today reminds us strongly of Graham Greene's distinctive country of the mind, 'Greeneland'. George Wing's extensive article in the same volume warns against oversimplifying the phenomenon of Hardy's Wessex, that 'his imaginative world is different from the existing Dorset and adjacent counties', providing 'challenging ambiguities';[65] despite its solid origins, 'it can also be located on maps of heaven and hell and poetry'.[66] However, it is a real landscape sure enough which Hardy employs in his art, intimately connected with the theme of the passage of time: Sophie Gilmartin writes that 'the layers of soil and stone in his writing work on a literal and figurative

---

[61] Florence Emily Hardy, The Life of Thomas Hardy (London: Macmillan, 1962), pp.122/123.
[62] Millgate, Career, p.248.
[63] Millgate, Career, p.351.
[64] Richard H. Taylor, 'Thomas Hardy: A Reader's Guide', Page, p.223.
[65] George Wing, 'Hardy and Regionalism', Page, p.78.
[66] Wing, 'Regionalism', Page, p.82.

level as the very substance of place and time.'⁶⁷ Hardy's earlier critics, like the first visitors who toured the region to 'find' the settings of the books, regarded Wessex as a real region, but given a new significance and imaginative potency by Hardy's reaffirmation of its origins and by the superimposition of his fictional stratum. Lionel Johnson wrote in 1895 of

> Art gathering up the wonders and the powers, no longer living of themselves; but henceforth to live only in Art: which has the natural office of piety towards the past. Mr Hardy has done this service to a great region of England, to Wessex. ... Wessex is full of significance, and no outworn appellation of antiquity, without a living force. In calling the land of his birth and of his art after its ancient, the Land of the West Saxons, Mr Hardy would have us feel the sentiment of historical continuity from those old times to ours; the storms of violent fortune, the slow touches of change, which have left their trace upon the land, whilst leaving at heart the same: ... In Mr Hardy's books, all that succession of races, their fusion and confusion, are brought before the mind ... .⁶⁸

A look at the topography of Southern England quickly shows that these shires are contained by the sea and the courses of the Thames and the Avon, with Celtic Cornwall forming the Western limit. Dorothy Whitelock explains:

> ... Wessex similarly developed from small beginnings, in Hampshire, Wiltshire, and the upper Thames Valley, until it denotes the southern counties from Surrey to the Bristol Channel and the Cornish border.⁶⁹

Surrey was a late addition, and the old kingdoms of Kent and Sussex followed, but Hardy knew exactly where Wessex was, and, again to contradict Cunliffe, it does not seem to be an especially apt name for what he goes on to call 'the less emotive 'Central Southern England''; Cunliffe also includes the now-abolished artificial county of Avon in his Wessex. The Government's recently delineated development regions with the potential for regional self-government, not surprisingly, place Hampshire and Berkshire in the South East (formerly the 'Home Counties'?) clinging magnetically round London, while the rest of old Wessex is joined by Mercian Gloucestershire in the South West region which is more or less the familiar holiday area, the 'West Country' (though it should be noted that the ancient boundary of Berkshire with Mercian Oxfordshire, following the Thames, was changed in the 1974 boundary revisions, with all of the North of the County added to an enlarged Oxfordshire). Such variations may prove the first point in his book, but though Wessex may be all things to Barry Cunliffe, it certainly was not to Thomas Hardy!

The name Wessex is derived from the Old English (Anglo-Saxon) West-Seaxe, applied to either the people (the West Saxons) or their kingdom (Wessex).⁷⁰ Kenneth Cameron describes the word as a 'folk-name', and continues, '... Saxon may be a derivative of *seax* 'knife, sharp

---
⁶⁷ Sophie Gilmartin, 'Geology, Genealogy and Church Restoration in Hardy's Writing', The Achievement of Thomas Hardy, ed. Phillip Mallett (London: Macmillan, 2000), p.23.
⁶⁸ Lionel Johnson, The Art of Thomas Hardy (London: John Lane, 1895), pp.89-90.
⁶⁹ Dorothy Whitelock, The Pelican History of England: 2 –The Beginnings of English Society (London: Penguin Books, 1952), p.8.
⁷⁰ Revised Dorothy Whitelock, Sweet's Anglo-Saxon Primer (Oxford, 1967), vocabulary, p.404.

single-edged sword or dagger', the tribe taking its name from its characteristic weapon.'[71] This kingdom had no fewer than four foundation myths,[72] but in its historic, Christianised period, its significance was as the one kingdom of the English that, finally, defeated the Danes, and assumed the hegemony over the whole country, ultimately recovering and incorporating the Danelaw into a united, Christian England. Michael Wood records historians' scepticism, that this 'dramatic reversal of fortune is so extreme that some modern writers have refused to take Alfred seriously ... '.[73] The Anglo-Saxon Chronicle for 878 records Alfred's decisive victory at Edington tersely but definitely; Barry Cunliffe is a little more expansive, but equally sure of its result:

> ... at Edington, the two forces met and here Alfred achieved a decisive victory. ... Hostages were given, oaths were sworn and Guthrum submitted to Christian baptism. The formalities complete, the Great army moved back to Gloucester and finally, in 879, to East Anglia, leaving Wessex in peace.[74]

Hardy's mentor William Barnes was an Anglo-Saxon enthusiast; this, together with Hardy's own interest in history, is enough to inform Hardy of the significance and appropriateness of his use of the name Wessex for his home region, though Millgate notes 'Hardy's regionalism and Barnes's intense localism'[75] as a distinct contrast between the two men. Hardy's knowledge of the Germanic origins of the English language may be gauged by such a small example as his naming of Abel Whittle in *The Mayor of Casterbridge*. James Gibson, in discussing the book as a classical tragedy, notes: '... Abel Whittle (Lear's Fool – 'wittol' was a Middle English word for fool').[76] Wittol has an Anglo-Saxon root; and incidentally, Hardy's biblical knowledge is apparent in Abel, the innocent victim of Cain. Hardy felt strongly about the cultural origins of England in general; he might be described as an 'English Nationalist', deploring the Victorian fashion for 'British' as opposed to 'English' in everyday parlance.

The use of the largely forgotten name of an Anglo-Saxon kingdom for the novels' setting was, and remains, one of Hardy's most popularising facets, inextricably linked as it is with the aura of a lost rural past, a recent but irrevocably vanished culture. Bradbury's book summarises a frequent comment from critics that Hardy's most decidedly regional work has traditionally been regarded as his best. Gibson explains the origin of the phenomenon thus:

> The name 'Wessex' had not been in general use for many centuries when Hardy used it in *Far from the Madding Crowd,* but it was picked up by reviewers and he soon became 'the Wessex novelist'. Knowing, as he said, 'the pecuniary value of a reputation for a speciality', he exploited the commercial value of this by an increasing emphasis on the Wessex topography ... .[77]

However, Millgate notes that, in contradiction of this assumed pioneering use by Hardy,

---

[71] Kenneth Cameron, English Place-Names (London: Batsford, 1961), p.48.
[72] James Campbell, The Anglo-Saxons (Oxford: Phaidon, 1982), p.26.
[73] Michael Wood, In Search of the Dark Ages (London: BBC, 1981), p.117.
[74] Cunliffe, p.304.
[75] Millgate, Career, p.127.
[76] James Gibson, Thomas Hardy – A Literary Life (London: Macmillan 1996), p.96.
[77] Gibson, Life, p.86.

William Barnes had used the name Wessex as early as 1868 to denote the region with 'a more contemporary significance'[78] in his preface to *Poems of Rural Life in Common English*.

Hardy had at first, like George Eliot with Middlemarch, or Elizabeth Gaskell with Cranford, fictionalised a real place to give himself the freedom to alter what he would (flexibly, according to Hardy's Preface to *A Pair of Blue Eyes*, it had a 'vague border'), but capture the verisimilitude and convey the immediacy of an area he knew so well, and in times of particular historical and affective significance.

The result was a phenomenon that he could never have envisaged, for in the process, he had struck on what might nowadays be called a 'marketing name' or 'image'. Millgate notes that Hardy's friend Charles Kegan Paul, who knew and loved Dorset, and recommended the Wessex novels as a way of getting to know Dorset was warmly thanked by the author, despite any 'reservations in the use of his work as a kind of tourist prospectus'.[79] He went on to treat the ancient name in a most proprietorial fashion for the rest of his life. In a letter of 12th January 1904,[80] thirty years after *Far from the Madding Crowd* had re-introduced the name, Macmillans, the author's publishers, wrote to Hardy to check that he did not object to Messrs. Bryan and Co. of Oxford using the name Wessex. Hardy gave approval, provided that the name was only used in association with his own name, or with the title of one of the novels!

King Alfred, the statue in Winchester sculpted by Sir Hamo Thorneycroft

Apart from continued and pervasive use of the name in his works, including poetry (*Wessex Heights* for instance) and short stories (the first collection he called *Wessex Tales*), Hardy named the first collected edition of the novels *Wessex Novels* (1895-1896, in 16 volumes). For this, Hardy the draughtsman-architect drew the defining map, illustrating 'The Wessex of the Novels', a manuscript of which occupies an honoured place in the Dorset County Museum. The Museum also (1999) displayed a newspaper cutting declaring that Miss Sophie Rhys-Jones, following her marriage to Prince Edward, had been created 'the first Countess of Wessex'; this is accompanied by a reader's letter pointing out Hardy's short story *The First*

---

[78] Millgate, Career, p.128.
[79] Millgate, Career, p.121.
[80] Dorset County Museum, Thomas Hardy archives, Letter no. 1006.

Countess of Wessex! Perhaps the correspondent should have gone on to suggest that without Hardy's re-discovery of the name, the Queen, though heir to Alfred the Great, might never have considered such an title. Hardy himself seems aware of the virtual disappearance of the name before his own usage brought it back; in fact he suggests that this now-revived title was, even in his own fiction, a name re-created from the lost Anglo-Saxon past. In *Tess* chapter XIX, Crick the dairyman implies this by mentioning '… the lands out by King's Hintock now owned by the Earl of Wessex, afore even he or his was heard of.'

Gibson comments that 'For the Wessex Novels edition [Hardy] made a number of topographical changes which resulted in greater consistency and emphasised this Wessexness.'[81] A similar observation is made by Martin Ray in noting the changes made by Hardy to the short story *What the Shepherd Saw*: 'All of these changes illustrate Hardy's typical tendency at this date to make possible closer identifications between his Wessex and the actual landscape.'[82] Millgate notes that the suggestion by John Hutton for a sketch map of the landscape 'as a frontispiece to a good novel' led eventually to one for *The Return of the Native* (and later to the familiar fuller Wessex map) and was a sign of 'the slowly developing conception of Wessex.'[83] Millgate sums up his examination of the phenomenon that, despite some flexibility, Hardy observed fidelity to the topography, though the past time was generalised[84] – even the more precisely defined *The Trumpet-Major* was an 'exploratory probing of the Wessex past.'[85]

Hardy's keen sense of the financial advantages of having 'his own' identifiable region were at first at odds with his strong instinct for privacy, even secrecy, upon which all his biographers have commented, though perhaps it is possible to see Wessex, both literally and artistically, as a refuge, a private place that could be used as and when necessary: the *Life* (p.399) notes the elderly Hardy's 'withdrawal into Wessex'. However, the practical necessity which first encouraged him to write prose in order to earn a living won the day in the public promotion of the region. In the most recent of a long line of guide books to 'Hardy's Wessex', Fred Pitfield outlines the tradition of which he is a recent exponent:

> More than any other writer, Hardy made use of real buildings, features and places which were given fictitious names, often more apt or descriptive than the real ones, and this was to prove one of the most popular aspects of his work. At a time when tourism was beginning to become common, many readers eagerly set out to explore the 'Wessex' area with a view to identifying and discovering the real places behind the fictitious names and guide books to cater for this need soon began to appear.[86]

Bradbury's *Atlas* remarks of this phenomenon:

> Urban readers, moved by his persuasive presentation of rural habits, customs, speech and values, were intrigued to think that just a few hours' train ride away was a place

---

[81] Gibson, Life, p135.
[82] Martin Ray, Thomas Hardy: A Textual Study of the Short Stories (Aldershot: Ashgate, 1997), p.304.
[83] Millgate, Career, p.124.
[84] Millgate, Career, pp.244/245.
[85] Millgate, Career, p.157.
[86] F.P. Pitfield, Hardy's Wessex Locations (Wincanton: Dorset Publishing Company, 1992), p.7.

Grave of Hardy's dog Wessex

unvisited, almost unheard of, where such a way of life had existed within living memory and might in remote recesses be surviving still.[87]

Pitfield lists C.G. Harper, *The Hardy Country* (1904), B.C.A. Windle, *The Wessex of Thomas Hardy* (1906), also two more recent books, and

> the most authoritative work on the subject … *Thomas Hardy's Wessex* by Hermann Lea (1913), illustrated by the author's own photographs. A personal friend of Hardy, Lea had the advantage of the author's collaboration on the project, and they travelled around the region together … .[88]

The name is still today on view at Max Gate: Florence's notoriously indulged and fierce dog, apparently feared by most visitors apart from T.E. Lawrence, is buried in the pets' cemetery in the grounds under a stone declaring: 'THE FAMOUS DOG WESSEX'.

Another, abstruse, connection between Hardy and Alfred's Wessex is that the heroic statue of the King in his capital, Winchester, erected in 1901, is by Sir Hamo Thornycroft, one of Hardy's society friends whom he delighted in naming in the *Life,* and whose elegant wife was one of those he found attractive. The statue was erected to mark what was then thought to be the millennium of Alfred's death (it is now known to have occurred in 900) and symbolises the Victorians' lionising of the King. Hardy's popularising of his kingdom's name thus pre-

---

[87] Bradbury, p.136.
[88] Pitfield, p.7.

dates this adulation and must at least be seen as complementary to, if not a direct catalyst for, Alfred's popularity.

The archaeology of Wessex is celebrated, comparable with the most significant areas of archaeological remains anywhere in the world. For a British writer interested in the past, it could hardly be bettered as a home. Though 'Wessex' has long been the favoured descriptor for the South West region with Stonehenge as its focus (for example, Leslie V. Grinsell's *The Archaeology of Wessex*, 1958),[89] the term 'archaeology of Wessex' is really an anachronistic misnomer, for, in common with the rest of England, the Anglo-Saxon past of Wessex is represented very much by its cultural heritage, supremely, by language, far more than by physical remains. Anglo-Saxon archaeology consists principally of coins, burials, the shape and vestigial ramparts of Alfred's fortified towns of the burghal hidage, and by churches – mainly their towers that have survived the wholesale reconstruction in the Middle Ages (of the kind that the young Hardy was to be involved with in the nineteenth century). Ironically, the remains of earlier eras are so much more numerous and more massive than those of the age to which the name Wessex refers, that the very term 'Wessex archaeology' instantly conjures up the megaliths and huge landscape features that typify the region.

James Dyer's popular guide,[90] by its very nature concerned with sites that are both important and accessible, easily confirms the importance of the region in prehistoric archaeology. Hardy's own Dorset provides forty-two sites for the book, while neighbouring Wiltshire, which boasts World Heritage Sites like Stonehenge and Avebury, has no fewer than sixty-eight; this may be compared with the important Anglo-Saxon Kingdom of East Anglia (Norfolk and Suffolk), like Wessex one of the Heptarchy, which includes only fifteen, just two of which are in Suffolk. In Roman archaeology, Dorset has its share of notable sites, as my chapter on *The Mayor of Casterbridge* indicates, and Bath, also in Wessex, is one of the most important Roman towns in Britain (Hardy's poem uses its Roman name, *Aquae Sulis*).

An important archaeological term with which Hardy, owing to his championing of the name, can be indirectly credited is 'Wessex Culture'. This revived familiarity of the name made it an obvious choice for Stuart Piggott who coined the term Wessex Culture in 1938 for the era of the warrior aristocracy of South West England in the Early Bronze Age (mid-second millennium BC).[91] Barry Cunliffe, (who indicates only that the term is a mid-twentieth-century neologism to identify artefacts that had first been recovered many centuries ago), is more circumspect than the archaeologists who first used the term, and deals with it thus:

> Some time about 2000 BC rich graves began to appear and the tradition continued until as late as 1400 BC. In all about a hundred 'rich graves' have been identified, the majority of them being in Wessex. … When the rich Wessex burials were first discussed over half a century ago, it was suggested that they represent a distinct 'culture' which was probably introduced from Brittany and maintained links with the Mycenaean world of the Aegean. It is now generally agreed that the 'Wessex Culture' phenomenon simply resulted from the desire among the upper echelons of the in-

---

[89] Leslie V. Grinsell, The Archaeology of Wessex (London: Methuen, 1958).
[90] James Dyer, Guide to Prehistoric England and Wales (London: Allen Lane, 1981).
[91] Stuart Piggott, 'The Early Bronze Age in Wessex', Proceedings of the Prehistoric Society, no.4 (1938), pp.52-106.

digenous population to display the status of their lineage through exotic grave goods which now they had the means of acquiring.[92]

This 'phenomenon', then, which is not alluded to as such in earlier texts such as Dyer's *Guide*,[93] is the major flowering of the Early Bronze Age in Britain, which had begun in *c.*2200 BC. Its grave goods are of a physical and aesthetic quality that certainly appealed to the early antiquarians and to the putative archaeologists of Hardy's early years – very much the practitioners of 'treasure hunting' to the exclusion of true archaeological knowledge.

---

[92] Cunliffe, p.123.
[93] Dyer, p.30.

CHAPTER THREE

NOVELIST AND 'BORN ARCHAEOLOGIST': HARDY'S PERSONAL WRITINGS

'The proper study of mankind is man.'

Alexander Pope, *An Essay on Man*, Epistle 2.

Pope's maxim, quoted as this Chapter's epigraph, is singularly apposite for a writer who both utilised archaeology as an artistic resource and also wrote about the subject with scientific objectivity, for both are equally approaches to 'the proper study of mankind' and are united in Hardy's intellect and imagination.

A study of Hardy's personal interest in archaeology reveals that his fascination was not indiscriminate, either in its practical application or in its artistic use in his works. The enigma of a site like Stonehenge – clouded with centuries of ill-defined myth, but unburdened by the legends of a Trojan War and thus spared the determined depredations of a Schliemann, whatever the attentions of local antiquaries – proved far more suggestive and suitable to Hardy's artistic purposes than Classical or newly-revealed Mediterranean prehistoric models, and of course more immediately available and solid than a site remembered from a foreign tour or read from the pages of Homer. We can, I believe, assume that the great discoveries of Schliemann at Troy (1870–1873, 1878–1879) and Mycenae (1876–1877) when Hardy was in his early middle years, or of Sir Arthur Evans at Knossos (from 1900) when Hardy was entering old age, excited interest in the author. Schliemann, for example, was a star guest speaker in London when Hardy was already well-known in London society: the controversial German lectured to the Hellenic Society in 1886, the year of the publication of *The Mayor of Casterbridge* with its mass of archaeological reference. But of these and the other key discoveries in the later nineteenth century, Hardy's surviving writings are frustratingly devoid of direct reference. Not only were such geographical areas as those of the Classical civilisations outside Hardy's centre of interest, but the examples I quote are among those which stretched concrete, factual knowledge back into time periods previously shrouded in myth, a factor of little use to a novelist who used archaeological material in Hardy's way. This fact, as well as their distance from Wessex, precluded such developments from Hardy's artistic resource, however fascinating their reports may have been when Hardy may have encountered them in the press. That he admired and gained an intimate knowledge of modern scientific method is, of course, quite another matter

– but this facet of the author's acumen was also rooted deeply in his home area. The key point is that Hardy the artist had a quite different engagement with archaeology as part of his resource from Hardy the man of wide contemporary interests. Further, Hardy's championing of his home area and his predominant interest in its archaeology do not lead to any kind of general promotion in his fiction of the region's archaeological sites. When it comes to the artistic use of archaeology in Hardy's works, the artist sets the agenda rather than the archaeologist or ambassador of Wessex. Stonehenge and Maiden Castle might be on any tourist itinerary, but Roman Dorchester is of minor importance, and the Devil's Den is one of the more obscure of many hundreds of barrow ruins that one could visit: there is no 'Cook's tour' of Avebury,

Maiden Castle

Silbury Hill, and the other notable places that the author must have visited. Indeed, two important types of prehistoric ritual monument, standing stones and circles (apart, of course, from the wholly exceptional Stonehenge), hardly figure in all of Hardy's work – whereas even his poetic hero Wordsworth, with no particular antiquarian interest, wrote a short piece about the Cumbrian circle Long Meg and her Daughters (Itinerary Poems of 1833, XLIII).

As I have noted, Hardy's lifetime coincided approximately with the development of archaeology out of antiquarianism. Hardy's non-fictional writings on archaeological subjects are few, and so commensurately are his uses of the word archaeology and its lexical derivatives. His prose fiction is vast by comparison, and because the novels and stories are generally set in the first half of the nineteenth century, Hardy uses – on the rare occasions when it is called for – the word antiquary for someone engaged in what would later be the specialised activity of the archaeologist. Antiquary, defined by the OED as 'a student or collector of antiques or antiquities', is thus assigned a much broader range of interest than any scientist, and was even taken in everyday terminology to include those interested in researching local history or genealogy and the like. Crucially, there is a distinct connotation of the amateur or the dilettante about the word, for most of those described as antiquaries were country clergymen or landowners, men with time on their hands, financial security, and sometimes servants to help with the manual work; with libraries at their disposal, and invariably with a Classical education which coloured their thinking about the past of this country. For the modern archaeologist, the antiquary is, to a greater or lesser extent, coloured by the pejorative connotation of amateurism and careless-

The Roman Temple remains in Maiden Castle

ness, and though a somewhat primitive antecedent, was nonetheless a necessary evolutionary step towards the true science of archaeology. Hardy's attitude is the more negative because of his personal animosity to Edward Cunnington, and because of his friendship and admiration for Pitt-Rivers, the founder of modern archaeology, who made Cunnington look both methodologically primitive and intellectually suspect.

Cunnington is the apparent model for the antiquary in *A Tryst at an Ancient Earthwork*, Hardy's only fictional piece based on the practice of archaeology. Following the brooding presence of Rainbarrow in *The Return of the Native* (1878) and the re-creation of the past achieved in *The Trumpet-Major* of 1880, the 1880s saw the other substantial works with major archaeological content, and the first two pieces of journalism about the subject. *What the Shepherd Saw* appeared in *The Illustrated London News*, the journal that did so much to promote popular interest in archaeology, at Christmas 1881; Hardy joined the Field Club (1882), wrote the Max Gate excavation report for presentation to the Field Club (1884, the same year as *A Tryst*, and *The Mayor of Casterbridge*, subsequently published 1886), and probably wrote an article based on Max Gate for *The World* with details about antiquities on display (February 1886). The Hardys viewed substantial relics of the past on holiday in Italy in 1887 and visited Flinders Petrie's Egyptian Exhibition in London on 14th July 1888. The first of the short stories collected in *A Group of Noble Dames*, 'The First Countess of Wessex', appeared in *Harper's New Monthly Magazine* in December 1889; these stories are linked by the device of being narrated in the Casterbridge Museum by members of the South Wessex Field and Antiquarian Club,

Max Gate, Hardy's home on the outskirts of Dorchester

based on its real Dorset equivalent, and were finished in May 1890 for publication in *The Daily Graphic*. Hardy then wrote *Tess* with its celebrated Stonehenge scene in 1890 (planned from autumn 1888 but interrupted by short stories; published 1891). The three later pieces (an interview about Stonehenge published in *The Daily Chronicle*, the Introduction to Henry J. Moule's *Dorchester Antiquities*, and the article 'Maumbury Ring' for *The Times*), together with Hardy's noted enthusiasm for archaeological activity, provide evidence that the interest more than survived the end of his fiction writing.

Hardy's increasing archaeological interest coincides with developments in the career of General Pitt-Rivers and the author's friendship with him and his family. The only reference to the relationship in the *Life* is evidently to its mature phase, in September 1895, when 'they paid a week's visit to General and Mrs Pitt-Rivers at Rushmore, and much enjoyed the time'.[1] The two biographies of the General give no more help: M.W. Thomson[2] makes no reference at all, and Mark Bowden mentions only the visit quoted above and the poem 'Concerning Agnes' about the General's third daughter.[3] But Andrew D. Radford tells us that Hardy the artist 'repudiated Pitt-Rivers's naïve, early optimism that the uncovered remains of outmoded cultures might enrich and irradiate the modern moment'[4] and that he was opposed to the destructiveness of archaeology because it could destroy the emotional associations of the place[5] – wholly understandable caveats from a writer, but for our 'born archaeologist' who carried out excavations they are a powerful reminder of the fundamental ambivalence and contradictions of this fascinating personality.

However, apart from the very evident influence of the General on Hardy which I shall explore in detail, Pitt-Rivers' career marked the end of the era of polymathy, the time before modern specialisation made eminence in more than a limited field all but impossible; this meant that he was part of a circle of experts who all knew each other and this in its turn meant that Hardy could readily meet many of the leading thinkers and practitioners of his day in a range of developing sciences in sympathy with Pitt-Rivers' advanced ideas.

Harold Orel asserts in his article: 'It is therefore no accident that Hardy's most interesting writings based upon archaeological insights and data began in the 1880s, when the full implications of General Augustus Henry Lane-Fox Pitt-Rivers' work were exciting a new generation of barrow-diggers and antiquarians.'[6] Long before this time, both Hardy and Pitt-Rivers had become celebrities in their fields; the General was near the end of his career, for he died in 1900. The biographies give no clue as to when the two first met (though the first invitation to Pitt-Rivers' home was possibly in September 1895), but Hardy's more intense 'archaeological' phase closely matches the increased practical archaeological work of the General in Wessex whose celebrated excavations of the huge inherited estate on Cranborne Chase in Dorset started in 1880. Orel continues that 'Hardy's knowledge of the General's contributions to taxonomy, typology, ethnography, and prehistoric archaeology, and of his emphasis on scientific stratigraphy at any dig, was extensive. The General had 'devotedly crawled among the stones on his hands & knees inspecting rabbit holes &c.', Hardy wrote to Mrs Henniker ... '.[7]

Born Augustus Henry Lane-Fox, he added the Pitt-Rivers when he inherited the estate from his uncle Lord Rivers in 1880. His excavations of the Cranborne Chase estate continued until his death. The histories of archaeology concur in the prominence they give to the importance of Pitt-Rivers' achievements in the development of the science. His influence was both recognised and extended by his appointment as the first Inspector of Ancient Monuments in January 1883. Glyn Daniel's *A Hundred Years of Archaeology* explains that the General was not only the *sine qua non* of modern archaeology, but his was the culmination of the developing work of the later antiquaries. He made two crucial contributions to archaeology: the analysis of artefacts by their typological classification along evolutionary lines, and the technique of

---

[1] *Life*, p.269.
[2] M.W. Thomson, *General Pitt-Rivers* (Bradford-on-Avon: Moonraker, 1977).
[3] Mark Bowden, *Pitt Rivers* [sic] (Cambridge: CUP, 1991), pp.33, 35, 149.
[4] Radford, p.22.
[5] Radford, p.15.
[6] Orel, 'Archaeology', p.30.
[7] Orel, 'Archaeology', p.33.

highly organised, thoroughly executed and minutely recorded excavations which were published in full as swiftly as possible after the event. His impulse to educate informed all his endeavours, and in all his work he was conditioned by a military rigour and facilitated by the virtually unlimited funds of his inheritance. Daniel comments on his 'great talents for organisation and for experimental research', and notes that he 'began what may justly be called a sociological approach to artefacts.'[8] Typical of his bold, uncompromising approach were remarks made in his address at the opening of the new Dorset County Museum on January 7th 1884, an event attended by Hardy (who later became a trustee) and just before the author began writing his most 'archaeological' novel, *The Mayor of Casterbridge*. The General commented:

> The remarks which I have to make may be divided under two heads, embracing the two principal functions which a Local Museum [sic] may be expected to serve. Firstly, its utility in subordination to the interests of science in general as a means in aiding scientific men in their researches, and secondly, its utility as a means of instruction in the town or district in which it is established. All museum space is necessarily limited and in a local Museum [sic], notwithstanding the liberality of the gentry and others in this neighbourhood by which you have been enabled to construct a building which will do credit to the town, the space must be very limited, and the attention of the curators will have to be drawn, not merely to the collection of useful specimens, but quite as much to the exclusion of objects which serve neither of the two purposes which I have named. I speak, I am sorry to say, in ignorance of what this museum actually does contain, and therefore my observations must be considered to refer to local museums in general rather than to this museum in particular. But I am certain that unless a hard and fast line is drawn from the commencement for the guidance of those who are in charge of the collections, local influence will be put upon them to fill your valuable space with things that are of more interest to the donors either to preserve or to get rid of, than of value to the public or for any scientific purpose.[9]

Of particular relevance to Hardy's use of the archaeological, the *Life* says, 'Pitt-Rivers and Petrie [both personal friends of Hardy] were the leaders of the revolution in archaeology which led it away from the contemplation of *art* objects to the contemplation of *all* objects'[10] – an approach which had a natural appeal to the cottage-born son of a mason and one who so readily imbibed folklore. Again, Hardy's evident lack of interest in the treasure-hunting expeditions of the Mediterranean archaeologists is made forcefully understandable: such activities and motivation had no appeal nor place in this author's world-view, whereas his sympathy and admiration for the approach of General Pitt-Rivers seem inevitable by comparison.

The Pitt-Rivers Collection was donated for public display and edification, eventually moving to a purpose-built extension to the University Museum in Oxford where it remains to this day. Its taxonomical arrangement of all manner of artefacts ('The Evolution of Firearms' is a typical section and was one of Pitt-Rivers' earliest expositions of his method) was far ahead of its day, and the Darwinian origins and approach of its founder were very much in keeping with Hardy's enthusiasm for all that was new in the sciences; and this socially elite family with

---

[8] Daniel, *Hundred*, pp.169-174.
[9] Jo Draper, ed., *Address by Lt.-General A.H.L.F.Pitt-Rivers at the Opening of the Dorset County Museum, 1884* (Dorchester: Dorset Natural History and Archaeological Society, 1984), p.4.
[10] Daniel, *Hundred*, p.171.

its charismatic head (and attractive women) were just the sort of people whom Hardy loved to know – and to mention in the *Life*. Although the General recognised the possibility of regression, his was a Victorian belief in the overall March of Progress. Whatever Hardy's sympathies in the factual realm, the overwhelming impression of his fiction is quite the opposite of optimism, and his interest in archaeology and friendship with Pitt-Rivers and other contemporary luminaries offer one of those striking paradoxes about Hardy, though – as with so many of his generation – the older Hardy was reduced to grim despair by the Great War.

Hardy's friendships with Petrie and Pitt-Rivers, both, like Hardy, admirers of, and in their scientific method and creed, avowed followers of, Charles Darwin, make it remarkable and frustrating that there seems to have been no contact between Hardy and his equally celebrated near-contemporary Arthur Evans, even though they became equally well-known in social and academic circles. John Evans and his son Arthur Evans were both noted archaeologists and collectors and the son later became the discoverer of the Minoan Civilisation of Crete, a name of his own coining. Evans senior was a friend of Darwin and of Pitt-Rivers, Evans junior a friend of Petrie and follower (in his maturity) of Pitt-Rivers' methods; Hardy was an admirer of Darwin and a friend of both Pitt-Rivers and Petrie. The Evanses' Oxford University culture, together with Arthur's very different social background might be enough reason for their never having met and his passion for the archaeology of the Aegean was an obvious geographical barrier – though he shared Hardy's distaste for the perceived superiority of Classical culture which in part motivated his search for the prehistoric civilisation of Crete.

***

A Tryst at an Ancient Earthwork (*Complete Stories* pp. 645–654) is assuredly a minor piece among Hardy's fictional utterances, but its importance as a pointer to Hardy's interest in archaeology and his attitude to the changing nature of the subject in its formative period is considerable, and its composition date of early 1885 – in the midst of writing *The Mayor* – is significant; in fact, the novel was finished the month after the story's first publication. Harold Orel dubs it a 'slight but striking anecdote',[11] while for Josephine Dool, 'the story is slight but as an evocative description of a hillfort on a stormy night it is superb.'[12] Without a specific interest in Hardy's involvement with archaeology, Martin Ray is more ruthlessly dismissive, starting his chapter on the piece: "A Tryst' is one of Hardy's least successful short stories.'[13] While accepting it is 'a moody, evocative sketch', he finds the narrative merely 'stage business at the end'. I would disagree, however, that the piece shows in itself that Hardy found first-person narrative 'not a form that was at all congenial to him' – though the small number of examples might suggest disaffection. The story is certainly most unusual for its author in being a first person narrative, as Ray points out, and in the voice of an adopted persona to boot, but it is also remarkable in being told in the present tense. This mode provides a dramatic immediacy, but Hardy gives the whole a longer perspective by adding a brief narrative postscript in the past tense, as if he later reflected on the curious events of that night. Ray notes that the 1913 version has the archaeologist dying seven rather than five years after the meeting, 'thereby casting

---

[11] Orel, 'Archaeology', p.24.
[12] Dool, 'Archaeology and Thomas Hardy'.
[13] Ray, p.291.

the story backwards in time and showing the tryst in a longer historical perspective, making the tale itself, as it were, a kind of relic which the narrator has unearthed for us.'[14]

The story in its final form is an evocative account of a secret meeting between the narrator and a local antiquary who is obsessed with proving his theory about the true nature of the hill-fort, in reality, Maiden Castle. Before they leave the spot, our narrator suspects that the elderly fanatic surreptitiously secretes a small figurine in his coat pocket for his personal collection, an item which is subsequently (in the closing words of the postscript) 'bequeathed to the Casterbridge Museum'.

The persona adopted for the narrator is clearly not Hardy himself, his home – although it is not called such and may be just temporary shelter before the meeting – ('a cottage ... a mile away ...') being at least a mile distant from and much more modest than Max Gate. An anonymous article from *The World* in February 1886, judged by James Gibson to be likely 'written by Hardy or is based largely upon notes supplied by him',[15] mentions the clear view of Maiden Castle from Max Gate before the trees obscured the surroundings: '... from a lower window at the side, however, we have a full view of the immense ramparts of Maiden Castle, which, to quote from one of this writer's stories describing the place, 'rises against the sky with a Titanic personality [this ascription, so like that for Egdon Heath in *The Return of the Native*, is, of course, from the original 1885 version and was later changed to 'obtrusive personality'] that compels the senses to regard it and consider.' Although the spot is more than a mile distant, the sentence does not exaggerate the strange force with which the magnificent earthwork impresses its presence upon the occupants of this room.' Impressive evidence that Hardy 'wrote' the article comes at the end when a storm brewing over Maiden Castle is described in terms strongly reminiscent of those in *A Tryst*: '... we note, low-lying about Maiden Castle, huge masses of cloud, now luminous with the splendour of sunset, anon livid with the tones of approaching night and tempest.'[16] And Hardy knew Maiden Castle intimately at close hand as well, as details in the story clearly show. The first person narration might, nevertheless, suggest the author's commitment to the sub-text, which is a very trenchant critique of the cavalier and obsolete attitude and methods of the antiquarian compared with the new, fully-fledged science of the archaeologist. Moreover, his evidently nefarious midnight appointment, he tells the reader, 'I rather regret my decision to keep now that night is come'.

For the general reader, perhaps discovering Wessex sights as a result of reading the novels, Henry J. Moule, brother of Hardy's mentor, enticingly describes the fort thus: 'The largest of these Dorset camps is, you know, close enough to us – Maiden Castle. It is one of the finest and best preserved in England – nay, in the world.'[17] Hardy's evocative opening shows his knowledge of palaeontology in describing the fort with its partaking of the cephalopod in shape which 'may be likened to an enormous many-limbed organism of the antediluvian time'. We are reminded of the famous description of Egdon Heath at the start of *The Return of the Native*; the hill-fort is personified as a monstrous being with its 'heavy high-shouldered presence' which 'looms up out of the shade by degrees, like a thing waking up and asking what I want there.' Hardy goes on to create a marvellously atmospheric scene in the shifting play of light:

---

[14] Ray, p.300.
[15] Gibson, *Interviews*, pp.19/20.
[16] Gibson, *Interviews*, p.23.
[17] H. J. Moule, *Old Dorset: Chapters in the History of the County* (London: Cassell, 1893), p.97.

'With the shifting of the clouds the faces of the steeps vary in colour and in shade, broad lights appearing where mist and vagueness had prevailed, dissolving in their turn into melancholy gray [sic], which spreads over and eclipses the luminous bluffs.' The description of the near approach to the fort reveals not only Hardy's acute descriptive power, but his knowledge of one of the most significant causes of archaeological degradation: 'the ploughs' which have 'essayed for centuries to creep up near and yet nearer to the base … '. It is typically Hardyesque in nature,

Badbury Rings, Wimborne

as well, for with 'its solitude, it becomes appallingly mournful in its growing closeness.' Other aspects of the evocation accord with the archaeological subject-matter: the 'transitoriness' of the storm and the very furtiveness of their entry are set ironically against the age, permanence, and overtness of the hill-fort in the midst of a very open landscape. The roar of the storm 'travelling the complete circuit of the castle … Like a circumambulating column of infantry', the lightning's 'resemblance to swords moving in combat … [which] has the very brassy hue of the weapons that here were used', the soaking aftermath of the storm which 'sparkles on every wet grass-blade', and the memory of 'hail shot with lightning' – resembling, surely, slingshot ammunition – re-emphasise Hardy's informed sense of the history and original purpose of the place.

I shall deal with the origins and understanding of the 'stupendous ruin' of Maiden Castle in some detail, not least because it illuminates Hardy's own knowledge of the site and places him in its archaeological history at a nodal point between the tinkerings of antiquarians and the scientific investigations of Wheeler and his more recent successors. Indeed, Maiden Castle is perhaps the best known and one of the most thoroughly studied of any of the hill-forts in Britain. Hill-forts, which were first constructed in the insecurity of the late Bronze Age, are the archetypal visible remains of the Iron Age in Britain, and formed the most formidable obstacles to the conquest of the island by the Romans from AD 43.

Richard Muir's and Humphrey Welfare's chapter on this last prehistoric period is called simply 'An Age of Hillforts' [In this study I have preferred the hyphenated form as given in the OED].[18] Their vast scale, intricate design, and sheer number in the landscape make them among the most impressive features of prehistory. Many of the most famous and best explored are in Wessex, several of them in Dorset. Hardy had, of course, been familiar with Maiden Castle since childhood; in July 1881, Hardy took Emma to visit Badbury Rings, another Dorset example, near Wimborne. Maiden Castle shows traces of Neolithic occupation from $c.$ 3000 BC, then was developed in $c.$ 350 BC as a single rampart and ditch Iron Age hill-fort. The defences declined into disrepair in safer times and had to be rebuilt in about 250 BC when 'elaborate entrances were constructed at both east and west ends of the hill', and again in about 150 BC when 'Double ramparts were constructed on the north and treble on the south [sides].' ... 'By 100 BC it was necessary to remodel all the defences on the scale of the inner rampart ... with platforms for slingers and sentry boxes at the excavated eastern entrance.'[19] The Legio II Augusta under Vespasian overwhelmed the fort after a siege in AD 44, but habitation continued for twenty years, and in the 4th C AD, a temple with a mosaic over the *cella* floor and a (?priest's) house were constructed on the hill top.

It is interesting that Moule's descriptor for Maiden Castle, already quoted, is a 'camp'. The most recent research points to the sheer variety of purpose and nature of these 'forts', ranging from settlements to ritual places, markets to tribal assemblies – with defence by no means being necessarily a primary function.

A beautifully drawn scale plan of the fort accompanies Hutchins' description of the site. What Josephine Dool calls the 'unpublished and ill-recorded excavations'[20] of Edward Cunnington, clearly identifying him with outdated and unscientific antiquarianism, were carried out in 1882–1884. The thorough and scientific work of Sir Mortimer Wheeler, whose publication *Maiden Castle*[21] is dubbed 'a classic of archaeological literature' by Glyn Daniel in his *A Short History of Archaeology,*[22] re-opened and extended Cunnington's dig from 1934 to 1937. The contrast between the two, though the second was nearly a decade after Hardy's death, forms an important part of the inferential discussion of Hardy's attitude to archaeology which may be drawn from *A Tryst at an Ancient Earthwork*. The details of the finds and results may be briefly clarified. Cunnington believed that his discovery of a building with a mosaic floor, as in the story, was a Roman villa, and this was disproved by Wheeler's more extensive re-examination. Cunnington found a small bronze plaque depicting the Roman goddess Minerva, but Hardy chose to transpose to the story a more notable *objet*, a figurine of Mercury which he no doubt knew from the Museum collection and from Hutchins who describes it

---

[18] Richard Muir and Humphrey Welfare, *The National Trust Guide to Prehistoric and Roman Britain* (London: George Philip,1983), chapter 7.
[19] Dyer, p.126.
[20] Dool, 'Archaeology'.
[21] Originally, R.E.M. Wheeler, *Reports of the Research Committee of the Society of Antiquaries of London No. XII – Maiden Castle, Dorset* (London: Society of Antiquaries, 1943).
[22] Daniel, *Archaeology*, pp.168/169.

and includes an illustration. This was found in 1747 by a Mr Cozens in the garden of the old Grammar School in Dorchester.

Hardy styles the name of the fort Mai-Dun, a supposedly ancient form that he clearly took from Hutchins, and to which he remained loyal in all his writings. Hutchins' account of the origins of the place and its name is both thorough and objectively non-committal; no wonder that not only did Hardy rely on Hutchins, but later commentators cite him as a notable example of a pioneering earlier generation of good local historians. Hutchins' entry on Maiden Castle is part of his article on the parish of Winterbourne St Martin and starts thus:

> On this farm a little north of Ashton, on a hill which it entirely occupies, stands Maiden Castle, one of the largest and most complete Roman (British) camps in the West of England. It is so called on a tradition, says Mr Coker, that it was never lost or won. Thus Edinburgh Castle was supposed to be called Maiden Castle, because formerly scarce ever taken, or because the daughters of the King and nobility were kept there till married. But this is a mistake; for maiden, in the Highland language, signifies a castle on a rock. Besides, Maiden Castle, Maiden Way, Maiden Hold and Maiden Bower occur in several places in the North of England. Dr Gale mentions a Maiden Castle at Bowes in Richmondshire, co. York; and Leland another, being on a hill diked in, near the Borough co. Westmerland [sic]. Some derive the word Maiden from the British Mad, fair or beautiful (whence the Saxon word Maid or Maiden), and thence conclude that fortifications so called were deemed impregnable. Mr Baxter's derivation is more probable, who deduced it from the British Mai-Dun the castle of the great hill; in his opinion, it is the Dunium of Ptolemy; the capital of the Durotriges. ... Camden changes this into Durnium to make it correspond with Durnovaria. Dunium is mentioned only by Ptolemy ... .[23]

An exhaustive etymological study included in Wheeler's *Maiden Castle* fails to find any substantive evidence for these traditional claims discussed by Hutchins, nor hence of Hardy's. He concurs in many details with his predecessor, but, having the benefit of much more recent scholarship, regards as, at best, unreliable the traditional old name beloved by Hardy and others such as John Ireland. Like Hutchins, Wheeler points to the *widespread* use of the same name in Britain, but as far back as the twelfth century, and in addition (in their respective languages) in other European countries even further back as the ninth century in Germany, so rendering untenable, as implicitly did Hutchins, the possibility of an exclusive meaning for this one site in one country. Wheeler concludes his three-page note 'The Present Name': 'In summary, the ultimate origin of the name 'Maiden Castle' is uncertain, and no attempt to derive it from Celtic or other originals is of substantive value.'[24]

Thirteen years before Wheeler's excavation, in 1921, the composer John Ireland, who had an intense interest in the mysterious, immanent character of ancient sites, chose to follow Hardy's lead in the title of his yearning and passionate symphonic rhapsody *Mai-Dun*. John Burke writes:

> Ireland shared Housman's ironic pessimism about the world and he found another

---
[23] Hutchins, p.575.
[24] Wheeler R.E.M., 'Maiden Castle, Dorset' (London: Society of Antiquaries, 1943), p.11.

kindred spirit in the fatalistic Hardy … Grim echoes of a prehistoric past always argued in Ireland's mind with wistful intimations of lost beauty.[25]

Burke's summary here accords well with the fascination with the place that Hardy demonstrates in *A Tryst*, but there is, of course, far more to Hardy's overall concern with the past than Ireland's romantic 'wistful intimations'. (This same chapter four of Burke's book discusses Edward Elgar's 1913 meeting with Hardy to plan an opera based on one of Hardy's works, and also Hardy's relationship with Gustav Holst to which I refer in Chapter Five.)

Hardy withholds his use of the name until his evocation of the place itself is complete, then his narrator states prosaically in the manner of a historical reference book: 'The peculiar place of which these are some of the features is 'Mai-Dun', 'The Castle of the Great Hill', said to be the Dunium of Ptolemy, the Capital of the Durotriges, which eventually came into Roman occupation, and was finally deserted on their withdrawal from the island.'

Hardy's extensive and far from inexpert knowledge of archaeology is amply shown in *A Tryst at an Ancient Earthwork*. His detailed first-hand local familiarity is revealed in the description of the extreme difficulty of the climb up the ramparts (a modern assault which incidentally serves to prove the excellence of the original defensive design, and also indicates the offensive nature of the antiquary's visit): 'The first was a surface to walk up, the second to stagger up, the third can only be ascended on the hands and toes.' The details of the construction confirm Hardy's account here, for the narrator ascends from the North side where there are two ramparts, meaning that he had to make three ascents including the final one to the main level of the fort. He notes that it is 'the largest ancient-British work in the kingdom' and observes 'the true entrance used by its occupants of old'; he speculates on whether the designer was 'some great one of the Belgae, or of the Durotriges, or the travelling engineer of Britain's united tribes', and claims in the person of his antiquary 'that it is not a Celtic stronghold exclusively, but also a Roman …'; he describes 'a complete mosaic – a pavement of minute tesserae of many colours' – all of which was at the limit of contemporary knowledge. With not a little pathos, as well as an accurate knowledge of the centuries-old tradition of quarrying archaeological sites for dressed stone, Hardy says that this was a 'long-violated retreat; all its corner stones … were carried away to build neighbouring villages … '. And in a typically wry note about Christianity, 'the corner stones of this heathen altar may form the base-course of some adjoining village church.' Other more purely imaginative possibilities of such an archaeological site are also fully explored. Like Keats contemplating the Grecian urn, the narrator is so engrossed in the experience of antiquity that 'Past and present have become so confusedly mingled under the associations of the spot that for a time it has escaped my memory …' and the signpost at the summit is the first evidence 'that the time is really the nineteenth century'. He visualises that here 'doubtless, spears and shields have frequently lain while their owners loosened their sandals and yawned and stretched their arms in the sun'. He hears in his mind's ear the songs of the Celtic warriors, and, reminding us that Hardy's breadth of material in his archaeological allusion, like the archaeology at Maiden Castle itself, encompasses both Roman and prehistoric, he declares that 'We seem to be standing in the Roman Forum and not on a hill in Wessex.' The crucial difference between the prehistoric and the historic Roman facets

---

[25] John Burke, *Musical Landscapes* (Exeter: Webb and Bower, 1983), p.65.

of archaeology is realised in the fact that Hardy makes it clear that not only do we know nothing of the architect of the fort, nor any definite details of its inhabitants, but their deeds are unrecorded in any form: hence the imaginative delight he shows in speculating on prehistoric archaeology.

Not least in this imaginative scheme is Hardy's musing upon the passage of time, and especially on *sic transit gloria mundi*. He declares, extending the audible nature of the storm sweeping round the fort, 'Acoustic possibilities multiply tonight. We can almost hear the stream of years that have borne those deeds away from us.' Where soldiers once marched, now do only 'columns of sheep and oxen'; 'its cunning, even where not obscured by dilapidation, is now wasted on the solitary forms of a few wild badgers, rabbits, and hares.' Prehistoric archaeology, the branch particularly developed by Pitt-Rivers, gives particular, and perhaps even more affective, scope to the imagination, and so Hardy reflects:

> Men must have often gone out by those gates in the morning to battle with the Roman legions under Vespasian; some to return no more, others to come back at evening, bringing with them the noise of their heroic deeds. But not a page, not a stone, has preserved their fame.

Martin Ray's exhaustive textual study of the story details five successive versions, starting with the original *Ancient Earthworks and What Two Enthusiastic Scientists Found Therein* published in *The Detroit Post* on 15th March 1885 (aptly for a newspaper, this sounds just like a headline); then the more local *Ancient Earthworks at Casterbridge* in *The English Illustrated Magazine* of December 1893, the identifying name apparently being added by the editor. The change of the original inaccurate, albeit aptly ironic, title was the first of many changes made for subsequent versions. Hardy's commitment to a piece that had lain dormant for over eight years is shown by his revisions and by his sending with the story three (Ray notes that four were reproduced in the magazine) photographs of Maiden Castle by W. Pouncy of Dorchester. This publication of the story is interesting in that, as Ray points out, the editor of that magazine, Clement King Shorter, was also the editor of *The Illustrated London News*, which, as I have noted, was well-known for its popular promotion of archaeology. Hardy submitted the piece for publication in the latter, and it was Shorter who wanted to use it in his other journal. I would speculate that Hardy's impulse was that the story had definite archaeological significance, but that Shorter felt that the mischievous satire on a strongly-suggested living subject required a transfer to the realm of entertainment. Publication under the present title, both as a single work and as part of *A Changed Man and Other Tales*, was in 1913, and then in the Wessex Edition of 1914.

Ray's analysis of the changes in the later editions reveals that considerable polish and improvement were achieved: 'The principal changes give a greater presence to the narrator and the shady antiquary ... turning a rather static sketch of Mai-Dun into a more dramatized work of fiction.' He also finds 'a clearer thematic perspective on his material' – a vital development in that this concerns his attitude to archaeology – and develops 'an impressionistic quality', 'enhanced prominence of the first-person narrator', and is concerned to 'animate the whole scene' with increased personification.

More specifically, I find that several of Hardy's alterations reveal a continuing concern with archaeological accuracy, updating details to match the rapidly improving knowledge of prehistory that Hardy surely kept abreast of in his reading and at meetings of the Society. Ray points out that the term 'Anglo-Romans' was deleted after the first version. This could show that Hardy realised he had been careless, or, I suggest, that he realised the term was historically meaningless. More substantially, Hardy refines the identity of the builders, which he reinforces in the final version, excluding the obsolete notion that Maiden Castle was Roman, and clarifying the situation of the Romans attacking the Celtic defenders of the fort from outside; he is also more definite in the details of the fort itself.

The main focus of the tale through the different versions is increasingly on the character of the antiquary, and hence on the theme of the inferiority, both scientifically and morally, of antiquarianism compared with modern scientific archaeology. Andrew D. Radford states that Hardy 'wished to incorporate into his artistic vision both the tenacious resolve … and the jovial dilettantism of the amateur antiquarian' also represented 'with effortless ease' by William Barnes.[26] Bearing in mind Hardy's reverence for his mentor Barnes and what this story clearly indicates of Hardy's attitude to the 'amateur antiquarian', it is vital that we distinguish in this comment Hardy's 'artistic vision' from his clear and modern scientific attitude.

In his study, Martin Ray generally refers to him as an 'antiquary', but once or twice uses 'archaeologist' which tends to confuse the argument a little: he states that the 'most substantial new material for *EIM* involves the dozen or so additions which give personal and invariably critical information about the archaeologist' giving him 'a much more prominent and satirical presence'. These clearly signify that Hardy was becoming progressively (in both senses) more concerned and enthusiastic for the modern scientific archaeology of his friend Pitt-Rivers. The final version of the story, however slight the narrative, is virtually a critique of the antiquarian's whole approach. Michael Millgate's biography explains that 'Hardy seems to have found himself at cross-purposes with Edward Cunnington, a local antiquary of what Hardy evidently took to be rather rapacious habits.'[27] It would be unfair to say that an antiquarian would be *ipso facto* 'rather rapacious', but that Hardy was by this time eager to assert the more careful and circumspect scientific methods of the true archaeologist is significant – and by the time of the 1893 revised version, he was in what Millgate calls a 'publish and be damned' mood.[28] Hardy was at first coy about identifying the place, since his antiquary was so readily identifiable with Cunnington ('almost libellously, one would think' – Millgate, see note 25). But the story in manuscript ended with 'Casterbridge Museum', and so his complaint that his editor had added 'Casterbridge' to the title of the *English Illustrated Magazine* version seems odd.

The 'charges' that Hardy levels at his antiquary are of two kinds: firstly that his methods are unscientific, and secondly that his motives and methods are morally reprehensible, the two intertwined in the story under the pall of an obsessive neurosis verging on the psychotic. Ray observes that there is

> a stark contrast between the technological foresight and ingenuity of those who built the earthwork and the myopic self-interest of the 'scientist' who scrapes about and digs in the dark. The pioneering brilliance of the ancient engineers has been replaced

---

[26] Radford, p 15
[27] Michael Millgate, *Thomas Hardy – A Biography* (Oxford: OUP, 1982), p.244.
[28] Millgate, *Biography*, p.342.

by the grubby and furtive work of the modern archaeologist [I must demur at the use of the term here], who can merely scratch at the surface of their world and plunder their valuables.[29]

Hardy's narrator, who sometimes ironically calls him his 'friend', says:

I remember to have heard of men who, in their enthusiasm for some special science, art, or hobby, have quite lost the moral sense which would restrain them from indulging it illegitimately; and I conjecture that here, at last, is an instance of such a one.

The description of the man paints him as not only 'a professed and well-known antiquary with capital letters at the tail of his name' (Hardy having a dig at the value of academia!), but a diminished and patently outdated spectacle of 'about sixty, small in figure, with gray old-fashioned whiskers cut to the shape of a pair of crumb-brushes. He is entirely in black broadcloth … '. The antiquary's 'dark lantern' and the very hour and secrecy of the tryst make it implicitly illicit. He states his theory as 'His eyes flash anew', which is that 'it is not a Celtic stronghold exclusively, but also a Roman;' [true, in fact, to the extent that a Roman presence existed for so long after its conquest] 'the former people probably contributed little more than the original framework which the latter took and adapted till it became the present imposing structure' – a view tending in exactly the opposite direction to modern knowledge, though supported by Cunnington's excavation, so aligning Hardy firmly with modern interpretation. In breathlessly free indirect discourse, Hardy quotes the old man's motive that 'it proves all the world to be wrong in this great argument, and himself alone to be right!' – a statement as hyperbolical as it is egocentric. He 'continually murmurs to himself how important, how very important this discovery is!' and 'digs on unconcernedly; he is living two thousand years ago, and despises things of the moment as dreams,' so very different from the narrator's harmlessly imaginative reverie. Hardy describes the dig (excavation would be too elegant a term) with heavy irony: '… he begins flourishing the tools anew with the skill of a navvy, this venerable scholar with letters after his name' and throws up 'a semi-transparent bottle of iridescent beauty [Millgate mentions that 'Cunnington made a number of significant archaeological 'finds' near Dorchester in the 1880s – including, according to a recent authority, 'an amber cup, allegedly complete till Cunnington trod on it'. This could be the original for the bottle. Such a cup can be seen in Brighton Museum.] … A piece of a weapon …' and '… A skeleton is uncovered, fairly perfect.' This latter '[falls] to pieces under his touch: the air has disintegrated them, and he can only sweep in fragments.' The careless destruction and discarding of the *human* remains compared with the eager seizing of the artefacts again underlines Hardy's disgust at both the moral and scientific failings of the antiquary. The purloined statue, Ray points out, is reduced from a gold example in the 1885 version to a gilt one in the later editions, and 'of the highest finish and detail' in the 1893 version to 'of good finish and detail' in the final text (though, on balance, he also points out that the antiquary's label of the statue as 'Debased Roman' for the piece would be calculated to deceive as to the known value of his theft).[30] These alterations may reduce the scale of the offence committed, but I believe also makes it a less sensational discovery (and

---

[29] Millgate, *Biography*, p.294.
[30] Ray, p.298.

theft) and perhaps morally belittles the act still further. Ray's thorough examination of the successive versions also shows that Hardy made the antiquary's action in keeping the statuette yet more deliberately deceitful: the 'friend' originally 'solemnly asserts that ... he intends to take away nothing – not a grain of sand' but in the manner of many true archaeological excavations, all will be re-covered after examination. However, his companion, suspecting that he has secreted an item, says, 'We must re-bury them *all*', the italic emphasis being added in

Second stone from the stone circle, Max Gate

the 1913 version. The most heinous act of archaeological heresy, aside from the lack of care in the digging, allowing the exposed bones to crumble, and wiping the artefacts on wet grass (and not to mention the antiquary '[wiping] the perspiration from his forehead with the same handkerchief he had used to mop the skeleton clean'!) must be in making no kind of record of the activity, of which the antiquary's leaving no recorded provenance for the statuette is but the worst facet.

The illegality of the act, ignoring the signpost, further nullifies any validity in the antiquary's actions. The wording of the signpost was expanded in the second edition of the story, in Ray's words 'making it emphatically clear that the archaeologist's removal of the statue is illegal.'[31] Although the man originally defends his action on guessing his companion's caveats, he 'chuckles' at his ignoring the new antiquities law because the authorities would not have given permission for the dig – implying that officialdom have now moved on decisively from the methods and motives of the antiquaries: in fact, the Ancient Monuments Preservation

---

[31] Ray, p.298.

Act was passed in 1882, just before Hardy wrote *A Tryst*, and the post of Inspector of Ancient Monuments was created as a result and filled by General Pitt-Rivers.

***

The piece of Hardy's non-fiction most closely associated with *A Tryst* is his paper *Some Romano-British Relics found at Max Gate, Dorchester*, given, by request, at the 1884 meeting of the Dorset Natural History and Archaeological Society, on 13th May. After returning to Dorchester, Hardy wanted to build himself a new home within easy reach of the town, and in 1883, negotiations were concluded to purchase a plot of land at Fordington Field from the Duchy of Cornwall. The house was constructed between October 1883 and June 1885 and named to reflect the history of the site, for Mack had been the toll keeper at the site years before; hence the pun Max Gate, though Hardy comically dubbed the house Porta Maxima as if to reflect a fake connection with the town's Roman origins. Hardy may have been attracted to the site initially by its view of Maiden Castle and a barrow-topped horizon, and of the prominent Bronze Age Conquer Barrow adjacent (both of which are now obscured by trees planted by Hardy and by other developments). Archaeological discoveries might be anticipated in such a location, but the choice proved richly endowed for one fascinated by antiquities. Hardy revels in the irony when the *Life* records (p.163) that the 'only drawback to the site seemed to him to be its newness. But before the well-diggers had got deeper than three feet they came upon Romano-British urns and skeletons. ... More of the sort were found in digging the house foundations.' Apparently, five further bodies were accidentally decapitated by workmen constructing the drive, an unfortunate echo of the antiquary's action in the story. Hardy's Druid Stone was found, according to the National Trust guide to the property, during digging for a soakaway under the middle lawn in 1885; its fellow, from the same Neolithic stone circle, was recovered during by-pass construction in 1988 and also placed in the garden. Josephine Dool's lecture notes state that Conquer Barrow sits on the sole surviving section of the bank of a great henge monument called Mount Pleasant, excavated by Geoffrey Wainwright in 1970-71; even before Hardy's purchase, all traces had disappeared under the onslaught of ploughing, however, and the only evidence now is from aerial photographs. She also mentions that Max Gate is now known to lie over another kind of earthwork, a Neolithic causewayed camp. And so Hardy's problematically 'new' plot continues to reveal a remarkably rich ancient heritage.

The excavation finds displayed at Max Gate were given, along with some other material, to the Dorset County Museum by Florence Hardy. In addition to the skeletons, they are listed by Miss Dool as: one ring-neck flagon of cream-coloured ware similar to Claudian examples from the Corfe Mullen kiln and six vessels of native black Durotrigian ware; two bronze penannular brooches linked by a bronze fibula with iron hinge pin from the forehead of one skeleton and probably a shroud fastening. The importance of the article from *The World* of February 1886 cited by James Gibson in *Interviews and Recollections*, and probably largely written by Hardy, is the emphasis given both to the 'archaeological view', and to the finds from the excavations. The pride and prominence given to these artefacts (both in the house and in the article) at this date indicates how importantly they were regarded by Hardy in his archaeologically significant setting (and Hardy's awareness of his personal past is not lacking either). Firstly, the house is placed in its historical setting as if designed specifically for it: '... we have a full view of the ramparts of Maiden Castle ... From the same window we discern, high on Blackdon, the monument to Sir Thomas Hardy, Nelson's captain, a circumstance which reminds us that the author is the third of the Thomas Hardys, born and resident in this immediate locality ... The drawing-room discloses a window so arranged as to form a frame to the imposing tumulus ... Conquer Barrow ... '. This is followed by a very detailed account of the artefacts from the dig, closely reminiscent of Hardy's paper, and pointedly implying that the Hardys had no time for more conventional bourgeois nick-nacks:

> Mr Hardy's collection of old china is of a very peculiar kind. In place of the regulation Nankin, crackled, and what not, we see groups of black urns and vases of various designs characteristic of Anglo-Roman [a slip, maybe, since this meaningless term was replaced in *A Tryst*] work of the third or fourth century [now known to be an error], vividly recalling the pots and pans in Mr Alma-Tadema's picture of 'The Visit of Hadrian to the British Potteries'. With some surprise we learn from our hostess that such urns as these abound in the earth beneath our feet, the specimens on the shelves having been dug up on excavating the foundations at the building of the house. Human skeletons were also discovered here, curiously interred in oval graves cut from the maiden chalk, each body lying on its right side, with the knees drawn up to the chest in a manner strongly suggestive of the chicken in the egg-shell [identical wording to the paper]. With these venerable pieces of crockery lie an iron blade, the head of a spear taken from the side of one of the same interred Roman warriors; with a gilt-bronze fibula – similar to those in the British Museum – which Mr Hardy himself unfastened from the forehead of a skull discovered under his kitchen, proving that these clasps were used to sustain some sort of head-fillet, and not only the cloak or other garment as usually supposed ... .[32]

It is notable that Hardy wants to show off his own personal discovery of archaeological knowledge here (about the use of fibulae) and quoted later in Gibson's same volume, Hardy explains in an interview with Frederick Dolman that the British Museum's labelling of 'cloak fastener' for an identical fibula to his own is clearly an error.[33] He is, however, uncharacteristically silent on his friendship with Alma-Tadema, a society friend who reacted with excitement on being told about the excavation finds 'as he was painting, or about to paint, a picture expressing the art of that date.'(*Life* p.164). Perhaps it was the work mentioned in the article.

Hardy's peak 'archaeological period' of the 1880s saw him at the height of his fame and before the opprobrium of Victorian censure descended on the author of *Tess* and *Jude*. Gibson's preamble to the article quoted declares: 'Hardy's need to make a living by his pen meant that in the 1880s he was keen to have publicity.' This is in stark contrast to the reticent Hardy of later years, at odds with the critics, and hidden behind the banks of Austrian pines he had planted which, incidentally, cut off the view of the archaeological setting of his home. When Siegfried Sassoon, one of the circle of later young friends which included T.E. Lawrence, wrote his poem 'At Max Gate', he met a quietly courteous mask hiding a reclusive celebrity:

> Old Mr Hardy, upright in his chair,
> Courteous to visiting acquaintance chatted

---

[32] Gibson, *Interviews*, p.21.
[33] Gibson, *Interviews*, p.44.

With unaloof alertness while he patted
The sheep dog whose society he preferred.
He wore an air of never having heard
That there was much that needed putting right.

Hardy, the Wessex wizard, wasn't there.
Good care was taken to keep him out of sight.
Head propped on hand, he sat with me alone,
Silent, the log fire flickering on his face.
Here was the seer whose words the world had known.
Someone had taken Mr Hardy's place.

1884, the year that Hardy read the paper to the Society, was the same year that he wrote *The Mayor of Casterbridge* and the year before he wrote *A Tryst*. In his biography, Michael Millgate calls it 'remarkable' that Hardy should have acceded to such an invitation 'in view of [his] later distaste for such public performances' and notes that 'the paper was mysteriously omitted from the Club's published *Proceedings* for a full six years [1890; listed in *Proceedings* of the DNH&AS, XI, 1884] – possibly because of animosity towards Hardy on the part of Cunnington or one of his friends'.[34] Harold Orel notes that the article was nonetheless reported in the *Dorset County Chronicle* for May 15th 1884.[35] This animosity must have an origin other than *A Tryst*, since the paper predated even the story's first publication in America by some ten months. In addition, Hardy pays Cunnington the compliment in the paper of referring to him anonymously by the periphrasis 'our local Schliemann'. Nowadays, with so much of Heinrich Schliemann's questionable motivation and dubious method so well-known, such an appellation would certainly be regarded as sarcastic. Modern archaeologists cannot but be ambivalent at the very least about the German 'visionary'; Wheeler notes: 'We may be grateful to Schliemann for plunging his spade into Troy ... because he showed us what a splendid book [i.e. layers of stratification] had in fact been buried there; but he tore it to pieces in snatching it from the earth, and it took us upwards of three-quarters of a century to stick it more or less together again and to read it aright, with the help of cribs from other places.'[36] At the time of Hardy's address, however, Schliemann was an international celebrity who had done much to reveal the background element of historical truth behind Homeric legend and who had carried out excavations of some of the most celebrated sites of antiquity. Even without the benefit of hearing the speaker's tone, we must regard this appellation for Cunnington as facetiously reductive antonomasia, at the very least. In Orel's article, he states in a paragraph of invective against the less scrupulous antiquarians (or diggers as he calls them – a useful distinguishing term to describe their primitive non-scientific activity) that 'Hardy saw Cunnington as a throwback to a pre-Pitt-Rivers period of archaeology. Not only was he aware of advances in scientific knowledge ... But he knew more than a little about the behaviour of diggers ... over the preceding century. ... A surprising number behaved like pirates ... They owed nothing to history ... Like Cunnington, they often stepped on, and ruined, the very objects they were

---

[34] Millgate, *Biography*, pp.244/245.
[35] Harold Orel, *Thomas Hardy's Personal Writings* (Wichita: Kansas UP, 1966), p.195.
[36] Wheeler, *Earth*, p.59.

seeking to unearth.'[37] It is surely likely that Hardy's attitude, as echoed in this passage, had become known to other members of the Society, and that, however intoned, his remark was taken as sarcastic by Cunnington's circle. In addition it must be remembered that Hardy was a relatively new member of only two years' standing, and less notable locals may have resented Hardy as an international celebrity of another discipline lecturing them on their own sphere of interest. A further point in estimating Hardy's attitude to such as Cunnington is that they *were* just diggers: their activity was not only an affront to Hardy's scientific instinct, but moreover to his contradictory imaginative impulse as well which loved the very closedness of ancient sites and their concomitant mystery.

The paper begins and ends with self-effacement typical of Hardy, and which confirms a certain anxiety about straying into just such a realm in which he was an enthusiastic amateur among perhaps dourly experienced quasi-professionals. The opening includes: '… as the subject of archaeology is one to a great extent foreign to my experience, my sole right to speak upon it at all, in the presence of the professed antiquarians around, … '. And the piece concludes: 'These are merely the curious questions of an outsider to initiated students of the period … which may well occupy the attention of the Club in future days.' The unselfconscious mixing of 'archaeology' with 'antiquarian' is in no way a slight on the status of members of the audience, however, but a reminder that Hardy is speaking during the transitional period from antiquarianism to modern archaeology.

What is particularly notable for one who calls himself 'an outsider' is the very modern and professional tone and content of his report. In all the following, Hardy shows himself, outsider, amateur or no, to be the absolute antithesis of the antiquarian in *A Tryst at an Ancient Earthwork*. He first makes the crucial scientific point that he 'saw most of the remains *in situ*', later reinforcing his approach with 'but as [the fibula] was taken away without my knowledge I am unable to give its exact position when unearthed.' He places the site of the dig in its topographical and archaeological context, in Fordington Field but beyond the area of 'the great Romano-British ['Anglo-Roman' has been definitively superseded] cemetery upon Fordington Hill', noting that despite the lack of a barrow, 'the fine and commanding tumulus called Conquer Barrow' is nearby to the east. He proposes his own theory about a recovered fibula, crucially *from his own careful on-the-spot observation*: 'This is, I believe, a somewhat unusual position for this kind of fastening, which seemed to have sustained a fillet for the hair.' The rest of the report shows abundant archaeological knowledge ('characteristic of Roman work of the third or fourth century'; 'the wild ox formerly inhabiting this island'; 'no systematic orientation of the interments' – showing that he knew them to be pre-Christian, a point he takes for granted of his audience) is a model of detail and objectivity of the careful (at least once their significance had been realised) excavation of 'about three feet below the surface, three human skeletons in three separate and distinct graves' and eight and one half urns. The following will serve as an example of Hardy's style in the report: 'Each grave was, as nearly as possible, an ellipse in plan, about 4ft. long and 2ft.6 wide, cut vertically into the solid chalk. The remains bore marks of careful interment. In two of the graves, and, I believe, in the third, a body lay on its right side, the knees being drawn up to the chest, and the arms extended straight downwards, so that the hands rested against the ankles.'

---

[37] Orel, 'Archaeology, p.26.

There are distinct echoes of Hardy's fiction in the piece, strongly, for instance, of the Roman burials found – apparently at the Fordington Hill site – in *The Mayor of Casterbridge*; and also of *A Tryst* in 'brick of the thin Roman kind, with some fragments of iridescent glass' and (though a bottle rather than a skeleton) 'fell into fragments on attempting to remove it.' At the end of the address, Hardy more or less challenges his audience to pursue the investigation of the Roman town in a more holistic way, to reconstruct 'these evidences into an unmutilated whole … this fascinating investigation which may well occupy the attention of the Club in future days'. But before those final words, Hardy switches in an imaginative coda to a more speculative, creative register as he muses on the appearance of Roman Durnovaria – and so reminiscent is it of the distant view of the extant Roman shape of Casterbridge in *The Mayor*, not to mention the emotive tone of the poetry, that we are surprised not to read the fictional name – ' as it actually appeared to the eyes of the then Dorchester men and women, under the rays of the same morning and evening sun which rises and sets over it now' and 'we may ask what kind of object did Dorchester then form in the summer landscape as viewed from such a point'.

The true nature and story of Maiden Castle were revealed by Mortimer Wheeler, as I have already stated. In *Maiden Castle*, already referred to, Wheeler begins his section headed 'The Site': 'It is inevitable that any description of Maiden Castle shall begin with Thomas Hardy's picture of the site.' He then quotes from the opening of *A Tryst at an Ancient Earthwork*. This is not merely a handsome compliment, but a compliment by none other than the modern heir to the mantle of Pitt-Rivers as the leading innovator in scientific archaeological method of his day, who, moreover, wrote so imaginatively about archaeology, matching the technical accuracy and detail with which Hardy as a great creative artist was able in his turn to write about archaeology. With this choice of quotation, and well understanding the import of the story's theme, Wheeler symbolically embraced Hardy in the community of modern scientific archaeology, dividing the writer definitively from the outmoded culture of antiquarianism.

One final rather frustrating reflection is that in John Schlesinger's famous 1967 film of *Far from the Madding Crowd* (in my view the best cinematic treatment of Hardy), the sword-drill scene is very obviously shot at Maiden Castle, offering added symbolic possibilities – what a pity Hardy did not think of that too!

***

Hardy's Preface to *Dorchester Antiquities* by Henry Joseph Moule (1825–1904), published posthumously in 1906,[38] is really a memoir, to quote the final words, 'of a friendship of between forty and fifty years.' As such, it contains little reference to the subject of archaeology, except to quote from a poem of Moule's imagining a departed Kelt (sic) wandering on Egdon, apparently inspired by *The Return of the Native*, and an extract from a thank-you note from Moule on being invited to stay in Max Gate while the residents were away, in which he commented that 'there will be a delight in having Conquer Barrow and the hedge-side track to Came Wood close at hand.' Harold Orel's notes appended to this piece begin: 'It is difficult to overestimate the influence of the Moule family on Hardy's life.' He comments on Hardy's great admiration for the Revd Henry Moule (1801-1880) who was the model for the parson

---

[38] Orel, *Writings*, pp.66-73.

in *A Changed Man*. Hardy knew the seven Moule children to a greater or lesser extent, Henry being the great friend, and Horatio the scholar-mentor who advised Hardy to give up Classics, but 'not to give up writing altogether'. It is inevitable that knowing the colossus of archaeology, Pitt-Rivers, should dominate consideration of Hardy's interest in archaeology, especially in the very modern turn it took. However, the very existence of Hardy's Preface to a book on an archaeological subject is evidence enough that it is too easy to underestimate, following Orel's injunction, the influence of that very long friendship for a scholar whom Hardy clearly valued so highly. Their correspondence was evidently considerable, and some revealing pieces survive in the Hardy Archive at the Dorset County Museum, including some written while Moule was the Curator (he was appointed in 1883). They indicate not only a mutual respect, but Moule's encouragement of Hardy's archaeological pursuits and his regard for the younger man's expertise in the field. Letters from Moule 857 and 858, of 17th and 20th September 1900 respectively, reveal by implication, in their detail and expert comment, the depth of Hardy's own specialist knowledge. In the first, Moule comments on 'your very interesting and valuable paper' and asks for further details of the fibulae since he had thought to have had a description of them 'viva voce'; a drawing of three connected pieces is inserted. The next letter indicates a swift response from Hardy: 'Very many thanks for your letter of yesterday and for what you tell me about the graves which you discovered on your property. I shall now be able to compile a short record of them. I am very glad to find that my recollection about the triplet of fibulae was right. I shall greatly value your capital sketch of them which I mean to enshrine in my commonplace book. As far as I know, the gold pins are most uncommon to say the least of it, as part of fibulae of bronze or iron.' There follows a detailed discussion of the 'great stone', comparing the similar find of a stone-with-burial made by Cunnington and 'in full view, of course, from your house.' He closes with 'a 'shot' pure and simple' that the great stone was 'set up as a menhir' then buried ages later as being 'a hindrance to the plough'. The tone of equality evident in these exchanges rather calls into question Carl Weber's assertion that Hardy 'never became as much of an antiquarian as Henry J. Moule … '.[39]

A far more 'high profile' indication of Hardy's well-known interest in archaeology had appeared as an interview in *The Daily Chronicle* for 24th August 1899 and headed 'Shall Stonehenge Go?' as a response, not as surprising as it may appear in view of the chequered history of the site in recent centuries, to its suggested sale by its private owner. Again, this 'interview' appears to be largely of Hardy's own composition, though signed cryptically by 'Our Special Correspondent', since Harold Orel cites a five page rough draft by Hardy in the Howard Bliss Collection.[40] The piece acclaims Hardy as 'the great novelist of Wessex', and because of this status, and of his 'special visits to Stonehenge to get his lights for the chapter [of *Tess*]', and though (as Sassoon pointed out with such beautiful succinctness) 'most timorous of appearing in any public way except through his writings' … 'Mr Hardy was all eagerness for [Wessex's] unique Stonehenge.' Hardy uses the interview as a plea for the extension of protection for ancient monuments, Stonehenge itself being 'a national relic … a sacred possession'; 'Emphatically Stonehenge should be purchased by the nation… '. Hardy also shows his considerable technical knowledge of both archaeology and of his own craft of architecture in explaining

---

[39] Weber, p.26.
[40] Orel, *Writings*, pp.200/201.

the cause of the erosion of the south-west face of the monument, the resultant undermining by water, and the ultimate collapse of the stones, that several indeed had suffered. He recommends the possibility of tree planting to fend off the winds, but notes the importance of the open landscape setting (which of course is a feature Hardy loved and made so significant in the evocative climax of *Tess*). After giving his own opinion that the monument 'was probably erected after the barrow period of interment in these islands from the fact that one or two barrows have been interfered with in its construction', he suggests a limited excavation to determine the scientific truth. Tellingly, however, the novelist, who loves the place in moonlight and at other times of dim light when the crowds are absent, prefers 'the state of dim conjecture in which we stand with regard to its history' – and this reminds us powerfully of the difference between Hardy the expert archaeology enthusiast and Hardy the imaginative, poetic user of archaeological traces. More detailed treatment of his celebrated evocation of Stonehenge at the climactic point of *Tess* is included in Chapter Five.

***

The last piece of Hardy's non-fiction on the subject of archaeology is the report on the excavations of Maumbury Ring (or Rings as it is generally known now) from 1908.[41] Moberley Bell, manager of *The Times*, wrote to ask Hardy for an article on the excavations at the Maumbury Ring on 30th September 1908 (Archive letter 1277) saying that 'it would be of great value to the public at large.' The piece was published in *The Times* on 9th September and on that date Sir Squire Bancroft wrote (Letter 1282) a note of appreciation to Hardy. The article is headed 'Maumbury Ring' By The Historian of Wessex, Thomas Hardy', using the epithet coined by J.M. Barrie in 1889. The text was eventually published in a limited edition of one hundred copies granted by the Trustees of Colby College Library, Waterville, Maine, in 1942. A review appeared in *The New York Times* of 15th November 1942, commenting that 'Hardy manifested an intense interest in the famous Roman Ring and he contributed to the fund for financing excavations. ... As an essay in re-creating the spirit of place it is one of Hardy's gems.' Blunden notes Hardy's debt to his mentor in mentioning that 'Hardy was following in the footsteps of William Barnes who had contributed to the 'Gentlemen's Magazine' for May 1839 a letter headed 'The Roman amphitheatre at Dorchester' and a plan'.[42]

It is interesting to note that the review mentions the *imaginative* power of the author's writing, more than a decade after he had abandoned prose, in a comment that could with equal validity be made about the Stonehenge scene in *Tess* or the ascent to Mai-Dun in *a Tryst*, for example. In contrast, Harold Orel's article comments that 'Hardy writes as an amateur scientist, in the precise manner of the General [Pitt-Rivers]: 'Of irregular shape and apparently excavated in the solid chalk subsoil, it diminished in size from a diameter of about 6ft.at the mouth to about 18in. by 15in. at the bottom. The picks exactly resemble those which Mr St George Gray found in the great fosse at Avebury last May. Roman deposits and specimens were found in the upper part of the pit down to the level of the chalk floor of the arena, but not below it.'[43] Most of Hardy's article is, nonetheless, an imaginative historical sketch of the place down the ages, showing the extraordinary historical continuity that such prehistoric sites

---
[41] Orel, *Writings*, p.225.
[42] Blunden, p.122.
[43] Orel, 'Archaeology', p.34.

embody. Furthermore, he cannot resist evoking the character of the place that so attracts him as an imaginative artist – in the kind of affective light that he found so aesthetically powerful – as opposed to Hardy the scientific enthusiast. 'While the antiquaries [Hardy even at this stage did not find the negative connotation in the word that we do] are musing on the puzzling problems' he allies himself in typical style with the persona of the mere observer who possesses a smattering of local history, and remembers local traditions recounted by people now dead and gone, may walk round the familiar arena and consider. And he is not, like the archaists, compelled to restrict his thoughts to the early centuries of our era. 'The sun has gone down on the Roman Via and modern road that adjoins, and the October moon is rising on the southeast behind the parapet, the two terminations of which by the north entrance jut against the sky like knuckles. The place is now in its normal state of repose and silence, save for the occasional bray of a motorist passing along outside in sublime ignorance of amphitheatrical lore, or the clang of shunting at the nearest railway station. The breeze is not strong enough to stir even the grass-bents with which the slopes are covered, and over which the loiterer's footsteps are quite noiseless.'

Many of the best and most familiar features of Hardy's writing are here: the allusion to 'people now dead and gone'; 'the Roman Via and modern road' hinting that humanity makes but little real 'progress'; the reference to a distinctive quality of the light; the ironic conjunction perceived between the noisy, heedless symbols respectively of twentieth-century and nineteenth-century technology – the motor car and the railway – and the silence of an ancient and ignored place; the strong, even rapt, sense of place, perhaps immanence, in such a location which ends the piece. A memory of how Hardy uses this site in *The Mayor of Casterbridge* lends it an even more affecting power. Whatever Hardy's technical knowledge of, and enthusiasm for, the science of archaeology, it is the creative artist who dominates; James Gibson comments: 'It is part of Hardy's wisdom that for him the heart is always more important than the mind.'[44] Furthermore, Blunden comments 'But Maumbury Ring meant more to Hardy than its appeal to his imagination of vanished civilisations ... It was one of those local landmarks with which all his actual experience, his life from earliest to latest, was deeply connected, and which held him as if timelessly watching what it had been his destiny to think and feel.'[45]

The excavation, to which Hardy subscribed, was requested by the Dorset Field and Antiquarian Club to determine 'the history and date of the ruins'. The excavator, whose project occupied 1908–1910 and 1912–1913, told the Field Club in 1908 that the work had been 'one of the deepest archaeological excavations in Great Britain.'[46] Harold St George Gray had been trained by Pitt-Rivers and became his chief assistant, so lending an unmistakable authority to the project for Hardy the forward-looking enthusiast. According to Orel, Hardy was fascinated 'by the confusion of dates in the remains', and this is the true fascination of the professional, refusing to be satisfied with the complacent preconceptions of previous ages. 'For centuries', Hardy writes, 'the town, the county, and England generally' have believed the place to be a Roman construction, with all the activities of 'the Colosseum programme on a smaller scale.' He notes 'a shiver' in the crowd when 'prehistoric implements, chipped flints, horns, and other remains' reveal that the place had a palaeolithic or neolithic origin. It was, Hardy states,

---

[44] Gibson, *Life*, p.90.
[45] Blunden, p.123.
[46] Orel, *Writings,* p.280.

'but a temporary and, it is believed, unnecessary alarm' – for Hardy never regarded the Roman Empire as more than an unmixed blessing at best, and treated it in his works with irony, though the connection with places far away, as revealed by the mention of the Colosseum, was fascinating. His second, but equal, focus was on the other body of archaeology all around him, and that was the indigenous prehistoric, which to him was the more powerful because of its unfathomable mysteriousness. The word 'alarm' we may regard, then, as tongue-in-cheek, for to the proud burghers of Dorchester, the Roman town, the idea of their own amphitheatre being merely prehistoric would be disappointment indeed! Moreover, in Edwardian England, there was still the lingering sense that the remains of the British Empire's august – and *Classical* – predecessor were of far greater innate value than the mysteries of earlier epochs. Hardy then proceeds to outline the facts of what the excavations revealed, that at Maumbury Ring, the earlier ideas of which were reproduced so tellingly in *The Mayor of Casterbridge*, the Romans 'to save labour, shaped and adapted to their own use some earthworks that were already on the spot.' He even, nearly half a century after he first read him, quotes Hutchins on the choice of site by the original prehistoric builders of such earthworks. In addition, Hardy introduces his historical outline of the place by stressing in the educative manner of good journalism that its 'history under the rule of the Romans would not extend to a longer period than two hundred or three hundred years, while it has had a history of 1,600 since they abandoned this island …'. Research tends to suggest that, built around AD 70–80, the Roman phase as an amphitheatre was in use for as little as fifty to eighty years.

What is so impressive in Hardy's approach to this subject is not merely the scope he gives to a potentially limited and academic subject, but that he mingles the evocative with the objectively scientific in the extremely clever fashion followed in the writings of the likes of Mortimer Wheeler, one of Hardy's admirers. Maumbury Rings will be discussed again in Chapter Four.

It may seem remarkable that this expert archaeology enthusiast wrote so little on the subject. However, Hardy was a professional architect then novelist, and regarded his vocation as poetry. Aside from the various prefaces to his works, a part of that business of earning a living, he wrote little of a non-fictional nature beyond his considerable correspondence: the contents of Harold Orel's invaluable *Thomas Hardy's Personal Writings*[47] includes in addition only thirty-six pieces, of which twenty are concerned, more or less directly, with literature (if not exclusively criticism) as one might expect of a great and versatile man of letters, and four on archaeological topics, to which may be added the *World* article of February 1886 apparently largely written by Hardy, a brief reference to local antiquities in a short preface to *Dorchester [Dorset] and its Surroundings* by F.R. and Sidney Heath (1905–6),[48] and *The Ancient Cottages of England* (1927)[49] on a related subject. In other words, of all the many interests that Hardy researched or pursued, archaeology alone occupies a significant place in his published writings alongside literature. And looking at the quality of his journalistic writings on the subject, it is surely regrettable that Hardy did not find the genre of journalism more sympathetic.

Nearly at the end of his long life, in October 1927, aged eighty-seven (as Edmund Blunden mentions[50]), Hardy went to see a newly discovered Roman pavement in Fordington High

---

[47] Orel, *Writings*.
[48] Orel, *Writings*, p.65.
[49] Orel, *Writings*, p.233.
[50] Blunden, p.175. See Chapter One.

Street. The mosaic, now in the Dorset County Museum, depicts sea currents surrounding the head of Neptune emerging from the waters, at which Hardy exclaimed in a fine combination of expertise and ecstasy, 'Oh, the vermiculation of the tesserae!' This remark is taken from Josephine Dool's lecture notes, which also comment on Hardy's 'insisting on going out to see the excavations, a walk of over a mile in a cold north wind';[51] Michael Millgate adds: 'On 25 October he attended a meeting at the Dorset County Museum summoned to take action to preserve a Roman mosaic pavement recently discovered in Fordington'[52] – ample testimony, if any were needed, to the strength of his abiding passion for the subject of archaeology.

---

[51] Dool, 'Archaeology and Thomas Hardy'.
[52] Millgate, *Biography*, p.567.

Chapter Four

Hardy's Roman Town:
The Setting for *The Mayor of Casterbridge*

'I do love these ancient ruins:
We never tread upon them, but we set
Our foot upon some reverend history ...'

John Webster, *The Duchess of Malfi*.

If the real Wessex, with its counties, towns, villages, and topography, was no mere readily available template upon which Hardy could carve a fictional pattern, Dorchester provided a very different model, though at the level of local colour and detail, Casterbridge really is Dorchester 'by any other name'.

Michael Millgate explains that 'Hardy sat down, in or about March 1884, to read his way systematically through the files of the local newspaper, *The Dorset County Chronicle*, for the period beginning January 1826. ... the entire exercise was part of a preconceived intention on Hardy's part to establish the fictional Casterbridge as a densely realized image ... of the historical Dorchester of the second quarter of the nineteenth century.'[1] Furthermore, as William Greenslade observes, Hardy made '... in the early 1880s ... [a] commitment that [he] would refamiliarize himself with the environment of his childhood in pre-railway Dorset ... '.[2]

It was important to Hardy that the setting for this, as in all his other novels, should be a place with a depth of history, a pedigree as it were. Sophie Gilmartin compares Hardy with Henry James who came to England 'to the presumably richer soil of Sussex', while (referring to Hardy's poem 'On an Invitation to the United States') Hardy declined to go to America 'where the inhabitants have no history, no tragedy, no 'centuried years' behind them.'[3] Even so, to regard Casterbridge as a real place with a fictional name is highly simplistic. Richard H. Taylor asserts: 'A coach trip to Dorchester is no substitute for imaginative transportation into Casterbridge.'[4]

Evelyn Hardy declares, 'As one might expect, knowing Hardy's love of the ancient, the aspect of Dorchester which he emphasizes is her Roman past.'[5] But Hardy had been aware of

---

[1] Millgate, Biography, p.248.
[2] Greenslade, pp. xvii – xviii.
[3] Gilmartin, 'Geology', Mallett, p.22.
[4] Taylor, 'Reader's Guide', Page, p.222.
[5] Hardy, p.194.

the ancient origins of Dorchester long before he set out to read the back numbers of his local newspaper. Evelyn Hardy continues:

> There had been spasmodic local 'digs' and discoveries during Hardy's childhood in the neighbourhood of Dorchester. ... These discoveries and collections [later, in Hardy's adulthood] merely added zest to memories stored in Hardy's mind – memories of Dorchester as he had heard it spoken of by the old people at home, by William Barnes and others, and as he had known it from childhood upwards. At the age of six he must have heard fragments of the controversy which agitated Dorchester as to whether Poundbury and Maumbury, her prehistoric fortress and amphitheatre (then believed to be Roman) were to be cut in half by the makers of the new railway.[6]

Edmund Blunden also saw the place as an artistic resource for Hardy, a canvas on which to paint a philosophical drama with a historical perspective: 'Here, like old Mr Barnes, [Hardy] considered gods and men from Dorchester as the centre, with the Hardyan difference that, for literary purposes, Dorchester was still a Roman as well as an English capital.'[7] The historian R.J. White noted 'Hardy's fascination by the local connection with old Rome,'[8] and indeed, Hardy had originally thought of writing a novel set in the Roman town. But by setting it in the period before and around his own birth, while retaining the Roman and prehistoric archaeology as an allusive *leitmotif*, he lent the historical perspective of the novel complexity as well as depth, and gave added prominence to the temporal theme. Indeed, Roger Robinson suggests, mentioning this novel in particular, that 'More obviously Darwinian in its connections, and even more diminishing than the physical setting, is the large-scale chronological background against which Hardy increasingly made his figures move.'[9]

Perhaps more than most narratives, *The Mayor of Casterbridge* is dominated by time: by a setting in a recent but past era including fleeting reference to the near-approach of the railway, the history of the town going back to its Roman origins, the ancient landscape which surrounds it, the past of the central character, Michael Henchard, and the threatening prospect of the future represented by Farfrae the newcomer with his methods and machinery – not to mention the unusual gap of time between the first fateful events and the main body of the story which leaves our questions about the mechanics of Henchard's rise to eminence unanswered.

Many commentators have seen the struggle of the characters in mythic terms, as figures in a kind of latter-day Greek tragedy imbued with the ancientness of Casterbridge and its environs. Philip Davis regards the book as 'an almost mythic account of the fate of belief in the physical, external reference of emotion and memory' and as 'a primal dramatic fable ... from emotion to thought ... '.[10] He even claims that Hardy himself feared *not* ending his life like Henchard;[11] Evelyn Hardy more plausibly links the character of Henchard directly with the Roman element in the novel:

---

[6] Hardy, p.196.
[7] Blunden, pp. 54/55.
[8] White, p.7.
[9] Robinson, 'Darwin', Page, p.131.
[10] Philip Davis, Memory and Writing from Wordsworth to Lawrence (Liverpool University Press, 1983), pp.354/355, 367.
[11] Davis, p.379.

> Hardy draws an implied parallel between the genius of Rome which was energy, and the sole talent of that blundering Titan of a self-made man, Michael Henchard. But here the parallel ceases. The Roman genius for law and order, and for submission to them, was lacking in Henchard and for this reason he fails.[12]

In this book, Hardy looks, as it were, through a vanishing perspective at ever more distant periods of the past. The town (both real and fictional) in Hardy's own day was very much a remnant of the past, a backwater by-passed by the onrush of the Industrial Revolution. The setting of the narrative is (at the time of the book's composition) in a recent past already hazy with myth and nostalgia, rather as the nineteen-sixties seem to the middle-aged in the early twenty-first century. The history of Casterbridge is alive in the minds of even illiterate inhabitants, and its farming practices and business methods are little changed from time immemorial, while the Roman origins of the town are inescapably apparent, for 'Casterbridge announced old Rome in every street' (p.140), and the prehistoric landscape from which the place grew surrounds and dominates it and is the physical background to events which unfold under the influence of a more recent past. 'Vanishing' may be the wrong epithet for Hardy's perspective, for the remoter epochs represented by Roman and prehistoric settings and allusions seem somehow no less real than much later eras in this novel. But, however exciting to the imagination and captivating to the intellect are the archaeological traces, those eras are most definitely past, and Hardy had 'no illusions as to the inevitability of change'[13] and a 'struggle to find a vital presence in 'survivals' ... whether they are tumuli or earthforts ... .'[14]

In this chapter, I shall consider the dominance of time in all its aspects. As I have indicated, the past casts an overwhelming shadow throughout the book, the ancient past in particular, but also Henchard's past. Firstly, then, I shall explore the novel as an example of a tragedy. Hardy's fictional name for a very real place will then be examined; this will be followed by an outline of the historical setting of the story and an exploration of the signal backwardness of the town – both real and fictional – in its relative isolation and the importance of this fact at the date of the story. Then the archaeological element of the novel will be discussed, looking at Casterbridge as a Roman town in a prehistoric landscape, and continuing to explore the way that Hardy uses all the prehistoric and Roman sites that are included in the book.

***

The grandest connection in the book with past time, moreover ancient time, is so embracing that it might be overlooked: that is, that this novel is a tragedy. Aristotle in the *Poetics* discussed four forms of poetry: epic, tragedy, comedy, and dithyrambic verse. Though tragedy and comedy developed into what we nowadays regard as the separate art of drama, all of these four genres of poetry were performance arts in the ancient world, and, together with their shadowy religious functions, their more practical artistic role was as the vehicle for narrative. Drama and epic continued to be twin media of narrative in various eras of history, but by the time of Hardy's birth, a lean period for the drama in England, the novel had superseded other art forms as the principal popular medium of narrative. It is therefore unsurprising that

---
[12] Hardy, p.196.
[13] Radford, p.38.
[14] Radford, p 27.

a nineteenth-century tragedy should be in the form of a novel, and that this book is but one of its author's experiments in the genre.

Michael Henchard is the dominant tragic hero, the eponymity indicating that he is the Oedipus of this story. His offence of wife-selling is the *primum mobile* of the plot, the murder of King Duncan, as it were; his weakness for alcohol is Othello's suspicion and jealousy. This dominant figure may invite comparisons with Lear, an earlier tragic hero moved by primal passions in a bleak landscape and destroyed as much by them as by an indifferent, if not antagonistic, Fate. Hardy himself introduces allusions to Caesar as Henchard follows 'the triumphal chariot of [Farfrae] to the Capitol' (p.264), and his rival at the *debacle* of Henchard at the royal visit notices that 'his Calphurnia's cheek was pale'(p.340). Like Lear, this hero also escapes to a heath – Egdon Heath – and away from both the town and the fertile landscape that had given him his earlier power and prosperity. The grandeur of Henchard's character is echoed in the strength and extremes of his emotions, his ardour of friendship for Farfrae as much as his outbursts of temper giving that sense of fateful 'tragic inevitability' to his story. Philip Davis points out in the passage already referred to (Note 9) that the character's later life is an attempt to forget the past which nonetheless re-emerges to destroy him as it does all 'tragic heroes'. Davis implicitly emphasises the role of the landscape in the novel, the continuing effects of the generations on the soil upon which they depend, by asserting that Henchard 'carries' his will to live 'along with him, making certain acts the distinctive mark of his being, his traces on the earth.' Ultimately, he suffers a 'just' downfall in payment for his offence, and his stoical nobility in the face of the decline and destruction of his fortune, reputation, and relationships befits any Classical equivalent. Like Arthur Miller's more recent 'tragic heroes', however, Henchard – for all his transitory power and success in Casterbridge – is not Henchard Rex, but a small scale notable, easily replaced, whose fall affects principally himself, and secondly (rather marginally, it must be said) his own family, but few others: in this sense, Hardy has written a 'modern' tragedy, and his references to Caesar and links with Lear may be seen as reductively ironic. Interestingly, Roger Robinson's persuasively trenchant article 'Hardy and Darwin' describes Henchard's battle with Farfrae as a Darwinian struggle for survival, an outmoded species in danger of extinction from a new, better adapted breed.[15] Our final emotional catharsis is, as Philip Davis puts it, through Henchard as 'the novel sends its memory and ... its heart out after its own exiled protagonist.'[16]

All narrative is, *ipso facto*, concerned with the passage and the effects of time; and with a tragedy, these effects are very much concerned with the past catching up with the malefactor-Hero. It is particularly significant and appropriate, then, that *The Mayor of Casterbridge*, which is so preoccupied with the past and is so coloured by the historical and topographical past of its locale, especially the ancient past, should clearly be modelled in important respects on Classical tragedy: as well as the Hero who is the leader of his community, there is his 'fatal flaw' (impetuosity perhaps, or violent temper, as much as weakness for alcohol), his unforeseeable rise then fall after the first error, and the inevitability of the course of events.

***

---

[15] Robinson, 'Darwin', Page p.136.
[16] Davis, p.358.

Dorchester, which with some slight geographical licence might be called Hardy's 'home town', awarded its most famous son the Freedom of the Borough on 16th November 1910, just five months after the author was received into the Order of Merit. The occasion demanded and received one of Hardy's rare public speeches in which he charmingly confessed that he felt he had 'possessed [the 'freedom' of the town] a long while ... '; and he continues, '... when I consider the liberties I have taken with its ancient walls, streets, and precincts through the medium of the printing press, I feel that I have treated its external features with the hand of freedom indeed.'[17]

Although Hardy gives himself the freedom to do what he will with otherwise 'real' places through the device of his fictionalised 'Wessex', even claiming that 'my Casterbridge ... is not Dorchester – not even the Dorchester as it existed sixty years ago, but a dream place ... ', nonetheless, the features of the town and its surroundings are so accurately reproduced in *The Mayor of Casterbridge* that one may even today find 'Henchard's house' and the King's Arms (still the name of a real hotel – now, inevitably, with 'Henchard's Bar'!) as one seeks Hardy associations in the streets. The archaeology of the area is similarly included in the novel and is used with a significance that outweighs the actual number of references in the narrative.

The dominant sense of the past is partly achieved through the not infrequent use of historical allusion. *Jude the Obscure* must be Hardy's most allusive novel, with a plethora of references in every chapter which bear testimony to his eclectic interests and wide reading. *The Mayor of Casterbridge* carries a range of allusions, typically to authors and artists, a few to his own profession of architecture; but a majority are to the past, including folklore and legends, and a majority of these refer to the ancient past, even in such a simile as 'the great sixteen-legged oak table, like the monolithic circle at Stonehenge in its pristine days' (p.304) which reminds us of Hardy's ready handling of archaeology as an imagistic resource and which simultaneously stresses the ancientness of Casterbridge. The town's medieval past is presented in 'Jopp's cottage by the Priory Mill ... built of old stones from the long dismantled Priory, scraps of tracery, moulded window-jambs, and arch-labels, being mixed in with the rubble of the walls.' (p.294) which is a convenient metaphor for Henchard's wrecked career at this stage of the novel. This medieval fragment is part of the town's historical continuity, for here, 'the river ... ran below a low cliff, the two together forming a defence which had rendered walls and artificial earthworks on this side unnecessary. Here were the ruins of a Franciscan priory ...' (p.197). All such references not only give a sense of a long history, but underscore the old-fashioned character of Casterbridge. The Three Mariners has 'Elizabethan gables' and a 'Tudor arch' (p.109) making it seem dated rather than quaint. The sinister and violent aspects of human nature and history and, by extension, Henchard's character, are not only given emphasis by the history of the Ring, but by fleeting allusions such as the 'large square called Bull Stake. A stone post rose in the midst, to which the oxen had formerly been tied for baiting with dogs to make them tender ... In a corner stood the stocks' (p.264). Andrew D. Radford sees the Ring as an ancient version of Henchard and Farfrae's arena of struggle which now takes place in the Cornmarket and hayloft. More generally of the book, Radford states: 'Casterbridge appears 'haunted by history', but specifically a history of conflict ...'[18] of which Henchard v. Farfrae is

---
[17] Life, pp.351-353.
[18] Radford, p.127.

but the latest enactment. Hardy also mentions more recent history: public hangings and the wife-selling, James II, and, by inference, Prince Albert's visit (of 1849). All of these colour the narrative with a distinct sense of harking back, a sense that such real events, already faded into the past by the time of the book's composition, are mere ephemera in the course of history no less than those of ancient epochs.

Among allusions to earlier eras, Hardy refers to, or quotes from, at least seven books of the Bible (which he knew thoroughly), and Classical literature and history, including a wealth of mythological characters such as Laocoön, Achilles and Chiron, Diana, Argus, and instances from Ovid's *Metamorphoses* – even humble Elizabeth-Jane has 'serene Minerva-eyes' (p.406). The use of Biblical and Classical allusions will be noted in most of Hardy's novels, always having this general effect, as well as having more specific significance in a variety of contexts. Such references are to a more or less unchanging cultural and ethical stock, having a permanence not unlike (or even greater than) the physical remains of the past such as archaeological features. In contrast, events are by their very nature transient phenomena. This distinction offers a parallel with individual lives in the novel, for the fleeting folly of Henchard's drunken actions in chapter I (like some precipitate words and actions later) cannot be erased, even by the passage of half a lifetime, and inevitably affect the remainder of his life and of those close to him. Hardy knew that, while events are lost on the flood of time, the new science of archaeology was revealing solid evidence of their occurrence; hence, the archaeological remains in the novel provide not just an ironic general commentary on the mortality of man, but a pointed counterbalance to the vanishing events of mere moments in the lives of the characters. People create both events and structures, and archaeology reveals this human causality which is quite different from that exposed by the astronomer, geologist, or palaeontologist.

In that same address of 1910, Hardy interjects that Casterbridge was 'a name coined offhand in a moment', a remarkable (and in view of Hardy's customary self-effacement, quite believable) claim, for this is a particularly apposite name for a Roman town in England.

According to F.B. Pinion, the name Dorchester derives from 'Dwrinwyr', 'the settlement by the Dwyr, or dark river'.[19] The second, Roman, element of the real town name is shared with its fictional equivalent. One of the most common elements of Roman origin in our present-day gazetteer derives from the Latin 'castra', a military camp. The precise origin of English names in -caster, -cester, and -chester (also frequently found as initial as well as terminal elements) is a little more abstruse, however. The Romans did not use the element as part of their own names for these towns, but purely as an identifying descriptor for a type of site. The neuter singular 'castrum' meant a fort, and the plural 'castra' was an alternative which seemed to apply to a more diffuse establishment which we may render in English by 'encampment'. The immediate origin of the element in place-names is from Old English 'ceaster', indicating an old Roman fort, so presumably the Anglo-Saxon settlers picked up the word from their Romano-British precursors. (I have made an etymological jump here, since, remarkably, *The Concise Oxford Dictionary of English Place-Names*[20] and Kenneth Cameron's classic *English Place-Names*[21] indicate the OE and British origin, while reputable Latin dictionaries must be consulted to confirm the Roman, 'ceaster' being cited as OE for 'Roman station'). However familiar may

---

[19] F.B. Pinion, A Hardy Companion (London: Macmillan, 1968), p.259.
[20] Eilert Ekwall, The Concise Oxford Dictionary of English Place-Names (Oxford: OUP, 1936), p.141.
[21] Kenneth Cameron, English Place-Names (London: Batsford, 1961), p.214.

be the 'castra' in our place-names nowadays, only someone of a scholarly bent could so readily coin such an apt name in 1884 when Hardy wrote the novel which used his name Casterbridge for the first time. Furthermore, the scattered allusions to the Roman and prehistoric archaeology of the district in *The Mayor of Casterbridge* are given in some detail, indicating that these are no mere ornaments or learned background to add colour to the narrative (as we may be tempted to suspect of the frequent highly allusive passages in the Wessex novels), but are references drawn from expert familiarity, and therefore demand some attention. A more transparent indication of Hardy's knowledge is his name for the workaday suburb of Casterbridge, Durnover, which is taken directly from the Roman name for Dorchester, Durnovaria.

The 'bridge' element is an obvious enough element for any invented English place-name (OE 'brycg'; and indeed Hardy makes significant use of the two bridges in the novel), but my point here is that Hardy's instant coining of such a name surely betrays both his absorbed Classical education, dating back to his Latin lessons in Dorchester from the age of eleven, and his lifelong familiarity with the archaeology of the district: the *Life* (p.21) describes, for instance, how 'when still a small boy he was taken by his father to witness the burning in effigy of the Pope [during the 'No Popery' riots of 1850 when Hardy was ten] in the old Roman amphitheatre at Dorchester'. Such familiarity with well-known and easily accessible ancient sites was, however, supplemented in the author's case by an intimate and detailed first-hand knowledge of the landscape of the area and its plethora of antiquities gained through exploration on foot and by bicycle, often over long distances, for his whole life until ill-health curtailed both activities in his eighties. His membership of the Dorset Natural History and Antiquarian Field Club, not to mention his friendships with archaeologists, gave Hardy a more academic and formal framework for his knowledge, and the stimulus to continue his researches as a hobby. Before writing *The Mayor of Casterbridge*, Hardy had long been familiar with John Hutchins' *History and Antiquities of the County of Dorset*, a work which figured in Chapter Two, but even this would have been a source of knowledge additional to his lifelong and immediate experience of the ancient sites which surrounded him, rather than the origin of new material. Hardy's early memories of ancient sites were augmented, therefore, by an innate enthusiasm and by the influence of the inchoate science of archaeology in the aftermath of Darwin - and of contemporary discoveries in Greece and Asia Minor, for instance. It is noteworthy, though, that Hardy deliberately eschews coldly scientific terms for archaeological sites, especially those which have become permanently blended into the landscape, preferring to depict them in a more impressionistic way: thus he uses 'burial mounds' or 'tumuli' rather than 'Bronze Age round barrows', for example. This is no poetic fancy, however, for modern technical names would, in context, be ineptly anachronistic in a work set long before such terminology was devised.

References to history and archaeology, then, are part of an intense temporal scheme in the book by which the characters are seen arising as ephemeral actors on the vast stage of an ancient landscape, soon to be forgotten as Hardy's indifferent universal force sweeps them away on the river of Time. There is a tension between their transience and the fact of their being memorialised by their creator, however, for allographic artistic creations like Henchard possess a permanence that potentially exceeds even that of archaeological sites. Hardy therefore uses his knowledge of the past as an integral component of both the narrative and the aesthetic scheme of his art.

In his preface to the collected Wessex Edition of his novels in 1912, Hardy counsels the reader of *The Mayor of Casterbridge* 'to bear in mind that, in the days recalled by the tale, the home Corn Trade, on which so much of the action turns, had an importance that can hardly be realized by those accustomed to the sixpenny loaf of the present date, and to the present indifference of the public to harvest weather' (p.67). Two things are apparent and significant in this remark: first, that the novel is set in a time both relatively recent (1850–1856) yet very different from 1886 (and even more different from 1912); second, that a fundamental concern - about the harvest - which had dominated much of human history since the inception of agriculture in the Neolithic (*c.*4500- *c.*2200 BC in Britain) had now been marginalised. In this context, the use of a historical and archaeological framework in the novel is vitally important. The novel is also set at a historical moment when new methods were on the brink of introduction in a backward area, methods which were changing agriculture everywhere for ever.

The Corn Laws were introduced in 1815, at the end of the Napoleonic Wars; the Anti-Corn Law League was set up in 1838, Hardy was born in 1840, and the Corn Laws were abolished in 1846. The author's preface indicates that the action is set around this period, the sale of Henchard's wife and the central character's death straddling the Repeal, with 'the uncertain harvests which immediately preceded' this event the cause of the rapidly fluctuating fortunes of Henchard and his rival Farfrae, with the latter's more ruthlessly efficient modern methods winning the day.

Though *The Mayor of Casterbridge* is set a generation before its composition, the archaic and conservative character of the town means that the place is trapped in a yet earlier era. Hardy's Dorset was a backwater, remote from the heartlands of the Industrial Revolution and away from the major arteries of communication, and so it remains, relatively speaking, today: the Southern Railway mainline to Exeter barely penetrates the northernmost fringe of the County, there are still no motorways (nor any planned) and only the egregious local authority boundary changes of 1974 brought a really large urban centre, Bournemouth, within Dorset's borders. Significant events in the Industrial Revolution happened elsewhere and long before the 1840s. James Watt's steam engine was patented in 1769 and Abraham Darby's iron bridge over the Severn was erected in 1779; and as late as 1837, a Dorset labourer earned just seven shillings and sixpence a week, while in Cheshire – between the burgeoning industrial conurbations of Lancashire and the Midlands – the wage was thirteen shillings a week. Hardy mentions in a letter to H. Rider Haggard in 1902 (*Life* pp.312-314): '... down to 1850 and 1855 [the era of the novel] [the Dorset farm labourer's] condition was one of the greatest hardship ... ', a situation which had already created Dorset's famous Tolpuddle Martyrs who were sentenced to transportation in 1834. Casterbridge, then – comprehensively based on Dorchester, whatever the author's defensive demurrers – is, by any reckoning, a town locked into the past.

The town is 'this antiquated borough, ... at that time, recent as it was, untouched by the faintest sprinkle of modernism' (p.94) with its 'old-fashioned ... houses' (p.128). Such a place, Hardy implies by this pejorative description, existing only a relatively short distance from the throbbing heart of the world's first industrial revolution, is ripe for the changes heralded by Donald Farfrae's significant first intervention in Michael Henchard's world. Like all 'outsiders' in Hardy's fiction, Farfrae, however inadvertently, causes first disruption, then destruction, of the settled, secluded ways of Wessex. We are told that 'The railway' – the great nineteenth-century symbol and promoter of industrialisation – ' had stretched out an arm towards Casterbridge at this time, but had not reached it by several miles as yet, …' (p.339) – and this was even after Henchard had ceased to be mayor (chapter XXXVII). Michael Millgate quotes from an anonymous article on Hardy in the *Examiner* of July 15th 1876 which notes 'Dorset as 'the very last county in England whose sacred soil was broken by a railroad, and those which now traverse it leave the very heart of the shire untouched.' Later it adds: 'Time in Dorset has stood still …'.[22] The lines actually reached Dorchester in 1847, after the 'little' and 'great' railway manias of 1835–6 and 1844–5 respectively. In the *Life* (p.20), Hardy remarks the cultural destruction wrought by the arrival of the railway at the time of his boyhood, just after the setting of the *Mayor*; he notes the end of the 'old traditional ballads' which were 'slain at a stroke' by 'the railway having been extended to Dorchester'. The novel therefore occupies the final phase of a pre-technological age whose knell is rung by Farfrae.

It was from the North that a direct influence on agriculture eventually came, in the form of agricultural machinery, a change which engendered surely the biggest shift in farming methods since the Bronze Age plough. In 1830, there occurred the 'Swing' Riots in rural areas against mechanisation in agriculture, and it took more than a generation for these powerful sentiments to be overcome in isolated Dorset. The Eddison Steam Plough Works in Dorchester, founded by a Northerner in the 1870s, and staffed by men from the industrial North and Midlands, disturbed Hardy with its factory hooter at 5.45 am while he was writing the novel. The 'red tyrant' in *Tess*, a steam engine with threshing machine, has its symbolic equivalent here in Farfrae's seed drill, a garishly colourful symptom of the owner's methods – and of his ultimate triumph – whose 'arrival created about as much sensation in the corn-market as a flying machine would create at Charing Cross'(p.238). Its owner is, to the locals, the proverbial 'colourful character' whose lustrous exterior (he is a singer, a charmer with a curious accent), like the seed drill, is only the alluring surface embodiment of an agent of profound change; for outsiders who invade the stable world of Wessex are almost always disruptive and ultimately destructive of that world. The force of this arrival in Casterbridge is multiplied if we know that the machine 'till then unknown in its modern shape in this part of the country' was in fact Jethro Tull's seed-drill which was introduced in 1701 – in other words, Casterbridge is presented as being some one hundred and forty years out of date. Lucetta, a sophisticated outsider, emphasises the town's backwardness forcefully in her exchange with Henchard about her opulent furniture: "Upon my life I didn't know such furniture as this could be bought in Casterbridge,' he said. 'Nor can it be,' said she. 'Nor will it till fifty years more of civilisation have passed over the town."

The town's outdated ways include the retention of a curfew, itself only made possible by the rigidly retained Roman boundaries of the place. After curfew, entry is only possible illegally via the plank bridge near the 'low dive', 'Peter's Finger' (perhaps a name dating back to medieval religious relics), the means by which Newson enters the town. The three-class structure of Casterbridge is represented by the three hostelries: 'Peter's Finger', 'The Three Mariners', and 'The King's Arms'. This scheme by chance stresses the town's ancient origins by

---

[22] Millgate, Career, pp. 96/97.

echoing the relative positions of the earlier and later Iron Age settlements as they gradually aspired to and then were metamorphosed into the Roman town on its eminence high above its beginnings. Long after Lucetta's observation, a sense that the real town of Dorchester remained locked in the past, and is thus, in this respect, very evidently the model for its fictional counterpart, is amusingly confirmed by a note in *The Life of Thomas Hardy*. At the age of eighty-one, Hardy met 'a group of film actors [who] arrived in Dorchester for the purpose of preparing a film of *The Mayor of Casterbridge*.' The author observed that 'Although the actors had their faces coloured yellow and were dressed in the fashion of some eighty years earlier, … the townsfolk passed by on their ordinary affairs and seemed not to notice … nor did any interest seem aroused when Hardy drove through the town with the actors to Maiden Castle.'

***

Throughout the novel, Hardy constantly reminds us that the characters are moving in the vast twin landscapes of history and the natural world. The novel opens with three anonymous figures 'before the nineteenth century had reached one third of its span … approaching … on foot … through the thick hoar of dust … from an obviously long journey' (p.69). After twenty-one years of 'a general drama of pain' (p.411), Henchard, in his hay-trusser's garb, returns with stoical resignation to the countryside, and later to Egdon Heath, abandoning the town for ever. Egdon's barrenness means that it has been untouched by the countless generations of human beings who have formed the agricultural landscape and the town of Casterbridge. Those many generations give the early Victorian town and its farming hinterland - its *raison d'être* since its foundation – both a continuity of venerable antiquity, and a discontinuity through their individual mortality. The sense of the past is overwhelming in this novel, and the past history of the individual characters is echoed and explored by Hardy's emphasis of the historical context.

With the exception of the very different *Jude the Obscure*, Hardy's Wessex novels and short stories are, in contrast to many works of his contemporaries, principally tales of the rural environment. Antipathy to what later became the author's hallmark led to him responding with the now all-but-forgotten *The Hand of Ethelberta*. In Hardy's great novels, visits to town by Gabriel Oak or by Giles Winterbourne are but interludes, whether for business or for pleasure, in a bucolic existence of seasonal routine and unremitting labour. The setting of *The Mayor of Casterbridge* is similarly decidedly rural, but the county town is the focus, and activity outside its bounds is subsidiary, the characters heading determinedly to or from Casterbridge, but rarely with anything like indifference to it. The action in the book moves from the mysterious, yet massive, evidences of prehistory to the ordered, historically recorded symmetry of the town's Roman origins.

Towns were a Roman innovation in this island and Dorchester was created as Durnovaria to be the civitas (tribal capital) of the conquered Durotriges which eventually replaced their old oppidum (tribal centre) at Maiden Castle. The process was by no means swift in the case of Durnovaria, nor is it fully understood by archaeologists and historians. Barry Cunliffe, in his volume of *A Regional History of England: Wessex to AD 1000*, notes the possibility that the transfer from hill-fort to new Roman town was via an intermediate stage of reusing some prehistoric enclosures, perhaps on the banks of the River Frome, before the settled site still seen today was adopted.[23]

Richard Muir and Humphrey Welfare are, if anything, even more assertive on this theme of the significance of towns in *The National Trust Guide to Prehistoric and Roman Britain*:

> The seed from which the Roman Empire grew was the city-state of Rome itself. ... with every new conquest ... by reproducing itself over and over again, introducing to each new province the institutions, conventions, and social structures of the Roman town ... it was the town which became the focus of a well-ordered, cultured and successful life: to Roman eyes, self-fulfilment was only to be found through membership of an urban community.[24]

And this is exactly the experience of Michael Henchard eighteen hundred years later. He leaves the countryside, a broken and chastened young man, and we next meet him as the 'urban success story', the teetotal mayor, wealthiest citizen (a Roman word), and a magistrate (another Roman title) of the town of Casterbridge.

Just as Durnovaria was a small replica of Rome, dominant over, yet dependent upon, its agricultural hinterland, so is Casterbridge / Dorchester, providing both the 'bread and circuses' of the Roman experience for its nineteenth-century citizens. Yet the relationship of the town and country is by no means simple: there is both sharp separation and total interdependence. Simon Gatrell, with unstated allusion to the town's Roman origins within its prehistoric hinterland, clarifies it thus:

> Architecturally and historically the antiquity of Casterbridge as an urban community is carefully established, its close clutter of shops and dwellings and public buildings physically opposes the scattered countryside, sharply divided from the surrounding fields by the dark square of avenues that encloses it.[25]

It is with an agricultural problem – a bread crisis – facing the town that Mayor Henchard addresses the public dinner at the start of chapter V when Farfrae, with his dispassionate, newfangled scientific ideas brought 'frae far', overhears the details of the problem and offers the embattled mayor a solution. Thus the ages-old practices of Henchard, as dependent on superstition as on a trusted handshake, are first brought, fatefully, into contact with the 'future', the Industrial Revolution through whose heartland Farfrae has travelled to bring him to Casterbridge. The ease with which Farfrae solves Henchard's problem over the poor grain at harvest illustrates the qualitative gap in their types of agricultural skill, but also the historical difference in their approach; the arrival of the new, modern world in this 'antiquated borough' is as sudden and simple as the passing of a note: 'When he heard Henchard's closing words, 'It can't be done', he smiled impulsively, drew out his pocket-book and wrote down a few words ... 'Give this to the mayor at once,' he said, handing in his hasty note' (p.106). The speed of this fateful action is in contrast to both the laboured, time-honoured ways of Casterbridge, and to

---

[23] Cunliffe, pp.222-227.
[24] Richard Muir and Humphrey Welfare, The National Trust Guide to Prehistoric and Roman Britain (London: George Philip, 1983), p.219.
[25] Simon Gatrell, Thomas Hardy and the Proper Study of Mankind (Charlottesville: UP of Virginia, 1993), p.76.

the immense distances of time represented by the ancient remains in the landscape and their extraordinary resilience in the face of the wind and weather of centuries compared with the life-spans and fragility of the story's protagonists.

***

There are certainly a number of references to, and settings in, prehistory, but Roman references and settings predominate: the novel is very much of the town, a Roman town; and the prehistoric landscape is in every sense decidedly outside this settled urban environment. The specific use of each archaeological site, or site-type, will now be examined in detail.

Unlike the use of single archaeological sites in *The Return of the Native* and *Tess of the*

Maumbury Rings, the Roman amphitheatre in Dorchester

d'Urbervilles, The *Mayor of Casterbridge* gives us a veritable gazetteer of archaeological sites in and around Dorchester. They may be enumerated as follows: prehistoric barrows, most likely Bronze Age round barrows, also called tumuli in the novel; earthworks, usually Iron Age forts, viz Poundbury Camp on the edge of Dorchester (but not named by Hardy), Maiden Castle, the major fort near the town (called by Hardy by an assumed ancient name, Mai-Dun – of which further use is made, as I have discussed in Chapter Three, in the short story *A Tryst at an Ancient Earthwork*), and The Ring, in reality, Maumbury Rings in Dorchester, originally a Neolithic monument with an extraordinarily long and varied continuity of use; the Roman walls of the town and its general plan, limits, and function; Roman burials and evidence of occupation dug up in the town; and finally, some reference to Roman roads in the district. Of these, Maiden Castle and Maumbury Rings provide symbolically important links between the prehistoric and the Roman, and with the present, Maumbury Rings assuming an important significance in the overall symbolic and narrative scheme of the book. Although the focus of the novel is very much on the Roman town of Casterbridge itself, the scattered references to the prehistoric environment are significant, as I shall show later.

Beyond the earliest bounds of human history, chapter I states that we are in a rural setting where people depend on Nature, which predates and outlives even the most ancient works of Mankind: the song of a bird 'might doubtless have been heard on the hill at the same hour, and with the self-same trills, quavers and breves, at any sunset of that season for centuries untold' (p.71).

The earliest evidences of human endeavour in the novel are of the Bronze Age. Prehistory

Poundbury Camp, Dorchester

is introduced to the time-scheme of the narrative as early as chapter II with a reference to Iron Age forts and Bronze Age barrows, both of which are repeated in chapter XIII. There are thousands of such mounds in Britain, and Wessex is especially rich in these. It is no surprise, therefore, that the view from the town walls of Casterbridge should feature such mounds, and this is also the character of view that Hardy enjoyed from Max Gate in the days before tree growth obscured it. In chapter II, Henchard awakens to the realisation of the terrible truth of what he had done in his drunken state the night before; the irony of this lowly young man's transient folly contrasted with the freshness of a new morning is heightened immeasurably, and poignantly, by the author's placing him so explicitly in the ancient landscape which surrounds the scene, a 'spot [which] stretched downward into valleys, and onward to other uplands, dotted with barrows and trenched with the remains of prehistoric forts. The whole scene lay under the rays of a newly risen sun...' (p.83).

The similar observations of 'the tumuli and earth forts of the distant uplands' at the start of chapter XIII (p.152) are added to a mention of the Roman remains of Casterbridge, thus giving the past-reference of a brief introductory paragraph an immense span of up to two-and-a-half thousand years of archaeology and nearly a further two millennia to the mid-nineteenth century. Hardy adds that this view of ancient remains has 'the usual touch of melancholy that a past-marked prospect lends' (p.152), so commenting on the mortality of the characters, and on the fragility and impermanence of their present situation, but also allowing the author to make a direct link between the transience of human beings and the relative permanence of what they place in the landscape, in this case, a landscape stolidly visible to the characters. Moreover, the author's dominant sombre mood is also made explicit. Furthermore, as in the earlier chapter, the diurnal passage of the sun gives a sharper, more immediately human time-scale as a contrast to the archaeological, whilst itself hinting at the immutable cycle of Nature which was introduced by Hardy at the start of the book with the reference to birdsong 'at any sunset of that season for centuries untold' (p.71). In this passage, the characters are placed in a densely archaeological setting:

> The cottage which Michael Henchard hired for his wife Susan under her name of Newson – in pursuance of their plan – was in the upper or Western part of the town, near the Roman wall, and the avenue which overshadowed it. The evening sun seemed to shine more yellowly there than anywhere else this autumn - stretching its rays, as the hours grew later, under the lowest sycamore boughs and steeping the ground-floor of the dwelling, with its green shutters, in the sub-stratum of radiance which the foliage screened from the upper parts. Beneath these sycamores on the town walls could be seen from the sitting-room the tumuli and earth forts of the distant uplands; making it altogether a pleasant spot, with the usual touch of melancholy that a past-marked prospect lends. (p.152)

Like the hill-forts of the Iron Age, prehistoric barrows blend verdantly with the landscape, suggesting not merely their age, but an ancient atrophy, and a closeness to Nature, to the soil. Long barrows, it might be noted, are among the typical marks of the Neolithic (New Stone Age), the era of the first agriculturalists, and generally contain chambers, passages, or simply an entrance area, for communal burials and many have later, secondary burials added. Although there are important examples in Wessex, such as West Kennet near Avebury, they are relatively few in number compared with the vast numbers of Bronze Age round barrows, and none is specifically mentioned in Hardy's works. Round barrows, first constructed in the Late Neolithic (the so-called Copper Age of the Beaker People), were generally raised over single burials, perhaps only those of important persons in an evidently more hierarchical, aristocratic society which has been given the name Wessex Culture because of the archetypes discovered in Hardy's region (see Chapter Two). In their passivity and apparent permanence (many barrows, like other archaeological sites, have in fact been obliterated by ploughing and natural erosion), barrows act as a contrast to the turmoil of Henchard's life and relationships; when he retreats from his troubles, a hay-trusser again, he is symbolically returning to the green landscape and away from the town – he is moving, as it were, closer to the greenness of the barrow-dotted landscape, and also closer to the quietness and inevitability of death to which they bear tacit witness. These burial mounds were venerated sites, honoured places for the dead, centres of long-forgotten ritual; indeed the vast majority of what we know of prehistory is concerned with burial practices. The reference to barrows is repeated in chapter XLV where the 'tumuli ... dun and shagged with heather' paradoxically resemble 'the full breasts of Diana Multimammia extended there' (p.406), an image of fecundity and new birth. This metaphori-

Bronze Age barrow near Dorchester (seen from Maiden Castle)

cal identification explicitly links the prehistoric with the Roman and gives the same sense of historical continuity that Hardy less deliberately achieves in his treatment of the Ring and of Mai-Dun. Such a reference so near to Henchard's death is ironic, but there is also the sense of the archetype returning to his roots, to be with his ancestors as it were, in 'that ancient country whose surface had never been stirred ... since brushed by the feet of the earliest tribes' (p.406). The barrow imagery aligns with the discovered Roman corpses of chapter XI and chapter XX, and the 'churchyard old as civilisation' in chapter XXI (p.214), underscoring the permanent shadow of mortality on human affairs. In this respect, the barrows augment the melancholy atmosphere of the novel and indicate the fatalism that is a necessary feature of tragedy.

A fleeting reference to barrows, rather in the manner of *The Mayor*, occurs in *The Trumpet-Major*, chapter XXXIII, with 'the elevation being only occasionally disturbed by the presence of a barrow, a thorn-bush, or a piece of dry wall which remained from some attempted enclosure' (p.311). As in *The Mayor*, this mention underlines the sense of historical temporal continuity (in this case, backward from Hardy's reader through the Napoleonic setting of the novel, into prehistory), the ominous indication of human mortality, and the link between natural and man-made landscape features. As with Henchard's final retreat, the hovel where he dies, all things human eventually return to nature. Near the very end of the novel when Henchard in despair forsakes the town, the scene of his rise and fall, he retreats far from the Roman-established limits of 'civilisation', beyond even the countryside where he had twice worked as a hay-trusser, to the ruined hovel in the wastes of Egdon Heath, the 'ancient country' – both

Surviving fragment of the Roman wall of Dorchester

metaphors for himself – where his nihilistic Will is found. This structure, 'built of kneaded clay originally faced with a trowel' (pp.407/408), is in the early stages of the physical degradation, 'its gray [sic] rents held together here and there by a leafy strap of ivy' which would lead to its becoming an archaeological trace, re-integrated into the landscape from which it was built. Like Lear, who also finds the minimal comfort of a hovel on a heath, Hardy's ageing tragic hero finds shelter from a storm, in Henchard's case, the wider moral and psychological storm of his past life.

***

Hardy's most significant practical involvement with archaeology was with the excavation of antiquities and skeletons in the grounds of Max Gate, an activity that brought him into close contact with the melancholy of ancient burials which figures so strongly in *The Mayor of Casterbridge*. An earlier such experience is recounted in the *Life* pp.44/45 when, as a young assistant to the architect Arthur Blomfield in 1865, Hardy supervised 'the removal of many hundreds of coffins, and bones in huge quantities' from the Old St Pancras Churchyard prior to work on a cutting for the Midland Railway. As well as its gloomy, fascinated inspiration for the writer (the account occupies nearly one and a half pages), this macabre task provided him with powerful evidence of the disruptive and destructive impetus of Victorian 'progress', which finds its fictional dialectic in the ominous approach of the railway and arrival of machines in the *Mayor*, in *A Laodicean*, and in *Tess*. As I have detailed in Chapter Three, Romano-British burials were discovered in the early stages of construction of the property. To reiterate, Hardy reported the discoveries in a paper to the Dorset Field Club in 1884 (printed in their Proceedings in 1890) while he was writing the novel. In March 1891, Hardy 'erected what he called 'The Druid Stone' [with romantically abandoned inaccuracy – but consciously adopting the popular idea of his time] on the lawn …' (*Life* p.233). It was a 'large block' buried three feet underground with 'a quantity of ashes and half charred bones' (*Life* p.234) and forms the subject of his poem 'The Shadow on the Stone'. Hardy dates it at 'perhaps two thousand years' (*Life* pp.233/234) old, placing it with the Romano-British remains; however, excavations in 1987 revealed a Neolithic causewayed enclosure that straddled the property, which is dated to the third millennium BC. A photograph of the stone with Hardy beside it certainly reveals it as much more a rough-hewn Neolithic block than the kind of work to be found in, for instance, Roman stone coffins. Hardy compares its retrieval as resembling the effort needed to build the Tower of Babel, rather than a more apt simile with Stonehenge; he actually mentions *Tess of the d'Urbervilles*, in which that monument is the scene of the climax, in the very next paragraph of the *Life*. In the field opposite Max Gate is Conquer Barrow, a very large Bronze Age barrow like those mentioned on the horizon in the novel. With burials all around his new home, ranging from Neolithic to Bronze Age to Iron Age / Romano-British, it is perhaps no wonder that a fatalistic melancholy pervades *The Mayor of Casterbridge*; indeed, the first macabre discoveries by the well-diggers on the site prompt the comment in the *Life* (p.163) that 'Hardy and his wife found the site steeped in antiquity, and thought the omens gloomy;' but interestingly, it continues, 'the extreme age of the relics dissipating any sense of gruesomeness.' Clearly, in this instance, art is not a reflection of life. In the novel, the peace of Susan Henchard's burial after her troubled life and the devoted visits of Elizabeth-Jane to the spot (chapter XX) also tend to dissipate 'any sense of gruesomeness' in the description of her 'dust mingled with the dust of [Roman] women' (p.204) which could otherwise be merely melancholy or simply macabre.

 Apart from 'the remains of prehistoric forts' in chapter II (p.83), and 'earth forts' (p.152) of chapter XIII, two particular examples of hill-forts feature in *The Mayor of Casterbridge*: Maiden Castle (Mai-Dun to Hardy), and Poundbury Camp (or 'Pummery' to give it its old name). Henchard is, pointedly, associated with both of these, even though their mention is but fleeting in the text. These forts are early evidence in prehistoric Britain of engagement in warfare on a massive scale and its associated need for defences. Although weapons date back to amongst the earliest artefacts, they could as easily have been for hunting and for defence against wild animals as for aggression against other people; and so the choice of hill-forts as settings symbolic of defence, and therefore of vulnerability, is particularly apt. Henchard and Farfrae are engaged in rivalry which is both individual and communal; reminiscent of prehistoric chieftains, their conflict has the mythic basis of agriculture, its battles occurring in the setting of disputed territory. In chapter XXVII, two heavily-laden wagons, one of each owner,

Roman milestone repositioned after construction of the Dorchester by-pass

meet at a narrow point in the Casterbridge streets and there develops a skirmish between representatives of the two rival factions: 'The thoroughfare leading to this spot was now blocked by two four-horse waggons and horses ... Instead of considering how to gather up the load, the two men closed in a fight with their fists' (pp.264/265).

At two different stages of this 'war', the setting is the quintessential prehistoric defence structure, an Iron Age hill-fort; in both cases, appropriately, Henchard is on the defensive. In the first, Henchard loses out to his ascendant rival by bad luck as much as imprudent planning; in the second, the defeated Henchard feels even his basic human need for love is threatened. In chapter XVI, the rivalry between Henchard and Farfrae reaches a turning point with their rival public entertainments 'worthy of the venerable town' (p.174). Henchard planned a lavish event on an 'elevated green spot surrounded by an ancient square earthwork – earthworks square and not square were as common as blackberries hereabout – ...' (p.174), a reference that underscores the town's place in a densely layered archaeological landscape. This particular site is the Iron Age hill-fort called Poundbury Camp. Typically of Henchard, he had chosen a traditional spot for 'merrymaking', and in the open air. With the tragic inevitability that accompanies the mayor's decline, the weather turns against him: the old-fashioned man in the prehistoric setting is rained off; the modern, efficient young rival, ironically employing covers borrowed from Henchard, wins the day - and the hearts of the fickle local crowd. Farfrae's covered site is on the Walks, the line of the Roman wall, which, although ancient, is, significantly, part of the much later, 'civilised' Casterbridge, the town that had triumphantly eclipsed its prehistoric forebears - and even in this situation, Farfrae is the innovator:

> ... towards a particular spot on the Walks [was] the enclosure that Farfrae had erected ... . The end towards the wind was enclosed, the other end was open. Henchard went round and saw the interior. ... All the town crowded to the Walk, such a delightful idea of a ballroom never having occurred to the inhabitants before. (p.176)

Just beneath Poundbury runs part of the long terrace engineered by the Romans to take the aqueduct to Durnovaria, an important archaeological relic, though probably unidentified until later, since Hardy would surely have made use of it in the novel; indeed, Poundbury Camp was not excavated until 1938.

Henchard is also associated with Maiden Castle, perhaps the most celebrated hill-fort of all; the site was fully discussed in Chapter Three. From this spot, in chapter XLIII, he sees the approach of Newson, and just as the rivalry with Farfrae destroyed his business empire and, with it, his social standing, so the advent of Newson is to rob the 'Man of Character' of his one scrap of emotional stability and warmth in the person of Elizabeth-Jane. Henchard is here dwarfed by the vast remains of the past, even as his own petty past misdemeanours are about to catch up with him, and the way is, like him, exposed ('hedgeless'), and Hardy uses a road as so often to indicate events moving on, as uncontrollable as the flow of time:

> Two miles out ... was the prehistoric fort called Mai-Dun, of huge dimensions and many ramparts, within or upon whose enclosures a human being ... was but an insignificant speck. Hitherward Henchard ... scanned the hedgeless *via* – for it was the original track laid out by the legions of the Empire ... (p.385).

This notion of being literally and metaphorically overshadowed by the past has an interesting parallel in the description of the tiny figure of Lucetta at the Ring; this will be discussed later. Hardy's personal knowledge of the hill-forts of the region includes one unnerving experience that may be reflected in the way he uses them in these incidents in this novel several years later. In the *Life* (p.116), he recalls this from September 1878:

> September 25. ... Coming back across Hambledon Hill ... a fog came on. I nearly got lost in the dark inside the earthworks, the old hump-backed man I had parted from on the other side of the hill, who was going somewhere else before coming across the earthworks in my direction, being at the bottom as soon as I. A man might go round and round all night in such a place.

Despite the celebrity of other hill-forts, Janet and Colin Bord, in their *A Guide to Ancient Sites in Britain*, describe Hambledon Hill as 'Undoubtedly the most impressive hillfort in Dorset after Maiden Castle'.[26] The looming presence of Hambledon Hill seems casually to dominate the lives of the villagers of Nuttlebury (Hazelbury Bryan) in a passing reference in *Tess of the d'Urbervilles* chapter L.

Maiden Castle is an implicit link between the prehistoric and the Roman, for not only does a Roman track lead to the town, but the siege and conquest of this important centre by the Romans led ultimately to its replacement by a Roman town. Roman roads themselves were sometimes, where convenient, laid on ancient trackways, of which there are famous examples in Wessex like the Ridgeway. The roads are slender links between Roman centres, built at first through a prehistoric landscape that took centuries to transform into the image of a Roman province. Peter Clayton's *Roman Britain* asserts: 'The origins of the road network must be found in the tribal capitals, for the main roads of Roman Britain run from capital to capital.'[27]

---
[26] Janet and Colin Bord: A Guide to Ancient Sites in Britain (London: Latimer New Dimensions, 1978), p.37.
[27] Peter Clayton, ed., A Companion to Roman Britain (Oxford: Phaidon, 1980), p.130.

Literal connections and historical links go together here, and parallel the affinity between the characters and events in the narrative.

Another reference, this time to a proverbially straight Roman road, what Richard Reece calls 'a straight line cutting across the modern landscape ... a lasting testament to Roman road building',[28] is in chapter XXIX, where Lucetta is walking along the road towards Port-Bredy (Bridport): 'The spot was a vale between two gentle acclivities, and the road, still adhering to its Roman foundation, stretched onward straight as a surveyor's line till lost to sight on the most distant ridge' (p.277). She stops at 'the end of the ranked trees which bordered the highway in this and other directions out of the town. This end marked a mile' – and is also surely a physical reminder of the carefully measured (Roman) mile lengths of their road system. The straightness metaphorically contradicts the vacillations of her relationships in the novel, for at this point in the story, she has just secretly married Farfrae, while ostensibly still promised to Henchard.

The 'old Western highway ... between the busy centres of novelty and the remote Wessex boroughs' (p.395), where Henchard in his decline finds employment on a pastoral farm, may be the Roman road towards Bridport and on to Exeter just mentioned. Its Eastward equivalent is the road that originally connected Durnovaria with Vindocladia, the modern Badbury Rings near Wimborne Minster, another Iron Age fort reused by the conquerors. This is the route that still provides the main East access to Dorchester, the road with two bridges, near one of which Henchard contemplated suicide until he saw the effigy 'with a sense of horror that it was *himself*' floating down the river (Chapter XLI p.372).

Not far from here is the spot where, with agonising slowness, the doomed and suffering Fanny Robin 'progressed till descending Mellstock Hill another milestone appeared'. This terrible final journey in *Far from the Madding Crowd* Chapter XL (p.324) is measured latterly in milestones, and this final one is very likely the Roman milestone, of the typical cylindrical style, which still stands, half-hidden by undergrowth, just near the roundabout with the Dorchester by-pass built in 1988. It was moved from its original position in about 1866 – just before the period in which the novel is set (could this have been to make it useful, to measure a modern mile rather than a Roman mile, I wonder?) – again in 1957, and again in 1986 prior to commencement of the by-pass construction. It now stands on the centre-line of the Roman road. The by-pass construction work also led, incidentally, to the excavation of the rest of the Neolithic stone circle near Max Gate, and the recovery of a companion for Hardy's 'Druid Stone' which was placed next to the lawn opposite that example excavated by the author himself. Only two Roman milestones survive *in situ* in Britain, one near Hadrian's Wall at Vindolanda (Chesterholm), Northumberland, and one near Temple Sowerby in Cumbria on the A66, another important Roman road route still in use. A slightly spurious claim might therefore be made for the Dorchester example, though the Ordnance Survey map of Roman Britain omits to show it. East beyond the aforementioned roundabout, the Roman road, with a portion of its *agger* well preserved (part of a designated footpath), runs through the woods which Hardy knew so well near his birthplace (the subject of the poem 'The Roman Road'), and on, quite close to the Rainbarrows of *The Return of the Native*.

Casterbridge and Henchard's story are in a district remote from the mainstream of Victo-

---

[28] Richard Reece, 'The Economy', Clayton, p.130.

rian England and its Industrial Revolution. Durnovaria was a junction of Roman roads, along one of which Lucetta is walking, but it was a town relatively distant from the centres of imperial power in the Province, and the major roads such as Watling Street are a long way to the East and North, rather as Dorchester is still on the sidelines of modern Britain.

The Ring, the most significantly employed archaeological site in the book which features in three chapters, is Hardy's name for the earthwork on the edge of Dorchester called Maumbury Rings. Like Maiden Castle, it is a site that embodies long historical continuity, but

Hambledon Hill Iron Age hillfort

it takes a far more prominent place in the novel, is presented in much greater detail, and is of an even longer pedigree – longer, in fact, and therefore even more appropriate than Hardy realised at the time of the book's composition. Between 1908 and 1913, the archaeologist H. St George Gray's excavations showed that 'one of the finest Roman amphitheatres, if not the very finest, remaining in Britain' (p.140) had, in fact, originally been created as a Neolithic henge monument. This, then, was a prehistoric ritual site, later considerably altered by the Romans to create their amphitheatre; as detailed in Chapter Three, Hardy wrote a celebrated article about these archaeological revelations. Thus, in *The Mayor of Casterbridge*, Hardy had serendipitously chosen a location of much greater antiquity than he realised, a fact – presented, for example in Martin Seymour-Smith's introduction to the Penguin Classics edition – that further emphasises Hardy's historical scheme in the novel and, like Maiden Castle, links the prehistoric with the Roman.

The Stone Age in Britain may be dated approximately to between 500,000 and 2100 BC; Palaeolithic, 500,000–10,000 BC, Mesolithic 10,000–4,500 BC, and Neolithic, 4,500–2100

BC. The Neolithic age of the Ring, therefore, although by no means giving the awe-inspiring geological time-scale to this novel that we find in the near-death experience of Stephen Smith in *A Pair of Blue Eyes,* let alone the astronomical reach in *Two on a Tower*, nevertheless – fortuitously – extends the temporal range of the novel beyond the brief references to the Bronze Age, and to over two millennia before the Roman occupation which is the dominant past-reference in the book.

Before the details of the Ring are enunciated in chapter XI, Hardy places the site in its Roman context within the town:

> Casterbridge announced old Rome in every street, alley, and precinct. It looked Roman, bespoke the art of Rome, concealed dead men of Rome. It was impossible to dig ... without coming upon some tall soldier or other of the Empire, who had lain there ... for a space of fifteen hundred years, lying on his side ... his spear against his arm; a fibula or brooch of bronze on his breast or forehead; an urn at his knees, a jar at his throat, a bottle at his mouth; and mystified conjecture pouring down upon him from the eyes of Casterbridge. (p.140)

[This passage matches that in chapter XX where Elizabeth-Jane visits her mother's grave which will be examined shortly.] Indeed such sights were so common that the inhabitants were 'quite unmoved by these hoary shapes' (p.140). Like the Hardys at Max Gate, the people of the fictionalised town believed that 'between them and the living there seemed to stretch a gulf too wide for even a spirit to pass' (p.140). This doleful, macabre note precedes the recital of the grim facts of the Ring's past, both ancient and more recent, and, as well as fitting the prevailing mood of the novel, tends to foreshadow the early demise of the frail Susan. In truth, though Maumbury Rings had been a place of solemn ritual and gathering for its first, Neolithic builders, the Romans radically remodelled it as a civil amphitheatre – that is, as a place for beast fights and gladiatorial contests, rather than as a military installation which would have been used primarily for parades and drill. This early, grim, change of function set the tone for most of what occurred there until very recent times in the later town of Dorchester when, long after Hardy's death, the new Queen Elizabeth II was greeted by the populace there in 1952. Such an account of the real site's morbid history between the first and twentieth centuries does, however, fit Hardy's intentions; not only does he select the more lurid and grim elements of its past (the execution of the woman was based on a real event) which match both his general and particular theme and mood, but he introduces an important irony: this public arena is used for personal meetings of the most imperatively private kind. The irony is emphasised by the size of the place, 'to Casterbridge what the ruined Coliseum is to ancient Rome ... and nearly of the same magnitude' (p.140); this is a guess that Hardy could have disproved and subsequently altered – but did not – after his visit to Rome in 1887. Henchard's two trysts are in fact typical of the place, whose tall banks make it a paradoxically secluded spot, though in keeping with the mood of the novel, Hardy notes that meetings of 'happy lovers ... seldom had a place ...' – an oblique pointer to the mayor's two unhappy relationships that bring him there: 'Standing in the middle of the arena at [dusk] there by degrees became apparent its real vastness. Melancholy, impressive, lonely, yet accessible from every part of the town, the historic circle was the frequent spot for appointments of the furtive kind ... intrigues ... divisions and feuds' (chapter XI pp.140/141). In X, Henchard writes a letter to Susan to arrange a meeting at 'the Ring on the Budmouth [Weymouth] road' (p.138); in XI the meeting takes place, accompanied by a detailed description of the arena, and associates it with the Roman character of the town; and in XXXV, Henchard meets Lucetta here in a similarly emotional scene in response to a letter of hers. Philip Davis believes that the place itself has an important influence on this event, mediated by Henchard's own memory, since he 'deals kindly with ... Lucetta ... not through moral introspection on his part but because she has come to plead with him in the same outside place, the old Roman amphitheatre, in which he became reconciled with the wife he had sold.'[29]

Hardy's outline of the two thousand-year history of the Ring that he knew in the 1880s thus re-emphasizes the novel's overall sense of historical continuity and simultaneously, presenting Henchard and Susan, then Lucetta, as tragic incidentals to that history, colours the narrative about these characters who meet there: the ancient site physically embraces two crucial personal meetings while itself being a grim microcosm of humanity's barbarism: 'the sanguinary nature of the games originally played therein ... in 1705 a woman who had murdered her husband was half-strangled and then burnt there (a more gruesome version of Hardy's own first boyhood experience of the place) ... pugilistic encounters ... there still remained ... cells for the reception of the wild animals'; even a boys' game of cricket in the arena might be deterred because 'some old people said that at certain moments in the summer time, in broad daylight, persons ... beheld the slopes lined with a gazing legion of Hadrian's soldiery as if watching the gladiatorial combat' (pp.141/142). Hardy has created a bizarre conjunction indeed in these scenes, but one that links this tragic novel with the prevailing bloody character of Classical tragedy. Interestingly, Hardy the artist was impressed by the spatial character of the amphitheatre in a quite different way; in his chapter 'Hardy and the Theatre', Michael Millgate quotes a letter of 1893 to Mrs Henniker in which the author anticipates theatre-in-the-round, suggesting 'the theatre would approach in arrangement the form of an old Roman amphitheatre ... .'[30] He is surely thinking of Maumbury Rings.

Both of Henchard's meetings at the Ring lead on to further personal disaster. In the first instance, his honourable intentions to Susan are nullified by her early death, and in the second, Henchard abandons his vengeful plans for Lucetta under the direct influence of the physical circumstances of the amphitheatre itself: 'The dusk of evening was the proper hour' (p.140) for the meeting with Susan, and so, luckily, it proves to be for the tremulous Lucetta:

> ... in appointing this spot, and this hour, for the rendezvous, Lucetta had unwittingly backed up her entreaty by the strongest argument she could have used outside words with this man of moods, glooms, and superstitions. Her figure in the midst of the huge enclosure, the unusual plainness of her dress, her attitude of hope and appeal, so strongly revived in his soul the memory of another ill-used woman who had stood there ... that he was unmanned ... (p.324)

Hardy even describes the setting sun as 'like a drop of blood on an eyelid' (p.323) as Lucetta approaches this tryst, and the interior of the Ring 'emphatic of the absence of every liv-

---

[29] Davis p.354.
[30] Millgate, Career, p.309.

ing thing' also stresses the grim and fatalistic character of the spot. Here, Hardy interweaves the personal history of his characters with the real history of others associated with the spot, and also with the more impersonal general record of the place's past, emphasising the totality of the continuous river of human existence made up of innumerable individual lives and tragedies. Further, as I shall explain in Chapter Five, the true archaeological origins of Maumbury Rings and its subsequent historical uses, as well as Hardy's use of the site in *The Mayor*

The Walks, Dorchester, preserving the line of the Roman walls

of Casterbridge, have important connections with the climactic scene at Stonehenge in *Tess of the d'Urbervilles*. Hardy, then, emphasises the Roman character of the town in his preamble to Henchard's meeting with Susan at the Ring, and in so doing, unwittingly links the historical Roman period with the long prehistoric past which was later revealed by the systematic excavation of Maumbury Rings.

British prehistory ends, effectively, with the Claudian invasion of AD 43, and the sharp division between pre-literate Celtic Britain and Roman, 'civilisation' (Latin 'civis', a citizen; 'civitas', city) is evident in the sharply defined geometric plan of the Roman town, clearly distinguished from the ancient agricultural countryside on which it depends and which, symbiotically, it controls: ' Its squareness was, indeed, the characteristic which most struck the eye ... It had no suburbs ... Country and town met at a mathematical line ... the stockade of gnarled trees ... was ... standing on a low green bank or escarpment, with a ditch yet visible without ... these external features were but the ancient defences of the town, planted as a promenade' (pp.94/95). The sharp physical divide between the Roman town and ancient agricultural countryside, which persisted into the nineteenth century, allows Hardy to distinguish between the 'Romanness' of the town and the 'prehistoric' countryside in his temporal-symbolic scheme; however, the relationship in the narrative (and for the book's characters) is assuredly reciprocal, the town being 'the complement of the rural life around, not its urban opposite' (p.126). This is also stressed in chapter XXVII in a reference that underscores the cultural-economic relationship between the two, and in which the imperatives of the farming year are the same as they had been for two millennia before the Romans arrived:

> The harvest had been so delayed by the capricious weather that whenever a fine day occurred all sinews were strained to save whatever could be saved of the damaged crops ... Nearly the whole town had gone into the fields. The Casterbridge populace still retained the primitive habit of helping one another in time of need; and thus, though the corn belonged to the farming section of the little community – that inhabiting the Durnover quarter – the remainder was no less interested in getting it home.
>
> Reaching the top of the lane Henchard crossed the shaded avenue on the walls, slid down the green rampart, and stood amongst the stubble ... (p.267)

We are reminded here of Hardy's comment in his Preface about the now-forgotten universal importance of the harvest, a feature of the novel that needed explaining to its readers of the 1912 Wessex Edition. The 'primitive habit' is surely an implied reference to the more ruthless new order that was being ushered in by Henchard's young rival Donald Farfrae, and, of course, it is to the old Roman-derived name Durnover that Hardy refers in this passage which looks back to a vanished world. Henchard slides down the rampart of the Roman walls and is immediately in the countryside, stressing that his twofold identity of town and country is as much a dichotomy as the other extremes of his existence, and as much of a contrast as that between Roman urbanity and prehistoric rusticity.

These defences, the walls, are of course the vestigial remnants of the Roman town walls which are nowhere near as substantial as those in London, Chester, or York; in fact, R.J.A. Wilson's *Guide* describes 'A rather wretched fragment of this [wall], penned behind railings ... visible in West Walk, a short distance south of the Hardy statue. Only the core of the wall is left standing, at most, eight feet high ... .'[31] This is the 'crusted grey stonework' mentioned in chapter IX (p.128); Thomas Hardy's statue was unveiled in 1931 in this most apt location. This sad remnant is as useless for its original purpose of defence as are Henchard's old values and personal secrecy, both of which are overwhelmed by the tide of innovation that sweeps in with his young rival in business and love. In chapter XIII, 'Susan under her name of Newson ... was in the upper or western part of the town, near the Roman wall' and 'the Walks – as the avenues on the walls were named' (p.153) are mentioned as places of recreation and of accidental meetings, such as that between Lucetta and Elizabeth-Jane. A chance meeting between these two women at the margin of the town occurs not long after they have each arrived from the countryside just beyond, and leads them both deep into the affairs of the town within. The melancholy of Susan Henchard's burial place is prefigured and given yet deeper historic resonance when Elizabeth-Jane approaches it along these 'avenues ... deserted as the avenues of

---

[31] Richard Wilson, A Guide to the Roman Remains in Britain (London: Constable, 1975), p.72.

Karnac [at Thebes on the Upper Nile]' (p.204). Indeed, the Roman walls not only constrict the modern town, but provide Hardy with a setting of claustrophobic intensity for the personal drama of the six main characters: what once gave a sure defence from enemies without has now trapped Henchard and his literal and metaphorical adversaries inescapably within – the whole town has become his very particular 'Ring'.

The sharp distinction between the clearly-defined Roman town in its superior physical position, with its continuing occupation, and the more hazy remains of the Bronze Age culture of round barrows and Iron Age culture of hill-forts which preceded it, now blended with the natural contours of the land, is emphasised by the view in both directions, from afar with its 'rectangular avenues' (p.312), and outward from the walls: 'Beneath these sycamores on

Roman stone face now in Dorset County Museum

the town walls could be seen … the tumuli and earth forts of the distant uplands …' (p.152). Hardy's physical distancing here of the prehistoric from the Roman 'civilised' past matches the distance that Henchard has travelled from dissolute young hay-trusser to First Citizen of Casterbridge, and the yet greater depths to which he sinks at the end of the novel.

The actual course of the Roman walls, then, defines the limits and shape of the subsequent nineteenth-century town, even though the ravages of time have reduced the substance of the walls to a mere vestige. Hardy visited the 'mournful relics of that city of the past' (*Life* p.292), Silchester, Hampshire, where there is a complete circuit of walls of a similar scale that had encompassed Dorchester in its later Roman phase. The one battered surviving fragment of these walls must have given added weight to Hardy's melancholy observations on the transience of the human past in such remarks. Excavations of Silchester started in 1864–1878 and continued in earnest in 1890–1909. The Hardys' visit was in early 1897, in the middle of the intensive investigations, but since the place is, even today, lost amidst the lanes, and the consolidation of the walls was not undertaken until the excavations of 1979–1985, the site must indeed have appeared as 'mournful relics'. Hardy would have undoubtedly been impressed and fascinated by Silchester's amphitheatre, also excavated and consolidated in 1979–1985.

The familiarity of the Casterbridge inhabitants with their Roman heritage is stressed, amusingly, by Buzzford, one of the 'Rustic Chorus', in chapter VIII, when he confuses the Romans with the Roman Catholics (in the reign of James II). His grasp of historical time is vague, to say the least, readily excusable since Hardy's country characters cannot have had anything like a formal education. The Forster Education Act of 1870 provided for universal elementary education for the first time; Buzzford's ''Tis recorded' indicates that his must be hearsay 'common knowledge', therefore, rather than learned or read knowledge: 'Casterbridge is a old hoary place of wickedness, by all account. 'Tis recorded that we rebelled against the King one or two hundred years ago, in the time of the Romans ...' (p.121).

In a rather more scholarly and thorough fashion than was possible or expected in the humble mass of the local populace, the pervasive influence of the town's Roman past informs the educational ambitions of the humble Elizabeth-Jane. In chapter XX, amongst other endeavours for self-improvement, 'she began the study of Latin, incited by the Roman characteristics of the town she lived in' (p.203). In this chapter also, in another typically melancholy and fatalistic note, the girl is said to visit her mother's grave; in this passage, the continuity of history is again contrasted with the transience of the individuals who exist in it: '... in the still-used burial-ground of the old Romano-British city, whose curious feature was this, its continuity as a place of sepulture, Mrs Henchard's dust mingled with the dust of women who lay ornamented with glass hair-pins and amber necklaces, and men who held in their mouths coins of Hadrian, Postumus, and the Constantines' (p.204). This burial ground is the one whose excavation the Revd Henry Moule, father of the family that had so much influence on Hardy, witnessed on Fordington Hill, occupying in part the graveyard of his church, St George's; one of the Roman tombstones (the marble memorial to one Carinus) is now displayed in the church. Coins are an accurate archaeo-historical indicator of the Roman Empire, from which relatively few written records survive. The two-fold irony here is subtle, but not abstruse: the plain, fragile Susan's dust is mingled with that of opulent, decorated Roman women, clearly of a decidedly higher social stratum than this humble, mistreated wife; Susan's mortal remains of a life of much misfortune and poverty mingle with all-but indestructible tokens of wealth and display anachronistically found in the 'churchyard as old as civilisation' (p.214). It is at this point that Elizabeth-Jane meets Lucetta and agrees to become her companion, a gloomily ironic setting for a new start. This resonates secondarily with the inference that, had Henchard not precipitately cast her off those many years ago, then perhaps Susan could have enjoyed the kind of social circumstances that were denied her until almost the end of her life, and which now surround her permanently in death.

One minor Roman feature is brought into play as a sombre portent for Elizabeth-Jane in Hardy's overall scheme of imagery: the keystone rescued from Colliton House (that until 1948 had been in an old brew house) is now preserved in the Dorchester Museum. Hardy transposes it to High-Place Hall, the house being taken by Lucetta. In Elizabeth-Jane's mind, Hardy comments explicitly, as if anticipating *Jude*, on 'the ultimate vanity of human architecture, no less than of other human things' (p.211). As she leaves the house, she notices the mask-keystone which once 'had exhibited a comic leer ... but generations of Casterbridge boys had thrown stones at the mask ... the blows thereon had chipped off the lips and jaws as if they had been eaten away by a disease' (p.212). The timid girl, not surprisingly, 'could not bear to look at it – the first unpleasant feature of her visit' (p.212). Beneath the demolished Colliton House, the opulent Roman town house that once occupied the site was excavated in 1937–1939 and further consolidated for public display under a new roof in 1999.

Though conveyed in few words, the frequency of allusion to the area's archaeological remains lends them significance in Hardy's overall philosophical scheme. Another means by which this prominence is achieved might easily be overlooked, and that is that so many of the references occur right at the start of a number of chapters. Hardy frequently opens a chapter by setting the scene, placing characters in the landscape; by introducing archaeological remains into the description, he presents us with a strongly temporal as well as topographical setting.

Roman tombstone, St George's Church, Fordington

Even in considering the living town of Dorchester, his address to the Town on accepting the Freedom (*Life* pp.351–353) reveals the quintessential melancholia of Hardy's fiction, a fatalism which is sensed early on in so many of his works:

> Where is the Dorchester of my early recollection – I mean the human Dorchester – ... of which the houses were but the shell? ... 'Nothing is permanent but change' ... the faces that used to be seen at the doors, the inhabitants, where are they? ... names on white stones ...'; and significantly from the point of view of the present study: ' ... after all the permanence or otherwise of inanimate Dorchester concerns but the permanence of what is minor and accessory. (*Life* pp.352/353)

This passage reminds us that historical and archaeological remains are only important as traces, as reminders of people; in the case of the novels, of individual people – otherwise, they are, to quote Mortimer Wheeler 'the driest dust that blows.'[32]

---

[32] Wheeler, *Earth*, p.13.

Chapter Five

Ancient and Modern Collide:
Tess of the d'Urbervilles and Stonehenge

'Love alters not with his brief hours and weeks,
But bears it out even to the edge of doom.'

William Shakespeare, Sonnet 116.

Hardy's worst novel must surely be *A Laodicean*: his greatest, perhaps, *Tess of the d'Urbervilles*. In one important respect, though, the two works are very comparable, and that is in their exploration of the clash of older worlds with the modernity of the Victorian era.

The focus of this chapter is on the great novel which has as its symbolic and narrative climax the arrest of Tess and Angel Clare at Stonehenge. Firstly, however, the artistic antecedent of *Tess* repays examination in revealing the way that Hardy's thinking developed over the course of ten years up to the completion of *Tess* in 1891.

Hardy's admirers will point out that *A Laodicean* (1880–1881) was written during a period of serious ill-health, but Trevor Johnson is not alone in dismissing it as Hardy's least successful novel, and describes it as '[a] society comedy which starts well and then collapses in ruins.'[1] Despite its congruity with *A Pair of Blue Eyes* (young architect, restoration project, problematic love, Wessex but not Dorset), it is a close, but cruder exposition of the clash of ancient and modern that followed in its more celebrated successor a decade later.

One particular aspect which is in parallel with *Tess*, and here of even greater importance, is the historical decline of an ancient family. This is physically represented by the crumbling Stancy Castle just as the Durbeyfields' poverty (and their humbled name – an Anglo-Saxon version of an aristocratic Norman moniker) indicates the decline of the true ancient d'Urbervilles. The opening chapter of *A Laodicean* presents the telegraph as an almost too-explicit symbol of modernity, and the entry of the wire into the fabric of the ancient and atrophied pile of the Castle is similarly obvious. Furthermore, Paula Power's late father had made his fortune from railways, which, as so often in Hardy, are the disruptive and destructive vanguard of modernity, though Hardy's enthusiasm for the new betrays his Janus-like feeling for such modernity. True, the railway had by-passed the Castle rather than destroying it (which was the Victorian fate of many ancient monuments that stood in the way of the iron road), but only so that Power

---
[1] Trevor Johnson, Literature in Perspective – Thomas Hardy (London: Evans Brothers, 1968), p.102.

acquire it in order to aggrandize himself and usurp the inheritance of the Castle's ancient owners. This is just what Alec Stoke d'Urberville seeks to do in *Tess* with his newly augmented name. As well as setting fire to the Castle, he uses the telegram to discredit Somerset in Paula's eyes and furthers this by means of a fake photograph, thus abusing his expertise in the new technological medium.

Names are significant in *A Laodicean*, but more obviously so: De Stancy is also an Anglo-Norman name indicating its ancient original builder, though the usurpation of the name is a subtlety that this book significantly lacks. And Power almost invites the prefixing 'Steam'.

Early in the book (Book First chapter IV), the proximity of the railway allows a direct statement of the ancient v. modern theme:

> She looked across the distant country, where undulations of dark-green foliage formed a prospect extending for mile. And as she watched, and Somerset's eyes, led by hers, watched also, a white streak of steam, thin as cotton thread, could be discerned ploughing that green expanse. 'Her father made *that*,' Miss De Stancy said, directing her finger towards the object.
>
> 'That what?'
>
> 'That railway. He was Mr John Power, the great railway contractor. And it was through making the railway that he discovered this castle – the railway was diverted a little on its account.'
>
> 'A clash between ancient and modern.' (p.27)

The irony here of the railway 'ploughing that green expanse' cannot be missed. Also in chapter IV, we learn that the late railway magnate's tunnel had uncovered the means for bringing further new industrialization to the locality which his daughter was subsequently intending to exploit – but her project is borne of the Grand Tour that the nouveau riche father had bought her, and of the yearning for the ancient past that it had instilled in her. In this instance, then, ancient and modern do not so much clash, as meet in an ironically humorous fashion, especially since the girl from the old family has been quite left behind by the modern young woman's education:

> 'Pottery! – how very practical she must be!'
>
> 'Oh no! no!' replied Miss De Stancy. In tones showing how supremely ignorant he must be of Miss Power's nature if he characterized her in those terms. 'It is Greek pottery she means – Hellenic pottery she tells me to call it, only I forget. There is beautiful clay at the place, her father told her: he found it in making the railway tunnel. She has visited the British Museum, continental museums, and Greece, and Spain: and hopes to imitate the old fictile work in time, especially the Greek of the best period,, four hundred years after Christ, or before Christ – I forget which it was Paula said … Oh no, she is not practical in the sense you mean, at all. (p.30)

For Hardy, the essentially pagan elegance of the Classical, the Greek ideal of Paula Power, is allied to the progressive non-Christian, while the up-to-the-minute fashion for Gothic, though quintessentially English, is associated with the Church that had been discredited by

Darwin. Presenting a polar opposite, Chris Brooks discusses Augustus Welby Pugin's 1836 *Contrasts* as the quintessence of the debate about which *A Laodicean* is in part concerned. Pugin, an ardent Roman Catholic, contrasts (in the 1841 edition) in a pair of prints an imaginary '[English] Catholic town in 1440' with 'The same town in 1840', the year of Hardy's birth, showing 'the debauching of taste and morality alike in the pagan riot of Neoclassicism'.[2] In a calculated insult that Hardy would no doubt have found more amusing than otherwise, Pugin dedicates the work to the architectural 'Trade'!

The state of many medieval Gothic buildings, spurned by the Georgian Classical taste, meant that two courses of action became inevitable for many: demolition (convenient if new

Stonehenge

development could be thus facilitated) or restoration, which might have to be radical to prevent collapse. Aesthetically and philosophically, however, Hardy's novel appears to deplore the destructive tendency of the modern and any restoration that is excessive. But we cannot oversimplify Hardy's attitudes, and not every facet of the book approaches the simplistic. Simon Gatrell notes 'modern pettiness and modern brilliance set against medieval splendour and medieval darkness and decay; and this theme operates through both characters and buildings … '.[3] These conflicting, equivocal tendencies in Hardy's outlook are explored in a clearer, more explicit schema in *Jude the Obscure*, but are evidenced years earlier in the radical shift in his attitude as a professional architect, away from extreme restoration and towards preservation.

---

[2] Chris Brooks, 'Introduction: Historicism and the Nineteenth Century', ed. Brand, pp. 8-10.
[3] Gatrell, p.55.

Stancy Castle is based on medieval Dunster Castle in Somerset; it was never burnt down, however, and while Paula Power agrees to her now-husband's (Somerset's) proposal to build a new eclectic-style house, she laments both the loss of the Castle and that her husband does not bear the ancient name de Stancy, a further anticipation of *Tess*. Dunster Castle is one of many in Britain that owe their continued preservation to the drastic work undertaken during the Victorian period – a paradox that echoes Hardy's shifting attitude to his own restoration work. In this, he was an echo of contemporary cultural debate on authenticity (is the substance or the shape the key consideration?), for Chris Miele states that the Victorians 'did not place as high a premium on genuine ancient remains as we do', rather, they felt that an authentic copy was an enhancement, and the whole restoration movement in fact led somewhat paradoxically to a 'cult of the original'.[4]

Claudius Beatty's succinct and fascinating work on Hardy and architecture[5] implies that within the architectural debate in the book, past and present are interwoven in a complex fashion: Paula, the forward-looking heiress, wishes to insert a Greek sculpture court in the midst of her restored medieval castle, much to Somerset's horror who is a Gothicist and one with the aesthetic sensibility to recognize a catastrophe in the making. The local architect and self-made man Havill has built the ugly Baptist chapel nearby which undoubtedly adheres more to Classical restraint then to the Gothic ornamentation of the Anglo-Catholic revival which – in artistic terms – was a facet of the Victorian Gothic movement.

As with Clym Yeobright in *The Return of the Native* and Angel Clare in *Tess of the d'Urbervilles*, both in a more profound and far-reaching context, it is education that has brought past and present on a collision course, and I shall return to this point shortly. Later in the book, however, it is the burning-down of Stancy Castle that marks symbolically the triumph of new over old. This act is perpetrated by William Dare, a character whose name is associated with 'daredevil' according to Pinion.[6] He is a sinister representative of the modern era, being a photographer, a practitioner of a new nineteenth-century phenomenon just as revolutionary as the railway. Dare is reminiscent of Donald Farfrae and Eustacia Vye, another of Hardy's disruptive outsiders, in his case having lived mainly in India, Malta, Australia, and Canada. Hardy loves allusion, especially references to the past drawn from his reading and assiduously recorded in his notebooks. These certainly appear in *Tess*, but in nowhere near the dense profusion of Classical and historical references in *The Mayor of Casterbridge*. In *Tess*, the predilection is for quotations from Shakespeare's tragedies which underline the nature of the heroine's history, and, importantly, by over fifty Biblical references which emphasize the moral themes in the book at a time of questioning and uncertainty about the truth of Christian doctrine in the author and society at large. In this philosophical realm, the novel is very much a presentation of the clash of ancient and modern, a conflict that Hardy had presented in *A Laodicean* and was to return to in *Jude*. But as in so many aspects of his art, I believe that it is in *Tess* that this theme is most finely expounded.

***

---

[4] Chris Miele, 'Real Antiquity and the Ancient Object: The Science of Gothic Architecture and the Restoration of Medieval Buildings', ed. Brand, p.103.
[5] Claudius J.P. Beatty, Thomas Hardy: Conservation Architect (Dorchester: Dorset Natural History and Archaeological Society, 1995).
[6] Pinion, Companion, p.292.

The cover of the Penguin Classics edition of *Tess of the d'Urbervilles* reproduces one of J.M.W. Turner's paintings of Stonehenge, yet the climactic scene at the monument occupies a maximum of just four sides in that volume. Rainbarrow in *The Return of the Native* is the most frequently recurring ancient motif in a single Hardy work, an image that dominates that book, yet most readers' first – or only – awareness of an archaeological site in Hardy must surely be that famous scene at Stonehenge: a paradox. Why is this? Does the answer lie in the shape and character of the particular work, the iconic status of the site, or in a combination of the two? I believe the last is the most helpful approach, as once again, Hardy's artistry and the material of archaeology achieve their alchemical synthesis. The very unusual nature of the incident and Hardy's powerful handling of it are combined with a unique and uniquely famous site to create 'that most beautiful and pathetic of all the scenes that Hardy ever invented.'[7]

The powerful imaginative effect of Stonehenge on the author might be guessed from his mentioning only this one of several visits by acting companies to Max Gate to perform dramatized versions of the novels; the Stonehenge scene occupies most of the brief account. This is from the *Life* (p.429):

> On December 6 [1925] the company of players from the Garrick Theatre arrived at Max Gate in the evening for the purpose of giving a performance of *Tess* in the drawing-room. ... – when the chairs and tables were removed the corner of the drawing-room became Stonehenge, and yet in some strange way those present said the play gained from the simplicity. ... Miss Ffrangcon-Davies's beautiful voice and exquisite playing of the Stonehenge scene in the shadows thrown by the firelight was a thing that I shall never forget.

Its fame is readily attested to by its dramatic representations. We can easily guess how prominent was the scene in a now-forgotten Italian opera of *Tess* with score by Frederic D'Erlanger, first performed in Naples in 1906; its London premier in 1909 was seen by the Hardys. The huge number of editions also underlines the novel's fame and with it the power of the Stonehenge climax. An American 'Photoplay Edition' 'partially illustrated by scenes from an American 'movie' ... shows Blanche Sweet as a very un-Dorset-like Tess at Stonehenge, surrounded by a posse of seven men, all obviously American in garb and posture.'[8]

Considering its brevity, the undeniable power of the climactic scene, then, is remarkable. However, that scene is but the high point of an integral scheme in which the clash of past and present is echoed in the emotional and moral conflict of Angel Clare, Tess, and Alec d'Urberville. More general in the earlier half of the novel is the conflict of an ancient world as it is overwhelmed by the nineteenth century: the myths of bucolic existence are evaporating under the hard, prosaic glare of the inchoate industrial age. In this context, the Stonehenge scene can be seen as both the most intense focus of this theme and the narrative and emotional climax of the novel.

Though the famous scene is so short, however, it can be seen as simply an offshoot of an intermittent spine of historicity binding the whole novel in the form of the d'Urberville lineage. This is introduced on the opening page by Parson Tringham.

---

[7] Weber, pp.172-173.
[8] Weber, p.189.

Tringham is an antiquary, that species of dilettanti satirized by Hardy in *A Tryst at an Ancient Earthwork* which was discussed in Chapter Three. Their eclectic interests included philology, anthropology, local history, genealogy, and antiquities. It is interesting that Hardy, an arch-opponent of unscientific antiquarianism, should use two of these disparate elements – genealogy and an archaeological site – as the past-reference of his overall temporal scheme in the novel.

Hardy's own interests were varied, and his own family history is not the least of his concerns in the *Life*. However, he is far more cautious than Jack Durbeyfield about the more aristocratic possibilities of his own ancestry, stating (p.5): 'Hardy often thought of restoring the 'le' to his name, and call himself 'Thomas le Hardy'; but never did so.' However, he is at pains to go into meticulous detail about his forebears, mentioning, but without undue insistence, that his was 'a family whose diverse Dorset sections included' four noted local Thomas Hardys, among them, 'Thomas Hardy captain of the *Victory* at Trafalgar' – one aspect of a lifelong interest that was the genesis of his 'Napoleonic' works, but a connection that is almost certainly false, for the author's ancestors were a Jersey family. Another Thomas Hardy (an Elizabethan, originally Hardye) was a philanthropist who founded a school. In 1927, the elderly author laid the foundation stone of a new school building in Dorchester and his address[9] largely concerned his ancestor.

Also important in Hardy's thinking about his immediate family past is the fact that his own father was among the last generation of players in the traditional West Gallery Choir, the personal inspiration behind *Under the Greenwood Tree*. Michael Millgate notes that in that novel, not only 'the conflict and ultimately the succession of the generations', but also 'the retrospective tendency of the conversation and the very antiquity of the customs being observed' at the tranter's party, all of which is a foreshadowing of the themes in *Tess*.[10]

However powerful the inspiration of the past, though, Hardy always had an eye to the future, even in lovingly recording the time around his own childhood that provided such a rich resource for his creative life. For his early years were a time of the historical upheaval that forms a key motif in *Tess*. On page 17 of the *Life*, he records 'an experience which became of interest in the light of after events. The Great Northern Railway to London [through Hertfordshire] was then only in the process of construction, and it was necessary to go thither by coach from Hertfordshire in order to take the train at Waterloo Station for Dorchester.' And so, his very first experience of travelling away from the secluded and time-honoured rural life of Bockhampton, 'at eight or nine years old', confronted his developing imagination with the kind of stark conjunction of old and new that we find between Talbothays and Flintcomb-Ash, and even the scene at Stonehenge.

Not all antiquaries were rogues or charlatans, of course; much valuable knowledge about the past we owe to the more reputable practitioners who formed the Society of Antiquaries of London, nowadays a distinguished learned society that celebrated its three-hundredth anniversary in 2007.

Tringham, however, is of a different and lower order altogether. Whereas a scholarly antiquary would be the antecedent of a scientific archaeologist, an expert who pursued knowledge

---

[9] Barber, D.F., ed., *Concerning Thomas Hardy* (London: Charles Skilton, 1968), pp.2-3, quoted.
[10] Millgate, *Career*, p.48.

and truth, Tringham's amateurish dabbling leads directly to the Durbeyfield family's catastrophe. The fateful opening encounter brings the past into play with the present as the indolent Jack Durbeyfield is flattered by Parson Tringham's flattering address to him. This inspires hope in an august past that distracts the man from the vagaries of an insecure future; for Durbeyfield is a lifeholder, so that though their immediate future is rendered problematic by his dissolute nature, the prospects for his large family in the event of his death are even less happy.

Durbeyfield's fatuous trust in the past is based on the belief that ancient lineage means historical continuity, and that wealth can be painlessly acquired by the simple expedient of re-establishing the forgotten link with wealthy members of the family. Thus the chance meeting on the first page introduces the significance of the past to the characters and leads with tragic inevitability to Tess's arrest on the 'sacrificial altar' at Stonehenge, the primary and very solid symbol of the permanent, immoveable importance of the past. Indeed, the two threads of allusion are brought together at the climax when Angel Clare remarks, with a touch of abandoned naivety, that Stonehenge is 'older than centuries; older than the d'Urbervilles!' Hardy thus returns us to this *primum mobile* of Tess's tragic career at the very end of the book: so, we start with the ostensible identification of the living descendants of the d'Urbervilles and finish with a reference to the old family's tombs. Between the first page and that final mention is a host of references, all of them tending to the 'sins of the fathers' mode of interpretation. Roger Robinson reminds readers of 'the finished novel' that it presented 'a drastic heightening of the heroine's ancestry ... In the final version, the theme is kept prominently in the front of the reader's attention.'[11] To Hardy's interest in his own family tree, amongst other kindred studies, may be added his reading of Darwin and of Weismann on heredity as sources for this important superadded strand in the book.

Even 'the spurious 'kinship' between heroine and villain was a late thought,'[12] developed after the original version of the book, entitled *Too Late Beloved*. Tess's tragedy, and that of her hapless family, is thus made all the more poignant by the revelation that Alec's family are parvenus, modern appropriators of an ancient title, with no more direct a claim on ancient wealth and honour, perhaps, than Jack Durbeyfield; indeed, Alec's blood line is no more secure than is his religious 'conversion'. Alec's destination of Abbot's Cernel for a preaching engagement as he overtakes Tess in chapter XLV and the irony in this context of what Hardy knew of the in-bred inhabitants of the place (the real Cerne Abbas) will be discussed in Chapter Six. The notion of Tess and her unhappy family being the modern descendants, 'a little debased', as Tringham puts it, of ancient wealth and social prestige, shadows the whole narrative and forms an intricately ironic counterpoint to many key events. The opening of the book gives due emphasis to the theme when the meddlesome parson meets feckless Durbeyfield.

Tringham's showing off what is possibly quite reputable scholarship (the Battle Abbey roll is a well-known source) is not the problem, and could be regarded as lightly mocking humour more than ostentation, but it is the seed of the unforeseen and unforeseeable effects on the flatterable Durbeyfield. Hardy rather implies a considerable contempt for the 'parson' who, instead of serving his flock, has become a self-regarding pedant who can recite a fantastic list of evidence ranging from 'one of the twelve knights who assisted the Lord of Estremavilla

---

[11] Robinson, 'Darwin', Page, p.137.
[12] Robinson, 'Darwin', Page, p.138.

in Normandy in his conquest of Glamorganshire' (p.44) right through to when 'in Charles the Second's reign you were made knights of the Royal Oak for your loyalty.' Previous to the present encounter, Tringham has persistently, as we have noted, from the first page addressed the subject of his researches as 'Sir John', perhaps in some frustration over a period of months, enticing the unfortunate inebriate to listen to him, merely in order to parade his scholarship before one too humble to rebuff the flattery and too ignorant to question the veracity or assess the implications of what he is being told.

The parson concludes, 'decisively smacking his leg with his switch, 'there's hardly such another family in England'', which draws the ominous response from Durbeyfield that, 'here have I been knocking about, year after year, form pillar to post, as if I was no more than the commonest feller in the parish ... '. Tringham must know that, at the very least, an ancient lineage is irrelevant to the present humble fortunes of the family, but this man of the cloth is of the kind that draws only cynicism from Hardy for his preference for researches into the dead to the welfare of the living.

Sophie Gilmartin, alluding to another of Hardy's modern Victorian enthusiasms that plays a more prominent role in other works, comments that 'geological time is frightening and alienating in its vastness, but even within *genealogical* [my italics] time, the human trace is at risk of being misread or forgotten'[13] – an observation that might equally be made of the prehistoric archaeology that fascinates Hardy, not least in *Tess*. In an unconsciously facetious reference later in the novel, in chapter L, Tess's dying father is still optimistically clinging to the empty hope he had once gained (and Hardy has his uneducated character use the inaccurate adjectival variant instead of 'antiquary', with Hardy's tongue-in-cheek mispronunciation as 'queer'):

> 'I'm thinking of sending round to all the old antiqueerians in this part of England,' he said, asking them to subscribe to a fund to maintain me. I'm sure they'd see it as a romantical, artistical, and proper thing to do. ... if Pa'son Tringham who discovered me, had lived, he'd ha' done it, I'm sure.' (pp.428–429)

But Tringham is as dead as the ancient d'Urbervilles and as useless as his scholarship has been to the Durbeyfields.

At first, Tringham's information would seem harmless enough if it were not for Durbeyfield's susceptibility, for he adds that the only adjunct is to 'chasten yourself with the thought of 'how are the mighty fallen'' (p.45). However, his caual meddling becomes culpable in Chapter V, after the Durbeyfields have hatched their hare-brained scheme for Tess to go to meet their 'relatives', when we read that 'he might have added, what he knew very well. That the Stoke-d'Urbervilles were no more d'Urbervilles of the true tree than he was himself' (p.78). In fact, Alec Stoke researched in the British Museum to find a name befitting his fortune, the name of an 'extinct, half extinct, obscure' or 'ruined' family to add cachet to his own and *'d'Urberville* looked and sounded as well as any of them' (p.78). Significantly, Alec's real name is that of a workaday Midland industrial town, Stoke-on-Trent, a place where new Victorian wealth could be made and a new aristocracy of wealth develop while the likes of the ancient d'Urbervilles decayed and disappeared in their rural fastnesses.

---

[13] Gilmartin, 'Geology', Mallett, p.37.

At the start of chapter XIII, Hardy calls them 'her [Tess's] bogus kinfolk' (p.132); indeed, the only link of any kind that is established at their first meeting in chapter V is Alec's lustful attraction to her 'beautiful feminine tissue' (words form the seduction scene at the end of chapter XI, p.119). More bitterly ironic is the only trait that he shares with the medieval nobility whose name he has misappropriated, for after Tess's defloration Hardy comments sardonically that 'Doubtless some of Tess d'Urbervilles's mailed ancestors rollicking home from a fray had dealt the same measure even more ruthlessly towards peasant girls of their time' (p.119) and Alec's reputation as a 'reckless gallant and heart-breaker was beginning to spread' (p.132) – as far away as Tess's home village, and it is known to the Clare family who discuss his 'most culpable passions' in chapter XXVI (p.228). In this connection, Simon Gatrell makes a neat observation about Tess's truer relationship to peasant ancestry compared with Alec's assumed lineage: 'She strikes Alec d'Urberville with a heavy leather glove just as her medieval forbears would have wielded in anger a mailed fist.'[14]

Tess parrots her father's trusting acceptance of the parson's claims in her introduction to Alec, but when she leaves the Trantridge estate, in bleak contrast to the perceived advantages of a noble birth, she declares, 'I wish I'd never been born' (p.124). So, in this theme which is so closely tied to Hardy's obsessive sensitivity to class, it is his humble victim-heroine who suffers most – from the inadequacies of her own poor family, from the tyranny of the life-hold system, and, interestingly, from the shadow rather than the substance of the nobility, and from the physical substance of Alec Stoke's fake aristocracy.

The link between social class and education, one of the prime concerns of Jude Fawley and intimately bound up with Hardy's own life, is never far from view and indeed the theme of the passage of historical time is symbolised by advances in education. If Durbeyfield had had more education, he might not have been so vulnerable to the effects of Tringham's 'learning' on his own situation. Angel Clare is anxious about Tess's social background, and anxious as a result to educate her beyond it. In her turn, Tess is far in advance of her own mother, Hardy noting in chapter III:

> Between the mother and her fast-perishing lumber of superstitions, folklore, dialect, and orally transmitted ballads, and the daughter, with her trained National [School] teachings and Standard knowledge under an infinitely Revised Code, there was a gap of two hundred years as ordinarily understood. When they were together he Jacobean and Victorian ages were juxtaposed. (p.61)

Hardy asks, then, as in *The Return of the Native*, that other of his novels so dominated by the image of a single archaeological site, how far people are educated out of a way of life as a catalyst to its own erosion (especially in the climate of accelerating change in Victorian England), – and just how far can those who are educated ever return, particularly in Clym Yeobright's case, as 'prophets in their own country'?

The fateful spectre of the d'Urberville ancestry reappears periodically throughout the novel, and serves a group of inter-related themes. Sometimes, the reference has a direct impact on event, but more often, Hardy emphasizes the dangerous delusion of the worth of ancient lineage in the gullible Jack, with which he has quickly infected his wife and (despite her better

---

[14] Gatrell, p.99.

education) eldest daughter. There are acid references to the contrast between old blood and new money, questioning the material value of lineage and position in a new world order of industry and its growing middle class. Overarching all these concerns is the emphatic deadness of the ancient d'Urbervilles and their inevitable resultant indifference to the fate of their real or assumed descendants. Hardy's long interest in family pedigree, and its associated social pretensions, probably connected to his anxiety to establish a connection with Admiral Thomas Hardy, occurs in many works. The differences between this theme in *Tess* and, say, the long lineage of Miller Loveday in *The Trumpet-Major* (in which that other Hardy appears), a 'representative of an ancient family of corn-grinders ... ramifying through the unwritten history of England' (*Trumpet-Major* p.10) are several: his ancestry is both continuous and genuine, and has contributed in a practical way to the well-being of society at large – all of which is a stark contrast to Alec d'Urberville.

The most direct intervention of the ancestry theme on events in *Tess* is when Angel, torn between love for Tess and his intense, hypocritical morality, nearly turns back to her room in chapter XXXV, but 'in the act he caught sight of one of the [portraits of the] d'Urberville dames ... In the candlelight the portrait was more than unpleasant. Sinister design lurked in the woman's features ... The Caroline bodice of the portrait was low – precisely as Tess's had been when he tucked it in to show the necklace; and again he experienced the distressing sensation of a resemblance between them' (p.305). The necklace is part of the Clare family jewels that Angel has inherited on his marriage and the irony of that unpropitious resemblance (surely occasioned principally by the sensual element that dominates his notice) cannot be missed. It echoes the earlier incident where Angel decks his new bride with the piece, the jewels gleaming 'somewhat ironically' (p.287), for whatever the superficial enhancement of jewellery, Tess is not of noble birth, neither can Angel be ennobled morally by the gesture. Hardy's emphasis is on the fragility of veneer that lacks any underpinning substance.

At their first meeting in chapter II, when Angel does not at first notice Tess among the other rustic wenches, Hardy comments wryly: 'Pedigree, ancestral skeletons, monumental record, the d'Urberville lineaments, did not help Tess in her life's battle as yet ... So much for Norman blood unaided by Victorian lucre' (p.54). Hardy was as interested by ancient names and what they signified as many other aspects of history: in a surviving 'Facts' Notebook, he jotted down, 'Families of the ancient Saxon and Norman race –'.[15] And of course it is Alec Stoke-d'Urberville who provides the latter and the ostensible help that the Durbeyfields so desperately need. The cynical, worldly Alec is quite sure of the benefit of a Norman name, albeit without the actual blood-line, while idealistic Angel is ambivalent. The reference to Alec, his assumed name, and 'colourful' reputation by Mr Clare in chapter XXVI is in the context of a discussion on whether nobility of name is necessarily coupled to nobility of character –this having as its literary antecedent the burden of the 'Sermon on Gentillesse' in Chaucer's *The Wife of Bath's Tale*. Angel, the ardent young thinker, is sceptical, but when in chapter XXX he is planning to marry Tess, she tells him of her ancestry and he declares: 'I do hate the aristocratic principle of blood before everything ... the only pedigrees we ought to respect are those spiritual ones ...' (p.253). Significantly, Tess only mentions her name to cover her admission of what Alec Quasi-d'Urberville has done to her, soon after they close to the old house. Shortly

---

[15] Ed. Greenslade, Note 2a.

afterwards, Angel tells her: 'Tess, you must spell your name *correctly*' [my italics] (p.254) for the improvement of her image in the eyes of his family in order to disguise her humble origins. The snobbish impression of him is confirmed by a stab at new 'Victorian lucre' when he adds, 'why dozens of mushroom millionaires would jump at such a possession!' In the following chapter, (XXXI), he exclaims, 'A d'Urberville hurt the dignity of a Clare! It is a grand card to play – that of your belonging to such a family, and I am reserving it for a grand effect when we are married' (p.259). In chapter XXXIII, Angel decides to remain cautious about Tess's name

St John's Church, Bere Regis

until he has made her more educated, equating social status with learning – as I have noted, an echo of Clym's mission in *The Return of the Native* and an anticipation of Jude's futile quest for self-advancement from a humble background. This most uncomfortably links Angel with Tess's dissolute father, for in chapter XXXVIII, Durbeyfield proposes that 'the couple should take Tess's own name, d'Urberville, as uncorrupted. It was better than her husband's' (p.329). His ignorant irony in believing the name 'uncorrupted' is noteworthy; further, this is at the very point where his wife mentions that 'no letter had come, but Tess had unfortunately come herself' following the couple's swift estrangement.

This 'What's in a name?' preoccupation from *Romeo and Juliet* is made an explicit connection at the end of chapter XXXIII when Hardy notes that 'Mrs Angel Clare ... was conscious of the notion expressed by Friar Lawrence: "These violent delights have violent ends"' (p.281). This of course is a remote foreshadowing of Tess's own fate and the *Romeo and Juliet* connections are again strong in the Stonehenge scene; importantly, the scene that Hardy quotes takes

Ancient and Modern Collide: *Tess of the d'Urbervilles* and Stonehenge

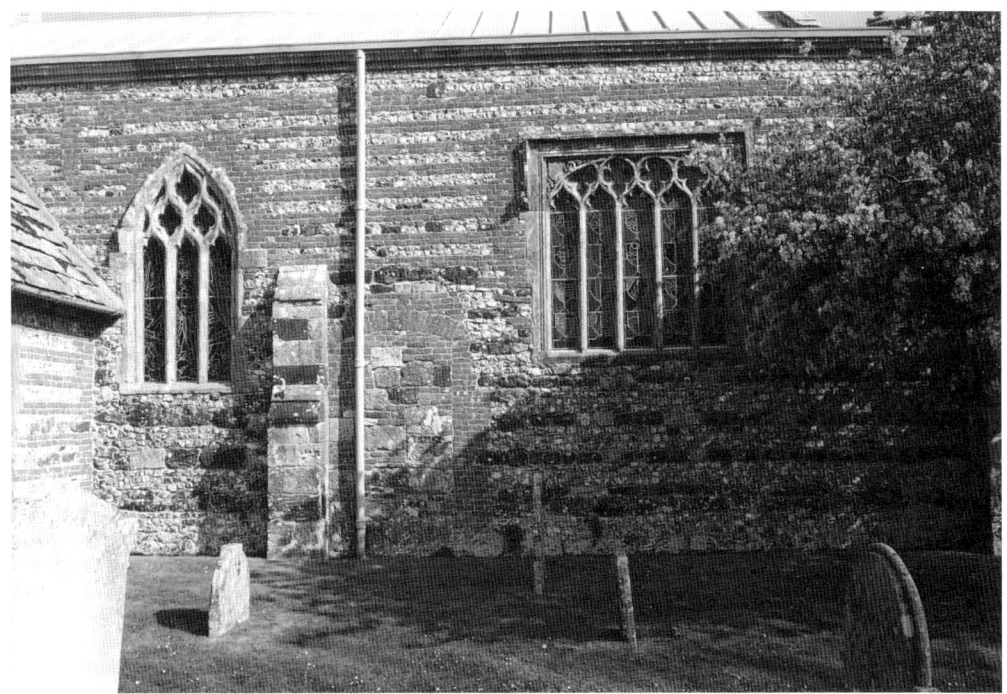

Bere Regis Church, the Turberville window

place in Friar Lawrence's cell at dawn, the very time that is repeatedly significant in the novel. There is even a suggestion that, just as Romeo and Juliet die to atone for the sins of the fathers, the fate of the latter-day d'Urbervilles is a kind of historic justice for what they had originally 'dealt ... ruthlessly' to their peasantry; in chapter L, Hardy interpolates: 'Thus the Durbeyfields, once d'Urbervilles, saw descending upon them the destiny which, no doubt, when they were among the Olympians of the county, they had caused to descend many a time, and severely enough, upon the heads of such landless ones as they themselves were now' (p.434).

All this confirms the essentially superficial nature of a name. Tess may be 'a rose by any other name', but in the nineteenth-century milieu, the plant's pedigree counts just as much - and however much this point accords with Hardy's social concerns, it remains a striking contradiction of that anxiety of his to align his own family with the ancient Hardys of his namesake, the Captain of HMS Victory later, Admiral Sir Thomas Masterman Hardy.

The most important motif in this theme of the ancient name is undoubtedly the d'Urberville tombs at Kingsbere. Hardy's use of these is another reminder of Shakespeare's fated lovers and their end in the Capulet vault, whose familial antagonism is just as powerful and destructive as the class gulf that ultimately destroys Hardy's latter-day equivalents. Additionally, there is some resonance with the sacrificial stone at Stonehenge where Tess is arrested. Hardy's originals are the Turberville family tombs in Bere Regis church, two sixteenth-century Purbeck marble monuments topped by alabaster effigies; and his etymology of the name may well be correct, for the ancestor of the family did indeed come over at the Norman Conquest as Parson Tringham says of the d'Urbervilles. Carl Weber notes that Hardy followed up his choice of name in his researches at the British Museum.[16]

Philip Larkin's celebrated and beautiful 'An Arundel Tomb' portrays two effigies surmounting the tomb in Chichester Cathedral; a copy of the poem is now displayed by it. The point of Larkin's piece is that the identity of the two figures, 'The earl and countess', has been eroded by time, but their love, shown by 'His hand withdrawn, holding her hand. / ... just a detail friends would see', is what has lasted, the one thing about the figures that still resonates for us in 'An unarmorial age'. The great irony is that the two cold figures are just as impersonally distant from their viewers as the Turbervilles, for what Larkin did not know at the time of writing in 1956 is that the 'sculptor's sweet commissioned grace' in portraying the held hands was actually an alteration made in the era of Hardy's novel, a Victorian sentimentalising. There is nothing at all sentimental about the Turberville tombs.

Most of the reference to the d'Urbervilles is, in fact, to these tombs, and accords with Hardy's fascination with tombs as symbolic of the transience of human life (and with it, of reputation) that he absorbed in the clearance of the old St Pancras churchyard as a young architect. Sophie Gilmartin's interesting article, already referred to, stresses the connections in Hardy's work between 'the earth's genealogical and geological layers and also those 'bare bones' of 'perished hands' and the skeletons buried in the earth, the human deposits which Hardy gives flesh to in his narratives'[17] through the repeated use of tombs and graveyards – Giles Winterbourne's and Fanny Robin's graves or the ancient graveyard in *A Pair of Blue Eyes* spring to mind. In what she perceives to be a strong tradition through Gray and Wordsworth, taken up in the Victorian arts, the 'graveyard could be viewed as the last bastion of pedigree for those families who had left their village. They could return to the graveyard to read their genealogical record on the tombstones.' So, 'This movement of return to the ancestral burial-place in *Tess of the d'Urbervilles* is an ironic reversal of the movement at this time away from the ancestral home.'[18] And we might also note the grotesque reversal that the impoverished living Durbeyfields are outside in the churchyard, while the aristocratic dead d'Urbervilles are snug and dry in the vault within the church!

Even the arrival of the newly-weds at 'their mouldy old habitation' (p.283) (where even the ancient family portraits cannot be moved 'owing to their being built into the wall' (p.284)) is an anticipation of the tomb, for this place, entered via an Elizabethan bridge, provides their 'lodgings at that very farmhouse which, before its mutilation, had been a mansion of a branch of the d'Urberville family' (quoted from Angel's inspection of the place in chapter XXXII, p.270). The deadness and decay of the family's property are a match for the dusty remains in the family vault, and, moreover, Kingsbere itself is a 'half-dead townlet' (p.445). This is reminiscent of the symbolically decayed state of Oxwell Hall in *The Trumpet-Major*; Simon Gatrell comments: 'Both man and house are crippled by miserliness, and the house seems as clearly condemned to slow decay and ultimate destruction as Derriman.'[19]

Hardy's favourite archaeological-mortality motif of the ancient barrows, in this case on the 'plateau, bosomed with semi-globular tumuli – as if Cybele the Many-breasted were su-

---

[16] Weber, p.171.
[17] Gilmartin, 'Geology', Mallett, pp.23/24.
[18] Gilmartin, 'Geology', Mallett, p.24.
[19] Gatrell, pp.52/53.

pinely extended there – which stretched between the valley of her birth and the valley of her love' (pp.355-356) gives an extended-temporal glimpse at the theme in chapter XLII, as well as being a milky mammary image appropriate to Tess's physical attributes as well as to her former occupation at the dairy.

By the beginning of chapter XXXVIII, it is apparent that Jack Durbeyfield's blusterings have made his noble ancestry well-known enough to have become a source of ribald humour among his social peers at Marlott (but, ironically, not those who sit in the House of Peers). Tess asks the turnpike-keeper for news and is told, *inter alia*, that 'John is a old and ancient nobleman himself by blood, with family skillentons in their own vaults to this day, but done out of his property in the times of the Romans [Hardy's joke repeated from *The Mayor of Casterbridge* meaning Roman Catholics]. However, Sir John, as we call 'n now …' (p.326). The key point is that the fatuous conceit of Durbeyfield's ancestry is inextricably bound up with the tombs, and, while constantly re-emphasising the deadness of the d'Urbervilles, the repeated allusion allows Hardy progressively, incrementally, to ironies – either in the authorial voice or through that of a character – right up to the events at Kingsbere church itself. By the end of the same chapter, Durbeyfield is lamenting the collapse of Tess's marriage solely in terms of the loss of his newly acquired ancestral reputation.

In chapter IV, Durbeyfield, 'sufficiently unsteady' with drink, and, 'like most comical effects, not quite so comic after all', trumpets in the middle of the village street: "I've got a family vault at Kingsbere!" (pp.68-69). However, his wife sensibly counsels that many other local families have such a pedigree, including (ironically) the Tringhams. By chapter XVI, Hardy is commenting that Tess notices in the distance 'the environs of Kingsbere – in the church of which parish the bones of her ancestors – her useless ancestors – lay entombed (p.156). Here, we are reminded that, unlike the invention of Alec Stoke for perceived advantage, Tess's ancestry is absolutely genuine, but completely valueless. At Talbothays, Tess, in 'an access of hunger for [Angel's] good opinion', remembers 'what she had latterly endeavoured to forget … – the identity of her family with the knightly d'Urbervilles. Barren attribute as it was … '. The ancestors are 'Purbeck marble and alabaster people', though she is 'no spurious d'Urberville, compounded of money and ambition like those at Trantridge, but true d'Urberville to the bone' (p.183). For the moment, 'she held her tongue about the d'Urberville vault (p.184), but not for long beyond this point, chapter XIX.

The ancestral lineage motif reaches its most complex and telling development in chapter LII, when Tess's destitute family with all their worldly goods arrive at Kingsbere – Mrs Durbeyfield in bold expectation that their pedigree would secure some advantage in this 'townlet', the 'spot of all spots in the world which could be considered the d'Urbervilles' home, since they had resided there for full five hundred years' (p.446). On announcing that she is the 'widow of the late Sir John d'Urberville … returning to the domain of his forefathers', she is summarily disabused by the messenger, who says, 'Oh? Well I know nothing about that', and informs them that their anticipated rooms have already been let. Impoverished supplicants rather than honoured descendants, the family are reduced to 'camping' outside the wall of the d'Urberville aisle of the church.

The irony of this would be perhaps too heavy were it not for Hardy's masterstroke in overshadowing this circumstance with the scene within the church. Tess enters to see the physical representation of her father's gullible trust in his ancestral heritage: broken carvings, stolen brasses: 'Of all the reminders that she had ever received that her people were socially extinct there was none so forcible as this spoliation' (p.448). One of the recumbent figures atop the tombs is Alec, who surprises Tess, and 'she sank down nigh to fainting' (p.449). Apart from the dark humour played on Tess, the incident is many-layered: it is at once an absurd parody of the tomb scene in *Romeo and Juliet*, and a grotesque metaphor of the difference between the old, dead, powerless but genuine d'Urbervilles, and this rich, lively, pseudo-descendant. Further, it is a foreshadowing of the deaths of both of them, the one entitled to lie here in the futile pomp of a plundered inheritance, the other no doubt to receive a lavish Victorian 'send-off' – but both of them as dead as the cold alabaster effigies. Alec is not such a villain as readers' memories would often suggest: though Hardy ends this 'modern tragedy' with a reference to Aeschylus, it is surely of Sophocles and the curse of Oedipus that we are reminded in the fate of Alec as well as of Tess, for he, no less than she, is a victim of the d'Urberville inheritance, perhaps even 'the family tradition of the coach and murder'. Angel, on learning that Tess has murdered Alec, wonders 'what obscure strain in the d'Urberville blood had led to this aberration' (both p.475).

***

In the conflict between the ancient world represented by agriculture (which developed in the Neolithic) and archaeology, and the new world of rapid travel and increasing mechanisation (not least in agriculture), Hardy clearly shows that the latter is overwhelming the former. This is made apparent throughout the novel and is indicated symbolically as a precursor to the Stonehenge scene by the incongruity, both of its nature and the rapidity of its development, of the modish new resort of Sandbourne (the real Bournemouth). Here, Alec takes Tess to a new bourgeois world both literally and metaphorically, a world to which he is perfectly attuned, but in which she is as much of an outsider as Eustacia Vye or Damon Wildeve are in Egdon Heath. Those two are destroyed by the Heath in their flight of rejection: Tess lashes out at this alien world in violence as she attempts to escape back into the ancient landscape to which she belongs. The vengeance of the 'new world' is, however, only postponed. Contradicting the violence of Tess's reaction, Roger Robinson's Darwinian analysis of the novel sees Tess's 'passivity'[20] at Sandbourne as symbolic of her 'spent family energies'; her failure to adapt leads her to 'become extinct in the exotic and artificial setting of a seaside resort'.

Sandbourne represents in microcosm the clash of ancient and modern that is central to the novel. Hardy knew many places that, apparently unchanged for centuries, were permanently altered by the impingement of modernity – the most persistent general instance in his works being the overwhelming effect of the new railways. The new world of Sandbourne (whose catalyst to growth was the railway) clashes rudely against the old, for it abuts and intrudes upon the ancient Egdon Heath with its archaeological traces, and there is the sense here in 'like a fairy place suddenly created by the stroke of wand' (p.463) of its being a wilful fantasy if not a mere whim, distant from the old solid ancient reality of Egdon:

> An outlying tract of the enormous Egdon waste was close at hand, yet on the very

---

[20] Robinson, 'Darwin', Page, pp.138, 136.

verge of that tawny piece of antiquity such a glittering novelty as this pleasure city had chosen to spring up. Within the space of a mile from its outskirts every irregularity of the soil was prehistoric, every channel an undisturbed British trackway; not a sod having been turned there since the days of the Caesars. Yet the exotic had grown here, suddenly as the prophet's gourd, and had drawn hither Tess. (p.463)

The sense of ancient human continuity blended all but invisibly with the natural landscape is strong here, further emphasising the contrast with the new resort - though it is ironic that 'the Caesars' had come to Britain from 'Mediterranean lounging places'. On the same page, Angel confuses the harmonious natural sounds of the sea and the pines, underlining his capacity for error, the error which had actually driven Tess to Sandbourne in the first place; but do we not feel that this mistake has been engendered by the artificiality of the place itself?

***

The nineteenth-century revolution in agriculture was profound and gives Hardy the opportunity to present the clash of worlds, of ancient and modern ways of life, through the medium of the two principal agricultural settings in the novel and his characters' involvement with them: Talbothays Dairy and Flintcomb-Ash. Indeed, Simon Gatrell states that the novel 'marks a climax of Hardy's exploration of the integration of characters with their environment … .'[21]

These two very different places are used symbolically to match the two contrasting situations in Tess's life and her extremes of emotional experience. They are not merely at opposite poles in their physical condition, however, but the whole character of the two sites and the activities that are pursued there represent the 'old' and the 'new' worlds of agriculture, two worlds that are in collision in the mid-nineteenth century. Just as Tragedy and Comedy are two extremes of reality, neither intended to be wholly real, so Hardy creates two polar opposite realities of rural existence, two mythic versions of the same cultural environment. In addition, this sense of cultural conflict shadows the moral conflicts among Tess and her two lovers. The grim sense of the rapidly evolving destruction of a way of life at Flintcomb-Ash, overwhelmed by the machine, both echoes and confirms the sense that Tess's life at Talbothays – and her unhappiness with it – could not last:

> Tess had never in her recent life been so happy as she was now, possibly never would be so happy again. She was, for one thing, physically and mentally suited among these new surroundings. ... Moreover, she and Clare also, stood as yet on the debatable land between predilection and love; where no profundities have been reached; no reflections have set in, awkwardly inquiring, 'Whither does this new current tend to carry me? What does it mean to my future?' (p.185)

Tess and Angel's first meeting is on different ground, however, in the 'beautiful Vale of Blakemoor or Blackmoor' in chapter II (p.48). This place is on the edge of the modern world, overlooked by hills which include 'the prominences of Hambledon Hill and Bulbarrow' with their hill-forts, and is 'for the most part untrodden as yet by tourist or landscape-painter,

---

[21] Gatrell, p.97.

though within four hours' journey from London' (a phrase which might apply to Stonehenge if it were not for Turner and Constable, though our fugitives' arrival is indeed much ahead of the later deluge of visitors). There is the sense here, then, of the near-approach of the modern world, mainly as a result of the revolution brought about by that prime Victorian symbol of modernity, the railway.

But the circumstances pertaining at the time of the lovers' first meeting in Tess's home in the Vale of Blackmoor are a confrontation rather than an approach – a collision of ancient and modern, the 'tourist' brothers coming across the ancient ritual of club-walking. Hardy emphasises the antiquity of the place by means of the customs that still persisted there, though these are on the wane. And the visitors are harbingers of a different age. His placing of a note of the history of this 'engirdled and secluded region' before an explanation of the club-walking – in reality an ages-old fertility rite particularly apt for the lovers' first meeting – unites myth with objective history in the place, and tends in retrospect to invest the 'yet' (quoted above) with a tone of foreboding about the arrival of the 'tourist' as a mobile harbinger and agent of modernity. Again, it is the sense of the pastness of a place that is notable in Hardy's painting its background, with the legendary 'killing by a certain Thomas de la Lynd of a beautiful white hart which the king had run down and spared' (p.49). From this mythic setting, the 'forests have departed, but some old customs of their shades remain. Many, however, linger only in a metamorphosed or disguised form' which include 'the club revel or 'club-walking' as it was there called.' The white gowns of the women were 'a gay survival from Old Style days' when life was simple, but the main point emphasises the mythic level, that 'the club of Marlott alone lived to uphold', in a Classical allusion, 'the local Cerealia' and, moreover, 'had walked for hundreds of years'.

The youthful merrymaking, then, is paradoxically in the form of an ancient custom. Michael Millgate remarks of *Under the Greenwood Tree* in connection with the dance: 'Much is made of the sequence, the conflict, and ultimately the succession of the generations ... the very antiquity of the customs being observed all promote a constant awareness that those who are old were once young ... '.[22] This seems just as relevant to the mature *Tess*. As today, the arrival of 'tourism' is not an unmixed blessing, with its potential to destroy or to ossify what it finds of the past. Hardy often appears in his Wessex works to be, as it were, the 'archaeologist of rural life', recording in the manner of true archaeology the traces of the past; and like that discipline and in contradiction of any sense of true nostalgia, R.J. White notes: 'There is no fuss or foolishness about the 'good old days' in Hardy's picture of a changing world.'[23] The evidences of that changing world recorded by Hardy, unlike archaeological traces, are still alive, like the Marlott club-walking, atrophied or moribund though they may be. This event is a vestigial fertility rite echoed in chapter X in the dance at Trantridge with its images of 'satyrs and nymphs – a multiplicity of Pans whirling a multiplicity of Syrinxes; Lotis attempting to elude Priapus, and always failing' (p.107) – a fine example of Hardy's giving both depth and scope to his sense of antiquity by mining his extensive Classical reading.

Tess and Angel become closely acquainted in chapter XX at Talbothays in the lush and fertile Frome Valley, the Vale of the Great Dairies. This setting is more than idyllic, it is a vi-

---

[22] Millgate, *Career*, p.48.
[23] White, p.6.

sion of Eden, and the two principal figures are Adam and Eve in their innocence – in both the colloquial and original meanings of the word. Being an Eden, the spot is both utopian and a world to be lost, both personally for the two lovers and historically. Millgate notes of *Far from the Madding Crowd*: 'the immemorial features of the domestic life and rural economy of an area still almost untouched by the economic or social consequences of the industrial revolution'[24] – a description that equally well suits Talbothays. Hardy eschews any sense that the real Talbothays – the actual name of a real farm let by his father – must suffer harsh winters and have its share of familial discord and economic uncertainty. Here, however, it is a mythic place where an idealised relationship can develop, where the practices of dairy farming can be carried on as from time immemorial, and where the blissful pair, bathed in a golden, unctuous light, are at one with Nature. Hardy's imagery of grey then pastel dawn light, creamy abundance, and luscious wetness creates a gorgeous sensuous impression, all this intermingled with Biblical allusion:

> They met continually, they could not help it. They met daily in that strange and solemn interval, the twilight of the morning in the violet or pink dawn; for it was necessary to rise early, so very early, here. Milking was done betimes; and before the milking came the skimming, which began at a little past three. ... No sooner had the hour of three struck and whizzed, than she left her room and ran to the dairyman's door; then up the ladder to Angel's, calling him in a loud whisper; then woke her fellow-milkmaids. By the time that Tess was dressed Clare was downstairs and out in the humid air. (p.186)

Hardy, at his most evocative in this chapter, particularly draws on his favourite painterly resource for his impressionistic use of light in 'The gray [sic] half-tones of daybreak' (p.186) and 'the twilight of the morning' being compared with 'the day's close' and 'twilight of evening'; his 'cold gleam of day' is an anticipation of their final dawn together at Stonehenge. The light imagery is closely woven with that of the Bible and of pagan mythology including their being named 'Adam and Eve' (p.186) and the quiet triumph of Easter at 'the Resurrection hour' (p.187) (– in Angel's mind, for at this stage, his conventional Christian upbringing is to the fore). The mythic sense is heightened by Tess's being dubbed 'Artemis' (p.187) and 'Demeter' by Angel (the Classical vein justified by the educated Clare's knowledge of Greek), though the authorial reference to Tess as 'Magdalen', a devoted, penitent 'fallen woman', is equally significant.

Talbothays is Paradise indeed, and the loss of innocence in the relationship when Angel (the name suddenly more ironic) learns the unpalatable truth of Tess's past makes it instantly Paradise Lost. The lack of machinery at the dairy also identifies it as a world which is being lost together with its culture. Even at Talbothays, however, Hardy keeps the modern world within reach with the brief but telling mention that the milk is taken to London by train. Nevertheless, the place is in its essence both beautiful and ancient, and thus presents a shocking contrast to Flintcomb-Ash.

Flintcomb-Ash is Tess's purgatory, but is presented more in the imagery of Hell, the very word 'ash' connoting destruction by fire; and flint, with its hard sharpness, epitomising the

---

[24] Millgate, *Career*, p.90.

character of the place and itself the means of making fire. Again, the real place, based on Dole's Ash in central Dorset, must have its fine summer days, but the novelist presents it in its worst light to emphasise it as a mythic extremity from the earlier site of innocent blissfulness. Every detail of the environment, and particularly the work that is pursued there, is a polar opposite to Talbothays. Hardy again has work beginning in the dawn light, but how different is the 'singularly inexpressive' (p.404) gloom in March. In Chapter XLVI, where this bleak new environment is introduced, 'The dry winter wind still blew' (p.392) over the 'wide acreage of blank agricultural brownness'; and Tess's work is dreariness under 'her hard taskmaster Farmer Groby' (p.393) in contrast to kindly dairyman Crick. Rather than flowing milk, the essence of nourishment, the farm produces, amongst other hardy crops, turnips. A reminder and symbol of modernity is the turnip-slicing machine, which in its lively assonant 'bright blue hue of new paint' (p.392) is reminiscent of Farfrae's new seed-drill, and may similarly have made the manual labour rather easier. Hardy suggests, however, that it merely enabled more to be done, since, 'For hours nothing relieved the joyless monotony of things' (p.392).

It is in another part of the farm where, in chapter XLVII, Hardy creates the real vision of Hell – and a decidedly modern image it is with another machine at its heart. Here, the contrast with Talbothays is made horrifyingly complete, the machine intensifying Hardy's sense of modernity as the focal point of that contrast. Again, light is an important resource for Hardy's bleak evocation, the 'dawn of the March morning is singularly inexpressive and there is nothing to show where the eastern horizon lies. Against the twilight rises the trapezoidal top of the stack which has stood forlornly here through the washing and bleaching of the wintry weather … Izz and Tess, with the other women workers in their whitey-brown pinners, stood waiting and shivering' (p.404). This is in contrast to the heat of the engine and he who works it, for Hardy draws on range of sensory impressions as in all his fine descriptive writing.

The literal and symbolic focus of this terrifyingly infernal scene is the steam traction engine, a machine whose presence is both mythic and historic. The length and detail of Hardy's description of the machine, and its relation to the rustics in its orbit of mechanistic control, is a measure of its significance to the temporal theme of the novel. Hardy's intensely wrought description makes it inextricably linked with the apparently sinister alien who operates it, a man who is as separated from the soil as the machine is from flesh-and-blood human beings.

The wandering operator, 'for as yet the steam threshing machine was itinerant in this part of Wessex' (thus making it more fixedly rooted in the ancient traditions of agriculture than other areas) (p.405), is an outsider who 'spoke in a strange northern accent'; he is a 'dark motionless being, a sooty and grimy embodiment of tallness, in a sort of trance … A creature from Tophet … he stood apathetic … the long strap which ran from the driving-wheel of his engine … was the sole tie-line between agriculture and him'; … if anyone 'asked him what he called himself, he replied shortly, 'an engineer'' – so, identified by industrial role, not personal name. Reminding us of Tess's fatal link with her ancestors, it was as if 'some ancient doom compelled him to wander here against his will in the service of his Plutonic master.'

The details Hardy gives of the seismic shift in agricultural life just beginning at Flintcomb-Ash tellingly resemble the changes wrought, not long before the historical setting of the novel, in Australia as among the latest of countries where prehistoric cultures had been gradually eroded and destroyed by 'advanced' industrial society: the local Wessex workers are 'aboriginals' (p.405), primitives compared with the itinerant outsider from the heartland of the Industrial Revolution who, it is thereby hinted, is merely the forerunner of more permanent colonists who will subjugate the locals and their ancient lifestyle. Even the local farmer Groby, the depersonalised 'he', bears the name of a village near Leicester, a distant industrial city. Hardy's mentor William Barnes was an Anglo-Saxon expert and philologist and it is more than likely that Hardy had long known that place-names ending in '-by' are far from Wessex, this being the Old Norse suffix for 'farmstead' or 'village'.

And it is this 'Plutonic master', the 'red tyrant' steam engine that is the dominant focus in this scene, the '*primum mobile* of this little world', rather than its denizen, the engineer. 'He had nothing to do with preparatory labour. His fire was waiting incandescent, his steam was at high pressure, in a few seconds he could make the long strap move at invisible velocity,' writes Hardy – but of course these are a machine's attributes that are enumerated, not a mere man's. The effect on the agricultural workers is as profound as on the efficiency of that most traditional agricultural activity, harvest:

> The rick was unhaled by full daylight; the men then took their places, the women mounted, and the work began. Farmer Groby – or, as they called him, 'he' – arrived ere this, and by his orders Tess was placed on the platform of the machine, close to the man who fed it, her business being to untie every sheaf of corn handed on to her by Izz Huett, who stood next, but on the rick; so that the feeder could seize it and spread it over the revolving drum, which whisked out every grain in one moment.
>
> They were soon in full progress, after a preparatory hitch or two, which rejoiced the hearts of those who hated machinery. (p.405)

Hardy's nightmare-machine might be seen as the much darker successor to the first train in Wordsworth's Lake District and the surveying for the new railway line in George Eliot's *Middlemarch* (1871–1872 – twenty years before *Tess*). In Chapter 56, a group of deeply conservative rustics, not unlike Hardy's later quasi-comic creations, discuss '[the] ruin of this country-side by railroads' followed by a headlong assault on the surveyors that is only halted by the timely intervention of Fred Vincy. The ageing Wordsworth's famous complaint was published in a pamphlet at the height of the 1840s 'great railway mania' and is a sonnet of October 1844, 'On the Projected Kendal and Windermere Railway'. In it he describes the railway as 'a blight' and 'ruthless change ... Mid ... fields at random thrown'. Hardy's ambivalence to modernity found no complaint against the arrival of the railway in Dorchester, but his abhorrence at the traction engine at Flintcomb-Ash is not, like these two predecessors, simply that it is spoiling the landscape (since a traction engine affects nothing but the silence): Hardy's horror is at its effect on the *people*.

The imagery of Hell which characterises Groby's farm with its unforgiving owner and unremitting work is largely associated with this alien innovation, and, emphasising the long working day, Hardy symbolically distances the farm both from the pagan ancient (represented by the Cerne Abbas Giant and Tess, identified with the moon, though not virgin) and the Christian medieval world (of Cerne Abbey and Milton Abbas) where work followed the natural diurnal, and not just an intensified seasonal cycle:

> But there was another hour's work ... as the evening light in the direction of the Giant's Hill by Abbot's-Cernel dissolved away, the white-faced moon of the season arose from the horizon that arose towards Middleton Abbey and Shottsford on the other side. (p. 414)

Like the turnip-cutter and Farfrae's seed-drill, steam traction engines were at the forefront of a profound change in agricultural methods that had been employed, to a large extent, since the Neolithic. The fact that railways have already become a normal part of the pattern of commerce and communication shows that the novelty of the steam traction engine and its associated machinery identifies Wessex as a backward – perhaps backward-looking – region in its culture. In both practical and symbolic terms, the main change is that the worker operating the equipment is not only singular, but is separated from the soil which produces the crop. The exclusive, modern title the operator gives himself instantly makes him innately incongruous, like the lapsed engineer Damon Wildeve in *The Return of the Native*; further, the other workers, though physically still in contact with the ground, are no more connected with the rhythms of Nature than is the 'engineer' himself: all are become automatons, predecessors of Chaplin's *Modern Times* character, compelled to work at a pace set by the machinery.

The notion of mechanisation in agriculture, Man separated from the Earth on which he depends and from which he has sprung, is a profound cultural shift, and continues to be a preoccupation of poets. R. S. Thomas's 1950s poem *Cynddylan on a Tractor* is from the time when virtually all field work had become physically separate from the ground:

> Ah you should see Cynddylan on a tractor.
> Gone the old look that yoked him to the soil;
> He's a new man now, part of the machine,
> His nerves of metal and his blood oil ...
> The sun comes over the tall trees
> Kindling all the hedges, but not for him
> Who runs his engine on a different fuel ...

How ironic it is that traction engines are now regarded as a quaint contrast with the internal combustion engine, not only slow and old-fashioned, but closer to Nature because they are surrounded by smoke and steam. There is no doubting Hardy's attitude to the arrival of machines in the ages-old environment of harvest which had occurred in Dorset some ten years before he wrote *Tess*. The steam engine is very much the infernal machine: it is of 'fire and smoke' (p.405), 'the red tyrant' (p.404), 'despotic', black with ... strength very much in reserve', its operator is 'grimy ... with a heap of coals ...'; as in Milton's Hell, there is heat without light, the engine 'with warmth ... Without the necessity of much daylight ... '. This imagery serves two purposes: that of indicating Tess's geographical and emotional flight from Eden as a result of her rejection, and by being associated with these machine-icons of the modern age, that of indicating the terrible and unnatural direction of Humanity as a whole away from the soil and its roots therein.

So, Talbothays and Flintcomb-Ash are Paradise and Hell, and it is the machine that is the distinguishing emblem of the latter. Mary Jacobus's observations on this theme in *The Woodlanders* could apply with equal force to *Tess*: '... Carlyle mourns the death of organicism.

Igdrasil has become a fiction, the Tree of Existence displaced by a demythologised and mechanistic world: 'The *Machine* of the Universe,' – alas, do but think of that in contrast!' The same reduction of myth to machine haunts *The Woodlanders*. Hardy laments a lost mythology as well as the rape of the woods by rootless predators from the modern world.'[25]

But what of Tess's home village of Marlott? The place seems outside this symbolic scheme, except that Hardy slips in what, at earlier stages of the book, seems the apparently insignificant detail of the 'revolving Maltese cross of the reaping machine' (p.136). Marlott is too backward to have received the full force of the Industrial Revolution in the form of the steam engine, for this other contraption is horse-drawn, but the 'paint with which [it was] smeared, intensified in hue by the sunlight, imparted to [it] a look of having been dipped in liquid fire'. This not only reflects something of Tess's present tormenting moral hobgoblins, having returned home pregnant by Alec, but also prefigures the fiery hellish character of the Flintcomb-Ash steam engine and all it stands for in that place where the machine is the more sinister by being further removed from Nature and those who work around it. And even here in Marlott, Tess (with the other female farm workers) is contrasted with the machine more than are the men because the women 'become part and parcel of outdoor nature ... a field-woman is a portion of the field ...' (P.137).

***

Beyond ancient and modern, and indeed all temporal concerns, Hardy places Tess in the frame of a vast, impersonal, indifferent Universe. In this way, we experience the diminution of the individual character to an even greater degree than is achieved through the use of quasi-permanent ancient man-made sites like Stonehenge. Her young brother Abraham's musings on the stars in the night resemble the use of the astronomical perspective in *Two on a Tower* in adding a huge extra dimension to the philosophic scheme. Once Angel is drawn in to share Tess's despair in chapter XXXV, as he lies alone in self-imposed estrangement, 'the night came in and took its place there, unconcerned and indifferent' (p.305). This, in its turn, is matched by the extraordinary juxtaposition of the desperately transient and the eternally fossilised as Henry Knight clings to the cliff in the climactic scene in *A Pair of Blue Eyes*. In *Tess* chapter IV, her little brother's 'childish prattle recurred to what impressed his imagination more than the wonders of creation' (p.69), and so the cold sky and questions of whether God is on the other side of the 'twinklers' and whether 'stars were worlds' are ironically juxtaposed with the question of Tess 'marrying a gentleman'. She brings both their expectations and natural imagery down to earth by likening the stars to 'apples on our stubbard-tree'; like people, she implies, some are 'splendid and sound – a few blighted.'

In the famous incident at Stonehenge, however, Hardy's symbolic scheme ignores the obvious astronomical possibilities, concentrating rather on the potential of the ancient site and, in particular, contrasting the arrival of dawn with the blackest of nights: 'But the moon had now sunk, the clouds seemed to settle on their heads, and the night grew as dark as a cave.' (p.483).

***

---

[25] Mary Jacobus, 'Tree and Machine: The Woodlanders', Critical Approaches to the Fiction of Thomas Hardy, ed. Dale Kramer (London: Macmillan, 1979), p.116.

The climactic scene in *Tess* in a bizarre drama brings into conflict an ancient site and the efficient modern police system. And the modern world wins. Andrew D. Radford admires Hardy's 'ambitiousness in embracing ... remotest antiquity ... and current events'[26].

But, alluding to the title of the present chapter, *Tess* presents not only a clash of the prehistoric with Victorian modernity: it offers us a microcosm of Hardy's preoccupation with Time and his fascination with the mysteriously ancient. Roger Robinson elucidates the significance of the chapter, observing that the 'thousand-year scale marked by the medieval and

Salisbury Cathedral

d'Urberville references, the Cistercian Abbey and the enigmatic monolith of the Cross-in-Hand, is itself diminished by the scene at Stonehenge and the many passages which convey the primeval antiquity of the natural landscape.'[27] In a similar vein but offering a different slant, Radford remarks Hardy's 'bold use of this ancient remnant as an opportunity imaginatively to revisit several different bygone periods and to contrive that that the modern moment is seen in relation to them ... .'[28]

Radford, in his exhaustive and fascinating examination, writes that the piece is 'immediate and accessible if often challenging in the signals it emits'[29] and the scene demands similar treatment in the present study.

There are many reasons that might be adduced to explain the celebrity of this scene; one of

---

[26] Radford, p.7.
[27] Robinson, 'Darwin', Page, p.139.
[28] Radford, p.3.
[29] Radford, p.2.

them is certainly the fact that the fame and archaeological importance of the site is in marked contrast to its very rare appearances in literature. Christopher Chippindale, in his fascinating and justly named *Stonehenge Complete*, points out that 'By contrast with the abundance of good Stonehenge paintings, the romantic literature of Stonehenge is very thin.'[30] Turner and Constable are but the most famous artists who painted the place, and Chippindale comments that their pictures are 'less pictures of Stonehenge than of fantastical storms'[31] (– the power of sheer *atmosphere* dominating, as in Hardy's response to the place, both in his own experience and in the novel). Chippindale continues, 'The only enduring novel of Stonehenge is Thomas Hardy's *Tess of the d'Urbervilles*.'[32] What is noteworthy about this comment is that the relatively short scene can so dominate the reader's memory that the whole work can without undue exaggeration be dubbed a 'novel of Stonehenge'. From a literary perspective, Radford characterises it as 'one of the best known and perhaps least fully appreciated episodes in Hardy's fictions.'[33]

This imbalance of artistic response is significant: haunting, mysterious image predominating over what words can express or evoke of the place. For Stonehenge is still, and will inevitably remain, a silent witness, prehistoric in the most literal sense – though with a vast later accretion of myth, folklore, and a history of its own. Furthermore, Hardy was an enthusiast for the visual arts and is often in his works a 'painter in words'; I believe, indeed, that his descriptive technique is one of his strongest claims to the mantle of a great writer.

One other work by a major artist that is relevant here is the rarely performed Ninth Symphony of Ralph Vaughan Williams – which is itself indebted to Hardy and underlines the inspirational power of the novel's climax. Unlike his close friend Gustav Holst, Vaughan Williams did not know Hardy personally, but fifty years before this last symphony, he corresponded with the author, writing three letters in 1904, 1908, and 1909 about setting some of Hardy's and William Barnes's poems to music. The composer's biographer Michael Kennedy wrote thus for notes to accompany Sir Adrian Boult's 1970 EMI recording:

> Original sketches are headed 'Wessex Prelude' and the last movement was once called 'Landscape'. Vaughan Williams planned a symphony about Salisbury and the surrounding area, a region he loved and visited in the last month of his life. The cathedral, Salisbury Plain and Stonehenge where Hardy's Tess spent her last night at liberty, each played a part in the genesis of this noble work.[34]

In a more recent (2000) recording of the work, with the same orchestra conducted by Bernard Haitink, Kennedy is more specific, writing:

> Two important superscriptions relate to the second movement – 'Stonehenge' and 'Tess'. This movement is clearly still an evocation of the arrest of Thomas Hardy's Tess of the D'Urbervilles [sic] at Stonehenge.[35]

---

[30] Christopher Chippindale, Stonehenge Complete (London: Thames and Hudson, 1983, revised 1994), p.112.
[31] Chippindale, p.105.
[32] Chippindale, p.112.
[33] Radford, p.1.
[34] Michael Kennedy, notes, Sir Adrian Boult, cond., Ralph Vaughan Williams Symphonies 8 and 9, London Philharmonic, EMI, 1970.
[35] Michael Kennedy, notes, Bernard Haitink, cond., Ralph Vaughan Williams Symphonies 8 and 9, London Philharmonic, EMI, 2001.

Before examining the scene in detail, it is important to outline the enormous importance of Stonehenge in archaeology which contrasts with its relative neglect by artists; indeed, it has been designated by UNESCO a World Heritage Site since the inception of that accolade in 1986 – along with such legendary contemporaneous prehistoric sites as Mycenae in Greece. The effect of modern tourism has been similar in both places – though the distance of the latter from main roads and the construction of a magnificent new site museum in 2003 provide a stark contrast.

The exact nature of the belief system that gave rise to the monument and any rituals that were performed there must of necessity remain unknown (of which more later), as indeed do the precise details of construction techniques, but modern archaeology has established more of the chronological facts of its origins. Recent research, including major new excavations in 2008, has narrowed and clarified the origins and uses of the site and keeps pushing the actual dates further back into prehistory, including Mesolithic occupation as far back as $c.7000$ BC. Received opinion distinguishes six principal stages of development, starting with a Neolithic structure of $c.3100$ BC, continuing through the Bronze Age until the final development in c1100 BC, the apogee being $c.2100-1900$ BC. The site continued in use for an unknown period after this.

Modern research has also tended to range more widely, revealing Stonehenge as the focus of an extensive, more complex landscape. An important new site was discovered in summer 2009 which has been dubbed 'Bluestonehenge'; this raised the possibility that a second, previously unknown, circle of bluestones (from the Preseli Mountains in West Wales) were removed to the main site to augment a remodelled, wider circle of bluestones perhaps as early as 2500 BC.

The modern history of Stonehenge, almost as chequered as its perilous passage through recent centuries, is thoroughly explored in *Stonehenge Complete*.[36] In 1967, with the stone circle open to hordes of casual visitors en route to the West Country, the archaeologist Jacquetta Hawkes (wife of J. B. Priestley) observed enigmatically that 'Every age has the Stonehenge it deserves – and desires.'[37] It has taken three further decades to address the issues. Following the continuous depredations through history, the twentieth century has exacerbated the site's problems. Significantly, the reliable James Dyer starts his lengthy entry on Stonehenge by commenting on this most unfortunate clash of ancient and modern at the famous stones:

> The most renowned and badly displayed archaeological site in Europe is something of an anticlimax to the uninitiated. Its isolation on Salisbury Plain dwarfs it almost to insignificance, and gasps of 'Isn't it tiny' greet one's ears from the incessant streams of tourists whose very presence in ever-increasing numbers is slowly eroding the site. So much so that the stone circle is closed to the general public, who may approach only one side of the monument. This is a tragedy caused by unsympathetic management, since it is impossible to view the circle intelligently with such restrictions. Visitors are strongly advised to carry binoculars.[38]

---

[36] Chippindale
[37] Chippindale, p.264.
[38] Dyer, pp.280-283.

Very obviously, Hardy's treatment of the site in *Tess* shows that he was not one of 'the uninitiated'.

In 1993, the House of Commons Public Accounts Committee described Stonehenge as 'a national disgrace', echoing Dyer's – and many others' – long-held opinion. As a result, English Heritage (what a glaring anachronism of a name for a prehistoric site! – reminiscent of the unsuitability of the Anglo-Saxon 'Wessex' for this context), the statutory guardians of the site and the National Trust, who own the surrounding land, drew up a controversial 'Master Plan' which would involve closing or tunnelling the main roads near the site, removing all fences, and moving the visitors (on arrival) and their facilities over the horizon. This Plan was accepted by the Government in July 1998 with a completion date of ten years hence. The chairmen of the two bodies write in their brochure about the scheme:

> Stonehenge ... stands at the centre of over 2,000 hectares of ancient landscape containing 450 Scheduled Ancient Monuments ... [We] will at last be able to reunite Stonehenge and its monuments in their unique and natural setting. ... People will be able to roam freely amongst the Stones, and, at no cost, to experience the mystery of one of the most powerful and distinctive places on Earth. ... [in] the awesome beauty of its natural setting.[39]

The planned completion date of 2008 was not met, however, because the Plan was abandoned on cost grounds in December 2007, the Government being unwilling to spend money on the costly road alterations involving putting the trunk A303 road into a tunnel. In early 2008, the Government announced that 'environmental improvements', including a new visitors' centre, would be carried out in time for the London Olympic Games in 2012 – possibly inspired by the extensive archaeological work in Athens preceding the 2004 Games there. In October 2009, the plans were made public. The A344 road will be re-routed to avoid the Stones and the landscape restored. The architects for the visitors' centre, Denton Corker Marshall, faced a daunting brief to create a design 'universally accessible, environmentally sensitive and almost transitory in nature: the aim [is] ... for visitors to remember their visit to the stones, not to the visitor centre.' This last comment is significant of the problems of presenting culture to the public with its echo of the infamous 1980s 'an ace café with quite a nice museum attached' publicity for the Victoria and Albert Museum. It is also a neatly ironic comment on the nature of a modern structure which echoes the fragile, vanished predecessors of the era of Stonehenge of which archaeologists can find only tantalising traces. At the time of writing, this latest scheme faces a crisis: after the election of the coalition Government in 2010, it became an early casualty in the battle to cut public expenditure, though English Heritage is pressing ahead and seeking alternative sources of finance.

The proposed restoration of the landscape would not only return the environs of Stonehenge to something approaching the ambience of prehistory, but pertinently for the present discussion, to more of the conditions that prevailed when Tess and Angel arrive on their fateful flight, for, as in all his novels, Hardy looks back to a recently vanished past. The open land, with its broad views unspoilt by the sound, sight, and fumes of motor traffic must have borne a stronger resemblance to its prehistoric state at the time of the henge's second phase of con-

---

[39] Brochure produced jointly by English Heritage and the National Trust, 1998.

struction in *c.*2000 BC (in view of more recent research, probably earlier) than to modern muddle at a major road junction on a holiday route. The railway reached Salisbury, the nearest major town to Stonehenge, in 1857; there had even been an earlier proposal to drive a line very close to the stones. After this quintessentially Victorian watershed, the place lost its remoteness for good. The setting of *Tess* in the 1870s means that Tess and Angel's arrival at the eerily deserted spot is actually *after* the place had already become a popular excursion destination, and with this in mind, the scene might be coloured for us by an additional vein of loss. Chippindale explains:

Old Sarum

> ... it was possible to reach Stonehenge from the metropolis [then the largest city in the world] on a day excursion. On a summer Saturday, the Baedeker advised, you should save the cost of a hired coach and join the excursion brake from the station for just 5 shillings return. If you stayed in Salisbury a few days, the Old Sarum and Stonehenge outing was inescapable ... a man who stayed a week in Salisbury *without* going near Old Sarum or Stonehenge was surely an especially interesting person.[40]

Ironically, perhaps unwittingly, the two fugitives take the same route from Salisbury to Stonehenge followed by the day-trippers – a fact of which Hardy and many of his first readers in 1891 must surely have been aware.

On their way to Stonehenge, Tess and Angel are 'obliged to pass through ... ancient

---

[40] Chippindale p.148.

Melchester [Salisbury] to take advantage of the town bridge for crossing a large river' (p.483). This is a well judged circumstance, since Hardy is able to exploit symbolically the contrast between 'the graceful pile of cathedral architecture' which was 'soon lost upon them' and the rougher prehistoric architecture that lies ahead. The pair are fleeing the Christian culture and morality that the city and its cathedral represent, and the socio-legal structure allied to it that is pursuing them. They have both abandoned themselves to more 'primitive' impulses – anger and fear – and will seek the haven of an ancient site which to a great extent defies rational explanation as they have eschewed any rational consideration of their course. As Radford reminds us, Tess, as a pagan, is at home at Stonehenge[41] in a way that she cannot be in the culture that condemns her to bury her baby in unhallowed ground.

This symbolic flight from Christianity is prefigured in chapter XLV by 'the spot called 'Cross-in-Hand'' (p.389), where 'a strange rude monolith, from a stratum unknown in any local quarry' reminds us of the much-travelled bluestones (spotted dolerite from the Preseli Hills in West Wales) at Stonehenge. Possibly a ruined Christian cross, the vestige is both symbolic and a link with the enigma of Stonehenge. Hardy comments that 'there was and is something sinister, or solemn … in the scene amid which it stands', confirmed later by the explanation of a local to Tess that ''twere not a cross! 'Tis a thing of ill-omen' (p.391).

Despite the paradoxically relative brevity of the great Stonehenge scene, which occurs in chapter LVIII, Hardy uses the setting in a particularly dense way, clearly showing his familiarity with the place and exploiting the aesthetic and connotative possibilities to the full. The solidity and longevity of Stonehenge and its fame provide a telling contrast with the transient, insignificant characters whom Hardy sends there; yet for the author, the complexity and mysteriousness of the site's history are surely matched in importance by the human condition that they parallel. Gillian Beer asserts that 'Hardy is acutely alert to diverse time-scales and to the extent to which the oblivious interaction of these differing scales make up the mesh of event and experience',[42] a comment that is nowhere more relevant than in relation to *Tess*. The quality of the light – or lack of light – again is important in Hardy's depiction, and accords with the couple's hazy understanding of the monument and, indeed, our inevitable lack of complete knowledge about all prehistoric sites which make archaeology a science to excite the imagination. Hardy's younger contemporary and friend Herman Lea expressed in his chapter on *Tess* the limits of what Hardy's generation could ascertain about the site in 1913, incidentally emphasising the aptness of Hardy's evocative treatment:

> They were now close to Stonehenge, the mysterious pagan temple, the greatest sight of its kind in the country. In the chronicles of Nennius (ninth century), the date of its origin is placed in the fifth century AD; but according to other and later writers it is supposed to have been erected one hundred years before Christ. Readers will not need to be reminded that there has been much controversy regarding its date and its origin; no authentic proofs are forth-coming [sic] to establish any of the various contentions.[43]

And here, we must remember that Hardy uses real names for both landscape features and

---

[41] Radford, p.2.
[42] Beer, pp.249/250.
[43] Herman Lea, *Thomas Hardy's Wessex* (London: Macmillan, 1913), p.29.

very ancient sites. Visually, they do often appear of a piece, and for Hardy it is of crucial importance that 'landmarks of local topography [which I take to include both categories] [are] crusted with ancestral imprints'.[44] This use of names achieves a fusion of identity and gives the man-made sites the same apparent permanence as the natural, a unity which reflects the fact that most ancient sites are literally built from the landscape in which they are set. The scientific fact that the sarsens and blue stones of Stonehenge are not actually local surely does not vitiate this identification of the two in this instance.

The Stonehenge scene is as intense and beautifully evocative a piece of narrative-description as any in Hardy's works; it is also the climax of the book's temporal tapestry. The choice of setting allows Hardy to utilise some favourite possibilities of such a setting. There is the irony and tension between the diachronic and the synchronic, a fixed and inscrutable ancient site as the scene of intensely personal and dramatic events in a developing narrative rapidly approaching its denouement. Moreover, Hardy enjoys placing the abstraction of his fictional characters in such a solidly real and venerable place, as if he were adding to the immeasurable river of events that has flowed past during several millennia. In a more recent novel that does the same, the nadir of Barney Flugelman's second marriage in Howard Jacobson's novel *Peeping Tom*[45] ('Tom' being Hardy!) is also the zenith of the book's sexual odyssey, an obscene parody of the climax of *Tess*, where the author, continuing his satirical motif, repeats some of the features of the original, including even a verbatim quotation of Hardy's final two sentences. Hardy's preoccupation in this scene is, equally, the climax of his thematic concerns, but could hardly be more different.

As one might expect of a west-countryman, and one interested in archaeology, Hardy knew Stonehenge well. Though there is no earlier reference in the *Life*, we read (p.296) of 'revisiting Stonehenge', and the site forms the subject of one of his few journalistic utterances on the subject of archaeology, as discussed in Chapter Three; it also looms ominously in the final stanza of 'Channel Firing'. Interestingly, it is to Stonehenge that Samuel Hynes, editor of the OUP edition of *The Dynasts*, turns to describe that 'English epic, perhaps the last one.'[46]

The *Life* extract continues with evidence of Hardy's often melancholy attitude to archaeological ruins in a brief remark quoted from his diary giving a different slant on his aesthetic interest in the past: 'The misfortune of ruins – to be beheld nearly always at noonday by visitors, and not at twilight' – a comment that insists that it is the special atmosphere of such places achieved by affective *lighting* conditions that is important. Thus, Tess and Angel arrive at Stonehenge in darkness and the arrest happens soon after dawn, neither event occurring in the stark, objective light of noon, but in far more suggestive, evocative conditions. It is noteworthy, incidentally, that in Hardy's brief account of the performance of *Tess* at Max Gate, mentioned earlier, he also stresses the more emotive light – the firelight – during the Stonehenge sequence, which is decidedly not in the revealing glare of 'noon-day'.

The climactic moment is the third of the significant dawns in the book, at once both a contrast and a match for Tess and Angel's prelapsarian dawns at Talbothays, but also the stark opposite of those at Flintcomb-Ash. Their journey has been aided by 'a diffused light from some fragment of a moon' (p.483), but their accidental arrival at a spot that so clearly embodies their

---

[44] Radford, p.4.
[45] Howard Jacobson, Peeping Tom (London: Chatto and Windus, 1984).
[46] Gibson, Life, p.150.

destiny in Hardy's scheme is in such blackness that 'They had almost struck themselves against it.' The lighting conditions are intimately enmeshed with the physical, topographical setting of the site, and the visual impressions are embellished with other sensory elements, auditory and tactile, for 'this pavilion of the night' (p.484) is also, in Clare's words, 'a 'very Temple of the Winds''; indeed, 'the wind, playing upon the edifice, produced a booming tune, like the note of some gigantic one-stringed harp ... Clare felt the vertical surface of the structure' (p.483), and as they enter the circle, 'the surfaces echoed their soft rustle'. Hardy himself, like his favourite heroine, was particularly fascinated by the sounds made by the monument, and accurately records, in the expert fashion of the archaeological enthusiast not only the dispositions of the stones, but their rough solidity and texture, perfectly revealing the writer's marriage of his artistic and scientific impulses.

The light increases very gradually, for at first, 'something made the black sky blacker, which had the semblance of a vast architrave' (pp.483-484). As the darkness dissolves, their predicament – and physical vulnerability – gradually become clear, for this place of refuge in the night is paradoxically 'open loneliness and black solitude' (p.483). As in *Romeo and Juliet*, Hardy inverts the customary alignment of light with good and dark with evil, for as in that other tragedy of fated young lovers, dawn is threatening and dangerous, exposing the pair to their enemies and to the wrath of the Law. Angel notices the first sign of their doom: 'In the far north-east sky he could see between the pillars a level streak of light. The uniform concavity of black cloud was lifting bodily like the lid of a pot, letting in at the earth's edge the coming day, against which the towering monoliths began to be blackly defined' (p.485), again integrating the permanent yet unceasing processes of Nature with the indestructible solidity of an edifice built by transient beings. Slowly, the 'band of silver paleness along the eastern horizon made even the distant parts of the plain appear dark and near' (p.486); and finally, the 'eastward pillars and their architraves stood up blackly against the light, and the great flame-shaped Sunstone beyond them and the Stone of Sacrifice midway', the traditional names perfectly fitting Hardy's symbolic and dramatic-poetic intentions.

The debt to Wordsworth of Hardy's early poem 'Domicilium' and his admiration for the major Romantic poets are noted in other chapters. In the scene at Stonehenge, it is once again Hardy's well documented wide reading that gives the hint of a source for the imagery. In this descriptive treatment there are remarkable similarities to a part of one of Wordsworth's early poems, 'Guilt and Sorrow; or, Incidents upon Salisbury Plain' – and what a fascinatingly apt subtitle that would be for this climactic chapter! This quasi-autobiographical work had its origins in a walking tour Wordsworth took from Salisbury to North Wales in the summer 1793 during a time of unhappiness and uncertainty; it was published in the *Lyrical Ballads* of 1798. With Hardy's passion for Wessex and admiration for his Romantic progenitor, it seems unlikely that he was not at some conscious level echoing the images and mood of this poem; these are some relevant lines from stanzas XIII, XIV, XV:

> The weary eye ...
> Marks nothing but the red sun's setting round,
>
> ...

> Hoary and naked are its walls, ...
> ... in shelter there to bide
> He turned, ...
>
> Pile of Stonehenge! So proud to hint yet keep
> Thy secrets, thou that lov'st to stand and hear
> The plain resounding to the whirlwinds sweep,
>
> ...
>
> Who in his heart had groaned with deadlier pain
> Than he who, tempest-driven, thy shelter now would gain?
>
> Within that fabric of mysterious form
> Winds met in conflict, each by turns supreme;
>
> ...

The winds, the darkness, the isolation, the myth of sacrifice and the suggestive yet opaque mysteriousness are all here, and even though the traveller is alone, his mental state is no less troubled than that of Tess and Angel, though very different in kind. For Wordsworth's hero, there is 'no moon to stream', but a minimal source of light more sinister is presented by 'the lightning's faint disastrous gleam'. Unlike Hardy's pair, he does not remain at the ruin, but finds rude accommodation in the form of a 'lonely Spital' reminiscent of the shepherds' shelters in *A Tradition of Eighteen Hundred and Four* and *What the Shepherd Saw*. Here, he has a dream which is uncannily like the experience of Tess and Angel at the nearby stones (stanza XIX):

> When hearing a deep sigh, that seemed to come
> From one who mourned in sleep, he raised his head
> And saw a woman in the naked room
> Outstretched, and turning on a restless bed:
> The moon a wan dead light around her shed.
> He waked her – spake intone that would not fail,
> He hoped, to calm her mind; but ill he sped,
> For of that ruin she had heard a tale
> Which now with freezing thoughts did all her powers assail;

As the night passes, Hardy's narrative diverges from any Wordsworthian influence, and we are confronted bluntly with the reality of the present. The police close in with ease; they are a quintessential symbol of an ordered modern society, and a key social advance of the nineteenth century. Their inexorably efficient pursuit and rapid arrival, so incongruous in the beautiful light of dawn at a famously ancient, isolated (and tranquil) spot, is indeed the culminating clash of the modern against the ancient. The setting might offer the potential for Tess's death in a desperate, violent climax; but Hardy, while disappointing such an expectation in giving us no transcendent moment over the prosaic course of justice, opts for drama of a poetic nature – but drama nonetheless. Michael Millgate goes so far as to call it 'the sacrificial apotheosis at Stonehenge.'[47] Radford reminds us of Hardy's explicitly tragic frame of reference, noting 'the *artifice* of ancient Greek tragedy' in the scene, for instance that the deputies seem to be wearing ritual masks as in the Greek drama.[48] Unlike Millgate, however, he acknowledges that the actual 'sacrificial apotheosis' takes place when Tess is hanged; for (he is without strict archaeological justification) there is 'little separating the rites enacted in the temple of primitive blood sacrifice and the atrocities committed at Wintoncester gaol ...' which stresses that Hardy's attitude was anti-ameliorist.[49]

As always in Hardy's use of archaeology, transient contemporary human beings are set ironically before the apparently immutable, impersonal traces of their forebears' endeavours and beliefs - and the effect is, I think, curiously heightened by the paradox of these fictional people, about whom we know a great deal, being placed in a real and well-known place which perforce remains an enigma. Stonehenge is part of our collective imagination, a site of eternal, if enigmatic, meaning which reminds us of Lear on the 'blasted heath' and Hardy's own Egdon Heath (and does not Wordsworth's hero seem rather a 'young Lear'?). Both Tess and Lear are transformed, reconciled to themselves by suffering in these special settings.

Whether from its obvious astronomical alignment or its lack of any apparent 'practical' function, and even discounting the dubious devotion of modern-day 'Druids', Stonehenge was once, very evidently, an important place of now-obscure rituals. Even reputable textbooks refer to it and other henges as temples (*without* inverted commas). Drama itself came from the equally misty origins of prehistoric Greek religion, developing into a more defined system during the Bronze Age perhaps at a not dissimilar date to whatever rites were practised at Stonehenge. (The carvings of an axe and a Mycenaean-style dagger on one of the sarsen uprights have been adduced as possible evidence of significant contacts with Greece in *c*.1500 BC). Tess feels at one with the place, despite her incomprehension and speculation about the site, for she too identifies it, in traditional fashion, as the 'heathen temple'. She anticipates 'when we are spirits' (p.485), asking Angel, 'do you think we shall meet again after we are dead? I want to know.' He kissed her to avoid reply at such a time (p.486), for Angel's agnosticism approaches that of his author's. The dawn rises, and Angel conveys some slightly more specific ideas about the true nature of Stonehenge as a part of the couple's remarks about religious belief, mingling pagan with Christian imagery, and he explains the idea of 'heliolatry': 'I believe [they sacrificed] to the sun. That lofty stone set away by itself is in the direction of the sun, which will presently rise behind it' (p.485). Again, Hardy integrates the setting intimately with his characters and their narrative.

Yet despite the pagan connotations of the setting and of the couple's aversion to traditional Christian morality, Hardy employs his Biblical knowledge as well as the Classical as he echoes the dawn arrest of Jesus (the police being the equivalent of the Temple Guard), confirming it by 'Like a greater than himself, to the critical question at the critical time, he did

---

[47] Millgate, Career, p.273.
[48] Radford, p.3.
[49] Radford, p.5.

not answer' (p.486), a second allusion to the events of Good Friday – and for the attentive reader, the Good Friday imagery is a reminder of the fateful afternoon cock-crows at the end of chapter XXXIII just as the newly-weds are leaving Talbothays. That eerie occurrence is not as Biblical as it appears, however. Hardy can have made no mistake in his allusion in transposing the thrice-repeated cock-crow in the afternoon for Peter's thrice-repeated denial of Christ before the single cock-crow at dawn (Mark chapter XIV, vv66-72): Hardy is reciting here a specifically pagan superstition, in keeping with the 'primitive' character of Talbothays, while simultaneously making the New Testament reference absolutely clear. Furthering the Good Friday echoes, Hardy's placing of Tess on 'an altar' (p.484) marks her as a sacrificial victim. Just as Alec d'Urberville lay in grim jest on one of Tess's true ancestral tombs at Kingsbere, unwittingly foreshadowing his own death, and Angel laid Tess in the abbot's tomb to anticipate his own unintentional part in her death, so Tess, exhausted, 'flung herself upon an oblong slab' (the altar, but resembling the tomb in the church), in seemingly willing anticipation of her own. Desmond Hawkins declares: 'There she could act out again some profound ritual of sacrifice and expiation, echoing that earlier cry of hers, 'Once a victim, always a victim – that's the law!'[50] This identification continues a venerable, though not ancient, tradition that the rituals carried on at Stonehenge included human sacrifice.

The mystery and uniqueness of Stonehenge aroused the interest of antiquaries and travellers – some of them by no means completely unscientific – from an early date, and just as myths and folk legends have given names to ancient sites in order to explain their origins, so these proto-archaeologists suggested names for features as they attempted to understand them. John Aubrey in *Monumenta Britannica* (seventeenth century, precise date unknown), William Stukeley in *Stonehenge, a Temple Restored to the British Druids* (1740), and Sir Richard Colt Hoare (accompanied by William Cunnington) who wrote his *History of Ancient Wiltshire* in 1810–1821, between them explored and further fuelled the ageless fascination that Stonehenge excites and added or confirmed speculative names to the various stones. Hardy may well be alluding here by his 'altar' to one of these traditionally named stones; the Slaughter Stone, a fallen entrance pillar, sounds appropriate. Chippindale, who notes that these names are a 'modern fancy,'[51] explains: 'Its upper surface, all humps, bumps and hollows often filled with rainwater, gave it its name, as it seemed in the eighteenth century so obviously suited to catch the blood of victims sacrificed on it.'[52] Fantastic notions like this abounded concerning the practices for which Stonehenge had been designed.

In thrall to erroneous traditions and necessarily ignorant of the much more ancient origins of the site, Stukeley and other antiquaries could refer only to one authority, the Roman historian Tacitus, for the source of their ideas about ancient Britons who apparently built Stonehenge, and history is, proverbially, written by the victors. Further, Tacitus was writing about Iron Age Celts many centuries removed from the builders of Stonehenge. Chippindale states: 'When the fighting was done, Tacitus says, 'this inhuman people were accustomed to shed the blood of their prisoners on their altars and consult their gods over the reeking bowels of men'. And Caesar found the Druids of Gaul as sinister; besides judging and settling disputes,

---

[50] Desmond Hawkins, Hardy's Wessex (London: Macmillan, 1983), p.168.
[51] Chippindale, p.15.
[52] Chippindale, p.15.

they were the priests of human sacrifice.'[53] This harsh image of the Druids was accepted by John Aubrey, while Stukeley invented a softer mythology, suitable as a kind of ancestral faith to Christianity, though 'Crucifixion and human sacrifice were an admitted failing, 'a most extravagant act of superstition'.'[54] Hardy had no doubt read, or was aware of the substance of, this material, but Chippindale's comments about the persistence of a particular vein of Druidism are particularly pertinent to the imagery Hardy invokes in his scene at the stones:

> Phoney or not, the Druids did not easily go away, especially as the nineteenth century produced no clear understanding of Stonehenge to take their place. ... And of the rival varieties of ancient Druid, it was fire, blood and human sacrifice that prevailed over Stukeley's amiable sages ... The image that lingered was of the sweet maiden, expired on the altar slab with her guts pulled across the grass, with the Druid priests crowded around in metaphorical darkness like a Wright of Derby painting.[55]

Hardy's actual model, however, by its more central position, as well as its name, must be the grey-green sandstone Altar Stone. The English Heritage guidebook states:

> The largest bluestone of all, the Altar Stone, probably stood as a tall pillar on the axial line inside the central and highest trilithon, and has since fallen down. There is no reason to suppose that its present position, or its name, is more than accidental.[56]

So the Altar Stone was originally an upright, belying its traditional name. It is about sixteen feet long, and though snapped in two and partly hidden by the upright and lintel of the great central trilithon which fell in 1797, could still provide Tess with room enough to lie wholly or partially stretched out.

As detailed in Chapter Two, Stukeley, who was important in the earlier part of his career in the development of archaeology out of antiquarianism, latterly became the Reverend Stukeley who engaged in the earnest propagation of Druidic fantasies. This has attracted the opprobrium of modern archaeologists at the expense of all his many genuine achievements. Christopher Chippindale comments that although Aubrey and others must bear some responsibility, Stukeley was the prime mover in the creation of Druidism: 'Even as he joined the Church, Stukeley began to take Druids for religious reality ... Stonehenge has never entirely recovered from [his] vision ... He set Stonehenge under a fog-bank of mystification which lasted a century.'[57] Taking the century literally, with Stukeley's Druids book dating from 1740, we are brought to the year of Hardy's birth for the waning of the pernicious influence. Yet Hardy unselfconsciously, if whimsically, adopts the name Druid Stone for the monolith found in his own scientific Max Gate excavations some forty-five years later: the 'born archaeologist' was also steeped in ancient lore. The echoes clearly reverberated much longer in the popular imagination, if not among the cognoscenti, up to the present day – indeed, Chippindale mentions that reputable authorities and reference works were still labelling the site as 'Druidic'

---

[53] Chippindale, p.83.
[54] Chippindale, p.86.
[55] Chippindale, p.95.
[56] Atkinson R.J.C., Stonehenge and Neighbouring Monuments. (London: English Heritage, 1987), p.13.
[57] Chippindale, pp.85/86.

well beyond the middle of the nineteenth century,[58] and 'right up to the First World War, the favourite postcard of Stonehenge was entitled 'Druidical remains' … .'[59]

Another tantalising possibility in Hardy's intentions exists; it is in the connection between this crisis point and the denouement of the novel. In chapter LIX, Tess is hanged at Wintoncester (Winchester) Prison, and, despite this further, looser, connection with the Good Friday imagery preceding it at Stonehenge, Hardy is again drawn to Classical Tragedy for his allusion and context by explicitly quoting (what quickly became a notoriously controversial phrase) from the tragedian Aeschylus: "Justice' was done, and the President of the Immortals, in the Aeschylean phrase, had ended his sport with Tess' (p.489). The connection with Stonehenge lies with the etymology of the word 'henge', an archaeological term drawn by a reductive etymological back-formation by allusion to the name of this most famous example of the type. A more respectable memorial to Stukeley is his coining of the term 'trilithon' for that unique and most instantly recognisable feature of the monument which had early led to the name Stonehenge. James Dyer, amongst others, defines a henge as a Neolithic ritual monument, circular or oval in shape, formed of a bank and inner quarry ditch. The OED gives 'heng' as a variant of 'hang', and a Spenserian usage corrupting 'hinge', while shorter modern dictionaries seem to explain exclusively the archaeological term dating to the mid-twentieth century; all agree, however, that the word is an inflexion of 'hang'. Muir and Welfare explain:

> The traditional [earlier Neolithic] constructions were superseded by a new type of public ritual monument: the earthen henge, which appeared around 3400 BC. This was an exclusively British or British-Irish creation which was never exported to the continent. It has also inherited one of the most inappropriate names in a subject [archaeology] not given to imaginative labels, for although henges are circular earthworks, their name refers to one of the 'hanging' or lintel stones which are unique to Stonehenge, itself the least typical henge imaginable.[60]

Now, its visual similarity to a gallows is clearly the origin of the monument's nickname ('stone henge' = 'stone gallows'), a name which long predates its adaptation by the science of archaeology, and indeed is recognised as immemorial by Hardy since he retains it unaltered as he does with landscape features. The connection with the details of Tess's visit and her fate are both apt and remarkable. I believe that it is not impossible that Hardy, with his eclectic reading and detailed knowledge of the region and its folklore, not to mention the philological tutelage of William Barnes, realised and intended the connection. At the very least, it is surely quite plausible as being a subliminal connection, an instance of 'unconscious art'.

Yet much of the power of the passage is purely aesthetic in nature. The stillness of the sleeping girl halts the precipitate intent of her pursuers; the swiftly developing narrative, briefly pausing at Angel's request, confronts the timeless immovability of the stones; and their coldness warmed, as the characters are, by the rising sun, is both a contrast to the living beings among them, and in its brevity, a foreshadowing of the permanent coldness of death. Even the efficient representatives of the new order who 'walked as if trained … and closed in with evident purpose' (p.486) are made subservient to the author's symbolic and aesthetic scheme,

---

[58] Chippindale, p.135.
[59] Chippindale, p.95.
[60] Muir and Welfare, p.90.

for according with the well attested astronomical significance of the site, they arrive from the four points of the compass; there is no escape as 'The dawn shone full on the front of the man westward'. The tension dissipated, they 'stood watching her' (p.487), held in a brief tableau as Tess sleeps. Good Friday re-emerges in subtle form at the exquisite final moment of this most accomplished and celebrated of all Hardy's scenes, for 'like a greater than *herself*, [my italicised alteration] Tess is a willing sacrifice: 'She stood up, shook herself, and went forward, neither of the men having moved. 'I am ready,' she said quietly.' (p.487). Hardy makes no easy analogy here, however, for Tess's death is ultimately pointless – the death of the 'pure woman' of the novel's subtitle, a suitably spotless sacrifice in the Biblical ideal by Hardy's reckoning perhaps, but to no definable purpose other than the appeasement of contemporary mores. Michael Millgate notes the strong connections in Tess's last journey with both Milton's *Paradise Lost* and Bunyan's *The Pilgrim's Progress* (though she is a pilgrim with no destination), but again, '*Tess* is not an allegory. Its allusions, like its philosophical formulations, are unlikely to carry relevance for more than their immediate context.'[61]

With a cyclical inclination common to many narratives, the closing paragraph of the novel returns to the fateful original cause of Tess's doom on its first page: like the silent, immutable cosmos above her, and the solid impersonality of Stonehenge, 'the d'Urberville knights and dames slept on in their tombs unknowing' (p.489). Hardy concludes by echoing the emotional shape of Classical Tragedy with the death of the 'Hero', while the survivors of the period of suffering, Angel and Liza-Lou, look to the future as they 'joined hands again and went on' (p.490).

Theatre, drama, ritual both of movement and event, sacrifice – all are present in this scene, and whether unconsciously or sub-consciously, Hardy has brought to bear his Classical, literate learning on this climactic event at this most famous of 'northern', prehistoric archaeological sites. Resonances of both sources abound in the scene, though the Classical may easily be overshadowed in our awareness by the physical presence of the prehistoric. The shape of Stonehenge adds to the dramatic sense, for the climax of the tragedy takes place in a theatre, an amphitheatre in fact, and like the Colosseum in Rome, a place in this context also of both sport and death. It is a significant focus of verticals in the midst of a broad horizontal landscape. It is in no way pejorative to describe the arrest of Tess as theatrical: the ritualistic feel of the scene with the symmetrically placed participants, the extraordinarily dramatic hiatus as the watchers wait round the sleeping form of the girl – all this takes place in a setting of the same unfathomable antiquity as those where primitive Greek religion first gave birth to the very notion of the Drama in the form of Tragedy. Furthermore, although the tragic elements in this novel may be somewhat less overt than in some of its predecessors, this major element of Hardy's Classical repertoire is still marked by the overwhelming sense of tragic inevitability right from the first page to the telling reference to 'the Aeschylean phrase' (p.489) in the final paragraph.

In choosing to imbue his climactic scene at this most famous of archaeological sites with the stuff of myth (of whatever origin or none), Hardy lays bare the paradox, the ambivalence – or simply the versatility – of his nature by going diametrically against the grain of archaeology as an objective science.

---

[61] Millgate, *Career*, p.273.

Chapter Six

Barrows and Beyond: Landscapes of the Past

'The past is a foreign country: they do things differently there.'

L.P. Hartley, *The Go-Between*.

The landscape of Hardy's Wessex is the bedrock of his most characteristic works – both literally and metaphorically. For some, it is awkwardly and inextricably bound up with Hardy himself, a fatal encumbrance to his work as a writer; R. S. Thomas's poem 'Taste' (Poetry Review, 1970) includes Hardy 'shuffling about a bogus heath / Cobwebbed with his Victorian breath'.[1]

Hardy's is an ancient landscape, but far from being pristinely natural: it has been radically shaped by human beings over millennia. For Simon Gatrell, this is crucial; he quotes in his introduction from a note of Hardy's: 'An object or mark raised by man on a scene is worth ten times any such formed by unconscious nature.'[2] We can see, then, that it is much more than the backcloth to the stories: mankind has shaped this landscape and in turn, it has shaped them, including Hardy's characters. The landscape provides their sustenance, its activities provoke their situations and problems, its nature provides tacit commentary on them; it embodies an old and often obsolete culture and economy, is the setting for a long history, and it contains a wealth of archaeology. All of this is applicable even to that most primordial and dominantly natural part of Wessex, Egdon Heath.

Virginia Woolf, perhaps thinking particularly of *The Return of the Native*, asserts that the relationship of landscape to character is peculiar to Hardy:

> His light does not fall directly on the human heart. It passes over it and out on to the darkness of the heath and upon the trees swaying in the storm.[3]

In this chapter, I shall examine works in which the landscape is special in some important

---

[1] Donald Davie, Thomas Hardy and British Poetry (London: Routledge and Kegan Paul, 1973), p.13.
[2] Gatrell, p.1.
[3] Virginia Woolf, The Common Reader, second series, 1928 (London: the Hogarth Press, 1932), pp.250-257.

sense and where the past is closely involved with it (though there is little of Hardy's output that eschews landscape altogether).

In his *The Making of the English Landscape*, W.G. Hoskins wrote:

> This, we feel, is exactly as the first men saw it when they reached the shingled margin of the river a hundred generations ago. Nothing has changed. We are seeing the natural world through the eyes of men who died three or four thousand years ago, and for a moment or two we succeed in entering into the minds of the dead. Or on some desolate English moorland it is even easier to feel this identity with the dead of the Bronze Age who lie nearby under a piled-up cairn or under the heathery blanket of a burial mound. ... But there are not many places where one can feel with such complete assurance that this is exactly as the first inhabitants saw it in 'the freshness of the early world.'[a reference to Wordsworth's *Guide through the District of the Lakes* already quoted by Hoskins]. Not much of England, even in its more withdrawn, inhuman places, has escaped being altered by man in some subtle way or other, however untouched we may fancy it is at first sight.[4]

Hoskins here, in the lucid and evocative prose of his ground-breaking book, both recommends and demonstrates the imaginative approach we must take in understanding the landscape and the pervasive changes that mankind has wrought upon it – in other words, envisioning the human past by reference to the landscape upon which it has taken place. The extract above might well inform our view of the uniqueness of the setting of *The Return of the Native*.

Pertinently for this present study, Hoskins' reviser Christopher Taylor remarks of his predecessor's much admired work:

> Writing first in 1955 when field archaeology in this country can be said to have been in its infancy, neither he nor anyone else could have had any conception of the part which archaeological studies were to play in the understanding of the development of the landscape.[5]

Hoskins' maxim in his pioneering work is that 'everything is older than we think', quoted and emphasised by Taylor's revision (p.12), an aphorism that Hardy seems to grasp in so much of his presentation of landscape and of the human effects on it, even without the technical knowledge and hindsight that Taylor possesses.

Hardy, with his extensive and intimate knowledge of the landscape and history of his home county and region, and his generally eclectic reading, had gained much from those 'learned trades' which deal with topography. He well understood Hoskins' key point that the English landscape is the product of a long process of development over 'a hundred generations'. It is the business of the poet to use and to re-create imaginatively his chosen material - which in Hardy's case is very much a densely altered English landscape of the kind of which Hoskins writes, and the recent people who have added their own stratum to its immensely long history. For this landscape is the origin and continuing sustenance of his characters: Hardy uses the

---

[4] W.G. Hoskins, The Making of the English Landscape, revised Christopher Taylor, 1988 (London: Hodder and Stoughton, 1955), p.18.
[5] Hoskins, p.15.

landscape – and the archaeology it contains – not as a pretty background, nor as mere local colouring, but as an imaginative resource.

***

In most of Hardy's works, the landscape is of the very essence, and its description shows the author at his very best. In *The Woodlanders*, the very source of the situation and problems is the environment, as claustrophobic among the trees as Flintcombe-Ash is bleak and windswept and the symbolic and literal setting for the characters' (and Hardy's) preoccupations in that part of *Tess*. *The Woodlanders*, said to be the author's own favourite story, contains typically evocative descriptive writing, and the wonderfully satisfying, aesthetic ending in my view eclipses all the others. In this novel, however, the broad horizons and distant views of *Tess* or *The Mayor* are closed down in the first few pages as we are drawn, with barber Percomb, into the enclosed world of the woods. At the opening of the novel, we are 'on the skirts of Blackmoor Vale, where the bold brow of High-Stoy Hill is seen two or three miles ahead' (p.41), but already, 'the leaves lie so thick' that we are on the verge of that claustrophobic environment.

So, a different kind of landscape painting takes over – a term made especially apt by Hardy's great interest in and study of painting and one which was given early endorsement by the sub-title of *Under the Greenwood Tree, A Rural Painting of the Dutch School*. In chapter II of *The Woodlanders*, Hardy writes that 'the scene formed by the girlish spar-maker [Marty South] composed itself into an impression-picture of extremest type' (p.48). The author had become particularly attracted by the work of the French Impressionist School, so named after a critic's jibe at a Monet picture at their first exhibition in Paris in 1874. As with his interest in the developing science of archaeology, Hardy was right up-to-date in his sympathies, a nice counterpoint to his enduring interest in the past. His description of that scene at the very start of *The Woodlanders* shows how completely he had studied and admired these artists, for it provides a succinct summary of their style:

> … the girl's hair alone, as the focus of observation, was depicted with intensity and distinctness, while her face, shoulders, hands, and figure in general were a blurred mass of unimportant detail lost in haze and obscurity. (p.48)

Hardy's descriptive skill gorgeously evokes the arboreal ambience of the setting, which with its characteristic seasonal shifts in the play of light and shade through leaves and boughs, provides a natural rhythm to the passage of time in the novel. Chapter XX begins:

> The leaves over Hintock unrolled their creased tissues, and the woodland seemed to change from an open filigree to a solid opaque body of infinitely larger shape and importance. The boughs cast green shades … Such an appearance it had on Midsummer eve of this year … (p.193)

In chapter XL, the season has moved on:

> The leaves overhead were now in their latter green - so opaque, that it was darker in some of the denser spots than in winter time, scarce a crevice existing by which a ray

could get down to the ground. But in open places she could see well enough. Summer was ending ... (p.363)

Hardy's interest in the more distant time-perspective of history and archaeology is little evidenced in this great novel, however. Even the two references to ancient roads from the first page of *The Woodlanders* that I have already quoted in Chapter Four can be interpreted in other ways: 'the forsaken coach-road' (p.41) may possibly not be on the course of an ancient trackway, and 'the many gay charioteers now perished' could plausibly, therefore, be simply Hardy's jocular periphrasis for past travellers in horse-drawn vehicles generally rather than Romans in chariots.

The Cerne Giant, Cerne Abbas

A reference just after this point could well be an example of Hardy's oft-overlooked sense of humour, to which his biographers refer. Percomb asks directions to the tiny hamlet of Little Hintock, whose obscurity is emphasised by Mrs Dollery's 'I wouldn't live there if you paid me to. Now at Abbot's Cernel [Cerne Abbas] you do see the world a bit' (p.42). This comparison with the tiny village is ostensibly a little pleasantry at the former's expense, perhaps a smile at the rustic woman's naivety. Hardy, however, like any native of Dorset, would know that Cerne Abbas is famous for just one thing, for 'seeing the world a bit' too unashamedly for Victorian sensibility, in the form of one of Britain's most celebrated hill figures, the Cerne Abbas Giant. In *The Dynasts*, a woman declares that Napoleon eats 'rashers o' baby for breakfast, for all the world like the Cerne Giant in old ancient times' (*Dynasts* p.52); and in the compilation story *A Few Crusted Characters*, Old Andrey Satchel 'knew no more of music than the Giant o'

Cernel' (*Complete Stories* p.505). Interestingly, the Giant was owned by General Pitt-Rivers, Hardy's 'archaeological mentor'. James Dyer calls it 'a splendidly obscene male figure';[6] Janet and Colin Bord describe and comment upon it more explicitly thus:

> Here is a giant of untold antiquity cut into the hillside turf ... 180 feet high ... A remarkable feature of this figure is the erect phallus and testicles which undoubtedly indicates that fertility rites were practised here ... The giant is generally considered to represent the god Helith or Hercules and is thought to have been cut at the end of the second century AD when the emperor Commodus (who believed he was a reincarnation of Hercules) revived the worship of this ancient god ... It is remarkable that for 1,800 years the local people have maintained this figure against all those who, for their various reasons, would have gladly seen it fade into oblivion.[7]

What is not remarkable is that Hardy could not allude directly to the giant (one can imagine the letters in *The Times*!) – but I am convinced the intended joke is real, nonetheless, even if subconscious or forgotten on Hardy's part. In the *Life* (p.215), Hardy asks: 'Has the tradition that Cerne-Abbas men have no whiskers any foundation in the fact of their being descendants of a family or tribe or clan who have not intermarried with neighbours on account of their isolation? They are said to be hot-tempered people.' The sexual allusion here can only be more amusing if one speculates further on the heavily-bearded Hardy's thinking when he wrote *Tess* three years before this curious aside; for in that novel too, Abbot's Cernel is mentioned – twice. The first reference, in chapter XLV, is when Alec is en route from Evershead to preach at Abbot's Cernel (*Tess* p.389). A village with a Christian monastery and a famously pagan figure is a wonderfully chosen

Abbey Gate, Cerne Abbas

setting for this character who is torn between preaching and carnal desire. In-breeding is cer-

---

[6] Dyer, p.120.
[7] Bord, pp.35-36.

Rufus or Bow and Arrow Castle, Church Ope

tainly ironic in reference to Alec d'Urberville, since in reality he is not a blood relative of Tess, and yet their union has far more disastrous consequences for both of them than for the men of that village.

However ancient may be the woods and their skilful exploitation practised by the long-time residents of Little Hintock, Hardy emphasises the newness of human traces there, in contrast with the pervasive antiquity of the other novels. In chapter IV, Melbury's homestead, 'of the early Georgian time ...' whose 'reverberations ... were ... not, as with those of the castle and cloister, silent beyond the possibility of echo' (pp.62/63), are thus explicitly distanced from even the Middle Ages, immeasurably more recent than the barrows and earthworks so familiar elsewhere in Hardy's work. Gillian Beer notes the close identity of human and tree in the novel with the people at the service of the natural world and vice-versa, part of Hardy's seeking 'a scale for the human that will neither be unrealistically grandiose nor debilitatingly reductive.'[8] Trees certainly offer a manageable scale, but also an extended historical perspective because of their great age. It is interesting to note that one of the most widely used and reliable ways of dating prehistoric material available to the archaeologist is directly through the medium of trees. Tree-ring dating or dendrochronology (from the Greek; literally, 'tree time study') dates wood by the annual growth rings of trees and is thus able to offer an absolute date for wooden material found in archaeological contexts – with the proviso that very old timber may have been used, or re-used in any application; for example HMS *Victory*, as she sailed to Trafalgar in 1805 in the memorable description in *The Trumpet-Major* (chapter XXXIV), was already forty-six years from the laying of the keel and her timbers must have been seasoned and much older still. Dendrochronology is one of the earlier scientific techniques in the archaeologist's repertoire; the modern scientific method was developed by the American astronomer A.E. Douglass around the time of Hardy's death, though the principle had been in use since the late eighteenth century in the age of the antiquaries. It is highly likely, then, that Hardy knew of

---

[8] Beer, p.249.

dendrochronology, though any veiled allusion in *The Woodlanders* must, I feel, fall within the realm of unconscious art.

***

Other works particularly dependent on a special landscape are, however, much more closely tied into Hardy's interest in history and the passage of time. Probably by coincidence, Hardy's first and last published works of prose fiction are set, at least partly, on the Dorset coast. It is at Creston (later to become Budmouth – based on Weymouth – under Hardy's schematization of Wessex names) in *Desperate Remedies* that the crucial early meetings take place and where the seaside identity of the town, including boating and steamer excursions, is important. Of that first published novel, Andrew D. Radford remarks that Manston (first name Aeneas: one of Hardy's earlier essays at Classical allusion) has 'vestiges of primitive experience ... a chthonic potency'[9] which in a sense prefigures Clym Yeobright in *The Return of the Native* (the principal subject of this chapter) whose 'primitive rapport with the soil ... exceeds that possessed by any of his 'non-thinking' neighbours.'[10] In *The Well-Beloved* (Hardy's final novel if one considers this revision of *The Pursuit of the Well-Beloved* as a 'new' work), the Isle of Portland, 'the singular peninsula once an island' (p.179) is dubbed both 'The Isle of Slingers' – a supposed memory of the place as a source of slingshot ammunition in prehistoric and Roman times, and a name culled from Hardy's reading of the antiquary John Leland – and Vindilia, the Roman name for the peninsula. (Interestingly, Sir Mortimer Wheeler's excavations at Maiden Castle a generation after Hardy's death discovered slingshot ammunition that had come from Portland.) Both of these names were added to the 1897 book and give a sense of historical depth. For this is an historic place, for all its windswept bleakness, and an isolated spot, quite distinct even from the rest of South Wessex (Dorset) and locked in a primitive past. In his Preface for the 1912 re-working, little altered from that of the original 1897 work, Hardy explains that the distinctiveness of place and its past are intimately interwoven:

> The peninsula carved by Time out of a single stone, whereon most of the following scenes are laid, has been for centuries immemorial the home of a curious and well-nigh distinct people, cherishing strange beliefs and singular customs, now for the most part obsolescent. (p.173)

Here, 'strangers from the mainland of Wessex' are called "kimberlins' or 'foreigners" (p.187). Ancient marriage customs prevail, according with Hardy's many casually dismissive references to traditional Christian marriage, and:

> The church had slipped down with the rest of the cliff, and had long been a ruin. It seemed to say that in this last local stronghold of the Pagan divinities, where Pagan customs lingered yet, Christianity had established itself precariously at best. (p.186)

The natives, who speak a dialect peculiar to the Isle, are of ancient origins - 'Like his own, her family had been islanders for centuries – from Norman, Anglian, Roman, Balearic-British [?Celtic] times' (p.232) and 'The Caros, like some other local families, suggested a Roman

---

[9] Radford, p.45.
[10] Radford, p.91.

lineage, more or less grafted on the stock of the Slingers' – the reverse chronological order here reinforcing the sense of ancient hybridisation. Hardy's knowing that the Balearics were a source of slingers for the Roman Army is impressive. Here, therefore, it seems unsurprising that near the end of the story, the sculptor Jocelyn Pierston – reminiscent, in this regard, of Henchard – should change 'his style of dress entirely, appearing always in a homely suit of local make, and of the fashion of thirty years before'(p.334). Like Hardy and several others of his characters, Pierston is a native who returns; and the Isle, in Millgate's view, represents 'the essential Pierston'.[11] Tom Paulin, however, discussing the poem 'Rome The Vatican: Sala delle Muse', identifies Pierston with Hardy in his attitude to love.[12]

In this novel, Hardy develops a complex temporal scheme with several interlocking elements which Andrew D. Radford characterises as 'Hardy's restless time-voyaging'.[13] In addition to the time-span of narrative, he presents the pursuit by the sculptor of his ideal woman at three points in his life, by the means of three Parts: 'Part First: A Young Man of Twenty'; 'Part Second: A Young Man of Forty'; and 'Part Third: A Young Man Turned Sixty'. While he grows older, the ideal beloved takes the form of mother, daughter, then her daughter, ever young, therefore, and each called Avice. This whimsical procession of relationships is set against not only the atavistic tendencies of the Isle, but also the constantly revealed evidence of much earlier epochs: Hardy the architect knew all about the importance of Portland stone (which had first been popularised by Wren's use of it in his new St Paul's), and a good deal about the new science of geology, as the famous cliff scene in *A Pair of Blue Eyes* demonstrates. Portland is 'a solid and single block of limestone four miles long … All now stood dazzlingly unique and white against the tinted sea, and the sun flashed on infinitely stratified walls of oolite' (p.179). Later, we read:

> To find other trees between Pebble-Bank and Beal, it was necessary to recede a little in time – to dig down to a loose stratum of the underlying stone-beds, where a forest of conifers lay as petrifactions, their heads all in one direction, as blown down by a gale in the Secondary geologic epoch. (p.241)

Such an awareness of the immense span of geological time, like the use of astronomy in *Two on a Tower* and elsewhere, provides an unnerving background to the explicit archaeological-historical allusions in the book.

The Roman connections, always attractive to this writer from a 'Roman' town, are frequent: the 'long straight Roman street' (p.185) leads from 'the old Roman highway into the peninsula' (p.255). In London, Pierston 'thought of nothing but the Isle, and Avice the second' (p.238) who is innately connected in his febrile imagination with 'the haunted atmosphere of Roman Venus about and around the site of her perished temple there'. Later in this section, we read 'The church of the island had risen near the foundations of the pagan temple, and a Christian emanation might be wrathfully torturing him through the very false gods to whom he had devoted himself, both in his craft, like Demetrius of Ephesus, and in his heart' (p.261). Pierston dubs his fantasy-ideal 'Aphrodite, Ashtaroth, Freyja, or whoever the love-queen of his

---

[11] Millgate, Career, p.297.
[12] Paulin, pp.55-56.
[13] Radford, p.27.

isle might have been' (p.276). And aptly enough for a sculptor, in the final Part of the novel, Pierston has been studying in Rome itself. With these allusions to Rome embracing both the historical and the mythological, Hardy therefore manages to integrate his temporal scheme with both the aesthetic and the moral simultaneously. Another favourite theme of Hardy's is genealogy, and Sophie Gilmartin asserts of Pierston that the 'geological layers of this Portland stone serve his art, and also, by calling to his mind his father's quarry on his native isle, serve

Sandsfoot Castle near Weymouth

to connect him with the genealogical layers of the intermarrying families of his birthplace.'[14]

Apart from the symbolically ruined church (Hope churchyard – a sardonic choice of name – in reality, the place is Church Ope), the medieval period is represented by the two castles: Henry VIII's Castle (admittedly, a Renaissance fortification rather than a castle, the real-life Sandsfoot Castle south of Weymouth on the neck of the peninsula by Portland Harbour), and Red King's Castle, Hardy's name for the ruined Rufus Castle on Portland itself which together contribute to the sense of the immensely long and continuous history of this special landscape. Portland Castle, the Henrician twin of Sandsfoot, does not, however, appear in the book, and it may be significant that, while the two aforementioned castles are ruined and returning almost to the state of the quarries whence they originated, this monument is extremely well preserved and may thus be less suitable as a symbol of time irrevocably passing and leaving ruination in its wake.

In addition to these belittling perspectives that Hardy creates for his human characters,

---

[14] Gilmartin, 'Geology', Mallett, p.37.

Millgate notes an element in this novel which could be a parallel for his inclusion of archaeology in any of his works: 'There is, indeed, a sense in which *The Well-Beloved* incorporates within the framework of fable that counterpoint of seasonal and racial recurrence against the transitoriness of the individual life and experience which lies close to the heart of Hardy's greatest novels.'[15] And surely *The Return of the Native* fits this observation as well as the descriptor, fable.

A stone quarry on Portland

As in *The Mayor of Casterbridge* and elsewhere, the railway is symbolic of modernity and its inexorable, intrusive advance: at first it reaches only to Budmouth, then later, a line leads right onto the peninsula as the modern world, and a colder reality, reach the Isle, and Pierston and Marcia – long-time friends – get on with the humdrum business of living out their old age together.

***

In *The Hand of Ethelberta*, the seaside village of Knollsea (Swanage), not very far from Portland, is described in chapter XXXI as 'lying snug between two headlands' (p.233) and its inhabitants are either the inward-looking quarrymen who 'understood practical geology' (Hardy's Darwinian credentials included such close scrutiny of strata), or outward-looking sailors, who, like Captain Vye in *The Return of the Native*, were saved from the claustrophobia of an enclosed little world because they had 'a clearer notion of Alexandria, Constantinople,

---

[15] Millgate, *Career*, p.298.

the Cape, and the Indies than of any inland town in their own country.' Hardy well understood the dichotomy between his rural Wessex and the bustling metropolis which is a feature of this early novel, and the preceding chapter XXXII in London closes with 'Tall and swarthy columns of smoke were now soaring up ... spoiling the sweetness of the new atmosphere that had rolled in from the country overnight' (*The Hand of Ethelberta* p.233).

The landscape of *Two on a Tower* is around Warborne (Wimborne), 'a country of ragged woodland, which, though intruded on by the plough at places, remained largely intact from prehistoric times' (p.237). But more specifically, it is an unremarkable field 'in Wessex' (p.3), but made special by one remarkable feature, a memorial tower 'in the form of a classical col-

Rainbarrow

umn' built on a 'circular isolated hill of no great elevation' whose noble dedicatee is forgotten even by most of the local people; in fact, 'not a dozen people within the district knew the name of the person commemorated' (p.6) – though it is the great-grandfather of Viviette's husband. It is ironic in retrospect that Sir Sidney Cockerell had, according to James Gibson, the 'magnificent idea for a monument to Hardy on Rainbarrow to match that to Admiral Hardy on Blagdon Hill',[16] a proposal that would have given Dorset monuments to two of its notables who are very unlikely to be forgotten. And this provides a further fortuitous, if eccentric, link between two novels which feature prominent barrows. At once, in this first page, Hardy the architect indicates a specific revival style, one which harks back to an illustrious past that is – paradoxically – more celebrated and easily recognisable than either the 'respectable

---

[16] Gibson, *Life*, p.193.

officer who had fallen in the American War' (p.4), whose memory it should have perpetuated, or that war which is but a footnote of history – this was the War of 1812 which fell within the compass of Hardy's passionate interest, the Napoleonic period. By this amnesiac accident of history so similar in its force to the subject of Hardy's poem 'The Pyramid of Cestius', the true significance of the tower is rapidly becoming as obscure as that of any of the infinitely older archaeological remains that Hardy employs in his fiction, including the mound on which the tower stands. James Gibson comments on the book's 'constant reminder of the insignificance of human lives when seen against the vastness of space and time … a reminder of the little lives of men.'[17] This fascination with the passage of time, and its ironic, poignant placing behind the transient little events of two individual lives, is swiftly emphasised by a more detailed description of the tower:

> The fir-shrouded hill top was (according to some antiquaries) an old Roman castle, or (as the rest swore) an old Saxon field of Witenagemot – with remains of an outer and inner vallum, a winding path leading up between their overlapping ends by an easier ascent. The spikelets from the trees formed a soft carpet over the route, and occasionally a brake of brambles barred the interspaces of the trunks. Soon she stood immediately at the foot of the column.
>
> It had been built in the Tuscan order of Classic architecture, and was really a tower, being hollow with steps inside. The gloom and solitude which prevailed round the base were remarkable. … Above the trees the case was different; the pillar rose into the sky a bright and cheerful thing, unimpeded clean, and flushed with the sunlight. (p.5)

The author explains in his 1895 Preface that the site has not a single model, but is a conflation of 'two real spots in the part of the country specified, each of which has a column standing upon it' (pp289/290). Fred Pitfield mentions that Herman Lea identifies as the imported tree-clad earthwork of Rings-Hill an Iron Age hill-fort called Weatherby Castle near Milborne St Andrew. Pitfield and Kay-Robinson,[18] like Lea, identify Charborough Park as the fictional Welland Park, though 'Charborough Tower, being of early Gothic revival style and octagonal does not fit this description, but the Hood monument at Butleigh in Somerset is in the form of a Tuscan column.'[19] Hugh Brasnett gives a further detail that Hardy uses in his fictional tower, noting that 'The Weatherby Castle column, also a memorial to one man, likewise shares the oblivion accorded the Rings-Hill Speer monument.'[20] The Hardys saw the tower at Charborough House near Wimborne on their visit to Badbury Rings in July 1881, in a social milieu when landowners would never admit casual visitors like them. The big house, the spinster living there in seclusion, the tower – all tend to suggest that the place is the principal model for the setting of *Two on a Tower*.

Hardy's description of the hill seems to fit the tumescent distinctiveness of the Bronze Age round barrow, familiar from *The Mayor of Casterbridge* and *The Return of the Native* (which will be examined shortly), but it is love and its problems which concern the author and his two

---

[17] Gibson, Life, p.88.
[18] Denys Kay-Robinson, Hardy's Wessex Re-appraised (Newton Abbot: David & Charles, 1972), p.98.
[19] Pitfield, p.41.
[20] Hugh Brasnett, Thomas Hardy: A Pictorial Guide (Ivychurch: John Waite, 1984), p.54.

protagonists here, not any overwhelming sense of mortality, despite the long and dense history of their meeting place, and the frighteningly belittling effect of astronomy.

The site's physical nature is carefully delineated. The hill is surrounded by ploughed field, symbol of Mankind's moulding of nature since the Neolithic, making it difficult of access; the base of the tower is in the gloom of the past, in its Roman or Saxon origins – though Hardy leaves the 'expert' opinion inconclusive enough for us to posit a prehistoric pedigree and indeed, in chapter VIII, Hardy passingly calls it 'the prehistoric earthwork' (p.54) under which 'many ancient Britons lie buried'. These archaeological details make the site and its transient inhabitants parts of a long temporal continuum of human activity amid the greater vastness of nature: from the geological level of the earth, up through the archaeological level of the mound, then the historical monument with its ancient stylistic allusion, then finally the state-of-the-art telescope bought by Viviette which penetrates the remoteness of space and its very ancient light. Indeed, the whole range of Hardy's Darwinian interests – and beyond – is encapsulated in this one setting. The top of the column is in the bright light of the present and future, and paradoxically in the realm of the stars with their incalculably ancient light – for Swithin St Cleeve, Viviette's young lover, is an astronomer. Astronomy brings the two together, and so these two illicit lovers are more literally star-cross'd than Shakespeare's proverbial pair. Thus, Hardy introduces a vast extra dimension to the story, just as he introduced the immense time-span of geology to *A Pair of Blue Eyes*, and was later to do in *The Well-Beloved* – though astronomy is used here as a much more significant element than geology is in those novels. In both cases, the author's enthusiasm for the new sciences is invoked.

Hardy explains the purpose of this important motif thus in his 1895 Preface:

> This slightly-built romance was an outcome of a wish to set the emotional history of two infinitesimal lives against the stupendous background of the stellar universe, and to impart to readers the sentiment that of these contrasting magnitudes the smaller might be the greater to them as men. (p.289)

I believe that the author was being unduly reductive in the choice of the word 'slightly', perhaps diffident because of the failure of the previous *A Laodicean*. I find that the touching portrayal of the two lovers and the psychological realism of their relationship make this a most rewardingly memorable novel and unjustly neglected. The philosophical content with which the author endows the book certainly contradicts the notion of 'slightness'. Gibson quotes a letter of Hardy's in which he states that he wanted 'to make science, not the mere padding of a romance, but the actual vehicle of romance',[21] and I believe he succeeded. The tower is an obvious phallic symbol, and not the least touchingly emotive element is the divergent symbolic associations of the two protagonists with it. Viviette, the spinster-owner, provides a place of monastic hermitage for the scholarly Swithin, but in so doing, creates the conditions for their union.

The reference in *Tess* to contemplation of the stars may suggest a passing interest in the author, but for *Two on a Tower*, Hardy made thorough researches into the subject, reading his own copy of Richard A. Proctor's *Essays on Astronomy* (1872), and the young astronomer's work is described in impressive detail. This was no new enthusiasm, however, for the memo-

---
[21] Gibson, Life, p.89.

rable scene in *Far from the Madding Crowd* chapter II, where Gabriel Oak and his sheep are depicted under a starlit sky, was created eight years before Swithin cast his expert eye into the firmament. Hardy seems to show here that his interest in astronomy was as important to him as archaeology, and that, concerning this science with more ancient origins, he could unfold an impressive command of terminology – much of it, incidentally, as ancient as the traditional names for archaeological sites:

> A difference of colour in the stars – oftener read of than seen in England – was really perceptible here. The sovereign brilliance of Sirius pierced the eye with a steely glitter, the star called Capella was yellow, Aldebaran and Betelgueux shone with a fiery red. (*Far from the Madding Crowd* p.58)

Though he lacks Swithin's professional fascination and Viviette's intimate reason for fearing the heavens (and incidentally, St Swithin is famously associated with climatic foreboding), Gabriel (the messenger of the Bible) shares in the awe-inspiring experience of contemplating the cosmos (though Hardy only implies his participation) with young Abraham d'Urberville and with Clym gazing at the eclipse in *The Return of the Native* when he 'flung himself down upon the barrow, his face towards the moon, which depicted a small image of herself in each of his eyes' (*The Return of the Native* p.193).

In *Two on a Tower*, Viviette is awed by the revelatory power of the telescope which she likens to 'a great magician' (p.57); the very nature of the subject, as well as the young man's absorption in it, means that 'she felt her influence over him diminishing to nothing' (p.58) and she says that the telescope is 'an instrument to effect my own annihilation.' The awesomeness of the subject is given added depth by Hardy's agnosticism. In the same chapter, Hardy includes a passage that strikingly anticipates one in Peter Ackroyd's *First Light* (a novel which will offer a further comparison, with *The Return of the Native*) when the astronomer Damian Fall suffers abject terror in the face of the vastness before him and commits suicide; this passage certainly provides a stark contrast with the rapt musings of Gabriel Oak just quoted:

> At night, when human discords and harmonies are hushed, in a general sense, for the greater part of twelve hours, there is nothing to moderate the blow with which the infinitely great, the stellar universe, strikes down upon the infinitely little, the mind of the beholder; and this was the case now. Having got closer to immensity than their fellow-creatures, they saw at once its beauty and its frightfulness. They more and more felt the contrast between their own tiny magnitudes and those among which they had recklessly plunged, till they were oppressed with the presence of a vastness they could not cope with even as an idea, and which hung about them like a nightmare. (*Two on a Tower* pp.57/58)

Here, the striking feature is not that their feelings are simply the opposite of Oak's, but that they perceive an *ambivalence* borne of the Promethean closeness of approach that they have 'recklessly' achieved through the telescope. In a more concise expression of the terrible facet, Viviette declares that astronomy 'makes you feel human insignificance too plainly' (p.28). Hardy also makes the pair insignificant on a terrestrial plain, compared with the ancient landscape. Later, Viviette is going to the tower and 'appeared a mere spot, hardly distinguishable from the sod, as she crossed the open ground' (p.153). In the tower itself, she 'might have felt a nameless fear in thus sitting aloft on a lonely column, with a forest groaning under her feet, and palaeolithic dead men feeding its roots ...' (p.102). The use of the technical term 'palaeolithic' ('old stone-age'), dating only from 1865 in a novel of 1882, will be noted as indicating Hardy's keeping abreast of developments in the new science of archaeology, and is a reminder that Hardy's 'archaeological period', under the influence of the new friendship with General Pitt-Rivers, had now begun.

Michael Millgate notes that Hardy's use of the stars, as he himself asserts, though apprehended through a science via the medium of sophisticated technology, is nonetheless 'inescapably associated with ancient mythologies and with lingering and perhaps inextinguishable superstitions'.[22] This provides another paradox in the novel, and reinforces the circular links between ancient and modern in its themes (as well as being an unexpected link with the 'ancient, instinctual vitality'[23] of the specifically pagan culture of Egdon Heath in *The Return of the Native*). There is, however, a more subtle, but nonetheless direct, connection between the long and continuous archaeological origins of the site and the other new science whose pursuit gives the tower-folly, ironically, a practical use for which it was never intended, but which it anticipates by being telescope-shaped (as well as being inevitably phallic). For its builders, it is, in Simon Gatrell's words an 'aspirational structure',[24] with its upper level in the light while its lower level remains deeply shaded, and it continues thus for both Swithin and Viviette in their different ways. Gatrell also points out how the Tower is rooted in its pagan archaeological spot while looking at the godless heavens of astronomy, while the local church with its 'semi-norman arches', is Viviette's spiritual home with its tower pointing traditionally to the Christian Heaven.[25]

In the few years up to and including that of Hardy's birth, three scientists were independently working to establish the distance of stars from the Earth for the first time, using simple geometry and measuring their parallax motion. Friedrich Bessel in Konigsberg achieved and published his results in 1838, though F.G.W. Struve at Dorpat had come to the same conclusion earlier and published in 1840; the Scot Thomas Henderson published his findings after working in South Africa (where Swithin St Cleve went to pursue his studies) and at home in 1839. I have already mentioned that Hardy's earlier interest in astronomy is evident in the passage in *Far from the Madding Crowd*; in fact, that interest started at fifteen, and he learnt much from *The Popular Educator*, three volumes of which are among his books. On 25th June 1881, the Hardys observed Tebbutt's comet, recently discovered, the immediate catalyst for writing the book, and his research included a visit to the Royal Observatory at Greenwich. By the time Hardy wrote this novel, the connection between space and time revealed by those scientists was well known. By 1890, about two dozen stellar distances were known to science, the greatest being only 12.5 light years from Earth. With a modern knowledge of astronomy (in the 1990s, by vastly more sophisticated methods, stars have been discovered that are millions of light years from Earth), we can make the delightful inference that the light of some of the stars viewed by Swithin through Viviette's telescope might be literally contemporary with

---

[22] Millgate, Career, p.186.
[23] Millgate, Career, p.135.
[24] Gatrell, p.60.
[25] Gatrell, pp.62/63.

some of the archaeological levels just beneath the tower. With his knowledge and interest in the subject, Hardy may have guessed this possibility, but he could not have known for sure, any more than could the scientists of his day. Nonetheless, Hardy may well have been making a more subtle link in his temporal scheme in this novel than is at first apparent.

***

Both of Hardy's short stories which have a direct relevance to the present study were first published collectively in *A Changed Man and Other Tales* in 1913. *A Tryst at an Ancient Earthwork* is so significant to our understanding of Hardy's interest in the developing science of archaeology that it has already received detailed attention in Chapter Three. The other also

The Devil's Den, Clatford Bottom

concerns a tryst, but one of far different character – though both stories exploit the affective potential of moonlight eerily illuminating the prehistoric setting for the tale. *What the Shepherd Saw* (*Complete Stories* pp.655-672) first appeared in the Christmas 1881 edition of *The Illustrated London News,* a publication that, perhaps not entirely coincidentally, was crucial to the increasing popularisation of archaeology, as I noted in Chapter Two. It is a quintessentially Hardyesque story of circumstance and fatal misunderstanding set at a ruined barrow on the Marlbury [Marlborough] Downs, the monument in question being described as 'a Druidical trilithon, consisting of three oblong stones in the form of a doorway, two on end, and one across as lintel. ... The ruin was locally called the Devil's Door' (p.656). Here, the author refers to the monument as it would have been known to local folk of the time, rather than as it would be described by the archaeologist. Hardy bases the stones on a real site, a ruined barrow called the Devil's Den in Clatford Bottom on the Marlborough Downs.[26] James Dyer notes that the capstone of the chamber was re-erected in 1921, but 'the chamber was complete when Stukeley drew it in the eighteenth century.'[27] This means that the erosion that had so damaged the original barrow (destroying the burial chamber within) had further reduced the structure after Hardy had written the story, and after he had revised the piece in 1913. Denys Kay-Robinson, in her 'revision' of Herman Lea of 1972, notes that 'Hardy describes the arch as it is today – two uprights bridged by a horizontal. They stood thus when Bradley wrote in 1907 [A.G. Bradley, *Rambles in Wiltshire* (London: 1907)]'.[28] This is significant in that, in its original form as written in 1881, as Martin Ray explains, the story was not set on the Marlborough Downs at all, but on 'Verncombe Down'.[29] The revision therefore makes the prehistoric site

Corfe Castle

not merely a real one, but sets it in its real location. The shape of the original covering mound is invisible on the ground, but stones possibly once standing at the other end of it from the trilithon are still present by the footpath leading to the site, though the guidebooks do not allude to them. The stones are just three-quarters of a mile North of 'the turnpike-road across Mid-Wessex from London' (p.655), today the A4, which, notwithstanding the relief afforded by the M4, is still a busy route. The site remains an isolated spot, however, and the silence on a still day is palpable. The topography, though not easy to match to the story, is as Hardy de-

---

[26] Pitfield, p.40.
[27] Dyer, p.266.
[28] Kay-Robinson, p.218.
[29] Ray, p.304.

scribes it, but the downland here is now devoid of 'furze' (gorse) and the trilithon stands in a field sown with crops.

As with many occurrences, of lesser significance, in Hardy's oeuvre, the lethal events here are seen by an observer through an opening, in this case, from the shepherd's hut, with the reader given the superior and ironic overview of an omniscient presence. Although Hardy's altering of a real traditional place name for a prehistoric site (he usually retains such, for example, Stonehenge) may seem unnecessarily perverse here, the image of a 'door' opening for us on secret events, kept so by the shepherd-boy Bill Mills for twenty-two years, is certainly appropriate. Furthermore, the Devil's Den imparts nothing of the events of the tale, but Hardy's Devil's Door gives a hint that the site provides the accidental or even mischievous entrée for the deadly evil that breaks in upon the lives of the fated trio.

Hardy's Janus-like ambivalence towards antiquities is well shown by this story, a piece that reminds us of his forward-looking interest in the new science of archaeology, while he imaginatively looks backward to the mythic associations of ancient remains, exploiting them in the imagery and allusions of his art. For this is a story of a mythic nature, based on the primeval human passions of love, jealousy, and guilt – as well as on Hardy's preoccupation with the gulf between social classes – and so the author describes the stones in the terms in which they were known to local mythology, as 'Druidical' remains. This was an ascription perpetuated by the more primitive antiquarians, but their true identity had long been known by the developing science of archaeology: this site is typical of the many long barrows which have been so reduced by natural erosion or by ploughing that only the internal structure of the burial chamber remains, looking therefore like a tiny replica of the trilithons of Stonehenge. That Hardy realised the site's real origins is, I believe, attested by the clear connotations within the story of the two deaths that occur at the monument, the Duke's crime of passion and his own just end there years later.

In British archaeology, there are two principal forms of barrow which are themselves perhaps the most prolific and persistent of archaeological remains in this country. The relatively rarer long barrows were built in the Neolithic (New Stone Age), and were used for communal burial over generations. They often contained stone-built burial chambers like the Devil's Den, and are classified as entrance graves, passage graves, or gallery graves, according to the design of the chambers. The equivalent structures in the northern parts of Britain where turf is rarer than stone is the chambered cairn. In both cases, these burial sites were honoured for many centuries, with the Beaker people (of the so-called Copper Age, transitional between Stone and Bronze), and Bronze Age communities adding their own interments, often in stone cists, to the ancient structures. The archetypal Bronze Age monument is the round barrow, a mound constructed over a single – usually high status – burial and often occurring in groups called barrow cemeteries. (Some were built in the Iron Age/Roman period as well, and the shape was also more or less that of pagan Anglo-Saxon grave mounds such as at Sutton Hoo). Such tumuli formed, as we have seen, a significant element in the landscape, and resultant atmosphere, of *The Mayor of Casterbridge*. In *The Hand of Ethelberta*, the heroine rides through just such a group (named as Nine-Barrow Down in later editions, added parenthetically to p.237), which is the real Nine Barrows near Corfe Castle, a group of seventeen round barrows and one long barrow. Hardy cannot resist a typical comment on the ironic longevity of the site compared with the transience of individual humans such as Ethelberta with her muddled and troublesome life: 'Thence she ambled along through a huge cemetery of barrows, containing human dust from prehistoric times' (p.237). Later in the novel, during Sol and young Mountclere's desperate journey through the storm to prevent Ethelberta's marriage, other barrows are described in a fittingly ugly simile as befits the situation on 'the everlasting heath, the black hills bulging against the sky, the barrows upon their round summits like warts on a swarthy skin' (p.354). This provides a fascinating contrast to the elegantly Classical 'full breasts of Diana Multimammia' simile in *The Mayor of Casterbridge* (p.406), and how Hardy rises to his favourite skill in evoking landscape and atmosphere in such a scene! Ethelberta, in that same chapter, 'standing on top of a giant's grave in this antique land' (p.237) seems nothing if not an anticipation in Hardy's mind of Eustacia in her first appearance two years later in the much darker and more highly wrought successor to *The Hand of Ethelberta*.

***

Hardy sets one of his greatest novels, *The Return of the Native*, written and published in 1878, in a highly distinctive landscape with a barrow at its centre. James Gibson states that this book was Hardy's unsuccessful attempt at a 'great tragic novel in the classical tradition' which was subsequently achieved in *The Mayor of Casterbridge*.[30] I believe he underrates the power of the work, especially in the fine use and handling of this special landscape as its setting. Further, the powerful echoes of Shakespeare's greatest tragedy, *King Lear*, are unmistakable: tormented characters torn emotionally asunder on the pagan, elemental bleakness of a heath. Rainbarrow is a large Bronze Age mound on a hillside at the very edge of Egdon Heath, in fact in an area called Duddle Heath, overlooking the valley of the River Frome. In the first volume edition of 1878, chosen for Penguin Classics, it is called Blackbarrow – a name which fits the imagery of Egdon Heath well, though Hardy decided to revert to his usual practice of giving real names to prehistoric and landscape features in later editions, though in the singular rather than 'Rainbarrows'. Egdon Heath is one of the best-known of Hardy's topographical names, a conflation of the various heaths between Dorchester and Bournemouth that were once wild and desolate, but are now occupied by the extensive tank training grounds (next to which Hardy's young friend T.E. Lawrence lived at Clouds Hill), Winfrith nuclear power station, numerous caravan parks, busy main roads, and other impedimenta of twentieth century development. When Hardy showed the area to Gustav Holst on a motor tour in 1927, while the composer was in the midst of composing *Egdon Heath*, this, the subject of one of Holst's bleakest and most powerful works, was still untamed enough to inspire and emphasise the character of the score rather than to vitiate it. Indeed, Colin Matthews writes:

> It is Holst's most austere and personal work, and probably his masterpiece. Subtitled 'Homage to Hardy', the score quotes a passage from *The Return of the Native*.[31]

The passage Holst quotes is from the opening chapter of Book First of the novel – one that surely prefigures the creation of Michael Henchard:

---

[30] Gibson, Life, p.96.
[31] Colin Matthews, notes, Gustav Holst Orchestral Works, various artists, compilation CD, EMI, 1988.

> It was at present a place perfectly accordant with man's nature – neither ghastly, hateful, nor ugly: neither commonplace, unmeaning nor tame; but, like man, slighted and enduring; and withal singularly colossal and mysterious in its swarthy monotony. (p.11)

Holst describes his visit to Hardy in a letter to a friend thus: '… on Tuesday [9th August 1927] I had an unforgettable lunch and motor trip with Thomas Hardy himself, who showed me Mellstock, Rainbarrow and Egdon in general.' The composer continues, showing something of Hardy as well as his own working methods, 'I've promised to go up Rainbarrow by night. He is sorry I'm seeing it in summer weather, and wants me to come again in November.' The work received its premiere on February 27th 1928, just over a month after Hardy's death.[32]

Isle of Portland

Simon Gatrell notes the Heath's own peculiar temporal character, in 'geological and historical time'[33] with its 'ability to control or ignore the effects of time';[34] in summary, it is 'untouched Egdon [which] encompasses all conceivable scales of time from the geological to the hour by hour passing of each day.'[35] He conceives of the Heath as being like an island, 'distinctly cut off … inviolate, and inviolable.'[36] We might also reflect that, in this respect, it resembles the Isle of Slingers (Portland) in *The Well-Beloved*. Even today, and despite Hardy's

---

[32] Gibson, Interviews, pp.208/209.
[33] Gatrell, p.43.
[34] Gatrell, p.44.
[35] Gatrell, p.44.
[36] Gatrell, p.43.

admission in later editions that Egdon was an amalgam of heaths intruded upon by agriculture and forestry planting, the haunting character of the heath before such modern intrusions can readily be grasped on the walk to Rainbarrow and in a few other spots away from traffic. Despite its more sinister, brooding associations in his fiction, this special landscape formed an untroubled element of the author's childhood as recalled in the early, affectionately nostalgic, Wordsworthian poem 'Domicilium'; this is the third stanza:

> Behind, the scene is wilder. Heath and furze
> Are everything that seems to grow and thrive
> Upon the uneven ground. A stunted thorn
> Stands here and there, indeed; and from a pit
> An oak uprises, springing from a seed
> Dropped by some bird a hundred years ago. (ll.13-18)

The fascination with the passage of time is important in this piece, inevitably so, for Hardy's family and their memories are rooted in the spot: the cottage was built by Hardy's great-grandfather John Hardy in 1800 in the thick of the Napoleonic Wars – which fact, incidentally, perhaps adds to our understanding of the author's abiding interest in that period. It is no surprise that nearby Rainbarrow should appear in Hardy's Napoleonic *The Dynasts* (pp. 48/53), for Hardy mentions in the *Life* (p.162) that he met in 1883 a man whose 'father or grandfather had been one of the keepers of the Rainbarrows' Beacon, 1800-1815 …'; indeed, Hardy's epic verse drama combines intensely personal, family and local elements within its historical and cosmic dimension. Also important in this extract from 'Domicilium' is the sense that human habitation has been hard-won from the grasp of wild nature on the heathland; his 'father's mother' is quoted as saying that 'fifty years have passed since then, … Yonder garden-plots /And orchards were uncultivated slopes /O'ergrown with bramble bushes, furze and thorn. … /So wild it was when first we settled here' (ll.20-23). This sense that the heath is beyond cultivation, beyond human control, a wild region that distinguishes the human world from an untamed environment that embodies primeval forces, I have already noted in my discussion of both *The Mayor of Casterbridge*, when Henchard retreats from humanity to the heath, and of *Tess of the d'Urbervilles*, when Tess is in urbane, bourgeois Sandbourne, which is so sharply distinguished both from the wild heath at its very margin, and the passionate turmoil within the heroine herself.

In *The Hand of Ethelberta*, though a slighter work, a similar symbolic use is made of the heath near the start of the story. Ethelberta runs onto the heath away from the town of Anglebury (Wareham) where she is in temporary residence. In a comparable way to the ironic contiguity of Sandbourne with the surrounding wildness of the heath, the settled nature of this ancient town is contrasted with the heath that abuts its ramparts. Wareham is an Anglo-Saxon town with two Saxon churches, St Mary's (largely destroyed in the 1840s) and St Martin's, and a fine circuit of ramparts built by Alfred the Great in creating one of his fortified burghs. One rampart was omitted since the South side is protected by the River Frome that flows from near Hardy's home territory to the sea nearby. It is these geometrically planned defences (rather like those of Roman Casterbridge) which make Hardy's name so apt and which make the delineation of town and heath that much more sharply distinguished than in the case of the growing resort of Sandbourne. In chapter I, the eponymous heroine 'passed out of the town in a few moments and, following the highway across meadows fed by the Froom [sic], she crossed the railway and soon got into a lonely heath.' We see that the sharply defined limit of 'civilisation' is emphasised by the new railway here as well as the ancient town plan. Entranced by the lethal pursuit of a duck by a hawk, 'Ethelberta impulsively started off in a rapid run' to see the outcome of what can be seen as a sinisterly exaggerated symbolic version of her pursuit in the book by various suitors. Soon, 'the whole prospect was darkened to one uniform shade of approaching night' and she faces the frightening fact that she is lost in the bewildering

The Saxon walls of Wareham

heath. Her salvation by the aid of Christopher Julian, however, simply replaces one transient difficulty with the more irksome problem of her future life. Ethelberta flees the sedate order of the little town in obedience to a fascination with natural forces rather as her own and others' emotions are thrown into turmoil by the passions unleashed by her irresistible eligibility in London society. Like Eustacia, she is an outsider lost in this strange wilderness, though not desperately so. All of this is a tame anticipation of Tess submitting to her hatred of Alec, then fleeing her crime and her social pretence in Sandbourne for the wild uncertainty of the surrounding heath and life on the run beyond.

The setting of *The Return of the Native* is Egdon Heath, a 'Titanic form', an 'untameable, Ishmaelitish thing': 'the sea changed, the fields changed, the rivers, the villages, and the people changed, yet Egdon remained' (pp. 11/12). The focus of this landscape is explained as follows by Herman Lea, who evidently arrived at the spot from a different direction from the most practicable route today:

> ... we shall see on our left hand the tumuli called Rainbarrows, of which we may consider the largest as representative of the Rainbarrow of the story, although in our author's imagination it stood in a more central portion of Egdon Heath. ... Although the word barrow denotes a mound or hillock in its most literal sense, the term is now employed almost exclusively to signify a burial place. It was on top of Rainbarrow that the bonfire was kindled. This method of celebrating historic episodes of the past, which doubtless had its origins in prehistoric times and was directly connected with ceremonies of a religious nature, is now seldom seen.[37]

It might surprise Lea to know of the persistence of Guy Fawkes Night, let alone the nationwide chain of beacons which commemorated the four hundredth anniversary of the Spanish Armada in 1988 and the worldwide chain for the Queen's Golden Jubilee in 2002. It is interesting to note Lea's comment on prehistoric religion, however, for the quasi-pagan culture of the Heath, which matches and is sustained by its mythic character, is even more apparent in this novel than is the primitive culture of The Isle of Slingers in *The Well-Beloved*. Hardy firmly places the landscape and its inhabitants in his opening chapter in a past so primitive that 'Civilisation was its enemy' (p.12). Here, the Heath is personified in its 'antique brown dress'. 'With the exception of an aged highway and a still more aged barrow', the effects of humankind on the Heath are negligible: 'the trifling irregularities ... remained as the very finger-touches of the last geological age.' The fires on Rainbarrow have indeed their eerie pagan connotations:

> The ashes of the original British pyre which blazed from that summit lay fresh and undisturbed in the barrow beneath their tread. ... Festival fires to Thor and Woden had followed on the same ground and duly had their day. ... Indeed ... such blazes are rather the lineal descendants from jumbled Druidical rites and Saxon ceremonies than the invention of popular feeling about Gunpowder Plot ... The curfew is sounded ... a spontaneous Promethean rebelliousness against ... cold darkness, misery, and death. (pp.20/21)

Other references abound: 'going to church except to be married or buried was exceptional at Egdon' (p.89); Susan Nunsuch's 'ghastly invention of superstition' (p.347) in making and destroying the wax model of Eustacia is still 'a practice well-known on Egdon at that date'; and Hardy notes sardonically that the 'instincts of merry England lingered on here with exceptional vitality' ... where ... 'the impulses of all such outlandish hamlets are pagan still: in these spots, fragments of Teutonic rites to divinities whose names are forgotten, seem in some way or other to have survived mediaeval doctrine' (p.376) as a maypole is erected. Civilisation is invoked by the title of Book Sixth chapter II, 'Thomasin walks in a Green Place by the Roman Road', but the preceding chapter's emphasis on the power of the primitive is not entirely dispelled. The use of 'Teutonic rites' alongside 'Druidical' and 'Promethean' indicates that, although Hardy creates a very ancient and introspective world in *The Return of the Native*, Rainbarrow points upward to the cosmos, and he knows that there is a universality about

---

[37] Lea, p.72.

the mythic. Indeed, Roger Robinson declares that this is a novel which 'constantly evokes the Promethean myth of human aspiration' but 'in order to revoke it as something no longer possible to believe in.'[38] Rainbarrow is associated with all four of the Aristotelian elements as well as with the elemental forces that drive human beings. Containing cremated remains, it is also used as a beacon site; it suffers the lashing of millennia of rainfall and is a favourite meeting place for Damon and Eustacia who are drowned; it is built of earth; and it is raised higher into the air than any other spot on Egdon, 'a wart on an Atlantean brow, ... the pole and axis of this heathery world' (p.17). Impenetrable to the plough, Egdon Heath has as its most prominent feature a sterile monument to the dead. In the shifting shadows cast by the light of the ironically cheerful bonfire, the faces of the gathering have 'Shadowy eye-sockets deep as those of a death's head' (p.21).

Allied to the sense of the mythic, the archaeology is presented as being more widely representative of an ancient world rather than merely peculiar to this one enclosed little area of Britain; there are also numerous allusions to the Classical world, such as to the Cretan labyrinth, Oedipus, Pheidias, Alexander, and the Hellenic idea of life; and twice, Hardy the architect refers to 'Parian marble' from which the Parthenon was built; he also mentions the Chaldeans and Babylon. Such allusions also emphasise that the book is a tragedy on the Classical model. As I have already explained, the Dorset poet never in this, or his other works, infers any innate inferiority in the ancient remains of the North, in contrast with the world-view of his contemporary archaeologists who scoured the Mediterranean basin and filled museums with its artefacts long before equivalents from the North were thought worthy of a place. Hardy's deliberate use of specifically local archaeological allusion tacitly elevates the status of 'Northern' sites, and his presentation, or suggestion, of their enigmatic nature imbues them with an interest that circumvents or even subverts the norms and orthodoxy of contemporary received archaeological wisdom. For Michael Millgate, the Heath is 'a desert tract of pre-civilisation' and a moral wilderness into which standards of behaviour have to be imported; yet, at the same time, the novel is perhaps a Greek tragedy acted out, in observance of the Unities, on the open stage of the Heath.[39] Eustacia's first, anonymous, appearance identifies her intimately with the landscape and its ancient, pagan, inhabitants, as she appears on Rainbarrow as if 'one of the Celts who built the barrow ... The vale, the upland, the barrow, and the figure above it, all of these amounted only to unity' (p.17). The appearance is illusory, however, for, though a pagan, Eustacia is an outsider who is paradoxically at odds with the Heath and its inhabitants who are, as it were, prehistoric pagans; Eustacia is of partly Greek descent and therefore a pagan of the Classical world. She is familiar with Budmouth and Paris and, but does not realise that time on the Heath 'does not have the same significance.'[40] Significantly, she is unaware of the Druidical stones on the Heath. She cannot accept the Heath and ultimately, it destroys her and her lover/fellow-outsider Damon Wildeve. Her occupation of the heights of Rainbarrow gives her not command of the Heath, but the hope of a prospect well beyond it, to the resort of Budmouth and to the sea that can be but glimpsed by her grandfather Captain Vye (Captain Drew in the original version used for the Penguin Classics edition) through his telescope.

As in *The Well-Beloved*, and in *The Woodlanders*, the intense drama of the characters in

---

[38] Robinson, 'Darwin', Page, p.133.
[39] Millgate, Career, pp.130-132.
[40] Gatrell, p.45.

The Return of the Native is confined within a special landscape from which they find it difficult ever truly to escape and, in the case of outsiders, be accepted by. They may, like Clym, return changed (and uncomfortable in their old environment) but always, as the book's title implies, they are drawn magnetically back – back to the landscape and back to the more ancient culture that it embraces. In a Darwinian interpretation, Gillian Beer notes that 'the topic of the book is the near impossibility of return. In an evolutionary order it is not possible to choose to return to an earlier state.'[41] – yet the native (Clym) does return, though he cannot make the process of evolution accelerate for the other inhabitants through his attempts to educate; and those 'advanced' outsiders (Damon Wildeve and Eustacia Vye) who can neither settle nor escape are destroyed, perhaps because they anachronistically defy the evolutionary scheme in their primal passion. This ambivalence about the old-fashioned world of Wessex very much matches Hardy's own divided life, half the society celebrity in London, the world city, and half the local lad from Higher Bockhampton in its ancient, hidden landscape. Clym Yeobright is the native who returns, drawn irresistibly to his strange home environment. The story opens on Rainbarrow and ends with Clym starting his itinerant preaching there two-and-a-half years later, a cyclical structure that suggests the centrifugal force the heath exerts on its natives with the barrow at its epicentre.

Matching this is an ambiguity about the precise nature of the Heath: is it a rugged unspoilt tract, or is it an ancient landscape altered over millennia by the hand of Man? W.G. Hoskins' work emphasises that the natural appearance of the English landscape belies the intensive way in which it has been farmed and managed; the County Council information board on the nature trail, not far from Hardy's cottage, both explains the wildlife and explodes the illusion that this is virgin territory. Hardy uses both the appearance and the reality of the setting in the novel. Writing in apocalyptic terms in the book's opening chapter, he offers, as the only possible resolution of the paradox, the personification of the place as a sort of mythic monster reminiscent of a kind of insubstantial sphinx:

> The place became full of a kind of watchful intentness now; for when other things sank brooding to sleep the heath appeared slowly to awake and listen. Every night its Titanic form seemed to await something; but it had waited thus, unmoved, during so many centuries, through the crises of so many things, that it could only be imagined to await one last crisis – the final overthrow. ...

The untameable Ishmaelitish thing that Egdon now was it always had been. (pp.10-12)

This haunting, personified presence is reiterated later in the novel, and either by implication or explicitly, is set against the lives of the players in the tragedy in a similar fashion to the ironic use of Rainbarrow itself. In Book Fifth chapter II, we read of 'the imperturbable countenance of the heath, which having defied the cataclysmal onsets of centuries, reduced to insignificance by its seamed and antique features the wildest turmoil of a single man' (p.317); and immediately following in the next chapter, 'consciousness of a vast impassivity in all which lay around him took possession even of Yeobright in his wild walk ... overpowering the fervid by the inanimate'(p.317), reminding us of the universe that towers above Tess, above Gabriel and his sheep, and over Viviette and Swithin on their tower. Always, however, Hardy the humanist

---

[41] Beer, p.254.

keeps faith – and his focus – with his characters, defying the impersonal and the imponderable: to Thomasin, 'Egdon in the mass was no monster whatever, but impersonal open ground. Her fears of the place were rational, her dislikes of its worst moods reasonable' (p.355).

Since only 'in summer days of highest feather did its mood touch the level of gaiety' (p.11), it is unsurprising that only the 'most thorough-going ascetic could feel that he had a natural right to wander on Egdon.' Though populated sparsely, it is, then, with this small group of individuals that Hardy is concerned. Indeed, despite its appearance and antipathetic nature, and although 'the trifling irregularities were not caused by pickaxe, plough, or spade [i.e. by agriculture, the 'great leap forward' of the Neolithic], but remained as the very finger-touches of the last geological change' (p.12) (the Darwinian interest again), the heath is everywhere marked by traces of long and continuous human activity that give the novel the historic and prehistoric perspective characteristic of Hardy's works. And so it is archaeology that links the living characters with their curious environment: man-made features blend with the landscape, and some, like the track-ways and, particularly, Rainbarrow, still play a role in the seasonal cycle of people's lives. Rainbarrow is indeed typical of such man-made things which, very much in the nature of British archaeology, has the appearance of a landscape feature and as such seems to be a natural part of the physiognomy of the great mythic beast that is Egdon:

Ruins of St Andrew's Church, Church Ope

> This bossy projection of earth above its natural level occupied the loftiest ground of the loneliest height that the heath contained. Although from the vale it appeared but as a wart on an Atlantean brow, its actual bulk was great. It formed the pole and axis of this heathery world. (p.17)

So it is actually an ancient man-made object which symbolically dominates the scene and the book. Other traces of the long human involvement with the place are introduced early: 'an aged highway ... overlaid an old vicinal way, which branched from the great Western road of the Romans, the Via Iceniana, or Iknild Street' (p.12), the heath 'figures in Domesday' (p.11) and 'the right of cutting heath-turf occurs in charters relating to the district'; Leland, the antiquary to Henry VIII, writes of it; 'old churches' and 'decayed manor houses' (p.349) are mentioned in passing. The sense of Egdon being trapped in its past is emphasised by rituals like the bonfire, the maypole, and the mummers' play which continue unbroken tradition, by the heath's isolation from towns and good communications, by the inhabitants' pagan reluctance to attend church, and by their recalcitrance in the face of any attempted modernisation such as Clym's original scheme of starting a school to educate them out of their backwardness – though neither he nor his author wishes to reform them or convert them to Christianity; Donald Davie declares that for Hardy, very often 'The agnosticism, one perceives, is the crux.'[42]

The varied archaeological sites mentioned in *The Mayor of Casterbridge* form an integral part of the novel's temporal scheme; Stonehenge is the symbolic setting at the climax of *Tess of the Durbervilles*. In *The Return of the Native*, Rainbarrow is a symbolic presence which persists throughout the book. It represents a link between ancient and contemporary, as I have just explained, provides a physical focus for the action, and gloomily accords with the ominous character of the heath through its identity as a place of burial redolent of human mortality while providing underlying irony in that a man-made feature can last so incalculably longer than any individual human being. Hardy's sense of mortality, as I have discussed in Chapter Three, must have been greatly heightened by his work in clearing graves as a young architect as well as by other melancholy youthful experiences. R.J. White might be referring specifically to the barrows when he remarks: 'He was certainly well enough aware that his novels recorded the graveward descent of a civilisation or of an ancient way of life, although that was not why he wrote them.'[43] This comment could felicitously be applied to *The Return of the Native* or indeed to others, particularly *The Mayor of Casterbridge*.

Three more recent novels also have a barrow as a focus. Adam Thorpe's *Ulverton* has a Bronze Age round barrow, while in both Peter Ackroyd's *First Light* and Penelope Lively's *Treasures of Time*, there is a Neolithic long barrow. Like Rainbarrow, each is a symbolic device which comments on the transience of man while ironically, as a human trace, proving far more permanent than either the individual human beings who built it or who were buried within it. However, whereas Rainbarrow retains its mystery (in the book rather than in reality), all three tumuli in the other books are excavated: Hardy reserves the excavation of another, less prominent barrow to explore the symbolic and reflective possibilities of the activity, as well as adding a few extra colouring touches to the narrative.

Most indebted to Hardy, perhaps, is Adam Thorpe's *Ulverton*, an innovative work which chronicles the life of one imaginary English village from 1650 to 1988. The book starts and ends at a round barrow (its identity clear because it contains a single warrior) that dominates the skyline and extends the time-frame of the story by millennia. The final word in the book is 'tumulus'. Taking the time theme further and with wide symbolic potential, Thorpe has the barrow excavation beginning on the very day the Great War breaks out in 1914 in a chapter where its importance becomes emphasised; two items of pottery are the first finds. Of particular relevance to Hardy's own interest in excavation, Thorpe even has the archaeologist explain to a local rustic the difference between a 'treasure hunt' and searching for real treasure – for the

---
[42] Davie, p.182.
[43] White, p.5.

knowledge to be gained by finding the remains of a long-dead human being and the art that his age produced. But unlike that in Hardy's novel, the excavations in all three books by (more or less) professional archaeologists become a central part of the plot through which relationships and reputations wax and wane. In *The Return of the Native*, we are in the era of the antiquarian, and 'excavation' rather resembles tomb-robbing than a scientific pursuit of knowledge. Rainbarrow is certainly more than a symbol in Hardy's novel, but its use is more subtle and suggestive, and far less central to the plot than in these three modern works.

The prototype of Rainbarrow is a prominent mound, but it is now to be found in the surroundings of a plantation, difficult to distinguish from the rough terrain of the hillside from which it springs. A Hardy enthusiast has attached a small sign with its name, and the excavated gash in its top bears testimony to earlier antiquarian interest of the kind that takes place in the novel. Hardy must have known the spot for his whole life. It is difficult of access today, about a half-hour's walk from the birthplace, and cannot be found without specialised local knowledge; it is certainly more difficult to find nowadays than Lea implies, as quoted earlier in this section. The walk lies along silent woodland paths including a section of the Roman road that Hardy used in his poem of that name, its *agger* splendidly preserved, where, uncannily, one almost expects to encounter the characters from the novel.

The barrow rises from the heath, and its first appearance is in Book First chapter II following likewise, logically, from the description of the heath in chapter I. I have already noted the fact that this human construction appears to be an integral part of the landscape. This is emphasised by initially referring to the figure (of Eustacia Vye) as 'something' which 'rose ... like a spike from a helmet. The first instinct of an imaginative stranger might have been to suppose it the person of one of the Celts who built the barrow ... musing for a moment before dropping into eternal night with the rest of his race' (p.17). Hardy here presents us with one of his most affecting images, as mysterious as it is memorable. He creates a continuum between heath, barrow, and person (whose identity remains unknown until the next chapter) very reminiscent of the construct of field/earthwork/tower/astronomer in *Two on a Tower*. In Book Third chapter IV, the earlier novel is even more powerfully evoked when Clym watches the lunar eclipse from Rainbarrow, as entranced by it as is Swithin by the constellations seen through the telescope. When it reaches its fullest extent, Eustacia arrives, for the eclipse is the signal for their tryst, and Clym falls into her arms – an apt symbol, for the virgin goddess is eclipsed by their passionate embrace: 'Two on a Barrow', perhaps? This hauntingly poetic scene is the more layered in that they meet on a burial mound, with all its connotations of fatalism and mortality. That original purpose cannot long be absent from our consciousness when Rainbarrow is in view. It is emphasised by another key incident as the tragic events unfold. Eustacia in a downpour miserably awaits Clym on the well-named Rainbarrow, 'gradually crouching down under the umbrella as if she were drawn into the Barrow by a hand from beneath' (pp.345-346). She is pitiable, in 'isolation from all of humanity except the mouldered remains inside the Barrow ...' (p.346).

As in *The Well-Beloved* and in Ackroyd's *First Light*, the ancient inhabitants are the direct ancestors of the characters present in the narrative: Clym and the other 'natives' are presented, at least on an imaginative level, as descendants of the barrow-builders of the heath. Late in the novel, the symbolic and philosophical significance of the barrows is as strong as in the opening pages, as this passage from Book Sixth chapter I shows:

> He frequently walked the heath alone, when the past seized upon him with its shadowy hand, and held him there to listen to its tale. His imagination would then people the spot with its ancient inhabitants: forgotten Celtic tribes trod their tracks about him, and he could almost live among them, look in their faces, and see them standing beside the barrows which swelled around, untouched and perfect as at the time of their erection. Those of the dyed barbarians who had chosen the cultivable tracts were, in comparison with those who had left their marks here, as writers on paper beside writers on parchment. Their records had perished long ago by the plough, while the works of these remained. Yet they all had lived and died unconscious of the different fates awaiting their relics. It reminded him that unforeseen factors operate in the evolution of immortality. (p.373)

This kind of reflective passage is clearly important to the overall effect and character of the whole tragedy and is archetypal Hardy. Clym's being 'seized' by a personified past is clearly through the medium of the archaeological features all around him and by their operation upon his refined and acute sensitivity; indeed, the combination of archaeological knowledge with its imaginative effect makes a stronger case for identifying Clym Yeobright with Thomas Hardy. In Book V chapter II, 'Clym's grief, mitigated by wearing itself out' (p.308), is made to seem irrelevant by the 'seamed and antique features' (p.317) of the Heath; indeed, as in so many allusions by Hardy to archaeological features in the landscape – however focused we are on the drama of individuals – the ephemeral incident and the mortal life are placed in a new and temporally diminished perspective.

Later archaeologists and historians dismiss the idea that 'Celts' were the Bronze Age barrow builders, though Iron Age examples are of that origin; otherwise, Hardy's imaginative engagement with the past through the medium of archaeological remains anticipates the very best twentieth-century archaeology writers like Mortimer Wheeler. Moreover, Hardy's realisation that the archaeological record is partial, and can be crucially affected by a factor like ploughing (a detail also given in *A Tryst at an Ancient Earthwork*), gives a clear indication of his knowledge and perception of the subject, though perhaps claiming such an insight for the character – even an experienced and intelligent native like Clym – is stretching credibility.

Clym's upbringing in this uncultivated environment means, coincidentally, that he has been closely associating with archaeological remains all his life, and so his sombre reflections on the mortal remains of humanity is not solely because of his situation in the story. We read that 'his toys had been the flint knives and arrow-heads which he found there, wondering why stones should 'grow' to such odd shapes' (p.173). Again, although it could be coincidence, Hardy's knowledge of the subject seems impressive: it was only about eighty or ninety years since such artefacts of the Stone Age had been accepted as both man-made and very ancient, so Clym's childhood supposition is entirely fitting.

Following the tragic climax with the deaths of the outsiders who reject and are rejected by the special landscape, the novel moves to its serene coda, Book Sixth. Before the very end, which associates him specifically with the barrow, Clym the native is placed, as shown in the passage just quoted, in his native landscape as a whole and in his historic perspective, linking him with the countless forgotten generations of people who have populated Egdon Heath through the degraded but inescapable archaeological remains that are their affecting yet enigmatic testimony.

With an elegant cyclical symmetry, the book ends, as it begins, on Rainbarrow on which the solitary and tragic Eustacia is replaced by her marginally less tragic widower, Clym. In unmistakably powerful echoes of the Sermon on the Mount, he 'found his vocation in the career of an itinerant open-air preacher ... speaking not only in simple language on [Rainbarrow] and in the hamlets around, but in a more cultivated strain elsewhere ...' (p.396). As typical of the Biblical scholarship of such an allusion is Hardy the agnostic, for Clym 'left alone creeds and systems of philosophy ... '.

Archaeological artefacts are woven into the story in several other instances, for instance in 'Charley's ministrations to his former mistress [Eustacia] were unbounded. ... bringing home curious objects which he found in the heath, such as ... stone arrow-heads used by the old tribes on Egdon ...' (pp.329-330). More significant is the use of the cremation urns contained in the barrows which were among the most sought-after prizes of the antiquarians and other souvenir-diggers. Hardy the advanced scientific thinker and archaeological savant shows his disgust for this traditional – and, by the time of his maturity, largely discredited – practice by placing it alongside the profound significance, almost reverence, he attaches to the ancient tombs in the novel. His attitude to the use of Rainbarrow as a beacon may be ambivalent, the sombre and mythic connotations balancing any distaste for the irreverence implied by it; there can be no such doubt about 'a pair of ancient British urns which had been dug from a barrow near, and were used as flower pots for two razor-leaved cactuses' (p.121). One senses the disdain in Hardy's choice of both the casual use, and of such incongruously foreign plants. Much more important to the story is a 'slight touch in the shaping of Clym's destiny' (p.188) which comes when another 'barrow was opened on the heath and Yeobright attended the operation'. In the superstitious and heavily ironic words of Christian, one of the local rustics, to Clym's mother, 'they have found things like flower-pots upside down, mis'ess Yeobright; and inside these be real charnel bones. They have carried them off to men's houses; but I shouldn't like to sleep where they will bide. Dead men have been known to come and claim their own. Mr Yeobright had got one pot of the bones, and was going to bring them home – real skellington bones – but 'twas ordered otherwise. You'll be relieved to hear that he gave away his, pot and all ... ' (p.189) Clym has given the urn to Eustacia, bones and all, a macabrely prescient gift, and his mother challenges him about it forthwith.

The doyen of all writers in English who are inspired by archaeology is Sir Thomas Browne, whose works figured in Chapter Two, the Norwich doctor and philosopher who wrote two philosophical prose works inspired by the digging-up of urns (excavation is a term to be reserved for the scientific practice only): *Hydriotaphia – Urne Buriall* and *Concerning some Urnes found in Brampton-Field in Norfolk Anno 1667*. His knowledge of what we should call archaeology is impressive for his time, though factual understanding about these artefacts was virtually non-existent in the seventeenth century. However, his respect for the objects, and his profound reflections on the mortality of man inspired by them, is akin to Hardy's attitude evident in *The Return of the Native*. Browne's remark that the ancients were 'little expecting the curiosity of future ages should comment upon their ashes, and having no old experience of the duration of their Reliques, held no opinion of such after-consideration'[44] is very like Clym's thought in Book Sixth chapter I, already quoted, and in stark contrast to the casual way that he and others were engaged in digging up the urns. Perhaps this apparent inconsistency of attitude in him is a small instance of his ambivalence as the native who returned?

---

[44] Sir Thomas Browne, The Religio Medici and Other Writings, Prof. C.H. Hurford, introd., Everyman's Library no. 92 (London: Dent,1906), p.92.

Chapter Seven

Personal Memories and Ancient Remains: The Poetry

'Poetry unearths from among the speechless dead ...'

Geoffrey Hill, 'History as Poetry'.

Poem numbers cited are those allocated in *The Complete Poems*. Couplet (coup.) or stanza (st.) numbers are given as appropriate.

It is a truth universally acknowledged by biographers and commentators that Hardy the great novelist was a journeyman, and that Hardy the poet was the author's *soi-disant* identity. John Wain begins his introduction to his Hardy *Selected Poems*: 'Thomas Hardy was, constitutionally and by inclination, primarily a poet. Had he possessed private means, it is doubtful whether he would have written novels at all ... prose, for practical reasons, carried the day.'[1] David Wright's introduction to his selection remarks that 'when Thomas Hardy's first book of poems made its appearance in 1898 ... *Wessex Poems* was no more than a curiosity, the by-product of a famous elder novelist.' But he also states that Hardy 'once told his friend Sydney Cockerell that he would never have written a line of prose if he could have earned his living at poetry.'[2] Philip Davis perceives a personal aesthetic bias allied to Hardy's class consciousness that inevitably placed poetry in a superior position, 'because novel writing was still conceived of as a 'trade', while poetry was the voice of the solitary feeling soul.'[3] The disparity between the public perception of Hardy's poetry and his own is as fascinating as the author's determined lifelong reading and practice of the art. In the classic *Oxford Book of English Verse*, even in the 1927 edition[4] in which 'Q', Sir Arthur Quiller-Couch, acknowledges over forty contemporary or recent poets and published just months before Hardy's death, not a single one of his poems is printed in a selection numbering eight hundred and eighty-three. The equally venerable *The Golden Treasury* in its 1926 edition[5], and produced by Hardy's own publisher, Macmillan,

---
[1] Selected and edited John Wain, Selected Shorter Poems of Thomas Hardy (London: Macmillan, 1966), pp ix-x.
[2] Selected and edited David Wright, Thomas Hardy Selected Poetry (London: Penguin Books, 1978), p11.
[3] Davis, p370.
[4] Selected and edited Arthur Quiller-Couch, The Oxford Book of English Verse (Oxford: OUP, 1927).
[5] Francis T. Palgrave, ed. The Golden Treasury, 3rd ed. With Book V chosen L. Binyon (London: Macmillan, 1926).

includes just three Hardy poems. By contrast, in the popular *The Rattle Bag* of 1982,[6] Seamus Heaney and Ted Hughes choose sixteen Hardy poems. It is more than a little ironic, then, that Donald Davie summarises Hardy's place in the English poetic pantheon as 'this sort of cop-out, a modest (though proudly expert) workman in a corporate enterprise which from time to time publishes a balance-sheet called *The Golden Treasury* or *The Oxford Book of English Verse*.'[7] Hardy's credit as a poet, then, was certainly very limited indeed until long after his death.

Perhaps for 'Q' and his ilk, Hardy was just too individual, or too modern? The change in critical perception was slow, but not the least catalyst has been the admiration of extraordinarily varied fellow-poets; Merryn Williams writes that 'Poets as different as Sassoon, Pound, Auden, Dylan Thomas, Graves and Larkin have all expressed deep admiration for him.'[8] She continues, 'Donald Davie in *Thomas Hardy and British Poetry* (1973) wrote, 'In British poetry of the last fifty years ... the most far-reaching influence, for good and ill, had been not Yeats, still less Eliot or Pound, not Lawrence, but Hardy.'' Davie's book is really about the influence of Hardy on later poets, though the influence of Wordsworth is implicit throughout. The admiration that Hardy had for the Romantics is evident in the products of his Italian visit, that for Shakespeare in the many allusions in the novels, and his debt to other poets is apparent in the echoes one encounters in the surprisingly varied forms of his verse; some of these will be remarked upon.

So much for the way that time has treated Hardy's poetry, but what of the converse? It is a truism – and a temporal one – that Hardy is a nineteenth-century novelist and a twentieth-century poet, and this is not the least of the many paradoxes and ambiguities surrounding his complex personality and career. Commentators tend to emphasise Hardy's characteristic, often angular style in which some claim to find as many infelicities as in his prose. Not untypically, Philip Davis comments regarding 'The Voice' that in 'those words which hang together with the ghost of a syntax, there is something very like the staggering steps of Fanny Robin.'[9] John Wain in his introduction to *Selected Shorter Poems* typifies Hardy's admirers in declaring:

> ... Hardy's poems are very like the work of a village craftsman ... Like a rural workman, he built plainly and built to last, with no factory-tooled precision but with each new object shaped by the living hand ... His language is not elegant, his lines do not flow smoothly; when he sets himself a difficult metrical task and carries it out with a skill born of long practice, the result is never slick or varnished. There is always a certain stiff deliberation, the unhurried gait of the country man going about his immemorial business.[10]

All, however, agree on the importance of time, and especially of past time, in his poetic oeuvre. Donald Davie stresses the important connection of place with past or historic time in Hardy's poetry, and one might think particularly of the late works written after Emma's death in this connection:

---

[6] Selected and edited Seamus Heaney and Ted Hughes, The Rattle Bag (London: Faber and Faber, 1982).
[7] Davie, p.40.
[8] Merryn Williams, A Preface to Hardy, 2nd ed. (London: Longman, 1993), pp.132,134.
[9] Davis, p.386.
[10] Wain, pp.xii/xiii.

> For Hardy has the effect of locking any poet whom he influences into the world of historical contingency, a world of specific places at specific times.[11]

Central to his argument on Hardy's influence is the contrast to that of Yeats, for Davie sees the two as equally influential, each with his 'disciples', the crucial difference being in their respective treatment of the temporal element in their poetry:

> Hardy appears to have mistrusted, and certainly leads other poets to mistrust, the claims of poetry to transcend the linear unrolling of recorded time. This is at once Hardy's strength and his limitation, and it sets him at odds with, for instance, Yeats, who exerts himself repeatedly to transcend historical time by seeing it as cyclical, …[12]

The passage of time is not only the breath of much of Hardy's poetry, but it is also the wind that has winnowed away so many of the lesser voices that filled the old anthologies. Davie believes that such is Hardy's stature, that even notables among his followers will not fare so well by the same process: '… it is not true that it is merely the passage of time, and of atrocious history, which makes Roy Fuller or Philip Larkin unable to rise to Hardy's at once playful and mournful serenity.'[13]

***

I have already referred in Chapter Six to what is normally regarded as Hardy's earliest poem, 'Domicilium' (1), and its fascination with the past and the effects of time. This first piece with its acute visual details most assuredly justifies Tom Paulin's observation of Hardy's 'insistence throughout his work on what is authentically visible'[14] and it is the world he knew and observed so well that excites his memory and imagination of the past. Though the word 'time' is never mentioned, it is the substance, the medium of all the thoughts in the poem. Hardy's 'father's mother' of 'Domicilium' – whose vivid recollections of the Napoleonic Wars were such a powerful influence on his own passion for that period – is the subject of and again the inspiration for 'One we Knew' (227). Here, Hardy's much loved grandmother in great old age fascinates him with her inverted perception of time, where 'Past things were to her as things existent, / Things present but as a tale' (8th st.). Hardy's obsession with such perceptions of the nature of the enigmatic fourth dimension are nowhere more apparent than in his poetry. Joanna Cullen Brown states: 'To read his poetry is to become almost obsessively aware of time. Time, and particularly time past, is the character who dominates it … .'[15] Three of the collections bear titles which underline time as of paramount importance: *Poems of the Past and the Present*, *Time's Laughingstocks*, and *Moments of Vision*. And two other collections' titles imply the significance of time: *Satires of Circumstance* and *Winter Words*. Perusing the list of titles of Hardy's poems bears out this impression: such works as 'Evening Shadows' (833) and 'End of the Year 1912' (560), 'The Clock of the Years' (481) and 'June Leaves and Autumn' (900)

---

[11] Davie, p.3.
[12] Davie, p.4.
[13] Davie, p.182.
[14] Paulin, p.91.
[15] Joanna Cullen Brown, A Journey into Thomas Hardy's Poetry (London, Allison and Busby, 1990), p.38.

are typical. The much anthologised 'The Darkling Thrush' (119) is an exquisitely doleful New Year's Eve, and eve of a new century, poem subscribed '31 December 1900'.

But what kind of time is this 'character who dominates'? Patricia Ingham comments:

> In place of the sense of geological time and an accompanying impression of movement, another is obsessively present in the poems: of limited and characteristically human time, unrelated to anything outside itself.[16]

This broad generalisation points out a difference between the poetry and some aspects of the prose, but is really about the personal and individual temporal aspects of Hardy's poetry,

St Juliot Vicarage

not only the broad 'characteristically human', and omits entirely the historico-archaeological stratum that I shall demonstrate is another notable time-theme in the works. She notes that Hardy's mother escaped 'the cell / Of time' (4th st.) ('After the Last Breath (J.H. 1813–1904)' (223)) by death, and that it was only after Emma's death that Hardy found release in the poems of 1912–1913. Hardy had met his first wife Emma Lavinia Gifford at St Juliot Vicarage when he was sent to this remote spot in north Cornwall by the architect Crickmay of Weymouth in 1870 to draw up plans for restoring the crumbling church; Emma was the Vicar's sister-in-law. The passionate and regretful love poems he wrote after her death – dictated, bizarrely, to his

---

[16] Patricia Ingham, 'Hardy and 'The Cell of Time'', The Poetry of Thomas Hardy, ed. Patricia Clements and Juliet Grindle (London: Vision Press, 1980), p.120.

second wife Florence Emily (neé Dugdale) – are among the most celebrated of their kind in Literature.

Ignoring the relatively limited reference to the future in the poetry, Ingham makes a useful and important observation in stating: 'Hardy's treatment of time is revealed: its retrospective nature. The passing of time is seen when it has already taken place.'[17] Again, focusing on the personal poetry at the expense of the rest, she declares: 'Hardy's retrospective, negating, almost unmoving time leaves him usually on the wrong side of a limited stretch of existence. ... he is its prisoner, trapped already in the irretrievable. ... the past is dimly seen through the ravages of the present.'[18] And yet what is a work of art if it cannot be the opportunity both to reflect on what is or what has been, and to encapsulate in a permanent form? Inevitably, the power and intensity of the last works dominate our perception of Hardy's poetry and it is not unjustifiable to regard much of his output as the prelude to this climactic achievement. Philip Davis sees the switch from prose as a prerequisite, indeed the *sine qua non*, for the composition of the famous late works:

> He covered over his Henchard-like emotions until his emotions became buried in, and only revived by, his memory. ... Hardy had finally to turn from novel writing to confront through some form of autobiography the problems which he had evaded through the novelist's self-dispersal. ... He had given up writing tragedy in prose for autobiography in verse. ... When Hardy set his past moving again in verse it knocked him over as if it were now again present.[19]

And how that final remark on these intense, confessional poems about the guilt-ridden relationship with his dead wife reminds modern readers of Ted Hughes' *Birthday Letters*. Yet, despite Hardy's poetic preoccupation with the past, as in all his creative work he does offer far more variety in his treatment and use of time in his poetry than the important but limited focus evident in the very personal late works, and the historical and archaeological aspects provide an interesting extra perspective on his preoccupation with time.

Nine hundred and forty-seven poems are printed in the collected edition of Hardy's poems[20] (this excludes *The Dynasts*). Of the very large number that are concerned with time, thirteen are inspired by archaeological subjects, either places or objects; a further dozen or so include reference of some import to archaeological remains. To deal only with the poems which are to some degree concerned with archaeology would be to take an otherwise random and eccentric sample of Hardy's works: such pieces need to be seen as representative of Hardy's treatment of a dominant theme – time – using in an unselfconscious way one of his favourite subjects. In this chapter, then, I shall first examine a selection of Hardy's time-centred poems, then turn to those with some resonance with the past in an architectural subject; next come those which include some archaeological reference, and finally I shall deal in more detail with those which have an archaeological starting point.

---

[17] Ingham, Clements and Grindle, p.120.
[18] Ingham, Clements and Grindle, pp.125, 129.
[19] Davis, pp.373/374, p.378, p.404.
[20] Thomas Hardy, The Complete Poems, ed. James Gibson (London: Macmillan, 1976). The latest revised edition (Basingstoke: Palgrave, 2001) contains poem no. 948, 'The Sound of Her'.

Hardy's poetic interest in time is very much about the effects of this fourth dimension on people, whether individuals (including himself) or in general, and on their achievements and relationships. Many of Hardy's most famous poems come from the last period of his long poetic career and reflect mournfully on the relationship with and loss of his first wife Emma and on the general effects of the passing of time. Reference to the future is always ironic, envisaging the way that the future will look back on what is now the present. Most startling for the modern reader in this regard is the title '1967' (167), surprising and arresting for a poet preoccupied with time past, but a doleful anticipation of the mortal fate of the lovers a century hence 'With nothing left of me or you ... / Beyond a pinch of dust or two' (2nd st.). This typically bleak touch of Hardy humour is followed by an uncanny echo of Donne's flea in 'That thy worm should be my worm, Love!' (4th st.).

The concern with family continuity which is evident in 'Domicilium' (1) is a reflection of the poet's unswerving attachment to his roots and the lifelong social insecurity he felt, shown by his ambivalence to society people in his schizophrenic annual routine alternating between London and Dorset. This is echoed in Hardy's anxiety to establish as his ancestor the Captain Thomas Hardy of HMS *Victory*, a connection that he was never able to prove, and thus perhaps even helps to explain his whole preoccupation with the Napoleonic period. Hardy the agnostic wrote of family lineage in 'Heredity' (363), a poem of minimal consolation worthy of his Anglo-Saxon artistic and familial forebears – indeed, untitled, this work would have made a worthy successor to the Anglo-Saxon riddles. In it, he writes, 'Flesh perishes, I live on, ... / The eternal thing in man, / That heeds no call to die' (1st st.). The passage of historic time that is no respecter of the individual life is a theme in, amongst others, the moving and very un-jingoistic poems written about the Boer War. The wives in 'The Going of the Battery' (57) console themselves, waiting stoically 'in trust what Time's fulness shall show' (st. VII). But in 'Embarcation', 'upon the sea / Beyond which lies the tragical To-be' (3rd st.), a hint of Tennyson's 'Crossing the Bar', perhaps, Hardy is grimly realistic about the likely fate of men in this conflict, one 'Which this late age of thought, and pact, and code, / Still fails to mend' (2nd st.). In an echo of Byron's 'The Destruction of Sennacherib', the soldiers are 'Yellow as autumn leaves, alive as spring' (3rd st.). Hardy's pessimism about the immutable grimness of human experience, despite the extraordinary material and technological advances of his lifetime, is well shown here. Warfare – and domination of one nation over another – is seen as a grim, unchanging feature of human history, a decidedly radical note at the start of a war at the height of Victorian Empire:

> Here, where Vespasian's legions struck the sands,
> And Cerdic with his Saxons entered in,
> And Henry's army leapt afloat to win
> Convincing triumphs over neighbour lands,
>
> Vaster battalions press for further strands,
> To argue in the selfsame bloody mode ... (1st/2nd sts.)

Hardy clearly distinguishes the abstract concept and historic phenomenon of 'Time' with its capitalisation from the transient mundane 'time' of the individual person. In the third poem, 'The Colonel's Soliloquy' (56), subtitled 'Southampton Docks: October 1899', the eponym refers to his early career as 'my early time' (4th st.) which could almost be an alternative title for 'Domicilium' (1).

Hardy's own 'later time' was dominated by his poetry and by his drastically altered feelings for his late first wife. His difficulties in the latter part of their relationship were forgotten in the welter of regret and of yearning for the springtime of their love, all encapsulated in some of Hardy's most famous poems. The mind plays strange tricks, and though the details have vanished, the feelings of the young lovers 'At Castle Boterel'(292) are etched on the poet's mind, and what 'filled but a minute' (4th st.), recollected in tranquillity half a lifetime later (the poem is dated March 1913), inspired a yearningly beautiful poem about the puzzling nature of time and memory. The experience remains, but the moment has gone forever because of 'Time's unflinching rigour' (6th st.); Hardy closes, 'my sand is sinking, / And I shall traverse old love's domain / Never again' (7th st.). Even in such an intensely personal poem, Hardy's general sense of the recently discovered immensity of archaeological and geological time is present; Roger Robinson quotes, 'Primaeval rocks the road's steep border, / ... Of the transitory in earth's long order ... ', pointing out that, as in *The Dynasts*, such a different work, 'At many moments the historic perspective becomes a prehistoric, geological one. ... Against the scale of those newly-discovered 'immense lapses of time' which 'had known nothing of the dignity of man' (*A Pair of Blue Eyes* ch. 22) the grandest of human enterprises must seem trivial.'[21] 'Beeny Cliff' (291) bears the subscription 'March 1870 – March 1913'. Nature, whether represented by the cliff itself or by the waves in their 'ceaseless babbling' (st. II), has a permanence through continuity. Only the individual human being is irrecoverably lost; the poignant last stanza reads:

> What if still in chasmal beauty looms that wild weird western shore,
> The woman now is – elsewhere – the ambling pony bore,
> And nor knows nor cares for Beeny, and will laugh there nevermore. (st. V)

The last two pieces in *Moments of Vision* are time poems collected under the heading 'Finale', and both underline the transience of life, that theme which underpins Hardy's artistic interest in archaeology, indeed the whole of his preoccupation with time in so much of his work. 'The Coming of the End' (510) concerns the finite nature of all the daily round of activities that make up life, the 'housebuilding, furnishing, planting, / As if there were ages to spend / In welcoming, feasting and jaunting;' (3rd st.) but '/ It came to an end.' The fatalistic 'Afterwards' (511) expresses the hope that the poet will be remembered after his own death in association with the things in nature that he found beautiful and important in life, the unchanging cycle that brings 'glad green leaves' (1st st.) in May, 'such innocent creatures' (3rd st.) as the hedgehog that 'travels furtively over the lawn', and, as at many crucial points in Hardy's thought, 'the full-starred heavens' (4th st.).

***

Archaeology reveals, and consists of, the traces of vanished societies and the individuals that made them up. Donald Davie draws an interesting analogy with archaeology regarding

---
[21] Robinson, 'Darwin', Page, p.132.

the 'process' and the 'product' in Hardy's poetry, for he is 'so much the stonemason in his poetic imagination', but 'sometimes [the poems] make us think of industrial metalwork rather than carved stone. ... // ... The prehistoric shift from the stone age to the bronze age can still, in certain imaginative circumstances, be alive for modern man as distinguishing at least two different kinds of power, or even, it may be, of authority.'[22]

For a poet so concerned with time, archaeology provided an obvious source of inspiration just as did other indicators of the past. The few poems which have as their starting point an archaeological place or object include five written in Italy; several others include such material as a significant element in their ideas. These cannot be examined in isolation, however, for a number of other works present cross-connections in their thinking.

Hardy's architectural knowledge, and its resonance with geology and the past embodied in stone, inevitably found its way into many of his works. Hardy the future poet happened to be born in one of the several parts of Britain which are crammed with prehistoric relics, but the future architect born in *any* part of England would almost inevitably find a rich heritage of buildings – domestic, such as the old family cottage in 'Domicilium' built by his great-grandfather; commercial, as in the centre of Dorchester; fortifications like the two castles in *The Well-Beloved*; ecclesiastical monuments like Sherborne Abbey in *The Woodlanders*; and cultural-academic in *Jude the Obscure*. Hardy's depth of technical knowledge of architecture is immediately apparent in even the most fleeting allusion in the novels – and in four of these an architect is a leading character. In several poems he uses his professional background to reflect on the passage of time, and in particular, he sets the relative permanence of a substantial building against the transience of an individual in some way connected with it.

'The Abbey Mason' (332), for example, is a charming, rather whimsical, piece about the origins of the Perpendicular style, the apogee of the Medieval English Gothic, and gives the poet ample scope to recite some of the jargon of his youthful expertise, such as 'parpend ashlars' (5th coup.), 'ogees' and 'flexures' (20th coup.), 'jambs with transoms' (46th coup.), and 'mullions' (47th coup.). Tom Paulin, however, surely rates the piece too highly as 'one of Hardy's finest poems' because of its theme of 'cooperation between fact and imagination'.[23] However, in its deeply serious subject the poem is a form of meditation upon the nature of creativity and as such transcends its weaknesses. In his professional career, Hardy was engaged in the Victorian Gothic revival, recovering the past by imposing on crumbling medieval churches this quintessentially English style in the numerous restoration commissions given to his employer Hicks of Dorchester (the poem is sub-titled in brackets, 'With Memories of John Hicks, Architect') and his successor Crickmay of Weymouth (who sent him to St Juliot where he met Emma). This topic will receive fuller treatment in Chapter Eight. The narrative rhyming couplets in this poem may, aptly, suggest Chaucer, but the ecclesiastical subject is more reminiscent of, for instance, Richard Harris Barham's 'The Jackdaw of Rheims'. The starting point of this poem is the intriguing but ironic fact that the amount of factual information we have about historic periods does not increase proportionately with nearness to the present. As will become apparent later in this chapter, we know far more about the Parthenon in Athens and its architects in the fifth century BC, despite a residual level of ignorance about the rituals that took place

---
[22] Davie, p.177.
[23] Paulin, p.107.

there, than we do about those of the medieval English cathedrals which are the most enduring of our 'ancient monuments' (and still used for their original purpose). Hardy's notion is that the master mason of Gloucester Abbey (predecessor of the Cathedral with its massively Nor-

Gloucester Cathedral

man interior and elaborate Gothic without) drew up plans for a much altered style of architecture in re-styling the edifice; this is much the same process that Hardy himself was engaged in (and of course Hardy's own father was a master mason). But it was only when 'the hand of God' (55th coup.) intervened in a nocturnal rain shower that attenuated the chalk lines of his drawing, which then froze (so fixing the alteration), that the mason could see how the effect could be achieved. Hardy extends this idea to debate truth and the very nature of artistic creativity and the fame that accompanies it. As always, Hardy feels sympathy for the unfortunate artisan who lost out, and tacit derision for the man of power: the Abbot compels the jubilant mason to admit the origin of his design, so ensuring the 'oblivion dim' (91st coup.) of eternal anonymity, and so he 'wore in death no artist's crown' (84th coup.) (even though the populace acclaimed it as a discovery honestly made) – while the Abbot's name (Wygmore), like all those of his title and rank, is recorded for posterity (Hardy gives a different slant on this theme in 'At The Pyramid of Cestius' (71), where the eponymous and obscure Roman has achieved 'an ample fame' (6th st.) not by his opulent monument but by its proximity to the graves of Keats and Shelley). It is regrettable that Hardy's verse degenerates into McGonagall-esque doggerel for these serious observations (worst near the end with 'From Gloucester church it flew afar- / The style called Perpendicular, - / To Winton and to Westminster / It ranged, and grew still beautifuller' (95th/96th coups.)), but nevertheless, he does honour his family's antecedents and that whole class of creative people which he had left behind in becoming a writer and for whom he never lost his regard – they who, no less than writers, 'did but what all artists do, / Wait upon nature for [their] cue' (88th coup.). They are represented by the anonymous mason whose name was 'of some common kind / And now has faded out of mind' (92nd coup.), and Hardy the poet and mason's son exposes as fatuous the distinction between 'artist' and 'craftsman' – the latter amply and forcefully represented by Jude Fawley.

Wimborne Minster

Similarly forgotten by posterity is 'A Man' (123), perhaps in Dorchester, who refused to work on the demolition of 'a noble pile' from 'shrewd Eliza's' (st. I) reign because it was too beautiful to destroy – an indication of Hardy's conservationist tendency, in contradiction of much of Victorian modernisation. 'None sighed to hear his knell' (st. VI) and he was 'soon forgot', and Hardy pessimistically declares:

> Yet when I pass the spot I long to hold
> As truth what fancy saith:
> 'His protest lives where deathless things abide.' (st. VII)

A very different poem in a similar setting, 'In Sherborne Abbey' (726), is highly reminiscent of the kind of dramatic love incident that occurs in the Wessex novels with Hardy's typical match between lovers from different social strata – it also reflects on the passage of time, and on family lineage. Subtitled with the date (17–), and with the footing 'A Family Tradition', it is a short account of a couple's stratagem to marry – against family wishes – involving the poor young man riding pillion to his heiress-lover in their flight to the church so that he can claim that *she* had abducted *him*! Their pursuers are not the only consideration, however, but mortality distracts the panting fugitives in the Abbey pew as 'Forms round them loom, recumbent like their own' (2nd st.). In a scenario that echoes the bizarre meeting of Alec and Tess at Kingsbere church, Hardy thus cleverly sets the heated immediacy of the as-yet unmarried lovers' plight against the cold permanence of the effigies, the heat of their passion against the 'frigid stone' (2nd st.) of 'stately husbands and wives, side by side as they anciently slept'. The lively expectation that they 'soon shall be [married]' (3rd st.) is placed with tacit irony alongside the implication that, however favourable the turn of events, they must, as Hamlet said, 'to this favour come' when, symbolically, 'they are left in darkness unbroke and profound, / As likewise are left their chill and chiselled neighbours around' (6th st.).

'Copying Architecture in an Old Minster' (369) is also a vehicle for pondering mortality and the perceived insignificance of the mortal individual on finding himself surrounded by tombs, in this case those ranging from 'a Courtenay ... by his quatre-foiled tomb' (4th st.) right back to 'a Saxon king by the presbytery chamber', all to be found in Wimborne Minster which Hardy knew during his residence in the town from 1881 to 1883. The musings, probably autobiographical since it is in the first person, all take place 'In a moment's forgetfulness' (7th st.) and consider the whim that perhaps the dead 'have met for a parle on some plan / To better ail-stricken mankind', but the piece also encompasses the more reasonable and melancholy poetic notion that the architect-poet's visit is but a transient moment in the long history of an ancient building:

> Just so did he clang here before I came,
> And so will he clang when I'm gone
> Through the Minster's cavernous hollows – the same
> Tale of hours never more to be will he deliver
> To the speechless midnight and dawn! (2nd st.)

The same kind of melancholy thoughts come to the poet while 'Drawing Details in an Old Church' (655) reflecting the insignificance of the individual in the stream of Time. While he sits alone copying 'What some Gothic brain designed' (1st st.), he hears the tolling of the knell for some unknown parishioner and he anticipates that one day his own passing bell will sound in the ears of a stranger in the place – an idea that links with the earlier 'A Man' (123). Intimations of mortality in a robustly black-comedic vein are served up in Hardy's sombrely humorous 'The Levelled Churchyard' (127), also from the Wimborne interlude, but which clearly harks back to the poet's graveyard clearing work for Blomfield. Here the dead in the churchyard complain loudly that under their 'wrenched memorial stones' (1st st.) they are being 'Mixed to human jam' (2nd st.), the dust of a 'modest maiden elf' confused with 'some sturdy strumpet' (5th st.).

***

Hardy's lifelong interest in the Napoleonic era, perhaps the single most persistent manifestation of his preoccupation with the past, led the author to collect a Napoleonic library and to pursue research in the British Museum; indeed, in the Hardys' first visit to the London 'Season', in 1883, he deliberately found accommodation that was convenient for visiting the Museum. Weber comments that 'Hardy's historical research was done with extreme care,'[24] research that principally bore fruit eventually in the long-gestating *The Dynasts* as well as *The Trumpet-Major* and the short story *A Tradition of Eighteen Hundred and Four*. Nowadays, of course, Hardy would have done his chosen research at the British Library and would not have so frequently encountered the archaeological collections. However, incidental products of his research include an interesting short poem, 'In the British Museum' (315), a piece which shows exactly the kind of *imaginative* response to the traces of the past that the great archaeologists exhibit. It is not alone in betraying Hardy's close familiarity with the Museum's archaeological collections: in *A Pair of Blue Eyes* chapter 38, Henry Knight is found in 'the gloomy corridors of the British Museum' (*A Pair of Blue Eyes* p.353), and in *The Hand of Ethelberta*, Christopher and Faith have a conversation in the Museum while looking at 'bas-reliefs from Nineveh' (*The Hand of Ethelberta* p.177) where Hardy adds considerable detail, and has Faith respond to the sculptures, declaring, 'Don't you feel as if you were actually in Nineveh?'. The same monumental exhibits are fleetingly alluded to in the story *On the Western Circuit* in a simile that only an archaeology 'buff' would coin: the lawyer wears a wig 'curled in tiers, in the best fashion of Assyrian bas-reliefs' (*The Complete Stories* pp.429/430) – and the characters walk 'out of the city to the earthworks of Old Melchester [Old Sarum]', the nearby archaeological site, just a few lines later. In *A Laodicean*, the medieval Stancy Castle is to be made to conform to Classical taste with the addition of 'a Greek colonnade ... and statues like those in the British Museum' (*A Laodicean* p.71).

In the poem named for the venerable Museum ('In The British Museum', 315), Hardy conducts a dialogue with a 'labouring man' (7th st.), a class for whom Hardy retained an enduring respect in, for instance, 'The Dorsetshire Labourer', and whom he used as the source of so many minor characters and 'rustic choruses' in his fiction – though his often humorous take on them was not popular in his home area.. The two speculate on a stone in the Museum, 'the base of a pillar, they'll tell you, / That came to us / From a far old hill men used to name / Areopagus' (3rd st.). The precise identity of this stone is uncertain, and Hardy seems rather to be using the Museum's wealth of decontextualized archaeological material to draw poetic inspiration and make an imaginative and highly personal response. My inquiry to the Department of Greek and Roman Antiquities at the Museum received the following reply from Dr J. Lesley Fitton, Curator in the Department:

> I have consulted both our records of objects from Athens and my colleagues, but have not tracked down a column-base from the Areopagus. This is rather disappointing since the poem is so specific – but I suppose we must conclude that Hardy was using poetic licence. Perhaps he was struck by the thought that our fragments here might generally have echoed the voice of Paul, and then attached the thought specifically to an area where Athenian assemblies took place.[25]

The Areopagos, to use the Hellenised spelling, is the squat hill (probably from the Greek

---

[24] Weber, p.239.
[25] J. Lesley Fitton, Curator, British Museum Department of Greek and Roman Antiquities, letter dated 8/8/01.

Ares, god of war, though the etymology is not certain) opposite the Acropolis in Athens and the site (and thus, name) of an aristocratic council of great antiquity which lasted, shorn of all its previous political power, until the fourth century AD. The labourer, like Hardy the churchman, recognised the name from Acts chapter 17 when Paul addressed the Athenians there on the subject of the one true God in this noted centre of polytheism and idolatry. It is the voice of Hardy's humble labourer who has the sensitivity and imagination to respond to his interlocutor:

> I'm a labouring man, and know but little,
> Or nothing at all;
> But I can't help thinking that stone once echoed
> The voice of Paul. (7th st.)

A comparable imaginative response to a trace of the past is shown to a stuffed bird in 'In a Museum' (358), a mere 'mould of a musical bird long passed from light' (st. I) whose song is in some mystical way transmuted into immortality, like Keats's nightingale 'not born for death'. Here, 'Such a dream is Time', that the notes are blent 'In the full-fugued song of the universe unending', an inescapably Keatsian line. Paradoxically, Keats's late sonnet 'On Seeing the Elgin Marbles' seems to anticipate Hardyesque sentiments with the solidity of the ancient artefact 'That mingles Grecian grandeur with the rude / Wasting of old time' being a sharp reminder that 'mortality weighs heavily' on the young poet near to death, just as it continued to confront Hardy into old age; the philosophical melancholy of Keats's musing on the Grecian urn has been intensified into 'an indescribable feud … A most dizzy pain'.

However, 'In the British Museum' is more closely linked in its subject and theme with ''ΑΓΝΩΣΤΩΙ ΘΕΩΙ' (151) ("Agnostoi Theoi' – 'To the Unknown God'), which title Hardy gives like this in Greek characters. This poem is concerned specifically with the actual theme of St Paul's speech to the ancient Council of the Areopagos in Athens: the title is the phrase which the apostle included in the opening of his address: 'For as I passed along, and observed the objects of your worship, I found also an altar with this inscription, 'To an unknown god'. What therefore you worship as unknown, this I proclaim to you.' (Acts ch17 v23, RSV). Hardy the agnostic – the latter a term coined by T.H. Huxley (whom Hardy knew) in 1869 from the same Greek root as the poem's title – gives an ironic turn to Paul's use of the phrase by apostrophically musing on one of whom he has 'Long … framed weak phantasies' (1st st.) but 'Nought shows to us ephemeral ones' (2nd st.). Here, Hardy sets himself, one feels with some sadness as well as frustration, against the simple yet imaginative faith of the working man in the previous poem. We might also feel that this deity is the 'unknown god' whom Hardy could not know. The powerful ambivalence of Hardy's social and political sympathies are borne out in a quite contrary impression given in a remark in the *Life* (p.236), underlining Hardy's fatalism, but significantly in this context, showing some contempt for the mass of ordinary people who pay no attention, let alone any kind of intelligent imagination, to the Museum's rich legacy of the past:

> Next day – wet – at the British Museum: Crowds parading and gaily traipsing round the mummies, thinking today is forever, and the girls casting sly glances at the swathed dust of Mycerinus [?] [Hardy's own query in squared brackets – an indicator

of his concern for strict accuracy of fact in 1891 under the influence of Pitt-Rivers and Petrie]. They pass with flippant comments the illuminated MSS. – the labours of years [we might think of the similar labours of years of the novelist or stonemason here] – and stand under Rameses the Great, joking. Democratic government may be justice to man, but it will probably merge in proletarian, and when these people are our masters it will lead to more of this contempt, and possibly be the utter ruin of art and literature!

A late poem (dated '1905 and 1926'), 'Christmas in the Elgin Room' (917) returns to the 'British Museum: Early Last Century' as the subtitle declares. Unlike its predecessor 'In the British Museum' (315), there is no mystery about the archaeological objects referred to in this piece; they are among the best known and most controversial ancient artefacts in any museum. Lord Elgin had brought the Parthenon marble sculptures from Athens between 1801 and 1811 and made the celebrated artefacts a *cause célèbre* which stirs, if anything, greater passions today than ever, with all its connotations of cultural imperialism and national identity. There is a fortuitous Napoleonic connection here too, since Elgin, whose subsequent life was to be a catalogue of disasters, was arrested in 1803 on his way back from the Levant and held by the French until1806. The luckless peer sold the marbles, at a huge loss, to the Nation in 1816 and they were housed in the Elgin Gallery, at first a shed until a permanent room was provided where Hardy saw them (and where they remained until the Duveen Gallery was finished in 1938). The sculptures were made to adorn the Parthenon (the Temple of Athena Parthenos, Athena the virgin) on the Acropolis of Athens built in the late fifth century BC as the crowning glory of the triumphant city-state that led the defeat of the Persians. Pheidias was their sculptor, and the reference to him, and the use of the Classical Greek form of the feminine plural 'Athenai' for the City's name, forcefully remind us of Hardy's wide reading and not inconsiderable scholarship. In *A Laodicean*, Hardy alludes to the Parthenon sculptures with William Dare lying erotically like an 'unpedestaled Dionysus' (*A Laodicean* p.125). As with 'In the British Museum' (315), the poet in the Elgin Room piece again eschews pure abstraction or subjective debate, preferring a more imaginative approach, in this case, allowing these famous figurative sculptures the added dimensions of intellect and voice to be his medium for philosophical reflection. Again, Christianity is his theme; indeed two years before his death and living an old age in the wake of the Great War, Hardy was more than ever pessimistic about the world and sceptical of the faith which had been the unquestioned universal norm of his childhood. There is little overt agnosticism in this poem, however, and none of the barely restrained bitterness of 'And There Was a Great Calm' (545), which I shall mention shortly, though one of the statues says dismissively of Christmas, ''Tis said to have been a day of cheer, / And source of grace / To the human race' ('Christmas in the Elgin Room' 2nd st.) – rather, the poet presents a kind of tacit yearning for a golden age which happened to be pagan ('We are those whom Christmas overthrew ... (3rd st.) / Before this Christ was known, and we had men's goodwill' (5th st.)). The poem is about other concerns, too, musing on the principles underpinning archaeology and museology rather than solely a reflection on the passage of time. Hardy is clearly uneasy at the incongruity of these works ('us captives' (1st st.) in 'exile here' (2nd st.)), made in order to adorn a specific building in the Mediterranean sun, bought for hard cash and ranged in the gloom of a London room in mid-winter:

> O it is sad now we are sold –
> We gods! For Borean people's gold,
> And brought to the gloom
> Of this gaunt room
> Which sunlight shuns, and sweet Aurore but enters cold. (4th st.)

This aesthetic-archaeological sensibility is a modern attitude and shows Hardy, as always, to be very much up-to-date in his thinking. In it he anticipates not only the late twentieth-century policy of keeping artefacts as far as possible in their original context (whether *in situ* or in a local museum), but his words closely prefigure those of the Hellenophile Rex Warner in his 1953 book *Eternal Greece* when he wishes that the Elgin (Parthenon) Marbles could be restored to 'their proper place' because they were meant for the 'free and brilliant air and to be seen against a landscape that is absolutely unique', and not 'put ... in cages'; he declares: 'nor can I follow the argument of those to say that it is 'better' for these marbles to be seen in the wrong light, in the wrong place, at the wrong elevation and by the wrong people simply because such people are numerous.'[26]

By 1920, Hardy was a living legend, part of the fabric of English literary history, and still reflecting in his writings on immediate historic events as well as on those of the distant past. It might be instructive to compare his imaginative treatment of the Athenians' triumphal 'war memorial', the Parthenon, with his "And there was a Great Calm" (545) (to set against what had become known as the Great War, presumably) which was written at the request of the Times and published in its Armistice Supplement on 11th November 1920, the same day that Edwin Lutyens's Cenotaph was unveiled in Whitehall. The contrast in tone of this memorial could hardly be more different from the pious triumphalism of the Parthenon, and Hardy amplifies, rather than merely represents, the National mood about the War in this occasional 'public' poem, writing: 'The Spirit of Irony smirked' (st. VII) and 'Philosophies that sages long had taught, / And Selflessness, were as an unknown thought ...' (st. II).

Hardy's direct connection with the Classical world – beyond his wide reading and study of architecture, that is – was limited to a visit to Italy with Emma in March-April of 1887, a tour more limited but less final than those of his predecessors Byron, Keats, and Shelley. Here, as in Wessex, he was surrounded by monumental and decayed relics of the ancient past. He was also presented with one of the truisms of archaeology, that is the sharp distinction between the mysterious *prehistoric* nature of much of 'Northern' archaeology (a cloud which obscured a good deal of the subsequent Roman and Anglo-Saxon epochs as well) and the sunlit histori-cally-informed density of the Mediterranean world, replete with literary sources from the *Iliad* to Pausanias. This was the dichotomy which led to prehistoric archaeology being discounted as barbarous and unworthy by such institutions as the British Museum even long after the discovery of the Greek Bronze Age, which had the advantage of being legitimised by Homer.

The Hardys covered a good deal of ground in a relatively short time, but Hardy did manage to produce a group of seven poems from Italy alone, written retrospectively after returning to England (though the *Life*, p.189, notes of 'At The Pyramid of Cestius' (71): 'probably not written till later'). The origins of this group of works are explained in Chapter XV of the *Life*,

---

[26] Rex Warner and Martin Hurlimann (photographer), Eternal Greece (London: Thames and Hudson, 1953), p.17.

'Italian Journey'. The effect of Italy upon Hardy's sensibilities was powerful, almost to a morbid degree; he notes: 'After some days spent in the Holy City Hardy began to feel, he frequently said, its measureless layers of history to lie upon him like a physical weight.' (*Life* p.188). Carl J. Weber indicates Hardy's almost instinctively connecting things archaeological with human woes: 'In a quotation form Samuel Rogers's *Italy* , Hardy underlined 'The old cares are left clustering around the old objects' ... '.[27] For one of Hardy's sensitivity this might explain why he did not write more on this subject matter – and even why this archaeological enthusiast did not travel to the celebrated buried cities of the Bay of Naples. There is no hint of any definite reason in the *Life*. In Rome, Hardy explicitly confronts the ambivalence of his attitude to ruined buildings, his perception straining between the eye of the professional architect (and scientific archaeologist?) and the inner eye of the creative artist fascinated by time and its effects:

> The time of their visit was not so long after the peeling of the Colosseum and other ruins of their vast accumulations of parasitic growths, which, though Hardy as an architect defended the much-deplored process on the score of its absolute necessity if the walls were to be preserved, he yet wished had not been taken in hand till after his inspection of them. This made the ruins of the ancient city, the 'altae moenia Romae' as he called them from the *Aeneid,* more gaunt to the vision and more depressing to the mind than they had been to visitors when covered with greenery ... .[28]

One might speculate as to whether Hardy's preference for the aesthetically pleasing greenery does not betray a longing for the archaeology of Wessex, blent verdantly into the landscape, and whether this preference does not explain his relative artistic indifference to the vast stone remains of Classical antiquity. The same dichotomy of mind – at once the architect and the imaginative artist - is apparent in the note (*Life* p.189*)* that 'probably from some surviving architectural instinct, he made a few measurements in the Via Appia Antica, where he was obsessed by a vision of a chained file of prisoners plodding wearily along towards Rome, one of the most haggard of whom was to be famous through the ages as the founder of Pauline Christianity.' It must be regretted that this vision did not lead to a poem. In St Mark's, Venice, the combination of factual artistic knowledge with heightened artistic imagination is apparent in the comment (*Life* p.193) on '... wonderful diaphanous alabaster pillars that were once in Solomon's Temple.'

'Shelley's Skylark' (66), written 'In the neighbourhood of Leghorn' shows his acute awareness of the poignancy of his journey in respect of his artistic forebears. In a link with the stuffed bird 'In a Museum' (358), Hardy again recalls Keats's 'immortal bird' in this musing upon the 'The dust of the lark that Shelley heard, / And made immortal through times to be' (2nd st.). The birds in these two poems of Hardy's are, like so many of the individual human beings in his works, insubstantial glimmers of no account in the great sweep of time, unknowingly finding significance by chance. This creature 'knew not its immortality', but deserves 'a casket silver-lined / And framed of gold ('Shelley's Skylark' 5th st.) ... For it inspired a bard to win / Ecstatic heights in thought and rhyme' (6th st.).

In Rome, Hardy simultaneously expressed, through his enthusiasm for archaeology over

---
[27] Weber, p.43.
[28] Life p.188.

the more recent legacy of the Renaissance *et al* (and this despite his expert interest in the visual arts), his religious scepticism, declaring that (*Life* p.190*)* 'he was on the whole more interested in Pagan than in Christian Rome, of the latter preferring churches in which he could detect columns from ancient temples.' Even in more general observations, the same sentiments are conveyed: 'The quality of the faces in the streets of Rome: Satyrs: Emperors: Faustinas' (*Life* p.189). Five of the poems are inspired directly by archaeology, and 'Rome: At the Pyramid of Cestius near the Graves of Keats and Shelley' (71) is not only a homage, but also a comment on the ironies of fame and accidents of anonymity over the course of centuries: in fact, it is a human counterpart to Shelley's bird who by accident of time and place found 'an ample fame' (6th st.). The obscure Roman ('what is he to me?' (1st st.) asks Hardy), represented by his grandiose monument, 'Whose purpose was expressed not with its first design' (3rd sty.) is now known solely because of its ability to locate the graves of 'Those matchless singers' (5th st.). Hardy remarks the irony that 'through Time' (6th st.) Cestius has found a kind of immortality – not by the opulence and size of his memorial alone, but by its fortuitously convenient site. Years later, Hardy's admiration for Keats linked this poem with his home area in 'At Lulworth Cove a Century Back' (556) in which he plays the role of a wearily apathetic local man who has seen 'So commonplace a youth (2nd st.) ... an idling town-sort; thin ...' (3rd st.) pointed out to him: it is the unrecognised and doomed Keats pausing during his final voyage near Hardy's home in September 1820. The piece concludes 'A hundred years and the world will follow him there, / And bend with reverence where his ashes lie' (5th st.) – which is just what Hardy did.

Hardy had followed both Keats and Shelley a little earlier in his poetry-writing as well, for both of these 'matchless singers' had been inspired by visits to the British Museum: Shelley wrote his great sonnet 'Ozymandias' in response to seeing the huge dismembered granite head of Ramesses II which still dominates the Egyptian Sculpture Gallery at the Museum; Keats, with a more generalised inspiration from the large collection of Classical pottery, wrote his 'Ode on a Grecian Urn'.

Hardy grew up in a Roman district and lived in a Roman town. His fascination 'In the Old Theatre, Fiesole' (67) is transformed to delight by 'a child who showed an ancient coin / That bore the image of a Constantine' (1st st.). The poet in his 'distant plot of English loam' (3rd st.) found 'coins of like impress' and so this simple act by one of the species of humble, unremarkable persons who were so important to Hardy proved a revelation:

> ... As with one half blind
> Whom common simples cure, her act flashed home
> In that mute moment to my opened mind
> The power, the pride, the reach of perished Rome.

So it is the individual human being who becomes as important and powerful (in a sense) for Hardy as what the coin symbolises. Even the coin itself is made significant not by mere design, but by another individual, by the profile of a proud ancient, dead, emperor - a neatly ironic juxtaposition with the humble, modern, living child; Tom Paulin remarks that a 'memory is sparked by a profile.'[29]

Fiesole, not far from Florence, was ancient Faesulae, an Etruscan town – as Hardy puts

---

[29] Paulin, p.117.

it, 'Where Rome and dim Etruria interjoin' (1ˢᵗ st.). The distinctive culture of the Etruscans suffered the neglect of other ancient cultures outside the main Classical continuum, being eclipsed historically by the power of Rome and in artistic orthodoxy by its Graeco-Roman and Renaissance successors in Italy. Despite the discoveries of the nineteenth century, Etruria has always suffered a comparative neglect of interest as Hardy shows in his choice of the adjective 'dim' which perhaps betrays a hint of distaste at the hegemony of the city on the Tiber whither they were bound. Hardy's fascination with the Roman Empire was not unmixed: his awe at the achievement is set against his loathing of its oppression and brutality, and equalled by his strong perception here of the vanity and transience of human power – a sentiment which strongly resembles the thinking of Shelley in 'Ozymandias'. The recognition of the coin shown by the child also reminds us of Hardy's strong interest in archaeology and his practical involvement, albeit on a relatively small scale, in that discipline on his home ground. Incidentally, Hardy commits a familiar solecism in the *Life* (p.192) by referring to the theatre as 'the stone Amphitheatre' (sic), though the poem title corrects the *faux pas*. An amphitheatre is not simply any open-air or ancient theatre, but, according to its Greek etymology, a 'double theatre' like the Colosseum. The venerable Liddell and Scott (whose work forms the subject of Hardy's poem 'Liddell and Scott – on the Completion of their Lexicon' (828)) explain it as: 'a double theatre, a space wholly surrounded by seats rising one behind another, so as to command a view of the whole arena (the word, like the thing itself, first occurring after the introduction of Roman customs).'[30] This slip, though minor, is thrice surprising, since Hardy was not only a Classical scholar, but an architect, and a cognoscente of archaeology to boot!

A quite different experience is recounted while wandering in the ruins of 'Rome: On the Palatine' (68) (one of the ancient city's seven hills), 'investigating the remains of Caligula's palace' (*Life* p.189). At first, the poet is able, through his imaginative engagement, to visualise each ancient building at a superficial level 'as though / It wore its marble gleams, its pristine glow' (2ⁿᵈ st.); but it is with the aid of that most abstract and immediately affective of the arts, music, that the evocation is complete and he is transported, on hearing 'on strings nigh overhead, / ... [ironically, even bizarrely] A waltz by Strauss' (3ʳᵈ st.) which 'blended pulsing life with lives long done, / Till Time seemed fiction, Past and Present one' (closing couplet). Again, Time is personified and thereby accorded special phenomenal power over the individual lives that it embraces and then swallows. Byron in his Grand Tour poetry may have lamented the passing of the ancient world, and deplored the characteristic barbarism of the Colosseum where the gladiator was famously (in *Childe Harold's Pilgrimage* Canto 4 stanza 141) 'Butchered to make a Roman holiday', but Hardy is more interested in the general effects of the passage of time and the sobering lesson it teaches about the transience of the individual. The past also returns to haunt the present in 'Rome: Building a New Street in the Ancient Quarter' (69) in which the capital is dubbed 'Time's central City' (1ˢᵗ st.) (remembering Revd John William Burgon's 1845 poem 'Petra', 'a rose-red city 'half as old as time'', perhaps?). Here Hardy imagines, in what seems very much an architect's poem, a 'caustic monitory gnome' (2ⁿᵈ st.) – a kind of superintendent spirit of the ancient edifices – scorning the 'frail' (3ʳᵈ st.), insubstantial modern constructions rising among the solid but broken remnants. With more than a criticism of these 'feeble works', the spirit upbraids the builders, 'Dunces, here learn to

---

[30] Liddell and Scott, Greek-English Lexicon, 7th ed. (London, 1897).

spell Humanity!' (2nd st.) – if the gigantic piles of the past have been so degraded by time, then how much more importunate should be the lesson apparent in these latest, far more ephemeral constructions to their unthinking builders.

'The Vatican: Sala delle Muse' (70) provides a counterpart to the three English museum poems. One of the suite of Vatican antiquities museums, which house, *inter alia*, the world's largest collection of ancient sculpture, includes the 'Hall of the Muses' referred to here by its Italian name, in the sculpture section of the Museo Pio-Clementino which occupies two floors of the Belvedere Pavilion. The room contains seven of the nine muses from a villa near Tivoli, ancient Tibur, thought to be copies of possibly bronze originals from the school of Praxiteles, though probably not from the same group. Inspired by the fact that the group is arranged as if in conversation, Hardy is driven to exaggerated imaginative lengths and to an awkwardly self-conscious archaism of style in a dialogue with one of the muses in the heady ambience of ancient beauty. More prosaic, if not cynical, is his own explanation, that 'his nearly falling asleep in the Salla delle Muse in the Vatican was the source of another poem, the weariness being the effect of the deadly fatiguing size of St Peter's' – significantly for this sceptic, the world's premier Christian edifice (*Life* p.189). His anxiety expressed in the poem is clearly that he longs, in the presence of the muses, to be competent in other art forms as well as his own, inspired as he feels by such paradigms of ancient beauty. The consolation offered by the muse as the poem closes is that the author should be grateful to be proficient in even one sphere of creativity: 'Grieve not nor thyself becall, / Woo where thou wilt; and rejoice thou canst love at all' (6th st.). Speaking ghosts or personified visions are a not infrequent, and one of the less satisfactory, features of Hardy's poetry. Davie comments:

> The status of Hardy's ghosts is very hard to determine. On the one hand, they seem to be merely Virgilian stage properties ... some of Hardy's ghosts are more 'real' than others ... .[31]

***

An important inference can be drawn from Hardy's poems set in the British Museum and Italy. He was very evidently, as a trained architect and as an enthusiast for the arts and for the science of archaeology, very familiar with the archaeological and artistic legacy of the Classical world, much of which came to be understood more fully, if not discovered, in his own lifetime. The scarcity of his allusions to and use of specifically Classical *archaeology* (as opposed to the innumerable literary references drawn from his omnivorous reading) and the frequent and natural, one might almost claim inevitable, employment of Wessex archaeology, must therefore be seen as a matter of deliberate choice, a fundamental component of the underlying substance of Hardy's art. I include in this remark his use of the Roman component of Wessex archaeology, since the relative sparseness of documentary sources for Roman Britain make it a rather different case from the heart of the Roman world in the Mediterranean basin. I have already suggested that the archaeology of Wessex in its greenness is more appealing aesthetically to Hardy; his strong preference for that of his own home region specifically, together with its prehistoric and thus more enigmatic character, can therefore complete the rationale for

---

[31] Davie, p.45.

Hardy's eschewal of the dazzling archaeology of the Mediterranean world that so enthralled his contemporaries and was a catalyst for the popularisation of archaeology.

Commentators often refer to the mass of allusions in Hardy's works that are drawn from his reading. Michael Millgate, for instance, remarks:

> No reader can fail to notice – and few critics have failed to deplore – the ponderous allusions to literature and art which strew with their initial capitals pages of Hardy's early novels. Traces of his deliberate and painstaking acquisition of the knowledge that these allusions represent remain in the reading lists preserved in *Early Life* and in surviving notebooks.[32]

– and this acerbic comment could be made with almost equal force about the later prose as well. In contrast, neither Hardy's references to architecture nor his allusions to archaeology spring only – or even primarily – from book learning and notebooks, but from more immediate experience. His knowledge of and passion for these subjects is not that of the reader or dabbler, for architecture was Hardy's profession and he was surrounded by archaeological remains in which in later life he became increasingly and actively interested. As I have shown in Chapter Three, in his maturity he lived actually within an archaeological site which he excavated, he belonged to a venerable learned society, and it was deemed quite appropriate for the press to ask him to write with authority on the subject. But for all his evident expertise in archaeology, it is as a local man who is accustomed to ancient remains that he writes of and refers to the subject in his literary work quite naturally, and without any self-consciously learned terminology. 'Expert' Hardy may be to a degree, but – despite the listings from other subjects – he is too much the creative artist to enumerate slavishly the technicalities (many of them newly coined during his lifetime) about archaeological sites that are so much a part of his own cultural inheritance. Further, it is unsurprising that a poet so obsessed with the subject of time should not only find direct inspiration in the local archaeology for a number of poems, but also effortlessly include fleeting allusions to it in so many other works as we have seen, for example, in *The Mayor of Casterbridge*. Thus we find that the ubiquitous burial mounds and other evidences of the ancient past are seldom far from the poet's mind when he makes his home area his subject, whether the theme be time or otherwise. Isolated from the elements of character and narrative which dominate prose, the poems which include archaeological reference perhaps reveal more clearly the way Hardy regards the subject of archaeology and how he uses it in his art.

A range of such poems refers to the prehistoric and Roman remains familiar to Hardy in his Wessex surroundings; all of them use archaeology to in some way give a temporal depth to the subject, stressing the present as transitory in the great sweep of human history and firmly placing into such a context individuals and their lives. The anti-war piece 'Channel Firing' (247), written in early 1914 when conflict seemed inevitable, imagines that the gunnery practice off Portland naval base is quite literally enough to wake the dead. The dead aroused imagine that it is the last trump, and this bizarre idea allows Hardy some sardonic comments about the immutably destructive nature of war through the centuries – a kind of inverted perspective of 'In Time of "The Breaking of Nations"' (500), in which lovers' rites will long outlive 'War's

---

[32] Millgate, Career, p.39.

The Nine Stones, Winterbourne Abbas

annals' (st. III). The poem ends hauntingly in the remark that the guns' reports can be heard 'as far inland as Stourton Tower, / And Camelot and starlit Stonehenge' ('Channel Firing' 9th st.), a fleeting reminder of *Tess*. Camelot was probably identifiable to Hardy as Glastonbury, though this is much too far away, or as one of the Wessex hill-forts. However exaggerated the distance (Stonehenge is over forty miles from the coast near Portland), this surreal image of mythical places, serene in the night despite the booming omens of a new and terrible conflict, is beautifully calculated to emphasise the point of the poem while mitigating some of the weirdness of the dead conversing with God. Another poem reverberates with the fear of imminent conflict, in this case one that did not, in the event, transpire as anticipated. 'The Alarm' (26) also sets the peaceful permanence of the Wessex downlands against the threat of the traumatic violence of war, in this case the expected Napoleonic invasion that is the scenario of *A Tradition of Eighteen Hundred and Four,* and *The Trumpet-Major,* and which opens Part the First, Act One of *The Dynasts*. The false alarm that rouses the country is subtitled '(Traditional) In memory of one of the writer's family who was a volunteer during the war with Napoleon' indeed, this piece and other narrative poems in this section do possess much of the character of a ballad, reminding us that Hardy's first successful novel, *Under the Greenwood Tree,* has a celebration of traditional music-making in his own family as its subject, and one that provided undimmed fascination as he grew older. Hardy was fascinated with his forebears and their involvement with the conflict that so marked the generations immediately preceding his own birth – especially the possibility that he was a direct descendant of Captain Hardy of HMS *Victory*. Here, as in the novel in which that famous ship figures, the distant past is represented archaeologically by the immovable 'grim Mai-Don [sic]' ('The Alarm' 19th st.) as well as

The Roman Great Bath, Bath

by 'the steep Ridge-way'. The use of the highest-placed Bronze Age barrow as the convenient site for a beacon has a close parallel with *The Return of the Native,* of course, and the tumulus carries the usual sombre connotation of mortality. But in this case, the pointedly alliterative 'Barrow-Beacon burning' (13th st.) indicates an immediate and telling link between the long-undisturbed peace of the ancient dead and the dramatic immediacy of the threatened invasion: the barrow is thus both a general indicator of the brevity of individual lives (the Bronze Age barrow being originally the site of a single noble burial – a fact of which Hardy may well have been aware) and a solemn omen of the inevitable result of the battle that seems imminent. The beacon fire also connotes cremation and perhaps also the fiery hell of battle.

'After the Club-Dance' (196) and 'After the Fair' (200) are two of a sequence of seven short pieces entitled 'At Casterbridge Fair'. The former starts 'Black'on [Blackdown] frowns east on Maidon' (After the Club-Dance 1st st.), marking the long ancestry of the current fair and introducing a sombre note to the first person reflection of a girl who 'left the jocund bevy / And that young man o' mine' (2nd st,). The last of the four stanzas of the latter poem explicitly underlines the long continuity of the life of a Roman town like Casterbridge, its citizens being just 'the latest far back to those Roman hosts / Whose remains one yet sees, / Who loved, laughed, and fought, hailed their friends, drank their toasts / At their meeting-times here just as these!' ('After the Fair' 4th st.).

The age of the landscape and the affective possibilities of its association with the drama of individual lives are strong features of three first person narrative poems. 'Her Death and After' (27) is a somewhat mawkish tale of a man who achieves the guardianship of his late lover's child, as a kind of souvenir of her, by lying to the dead woman's remarried husband that he was actually the child's father. The man went to visit the dying wife in the absence of her uncaring husband 'By the way of the Western Wall' (1st st.) – the only surviving section of the Roman wall of Dorchester – to hear her wish that he should bring up the child: 'that I could insert a deed back in Time, I'd make her yours' (9th st.) she declares. She is buried 'where the earthworks [Maumbury Rings, 'Casterbridge Ring'] frowned' (11th st.). Another clear connection with the places as well as the themes and events of *The Mayor of Casterbridge* is that after one of his visits to the woman's grave, the lover meets the husband at the Ring, 'the cirque of the gladiators ... / That haggard mark of Imperial Rome, / Whose pagan echoes mock the chime / Of our Christian time' (16th st.) near the wife's grave (Again, Hardy rarely misses the chance of a sardonic remark about the 'newer' faith, especially in the context of a more ancient predecessor, nor is the barbarism of Rome omitted). The macabre associations of the place fit well the weird compact to be made and the cynical attitude of the husband in casually disposing of a life: 'The sun's gold touch was scarce displaced / From the vast arena where men once bled, / When her husband followed' (17th st.). One fleeting – and it must be admitted, tenuous, archaeological allusion is in the 'The Burghers' (23), one of several dramatic love narratives set in the past (this is subtitled '(17 -)'). In the second stanza, Hardy's narrator, betrayed in love, states: 'The level flare [of sunset] raked pane and pediment / And my wrecked face, ...' (2nd

Eggardon hillfort

st.). In context, this phrase 'wrecked face' could ambiguously refer not only to the distraught narrator's, but also to the grinning Roman mask sculpture (damaged by the elements and by the stones of generations of passing children) which had once seen service as a keystone on the front of Colliton House, and which is now in the Dorchester Museum, as mentioned in Chapter Four. Typically of Hardy, the grin is thus a coldly acid – and immutable – comment on the swift-moving and emotionally heated situation of the eternal triangle, as well as giving an extra historic dimension to the piece. It is indeed worth emphasising that so much of the archaeological material employed by Hardy is of cold, unchanging stone which provides an ironic contrast to the livid heat of transient human passions. 'My Cicely' (31) is a not dissimilar poem also set in the eighteenth century. Here, the lover, apparently in London ('the city / of frenzy-led factions' (3rd st.)) discovers that his sweetheart is not dead but living in 'far Exonb'ry' (6th st.) (Exeter). His impetuous ride at dawn to verify the shock news is made the more powerful by its passing the stolid permanence of archaeological features along the route: 'the bleak hill-graves of chieftains' (8th st.), 'Stour-bordered Forum [Blandford Forum] where legions had wayfared (10th st.)', 'Triple-ramparted Maidon [which] gloomed grayly' (13th st.) (– Hardy never forgot the sinister history of the place), 'The hill-fortress of Eggar', 'The nine-pillared cromlech'(14th st.). 'Eggar' is Eggardon Camp, an impressive hill-fort atop Eggardon Hill, West of Dorchester, and the 'cromlech' (Celtic for an arched, flat stone) must be the 'Nine Stones' circle near Winterborne Abbas – though, puzzlingly for sites so close to home, these two are listed here in the wrong sequence for travelling West. Beyond this point, Hardy is less secure in his topography; he knew his local landscape well, though his grasp of the wider Wessex is only secure in areas where he had made detailed visits: Hawkins notes that the ' 'nine-pillar'd cromlech' is the last precise landmark mentioned by Hardy as his itinerary passes into less familiar country.'[33] After discovering that the beloved is married – beneath her station – and is now a middle-aged hosteler, he retraces his steps, this time the long journey's archaeological landmarks condensed movingly into one telling stanza of ironic indifference to his own disappointment in the way in which Hardy so often employs archaeological allusion:

> Uptracking where legions had wayfared
> By cromlechs unstoried,
> And lynchets, and sepultured chieftains,
> In self-colloquy, (25th st.)

A lynchet is a familiar archaeological landscape feature, from the Old English for a ridge or ledge formed by ancient ploughing on a slope.

'The Revisitation' (152) is a comparable narrative, this time by a soldier who, finding himself again at a barracks which had been a youthful posting, decides on a whim to ride out at night to the site of a brief romance. After an enchanted night with the rediscovered lover, alas, 'Time's transforming chisel' (28th st.) has done its worst, for the daylight reveals her wrinkled features, and the magic is dispelled – as much, we feel, by the unrealistic expectations of the man as by the fact of ageing – by 'this trick on us of Time' (33rd st.) as he puts it. On the way to revisit his old haunts, he reaches the upland and tells how 'Round about me bulged the barrows / As before in antique silence – immemorial funeral piles – / Where the sleek herds trampled daily the remains of flint-tipt arrows (10th st.) / ... And the Sarsen stone there, dateless, / On whose breast we had sat ...' (11th st.). This brief inclusion of the 'silent', 'dateless' archaeology of the landscape is skilfully understated, woven into the personal details of the tale, and thereby lends a thought-provoking extra perspective to the piece that helps to make it a more successful, less sentimental poem than the two preceding works. Sarsen is the silicified sandstone (mostly found in Wiltshire) used for building many of the South's prehistoric monuments, most famously the trilithons of Stonehenge.

---

[33] Hawkins, p.110.

Personal Memories and Ancient Remains: The Poetry

The Druid Stone, Max Gate

***

Eight poems use archaeological subjects in Wessex as their starting point, or even their inspiration. They form an interesting complement to the group written in Rome on subjects more familiar and more traditionally appealing to the Romantic imagination of Hardy's artistic forebears. These home-based works, evenly divided between the prehistoric and the Roman legacy of the poet's home area, make use of the same archaeology as *The Mayor of Casterbridge.* However, they focus our attention more acutely on the implications of ancient remains in the manner of lyric, rather than as part of the complex of temporally significant allusion in the novel.

One poem is set in Somerset, near the northern edge of Wessex, in 'Aquae Sulis' (308) (The Waters of Sulis Minerva- which is the Roman name for Bath). Most of Britain's Roman towns are covered by their modern equivalents, and at Bath, as at York, a major Christian church lies directly over the centre of the Roman site. Bath's Roman remains began to be discovered as long ago as 1790 and the elegant Georgian spa echoed the sumptuous predecessor upon which it was built, for Bath is 'Rome's most famous witness in Britain after Hadrian's Wall. And rightly so, for it was no ordinary bathing station: it was a spa designed on the most elegant and ambitious scale.'[34] The place figures briefly in others of Hardy's works, notably as the location of the marriages of Bathsheba to Troy in *Far from the Madding Crowd* and of Swithin and Lady Constantine in *Two on a Tower,* as well as being the setting of the earlier poem 'Midnight on Beechen, 187– (733)'. In 'Aquae Sulis' (308), Hardy is probably looking back to the extensive excavations beneath the Georgian city which went on during the later decades of the nineteenth century and which he no doubt saw on his visits of the period. The poem uses the conjunction, indeed the superimposition, of the Minster on the pagan sanctuary (which went back to the pre-Roman rites of the British goddess Sul) to rehearse his agnostic scepticism about the ostensible triumph of Christianity. As in 'Christmas in the Elgin Room' (917), Hardy gives a voice to the pagan past when 'the goddess whose shrine was beneath the pile' ('Aquae Sulis' 3rd st.) says to 'the god of the baldachined altar overhead: / 'And what did you win by raising this nave and aisle / Close on the site of the Temple I tenanted?' The (male) Christian God is viewed as merely another

---

[34] Wilson, pp.102/103.

passing fashion, replying to her complaint that 'we are images both [i.e. equally superficial] - twitched by people's desires; / And that I, as you, fail like a song men yesterday sang!' (6th st.). Hardy's scenario for the little discourse now seems remarkably modern, even for the 1911 date of the piece, unwittingly anticipating the attitudes of the new so-called pagan movement of the later twentieth century: here, the (relatively) modern, scientific, practice of archaeology has, as it were, violated the sacred site and 'releases' 'a filmy shape unsepulchred' (2nd st.), the pagan spirit, as the ancient shrine is disturbed:

> And the daytime parle on the Roman investigations
> Was shut to silence, save for the husky tune
> The bubbling waters played near the excavations. (1st st.)

Roman Road near Hardy's Cottage

Further, he intimates that it is the susurration of the bubbling spring that first excited the idea of its betraying an immanent presence, and as the quiet darkness returns after the brief interruption of the midnight chimes, there comes the opportunity for the dialogue of the spirits. The exchange ends beautifully: 'And all was suspended and soundless as before, / Except for a gossamery noise ... And the boiling voice of the waters' medicinal pour' (8th st.).

Set at Max Gate, 'Evening Shadows' (833) is one of two poems that exploit the archaeological setting of the house itself. In it Hardy displays a scepticism about Christianity similar to 'Aquae Sulis' (308), this time without whimsicality. Hardy's fatalistic, often melancholy, artistic cast of mind found rich inspiration in the ubiquitous ancient burials that surrounded him throughout his life in Dorset, and in the brevity of a poem it can be brought tellingly into focus. Conquer Barrow, which is now obscured from Max Gate by trees, was in Hardy's day clearly visible nearby, and was a favourite destination for one of his shorter walks. It is mentioned in 'The Mound' (827) where it is 'the mound - / Now sheeted with snow – whereon we sat that June / When it was green and round' (ll. 4-6). In the first stanza of 'Evening Shadows' (833), Hardy reflects that the shadows of his house will still be seen after his death, as they are now, 'Though in my earthen cyst I shall not know' (1st st.). 'Cyst' is an archaeological term for a stone burial chamber or coffin; the spelling has more recently been fixed as 'cist' to distinguish it from the biological 'cyst'. The second stanza muses that the apparently permanent 'neighbouring pagan mound' (2nd st.) may one day cease to cast a shadow, 'Even as to-day when men will no more heed / The Gospel news than when the mound was made.' To the elderly Hardy, not only are we 'such stuff as dreams are made on', but so are the beliefs that sustain us, in whatever age of human history. 'The Clasped Skeletons' (858) is also set near Max Gate, but uses the ancient site to paint a much broader canvas – in fact, the piece provides a neat summary of the nineteenth century's discovery of the true extent of ancient time, both on the archaeological and geological scale. Further, we are reminded of the interests and depth of knowledge of Hardy the admirer of Darwin – and of Hardy the inchoate archaeologist who lived in an archaeological landscape: the poem is subtitled 'surmised date 1800 BC (In an ancient British Barrow near the writer's home)'. His treatment of the exploration of the barrow and the humane imaginative implications of its contents form an interesting contrast to the antiquarian trophy-hunting that is mentioned in *The Return of the Native*, set perhaps seventy years previously. A concern with individuals is equally evident, however, for, like a true modern archaeologist presenting 'Meet the Ancestors' or 'Time Team' on television, Hardy metaphorically puts flesh on these ancient bones, giving the anonymous couple a temporal status and significance because they are older than a whole catalogue of famous ancient lovers: 'Ere Paris lay with Helena ... Ere David bedded Bathsheba' (92nd st.); the list continues, showing off Hardy's Biblical and literary knowledge, but to good effect, with Jael and Sisera, Pericles and Aspasia, as well as more obvious examples like Antony and Cleopatra, Abelard and Heloise. All of them, however, pale into insignificance when compared with the antiquity of these two unknown lovers:

> So long beyond chronology,
> Lovers in death as 'twere,
> So long in placid dignity
> Have you lain here! (9th st.)

This climactic flourish does not end the poem, however, for Hardy concludes by placing the couple in the vastly longer impersonal context of geological time, the same context presented in Henry Knight's agonisingly long minutes on the cliff in *A Pair of Blue Eyes*:

> Yet what is length of time? But dream!
> Once breathed this atmosphere
> Those fossils near you, met the gleam
> Of day as you did here;
>
> But so far earlier theirs beside

> Your life-span and career,
> That they might style of yestertide
> Your coming here! (10th/11th sts.)

It is worth emphasising the difference for Hardy between the terrifyingly impersonal vastness of astronomy and geology, and the innately human context of the relatively shorter span of archaeological time. It is also notable that Hardy emphasises his interest in and regard for specifically *Northern* archaeology here, and implicitly its imaginative power, again dismissing the hierarchical superiority of the Mediterranean world which remained a scholarly orthodoxy even into the twentieth century – for these are prehistoric remains, and the poet pointedly ascribes to them an interest and status superior to that of celebrated literary Classical figures. The minor poem 'By the Runic Stone' (408) [Hardy's double quotation marks] may be mentioned here, for in this piece, a *living* anonymous couple, briefly pictured at a decisive point in their lives (perhaps it is the meeting when these 'Two who became a story', as the subtitle has it, become engaged) are set against the impersonal permanence of an ancient monument. Hardy may have used runes to indicate the mystery of love, though he may perhaps have been thinking of his own 'Druid Stone' at Max Gate. After they have heedlessly 'the die thrown' (3rd st.) at this fleeting moment, they could not foresee how personified Time would 'toss their history / From zone to zone' (4th st.).

The ambivalent attitude of a humane, imaginative man like Hardy to the vanished glory and excesses of the Roman Empire is shown once again in 'The Roman Gravemounds' (329), thematically almost a companion to 'In the Old Theatre, Fiesole' (67). The site here must be the Fordington district of Dorchester (Hardy's Durnover) where Roman burials were excavated in 1838 and of which Hardy learnt from the Revd Henry Moule. This would have been a burial ground, following normal Roman practice, outside the walls of the town. A Roman memorial stone discovered in 1908 under the porch is exhibited today in St George's Church; in view of Hardy's determination in the last year of his life to observe new excavations, it is surely more than likely that he took an interest in such an important discovery so near his home. The earlier burials uncovered in Fordington, as I have indicated, are the model for those recorded in *The Mayor of Casterbridge* and resembling those Hardy found on his own property at Max Gate. This poem, narrated in the first person, pictures a man seen as if engaged in that questionable sub-species of quasi-archaeological excavation, antiquarian digging, that Hardy satirised in *A Tryst at an Ancient Earthwork* and outspokenly criticised in his personal writings: 'I guess what impels him to scrape and scan; / Yea, his dreams of that Empire long delayed' ('The Roman Gravemounds' 1st st.). But the man is ignorant of the site until the narrator tells him, and he is in fact burying his dead cat, 'A little white furred thing, stiff of limb …' (3rd st.), a beloved pet. He cares nothing for the pomp of the ancient past, affirming 'could she but live, might the record die / Of Caesar, his legions, his aims, his end' (5th st.). Roger Robinson notes that 'the man furtively digging there sees the mounds as significant not for their archaeological fame but simply as the secluded grave of the pet cat whose death matters to him much more.'[35] Hardy's very evident concern for animal welfare (long before it became a liberal *cause célèbre*) recorded in *The Life*, and evident in Jude Fawley's revulsion at Arabella's preferred method of

---

[35] Robinson, 'Darwin', Page, p.146.

slaughtering the pig, and in the pets' cemetery at Max Gate, all imply genuine emotion rather than sentimentality; but in the piece itself, it is Hardy's use of the event to explore an historical context that saves it from that charge. He may dismiss the creature, commenting that 'the small furred life was worth no one's pen' (6th st.), but the conjunction of setting, pet, and distressed individual provokes the reflection that 'its mourner's mood has a charm for me' – and more, for it inspired a poem. In a fortuitous archaeological connection, Hardy mentions late in his life (*Life* p.435) that his own favourite pet, the 'Famous Dog Wessex', to quote the gravestone, used to sit atop the barrow on Frome Hill (one at a higher point than Conquer Barrow) while on their walks.

The curious Christmas poem 'The Paphian Ball' (796) (alluding to the important sanctuary of Aphrodite at Paphos on Cyprus, and subtitled 'Another Christmas Experience of the Mellstock Quire') makes an ironic link between the Christian feast and pagan midwinter festivals. In a style akin to a seasonal ballad with rhyming couplet verses, this piece has a homely Dickensian character, yet is quintessentially of Hardy's Wessex folklore, and without the heavy philosophising of 'Christmas in the Elgin Room' (917). The setting is on Hardy's home ground '… By Rushy pond / Where Egdon-Heath outstretched beyond' ('The Paphian Ball' 2nd coup.). The group's escape from the allurements of pagan revelry is presented symbolically by the Christmas dawn – the dawn of salvation – overwhelming the darkness of the pagan past symbolised by Rainbarrow in mammary imagery familiar from other references to tumuli:

> There, east, the Christmas dawn hung red,
>   And dark Rainbarrow with its dead
>
> Bulged like a supine negress' breast
> Against Clyffe-Clump's faint far-off crest (23rd/24th coups)

The quire's weird supernatural experience on Christmas Eve, recalling their traditional tour in *Under the Greenwood Tree*, thus ostensibly reinforces the Christian message, yet the mythic nature of the tale serves to underscore Hardy's agnosticism.'By the Barrows' (216), 'Not far from Mellstock' (1st st.) where 'all the upland round is called 'the He'th'' (2nd st.), is also set at Rainbarrows, as Lea confirms,[36] the actual group of three near Hardy's birthplace rather than the conflated single specimen of 'The Paphian Ball' (796) and *The Return of the Native*. Hardy's alliterative description, verging on the comical, is almost identical to a passage in *The Mayor of Casterbridge* in which '… barrows, bulging as they bosoms were / Of [Diana] Multimammia stretched supinely there, … '. Again, the possibility of absurdity is prevented by Hardy's theme: the significance of the drama of an individual life set ironically against apparently greater events and the solid resilience of ancient tombs with their fatalistic connotations. At this spot, 'a battle … / Was one time fought' ('By the Barrows' 2nd st.), but also 'once a woman, in our modern age, / Fought singlehandedly to shield a child – / One not her own – from a man's senseless rage' (3rd st.). Yet again, Hardy's sympathy for the humble human being is paramount over the grander imaginative facts and legends of the past – and in this case, we have a strong reminder of Hardy's concern and admiration for women, so memorably championed in

---

[36] Lea, p.72.

the person of Tess Durbeyfield, amongst others. In Hardy's opinion, 'no patriot's bones there piled / So consecrate the silence as her deed … '.

Hardy's close and very long relationship with his mother, so important in providing him with an education beyond his childhood social position, inspired another short poem in the archaeological landscape near the cottage, 'The Roman Road' (218). The opening simile is identical to that in *The Return of the Native*, capturing the most popularly familiar feature of Roman highways: 'The Roman Road runs straight and bare / As the pale parting-line in hair / Across the heath' (1st st.). The road is of course that referred to in the title of Book Sixth chapter II of the novel, 'Thomasin walks in a Green Place by the Roman Road', the well preserved section running for a couple of hundred yards not far from Rainbarrow. Again we find in this poem the concern with the individual life set in the large context of the past represented in archaeology, this time in a very personal sense. The achievement of Rome is here belittled against the emotional life of the author himself, for though 'thoughtful men [archaeologists or scholars, no doubt] / Contrast its days of Now and Then, / And delve, and measure, and compare' (1st st.), and seem to see again 'Helmed legionaries who proudly rear / The Eagle, as they pace' (2nd st.), the poet declares 'no tall brass helmed legionnaire / Haunts it for me' (3rd st.) – because however powerful the imaginative effect of the historical past upon Hardy, the influence of his own personal past is far greater: 'Uprises there / A mother's form upon my ken, / Guiding my infant steps, as when / We walked that ancient thoroughfare'.

Another very personal work deserves to conclude this survey. 'The Shadow on the Stone' (483) is in my view one of the most affectingly beautiful of Hardy's poems, even among those famous works written by the elderly Hardy about Emma - the more so because it lacks any hint of the occasional awkwardness of utterance as found in 'By the Barrows' (216) and is without the rather maudlin self-indulgence of, say, 'Evening Shadows' (833). Hardy is, as Donald Davie put it, 'usually envisaged as a crepuscular poet, the voice of those half-lit hours in which phantoms and apparitions glimmer uncertainly at the edge of vision.'[37] He is also, of course, in his more personal works, a profoundly emotional writer; Tom Paulin feels that this poem is directed as much at Emma as at the reader.[38] Here, an archaeological subject and an intensely emotional theme are perfectly integrated; in this piece, the irregular scatter of 'archaeological' poems and the late works which for many people *are* Hardy's poetry become one. The stone in question is the remnant of the Neolithic circle that Hardy himself excavated at Max Gate and which now stands, like its much later-discovered companion, in the garden. The poem is also very unusual in that extra-textual documentation of a singularly personal nature survived the bonfire so that, as Philip Davis notes, 'By an historical accident we know a little more explicitly about the life and memory behind the poem … than we do in the case of most of Hardy's other poems.' He explains:

> … Recorded in the Dorset County Museum: an annotation by Miss Irene Cooper Willis to p.306 of what was first published as *The Early Life of Thomas Hardy*, in the copy owned by Florence Emily Hardy herself: 'Mrs Hardy, the second, walking round the garden with me, the first time I stayed at Max Gate (1933) on coming to the

---

[37] Davie, p.177.
[38] Paulin, p.59.

erected stone, remarked: 'Hardy found his first wife burning all his love-letters to her behind that stone, one day". ... No wonder it felt like being haunted and tortured.[39]

The *Life* betrays a particular irony when (p.387) a quotation from Hardy's journal notes '... Several letters'. Among others was an interesting one from a lady who informed him that some years earlier she had been made the happiest woman in the world by accidentally meeting for the first time, by the 'Druid Stone' on his lawn, at the late Mrs Hardy's last garden-party, the man who was now her husband.' One can only speculate as to Hardy's motive for including such an item.

'The Shadow on the Stone' is dated 'Begun 1913: finished 1916', but whether the reason for the time elapsed is the painfulness of the subject, especially considering the above, must be speculation. The stone he still dubs romantically 'the Druid stone' (1st st.), and, like Hardy, it 'broods in the garden white and lone', hiding, as Davis reveals, 'the buried presence of memories';[40] and though the stone is excavated, the truth of its original Neolithic meaning is as buried today as Hardy thought was the painful truth of his own association with it. Looking at it, he senses his late wife's presence behind him when the shadows of a nearby tree fall on the monolith just as 'the shade of a well-known head and shoulders / Threw there'. Now that she is dead, 'his love for her is intense and – inevitably – Platonic or Shelleyan'[41] (Paulin finds a plethora of associations with Shelley in his study, pointing especially to 'Epipsychidion'). Shadow and shade: as Paulin points out, both words can be used in both senses, of a physical shadow and of a ghost. Hardy plays with both in the poem.[42] Joanna Cullen Brown notes of this poem that 'What happens when a past memory dominates an actual scene is another disjunction: we become positively dislocated from the present while we are only tenuously joined to the past.'[43] Hardy declares, "I am sure you are standing behind me" (2nd st.), but 'there was no sound but the fall of a leaf / As a sad response'. Yet Hardy knows that there is a 'perfectly rational explanation for the ghostly shadow ... '[44] and Paulin suggests the contrast with another very beautiful poem, 'A Sign-Seeker' (30), which ends 'when a man falls he lies.' This poem faces the grim reality of irreversible loss.

Though so distantly separated in time, the stone and Emma are both irrecoverably past – the mysterious ancient culture that raised the stone and their living emotional relationship being equally vanished. He minimises his grief by not turning to discover 'there was nothing in my belief'; so he leaves the garden, and the ancient stone, imagining still 'her behind me throwing her shade, ... / My head unturned lest my dream should fade' (3rd st.). As Paulin remarks, Hardy must surely have Orpheus in mind and attempts to evade the curse that befell Orpheus who did look back and lost his love; but for Hardy, 'ocular proof ... involves the dreary recognition of normality, the unvisioning of a shape he desperately wants to believe in.'[45] In Hardy's case, the loss is of a much less substantial kind of shade of the moment. In the longer term, Emma's shadow was cast on Hardy's life till its end.

---

[39] Davis, p.409.
[40] Davis, p.410.
[41] Paulin, p.59.
[42] Paulin, p.59.
[43] Cullen Brown p84.
[44] Paulin, p.59.
[45] Paulin, p.59.

Chapter Eight

Beyond Wessex: Architecture and Ideas in Oxford and Cornwall

'... you are not stones, but men ...'

William Shakespeare, *Julius Caesar* Act III Scene ii.

Although he was probably only subconsciously aware of the fact, Thomas Hardy's family had a peculiar affinity with his adult interest of archaeology, for the vast majority of the material studied by archaeologists was originally fashioned either by architects and builders or by craftsmen. Hardy's readers are used to his frequent allusions to architectural terminology and his draughtsman's eye for the detail of physical surroundings. Michael Millgate writes that 'Hardy was, as a young man, fascinated with technical terminology and eager to display his mastery not only of architecture but also of the kind of knowledge to be found in encyclopedias.'[1] In his final novel, through architectural allusion and subject-matter, he wrote large the acknowledgement that was never hidden in any of his works to those craftsmen who enabled the architect's ideas to become reality. Among these, of course, was his own father, the master mason and builder who, *inter alia*, built Max Gate to his son's design.

The most deliciously ironic event of Hardy's last years must surely have been his visit to Oxford in 1920 for the conferral of an honorary doctorate, by which 'everyone perceived what hitherto few had been able to perceive – that, in withholding her highest honour from the author of *The Dynasts* and *The Return of the Native* (perhaps, whispered Cambridge and the world, because he was also the author of *Jude the Obscure*), Christminster was making herself ridiculous', as the *Life* (pp. 399/400) so pointedly remarks. Hardy's last and most controversial novel, *Jude the Obscure*, drew inspiration both more widely and deeply from the author's origins, and from his dominant adult philosophical preoccupations: the value (and acquisition of) book learning, class divisions, sexual morality, and what Hardy saw as the unmerited influence and moribund state of Christianity. As such, the novel is not centrally relevant to the present study, indeed, some of the subjects touched upon – such as Hardy's architectural

---

[1] Millgate, Career, p.38.

career and his own experience of education, not to mention the powerful influence and role of railways in his works – are worthy of more detailed separate attention than they have perhaps hitherto received.

Architectural knowledge would have chimed very well with Hardy's Classical learning, for the orders of architecture would have given him an important insight into the ancient world and its artistic influence on his own and other centuries, even without the studies he pursued during the early period of his life. As a young architect in Dorchester, he notes (*Life* p.32) that his life was 'twisted of three strands – the professional life, the scholar's life and the rustic life', in other words, three influential sources of inspiration for his later artistic development. He would have known that specific architectural styles could symbolise particular historical periods, and, more importantly for this present chapter, that a change in architectural style or fashion could represent not merely an era, but an historic moment in the dynamic sense. Such a moment forms a key element of Hardy's thematic schema in *Jude the Obscure*.

Timothy Hands's useful and interesting article 'Hardy's Architecture: a General Perspective and a Personal View'[2] combines an introduction to Victorian architecture with a personal view on how Hardy's own profession influenced his creative work. On a superficial level, any perusal of Hardy's fiction will discover a mass of technical references and a draughtsman's eye for detail, especially of the built environment, and Hands's essay reveals much more. After Hardy had abandoned his architectural career for writing, he by no means disparaged his former occupation, the mass of architectural allusions being a clue; the unexceptionable architect-characters are stronger evidence. In *A Pair of Blue Eyes*, Henry Knight looks through Stephen Smith's sketchbooks (incidentally reminding us of the author's interest in archaeology as well): 'Antiquities had been copied, fragments of Indian columns, colossal statues, and outlandish ornament from the temples of Elephanta and Kenneri … everything, in short, which comes within the range of a practising architect's experience, who travels with his eyes open' (p.355). With no undue conceit, Hardy refers here to his own observational powers that enabled him to be a good draughtsman and a fine descriptive writer; to repeat Tom Paulin's assertion, Hardy demonstrated an 'insistence on what is authentically visible'.[3] Long after he had abandoned (even spurned) architecture after his marriage to Emma in 1874 to devote himself to writing, his interest led him to taking his sketchbook with him on long bicycle trips. In his late fifties, he sketched the landscape on the ancient Ridgeway towards Weymouth as well as the nave of Salisbury Cathedral and the twin towers of Exeter Cathedral.

Hardy's early works include architect-hero characters such as Stephen Smith in *A Pair of Blue Eyes*; in *Jude*, he identifies more with his social origins in making Fawley a craftsman. This is a deliberate part of his philosophical purpose in the novel, since by the later nineteenth century, architects would be more highly regarded, certainly not 'obscure', and it is Jude's lowly status that sets him apart from Christminster and prevents his being considered as suitable for admission – Hardy echoing his own youthful experience.

Hardy first learned architecture at the age of sixteen when he was articled to the Dorchester firm of John Hicks. At twenty-one, he moved to spend five years in London working for Arthur Blomfield and in 1863, at only twenty-three years of age, Hardy won first prize in the

---

[2] Timothy Hands, 'Hardy's Architecture: a General Perspective and a Personal View', Mallett, p.95.
[3] Paulin, p.91.

Architectural Association competition and a silver medal from the Institute of British Architects. Blomfield it was who set Hardy to supervise the clearing of St Pancras churchyard of bodies in preparation for the building of the Midland Railway, a crucial influence on Hardy's sensitivity as a writer; almost as importantly, Blomfield sent the meteorically successful young architect to Oxford in 1864 as his trusted assistant-architect on a commission to build a chapel for the Radcliffe Infirmary. Returning to Dorset, he became Hicks's assistant, and when he died, was taken on by George Crickmay of Weymouth who sent Hardy on the fateful assignment to St Juliot in Cornwall as detailed in the previous Chapter.

St Michael's, Oxford

In Oxford, Hardy was an outsider like Jude, observing at a distance the manners and mores of the privileged undergraduates. Much the oldest building in Oxford, older than any building that Jude could have worked on for the University, older indeed than the University, is the fine late Anglo-Saxon tower of St Michael's Church – an outsider, then, like Jude – but as much a part of Oxford's Christian heritage as is Hardy's fictional name, Christminster. Unlike the young architects of the earlier novels, Jude Fawley is by trade a stonemason like Hardy's father, but in common with the real-life young architect Hardy, this eponymous hero is frustrated in his quest for academic fulfilment at Christminster (Oxford) University, though through very different circumstances. Jude, as an artisan, is less lucky than Hardy would have been with a similar inquiry, being told quite explicitly in reply to a letter that a working man should seek success in life in his own sphere and occupation. Jude's home is at Marygreen, named after Hardy's paternal grandmother Mary (the powerful influence who figures in 'Domicilium' and in 'One We Knew'). Like Jude she grew up an orphan, and the hero's surname Fawley is the real name of the village near Wantage in Berkshire where she spent her childhood.

Jude Fawley, then, grew up in Hardy's North Wessex, Berkshire – in fact on the very Northern edge of Hardy's fictionalised world. The boundary with the neighbouring former Anglian Kingdom of Mercia, in which Oxford/Christminster is situated, is more than geographical, for Jude symbolically never manages to cross the social boundary between town and gown that divides him from the University while he is a working member of the City community that maintains its outward fabric. An irony dating to over seventy-five years after the composition of *Jude* in 1896 is that the Northern part of Berkshire was transferred to Oxfordshire in the boundary changes of 1974 (the Thames losing its ages-old liminal significance): thus, Hardy's dreary Northern fringe of Wessex was moved finally right into non-Wessex, as it were. The character of Berkshire is represented as very much that of this sombre novel with its 'frenetic railway-ridden restlessness';[4] the County's lack of historic and archaeological interest is noted

St Juliot Church

as a symptom if not a cause of the book's failings according to Edmund Gosse's review, quoted by Millgate:

> In choosing North Wessex as the scene of a novel Mr Hardy wilfully deprives himself of a great element of his strength. Where there are no prehistoric monuments, no ancient buildings, no mossed and immemorial woodlands, he is Sampson shorn.[5]

Millgate, however, adds that this 'criticism is an unwitting acknowledgement of Hardy's success' since he sees the thematic dislocation and rootlessness as key to the meaning of the book.

Hardy's fascination with the subject of time is as strong and intricate as ever in this final fictional utterance; the sense of place in Christminster is (though Millgate states that the book

---

[4] Robinson, 'Darwin', Page, p.130.
[5] Millgate, *Career*, p.332.

is 'deficient in the sense of place'[6]), as so often in Hardy, inextricably bound up with its 'pastness': we read that to Jude, 'Not as yet having mingled with the active life of the place it was largely non-existent to him' (p.132), but 'Like all new comers to a spot on which the past is deeply graven he heard that past announcing itself with an emphasis ... '. Perhaps, however, the most overt indication of the book's preoccupation with time is in the darkly jocular name of the child Little Father Time. Sophie Gilmartin quotes Edward Said's comment: '... the boy is neither really a son nor, of course, a father. He is an alteration in the course of life, a disruption of the archaeology that links one to the other.'[7] After the death of the children, the sequence of time is disrupted; seeing the novel in the light of *Tess*, Gillian Beer claims, 'The death of their children ... leaves Jude and Sue as aberrant, without succession, and therefore 'monstrous' in the sense that they can carry no cultural or physical mutations into the future and must live out their lives merely at odds with the present.'[8]

However, direct reference to archaeology *per se* is sparse: there is no persistent motif like Rainbarrow in *The Return of the Native*, no memorably symbolic antiquity as at the climactic Stonehenge scene in *Tess*, nor the recurrent scatter of allusions of *The Mayor*. Nonetheless, the abiding interest in the subject of archaeology is undiminished at this stage in the author's life, as I have shown in Chapter Three, and unsurprisingly, it takes its (rather limited) place as a natural component in the book's panoply of allusion, even though Hardy's focus and intentions are different again from his previous novels. Additionally, Simon Gatrell notes the lack of Hardy's customary Wessex-historical content in *Jude*[9] with the exception of Shaston (Shaftesbury) at the opening of Part Fourth with detailed description of 'its magnificent apsidal abbey' and 'gabled freestone mansions' – but these latter have been 'ruthlessly swept away', and it is as if Hardy is sweeping away his usual cultural template in this final novel.

Christminster is not in prosaic North Wessex, but beyond it, 'perched at the edge of his region but ... a crucial centre of *Jude*'[10] as George Wing's thesis has it. He believes that the landscape of the novel is intimately bound up with the disillusionment of the central character: 'Christminster becomes one dream further removed from 'reality' in that it seems to be presented as a false dream of Jude himself.'[11]

Hardy's gifted but tragic friend Horace Moule might in some respects be a model for Jude Fawley's *career*, but his discouragement of Hardy's academic ambition makes him a kind of negative image of Richard Phillotson. Phillotson is of particular interest among Hardy's potential biographical models for the book's characters in his hobby of researching Roman remains – and investigating the possible genesis of this character certainly underlines the dangers of an oversimplified autobiographical interpretation of Hardy's works. On his partial separation from Sue, Phillotson is 'trying to get together the materials for his long-neglected hobby of Roman antiquities. For the first time since reviving the subject he felt a return of his old interest in it' (p.289). Indeed, he declares to his departing wife: 'I have, too, this grand hobby in my head of writing 'The Roman Antiquities of Wessex' which will occupy all my spare hours' (p.297). The impersonal remains of the long-dead past here provide a distraction,

---

[6] Millgate, Career, p.332.
[7] Gilmartin, 'Geology', Mallett, p.38.
[8] Beer, p.251.
[9] Gatrell, p.165.
[10] Wing, 'Regionalism', Page, p.95.
[11] Wing, 'Regionalism',Page, p.93.

perhaps a consolation, for the dying of a recent personal relationship. Phillotson occupies himself 'going alone into fields where causeways, dykes and tumuli abounded, or shutting himself up in his house with a few urns, tiles, and mosaics he had collected' (pp.215-216) and '… [he] had begun to sit in his parlour during the dark winter nights and re-attempt some of his old studies [including] … Roman-Britannic antiquities' (p.215). The Wessex edition continues, '… a comparatively unworked mine … seen to compel inferences in startling contrast to accepted views on the civilisation at that time,' indicating a new focus on the historical changes in the study of archaeology rather than just on the artefacts – so there is no doubting here the inferences that Hardy wishes his readers to make about his own high Victorian civilisation.

Wardour Old Castle

Despite his own intense, forward-looking, and lively practical involvement in antiquities, Hardy too could 'make use' of them in a way divorced from their inherent interest; Edmund Blunden notes that the author, who valued his privacy, 'found it useful when interviewers were probing him about God and man, to deviate into this subject of the Roman legacy in Wessex.'[12] And, as Blunden observes, '… the Max Gate library naturally contained a selection of books splendid or modest on Dorset antiquities' reminding us that, unlike Phillotson's, Hardy's interest never became dormant. A touch of self-mocking humour that would surely delight Hardy's friends, who knew of his passion for archaeology, is introduced in a comment of Sue's to Jude, about a proposed outing: 'Not ruins, Jude – I don't care for them' (p.189)! The main point of this exchange, however, is that she believes that a suggestion to visit Wardour

---

[12] Blunden, p.52.

Castle in Wiltshire is inadmissible because it is 'Gothic ruins – and I hate Gothic!'. Jude, however, believes that Wardour is 'quite otherwise ... a Classic building – Corinthian' which for Sue is satisfactory, not just for its Classical style, but because it is both Classical *and* not ruined, for she views the Classical world as being more alive than dead. She declares, 'You ought to have learnt Classic. Gothic is barbaric art, after all.' (p.376). In a sense, they are both right, for their exchange is probably based on a confusion of identity: Wardour Old Castle (as it is now known) dates from about 1393, was badly damaged in the Civil War, and kept as a Romantic ruin to be viewed from (the new) Wardour Castle, a country house of neo-Classical style built in 1769–1776.

The Victorian period spanned a fundamental shift in taste from Georgian Neo-Classical to Gothic, though some architects like Decimus Burton managed to embrace both styles with distinction. The friction between the two inevitably receives attention in the works of Hardy the architect-novelist and this topic received attention in Chapter Five related to *A Laodicean*. The much more important aspect of architecture for Hardy the humane artist is not this stylistic debate but its human associations, as was noted in the discussion of the poem 'The Abbey Mason' in Chapter Seven. Referring to the older Hardy's mature reflection on his first career in the 1906 article 'Memories of Church Restoration', Tom Paulin stresses the 'uniqueness of each particular example of Gothic architecture and the human associations which accrue to it and which [Hardy] characteristically considers more valuable than its aesthetic qualities'.[13]

Whatever the ambivalence of Horace Moule's influence on Hardy's early adulthood, his elder brother Henry J. Moule with his 'friendship of between forty and fifty years', his curatorship of the Dorset County Museum, and his *Dorchester Antiquities* (Dorchester, 1906) with Hardy's Preface[14] must surely have been a part of the inspiration – especially since in the Preface, Hardy quotes a note from Moule 'relating to my novel of *Jude*, then being published serially.'[15] Hardy's other important, but untainted, mentor was William Barnes. Hardy's obituary of Barnes in the *Athenaeum* of October 16th 1886 makes reference to several subjects close to those in Hardy's own oeuvre, for, amongst that polymath's many pursuits, are his 'investigations of Roman remains, theories on the origin of Stonehenge, and kindred archaeological matters.'[16] Indeed, although the friendship with Pitt-Rivers and Petrie had an enormous influence on Hardy, we should not underestimate the importance of these two long-standing local friends.

Other references to the archaeological traces of the ancient past, though relatively few, crop up with an expected inevitability; but within the novel's overall temporal dialectic, they may be seen as far more than incidental – rather Hardy unconsciously slipping into a familiar strand of imagery. An early reference is to:

> ... a green 'ridgeway' – the Icknield Street and original Roman road through the district. This ancient track ran east and west for many miles, and down almost to within living memory had been used for driving flocks and herds to fairs and markets. But it was now neglected and overgrown. (p.59)

---

[13] Paulin, p. 118.
[14] Orel, Writings, p.66.
[15] Orel, Writings, p.70.
[16] Orel, Writings, p.102.

Within this part of a single sentence, Hardy encompasses a vast span of human prehistory and history: the ancient ridge tracks, all called 'ridgeways', are of immemorial date, and many were naturally chosen, where suitable, to be the line of the Roman roads; the familiar names for Roman roads like Icknield Street are Saxon, and Hardy links his own origins with this ancient past by implicitly including his grandparents' era ('almost to within living memory') – his favourite Napoleonic period – as the end of this trackway's story. Thus the end of a way of rural life that Hardy chronicled in *The Mayor of Casterbridge* is encapsulated here by the obsolescence of this ancient road. Moreover, the next sentence refers to Jude's being 'deposited by the carrier from a railway station southward' – by the intrusive life-changing icon of nineteenth century industrialisation that features so persistently in Hardy's temporal schemata. Perhaps the obvious and direct route of the prehistoric and Roman routes matches Jude's idea that there is a direct and obvious route for him to Christminster University; ironically, the modern world offers him no such thing, and in time, his ambition atrophies as the ancient trackway has done in the age of railways.

Later, a dominant theme is touched upon, that of the Classical world and its influence on the present and on the main characters. Again, the present is viewed in the grander perspective of the archaeological past, an easily accomplished device when characters are placed in the landscape of Wessex:

> In the afternoon Arabella met and walked with Jude, who had now for weeks ceased to look into a book of Greek, Latin, or any other tongue. They wandered up the slopes till they reached the green track along the ridge, which they followed to the circular British earth-bank adjoining, Jude thinking of the great age of the trackway, and of the drovers who had frequented it, probably before the Romans knew the country. (pp.98-99)

Again, there is more density of meaning than is first apparent. Hardy points up the sensitivity and education of his hero and the gulf of sensibility between the two characters while engaging the familiar device of placing the shifting and transient relationships and feelings of ephemeral individuals in the long perspective of their shared human past of which, in this case, Arabella is ignorant. Moreover, this incident is also that familiar Hardy device of placing his characters with their transient crises against the vast temporal backdrop of an archaeological site.

Much of the book, then, is not concerned with the detritus of past time in the form of its archaeological and historical remains, but rather with the contemporary clash of ideas between traditional Christian teaching and practice, and a more secular, neo-pagan philosophy that seemed more apposite in the wake of Darwin. But it is not only Christian commentators such as T.S. Eliot who have disliked the book, for *Jude the Obscure* manifests some of Hardy's worst failings of infelicitous style, including some ludicrously transparent devices (the absurd names for the Christminster colleges, for instance, even allowing for satirical intent), and needlessly persistent, painfully obvious polemic; it is almost as if Hardy were courting the precise hostile response that the book did indeed provoke in order to make his grand theatrical exit from prose fiction. There are subtle strands in the novel, however. In his dialectic, Hardy chooses architectural motifs to be his symbols: Gothic, the favoured English revival style of the Victorian Age and of the Anglo-Catholic movement within the Church of England is associated with the outmoded ideas of Christminster with its specifically Christian culture; and the Classical which originated of course in the pre-Christian world of Greece and Rome represents the pagan. Such is the symbolic scheme of the novel, but it would be simplistic in the extreme to identify its author with this rigid dichotomy of styles. Hardy himself by no means rejected Gothic in the categorical way that Sue does in the book; on the contrary, he famously defended (*Life* p.301) the perceived awkwardness of his poetry – which so repelled Eliot, for instance – in later life by 'thinking of the analogy of architecture', a defence that applies equally to aspects of the novels, 'that in architecture cunning irregularity is of enormous worth, and it is obvious that he carried on into his verse, perhaps in part unconsciously, the Gothic art-principle in which he had been trained … '.

In this novel, being concerned with a clash of specifically *literary* cultures, Hardy eschews reference to his beloved, enigmatic remains of prehistory that figure so largely in earlier works. In this light, Hardy's allusions to the Roman (and prehistoric, since they were, *ipso facto*, pagan) remains of Wessex and (in the poems) in Italy might be seen in a slightly different perspective and one of which the pre-*Jude* Hardy was probably not consciously aware (it is important not to equate Roman Wessex with 'the Classical world' too glibly, for Hardy clearly regarded the Roman Empire in a rather jaundiced way, at best as the debased, decadent inheritance of a grander, more truly civilised ancient Greece, though such a sentiment he does not make very explicit). In this book, however, there is a clear distinction between the archaeological remnants of the past which figure but little in the imagery, and the *literary* legacy of the past. Allusions to the Classics are dense, sometimes even cloying, in Hardy's works, and may be seen as no more than an element in the fabric of past-referential imagery, if not merely as Hardy showing off his reading in a rather awkward fashion. In *Jude,* however, such allusions are an essential part of the philosophical debate. This approach was to some extent prefigured, as discussed in Chapter Five, in the cultural-aesthetic conflict in *A Laodicean*: indeed, the hideous non-conformist chapel in that book, though probably *not* Gothic, is a precursor of the soulless new Marygreen church (of which more shortly).

Carla L. Peterson's densely argued essay, '*Jude the Obscure*: The Return of the Pagan',[17] proposes that amidst his debate over book learning and sexual morality and relationships (to which I would add, social class), Hardy is concerned with his characters' fluctuating rejection and acceptance of Christianity in favour of a more 'liberal-progressive' pagan viewpoint which is of course paradoxically a return to ancient, pre-Christian mores. In this analysis, Sue is revealed to be intimately identified with Artemis and she is aggressively anti-Biblical, declaring, 'There was nothing first-rate about the place [Jerusalem], or people, after all – as there was about Athens, Rome, Alexandria, and other old cities' (p.156). Jude himself in his later Christian mode perceives such an identification of her, saying: 'Sue, you seem ... to be one of the women of some grand old civilisation, whom I used to read about in my bygone, wasted, Classical days ...' (p.337). This model was an ideal for Hardy, too; in the *Life* (p.220) he comments on a girl's face seen on an omnibus, 'perfect in its softened classicality – a Greek face translated into English.' Later, more sombrely, Sue applies just such a Classical image (perhaps drawn by

---

[17] Carla L. Peterson, 'Jude the Obscure: The Return of the Pagan', New Casebooks: Jude the Obscure, ed. Penny Boumelha (London: Macmillan, 2000), p.75.

Hardy from Keats' 'Ode on a Grecian Urn') in describing the flowers carried by a bride they see in church as 'sadly like the garland which decked the heifers of sacrifice in old times!' (p.355). Overall, however, Sue believes that it is the Christian centuries that have stressed the misery of life and she says to Jude that 'I feel we have returned to Greek joyousness, and have blinded ourselves to sickness and sorrow ...' (p.366). Peterson explains:

> *Jude the Obscure* can be viewed as a fictional gloss on Matthew Arnold's argument over Hellenism and Hebraism in *Culture and Anarchy*. Hellenism and Hebraism are both ethical and social tendencies that pursue spiritual truths and moral modes of conduct. Hellenism is characterised above all by flexibility and spontaneity, by a straightforward acceptance of the difficulties involved in attaining moral goals ... Hebraism is much stricter and more inflexible in its philosophical outlook ...[18]

Of course, in accepting this analysis of Arnold's, Peterson is side-stepping the less palatable aspects of the Hellenic (Greek) model: its economic reliance on slavery, the destructive, indulgent tendency of Dionysian excess and so on – as well as forgetting the specifically Christian, New Testament development of Hebraism in its emphasis on the imperative of *agape*, self-sacrificial, undeserved love, a subverted example of which might be seen in Phillotson's 'release' of Sue from her marriage vows. Nevertheless, as a careful exposition of the feminist strands in the novel and in its detailed examination of some of Hardy's key poetic, mythological, and Biblical references, this article is a fascinating and revealing piece.

Sue's preference for the Classical (pagan) statues over the Christian images she is involved in producing at the ecclesiastical warehouse is a key metaphor. Contrary to the received art-historical perspective, ancient sculpture might be regarded as less important than pottery in historical-archaeological terms: there is less of it, and we learn rather less of the everyday lives of the societies that produced sculpture than from their pottery. Nonetheless, sculpture has the potential to provide more information about a culture's religious beliefs, political system, and historical identity. To simplify, most such products in the ancient world were not made merely for decoration, nor had they any alternative utilitarian purpose like pottery: they always had some religious or political function, as idols (or in some other way deistic representations), as representations of the dead, or as votive offerings or dedications at sanctuaries; images of leaders and their achievements were another important genre, especially in the imperial contexts of Mesopotamia, the Hellenistic age, and Rome.

Hardy's admired predecessor poets, Shakespeare, Milton, the Romantics, whatever their particular philosophical standpoint, did not generally see the Classical and the Christian in opposition, even if, like Milton, they regarded the pagan Classical age with its mythology as a time of ignorance superseded by Christianity – the main thrust of St Paul's address to the Athenians that Hardy used as the starting point for his poem 'In the British Museum'. Indeed, Milton with his intense Classical education acknowledged his Classical antecedents so far as to aspire to make of *Paradise Lost* the Christian Epic to match those of Homer and Virgil. However, Hardy chooses in *Jude* to adopt the aggressive stance of his contemporary Swinburne, whose description of Christ as the 'pale Galilean' in his poem 'Hymn to Proserpine' (1866), outraged Victorian opinion as much as his admirer's novel was to do thirty years later.

---

[18] Peterson, 'Return of the Pagan', Boumhela, p.75.

And so, Sue in her 'pagan' phase loves the pagan statuary – even lying about their identity – while loathing the Christian images. Hardy quotes that Swinburne line from 'the familiar poem' (p.143) which Sue reads at her lodgings at Miss Fontover's alongside her nefariously acquired of Venus and Apollo. Miss Fontover's smashing the two statues, which are to her idolatrous, precipitates Sue's departure. Hardy makes a sly jab at divided Christendom when, in free indirect quotation, Sue's evangelical aunt describes the 'ecclesiastical warehouse' as 'a perfect seed-bed of idolatry' (p.134). Interestingly, as discussed in Chapter Two, while Victorians, like their predecessors, admired the beauty of Classical art (whether discovered by archaeology or by treasure hunters), the prehistoric world and its art, which were a major new discovery of late nineteenth-century archaeology, were regarded charitably as 'primitive': no doubt the characters on both sides of the philosophical divide in *Jude* would agree.

The use of architecture as both a subject and as a vehicle for themes in *Jude the Obscure* starts in the first chapter. Hardy combatively (for he had, of course, known the doctrine of the Trinity since childhood) refers to the old, destroyed Marygreen church as 'the ancient temple of the Christian divinities' (p.50) and, to suggest that Christianity was less durable than its pagan forebears, ironically in an ancient landscape dotted with ancient barrows, its 'obliterated graves' had been replaced by 'eighteen penny cast-iron crosses warranted to last five years'. The new church is 'a tall new building of modern Gothic design unfamiliar to English eyes'. Even though this variation might be new, Gothic was taken up by the Victorian architects like Giles Gilbert Scott (who did much very radical 'restoration') because it was considered the quintessential English style, being an imitation of the majority of our medieval ecclesiastical buildings. The architect of this affront is dubbed 'a certain obliterator of historic records who had run down from London and back in a day' – by train of course, rather, one feels, like a predecessor of 'Mondeo Man' from head office who marks out some distant green field site for a new 'superstore'. In *A Pair of Blue Eyes*, Swancourt is proud of bringing a London man down to West Endelstow to commit a similar aesthetic affront. Hardy, as a young architect, had been engaged in very similar activities when he met Emma Gifford at St Juliot. Further, his experience of clearing graves at St Pancras as a young architect seems to have affected him deeply, judging by the recurrent tomb/grave/burial motifs in so many of his works of which 'The Levelled Churchyard' might be cited as an obvious poetic example. The link between graves, architecture, and stones in Hardy's works is no more eccentric than it is simplistic; it is made explicitly and discussed to good effect in 'Geology, Genealogy and Church Restoration in Hardy's Writing' by Sophie Gilmartin. She concludes her piece (in, alas, a rather tortured but still comprehensible sentence) with the important statement:

> While Hardy's writing is concerned intensively, almost obsessively with variously juxtaposed time-scales and cycles, those 'deposits' of history, generations and geology which provide him with a thick and fertile soil for narrative, he is less interested or inspired by continuity and ongoing generations than he is by a sterile repetition or a failure to continue a genealogical line. Enamoured as he is with 'the melancholy ruins of cancelled cycles', Hardy seems finally, with *Jude the Obscure* and *The Well-Beloved*, to have taken the decision to cancel his own narratives which rely so crucially upon cycles of generation.[19]

---

[19] Gilmartin, 'Geology', Mallett, pp.38/39.

Victorian church restoration was a very necessary activity after a long period of neglect, but it varied enormously in extent from re-pointing to the radical work undertaken at St Juliot (as represented in *A Pair of Blue Eyes* of which more later) to the kind of wholesale destruction (not unlike the actuality of much archaeology, in fact) at Marygreen. Hardy's attitude to the process shifted considerably over the years, as I shall outline shortly. Hardy's regret at the destruction of the old church is balanced by his acceptance, if not celebration, of the decline of the church's function. Christminster is crumbling and outdated both literally and metaphorically, but new towns are no more attractive aesthetically or culturally than Marygreen. Aldbrickham (Reading) is on the fringe of North Wessex, historically on the very boundary of Mercia since on the other bank of the Thames is Oxfordshire, part of Mercia during the Anglo-Saxon period. It is a workaday town which developed largely as a result of the railway and is presented throughout as a utilitarian, unattractive place. Its abbey was important in medieval times, but it is today one of the least attractive, worst situated monastic ruins for the visitor. Hardy refers to such a clash of ancient ruin and modernity at Stoke-Barehills (Basingstoke), and a melancholy hue he casts over the description:

> The most familiar object in Stoke-Barehills today is its cemetery, standing among some picturesque mediaeval ruins beside the railway; the modern chapels, modern tombs, and modern shrubs, having a look of intrusiveness amid the crumbling and ivy-covered decay of the ancient walls. (p.358)

Sue draws together three strands in Hardy's cultural-historic debate (the current status of Christianity, the rise of industrialisation, and the conflict between medieval Gothic and ancient Classical) in Part Third chapter one, as well as underlining her own identity, when she says to Jude at Melchester (Salisbury):

> 'Shall we go and sit in the Cathedral?' he asked, when their meal was finished.
>
> 'Cathedral? Yes. Though I think I'd rather sit in the railway station,' she answered, a remnant of vexation still in her voice. That's the centre of the town life now. The Cathedral has had its day!'
>
> 'How modern you are!'
>
> 'So would you be if you had lived so much in the Middle Ages as I have done these last few years! The Cathedral was a very good place four or five centuries ago; but it is played out now ... I am not modern, either. I am more ancient than mediaevalism if you only knew.' (p.187)

We might be reminded here of the later cliché that large railway stations are the 'cathedrals' of the Victorian age. Simon Gatrell comments that 'the station ... is the centrally symbolic building of modern civilisation'.[20] Similarly, the long walks which characterise so many of Hardy's works are in *Jude* largely superseded by railway journeys. Aldbrickham (Reading), an important railway junction on the Great Western, figures importantly, and Gatrell notes, for instance, that on Little Father Time's journey to the town, the 'boy's isolation seems intensi-

---

[20] Gatrell, p.170.

fied by the idea of the train as a capsule of folk being drawn at some speed by a machine on an invariable route through a landscape with which they have no contact'[21] – simultaneously a reminder of the symbolism of the 'red tyrant' traction engine in *Tess* and a contrast with the lovers' desperate flight on foot in the earlier novel.

Jude's employment at Christminster – so near and yet so far from fulfilling his real reason for being there – is as a mason engaged on restoring and maintaining the fabric of the satirically named colleges – Crozier (in Old-time Street, identifying it at once as outmoded), Cardinal, Rubric, Sarcophagus. He is, therefore, quite literally supporting the institution that so signally fails to support his own aspirations to learning. In so doing, he is handling and shaping the geology of immensely ancient epochs, stone that has a relevance as a building material that is more tangible and real to the mason than is the decayed and irrelevant institution and its perceived wisdom of which it is the physical embodiment and the vessel that holds the history of that institution. Commenting on the quarrying on The Isle of Slingers (Portland) in *The Well-Beloved*, Andrew D. Radford remarks how the stratifications of geology reach upwards through immense spans of time until they reach the strata that become buildings and hence stratifications of history.[22] The opening of Part Second chapter two is of crucial importance here, and Hardy has a great deal to say about the historic passage of time through the media of his narrative and his dominant themes. Jude is engaged in two ultimately hopeless struggles: first that of the artisan to gain access to the institution of the University; secondly, in one that Hardy the archaeologist would understand, that is the 'deadly struggle against weather, years, and man' (p.130). Later, Jude performs a similar function at Melchester (Salisbury) Cathedral, another symbolic pillar of orthodoxy that he leaves behind as swiftly as the lovers pass it by in *Tess*. Jude also shores up the past in a different and more positive sense by working on a less contentious institution, 'ashlaring ... a museum in Casterbridge' (p.379) – whose prototype can be none other than Hardy's own beloved Dorchester County Museum. Hardy makes it clear that there is a moral equivalence between the physical condition of the Christminster colleges and what was propounded and learnt within them; this makes the conscientious craftsman Jude's anxiety for their condition, in view of his yearning to be admitted, poignant as well as ironic. The deluded, romanticized view he has of the University by night – the symbolic obstruction of clear sight – is physically clear by day (and what a characteristic couplet the poet *manqué* gives us in the second quoted sentence!):

> The numberless architectural pages around him he read, naturally, less as an artist-critic of their forms than as an artizan [sic] and comrade of the dead handicraftsmen whose muscles had actually executed those forms. ... What at night had been perfect and ideal was by day the more or less defective real. The condition of several moved him as he would have been moved by maimed sentient beings. They were wounded, broken, sloughing off their outer shape in the deadly struggle against years, weather, and man. ... It was, in one sense, encouraging to think that in a place of crumbling stones there must be plenty for one of his trade to do in the business of renovation. ... The yard was a little centre of regeneration. (p.130)

---

[21] Gatrell, p.170.
[22] Radford, p.215.

In this passage, Jude identifies as closely with the stones as with their deceased fashioners, feeling in his personification of the buildings that his fellow-craftsmen have been let down by the injuries that their works have suffered. Only later does Jude gain the inner sight to match the external clarity with which he sees the buildings in the cold light of day. And Hardy uses a telling Darwinian fossil simile in his explanation, for the morbidity of the Gothic is allied in his mind to the wider development of 'post-Christian', agnostic scientific ideas about the origins of life:

> ... he perceived that at best only copying, patching and imitating went on here ... He did not at that time see that mediaevalism was as dead as a fern-leaf in a lump of coal; that other developments were shaping in the world around him, in which Gothic architecture and its associations had no place. The deadly animosity of contemporary logic and vision towards so much of what he held in reverence was not yet revealed to him. (p.131)

The craftsman/auto-didact Jude is a less exalted, less fortunate equivalent, and only the latest in a long list, of architect-characters in Hardy's fiction, here presented in a diminished form (a mason) to make his rejection from the institution he aspires to join as more of an inevitability than it would have been for someone of Hardy's own status. Owen Graye in *Desperate Remedies* is succeeded by Henry Knight in *A Pair of Blue Eyes*, and George Somerset in *A Laodicean*; there was also an architect in the unpublished and lost *The Poor Man and the Lady*. The third mentioned novel, discussed in Chapter Five, includes real debate about architecture which is closely integrated into the central theme of the clash of ancient and modern, and in its opening chapter anticipates, though in less fervid terms and without the same symbolic significance, the battle between Classical and Gothic that is so important in *Jude*. The narrator of *A Laodicean* notes that Somerset has studied all the styles of architecture, following with bemusement the shifting fashions, 'till quite bewildered on the question of style, he concluded that all styles were extinct, and with them all architecture as a living art. Somerset was not old enough at that time to know that ... ideal perfection was never achieved by Greek, Goth, or Hebrew Jew, and never would be' (*A Laodicean* p.5).

As the Victorian Age progressed, revealing new and ever longer perspectives of the past, so Hardy's attitude to old buildings shifted from the casual attention of a young working architect carrying out drastic restoration work to the conservation instinct of a celebrated author who could be consulted as something of an expert on archaeology, who was well versed in geology, and who was preoccupied with recognising the educative significance of the past, be it Stonehenge or the Napoleonic Wars.

Hardy's first published work was 'How I built Myself a House' of 1865, a charmingly light-hearted sketch written for the younger pupils of Arthur Blomfield; one could only wish that such material, not so far removed from the tone of much of *The Trumpet-Major*, had formed a greater part of Hardy's oeuvre. The fictitious narrator's lively and humorous account of a vertiginous climb to the pinnacle of the new house under construction, led by the droll foreman, surely reappears in more typically Hardyesque style as the fatal fall of the architect Ambrose Graye from a church spire in the opening chapter of Hardy's first published novel, *Desperate Remedies* of 1871. Towards the latter end of Hardy's career, in 1906, and long after he had ceased to practise as an architect, came a reflection on the work he had been engaged on in 'Memories of Church Restoration'. It is on this kind of work, and closely based on Hardy's own assignment in St Juliot for G.R. Crickmay, that Stephen Smith is engaged in *A Pair of Blue Eyes*. In the *Life* (p.79), Hardy records the demolition of the old St Juliot Church, where 'he much regretted the obliteration in this manner of the church's history', especially because of its personal associations for him. 'Yet his instrumentality was involuntary,' he continues. He acknowledges the 'dilapidated' state which meant some action had to be taken, but the 'old walls of the former nave, dating from Norman or even earlier times, might possibly have been preserved. A north door, much like a Saxon one, was inadvertently destroyed, but Hardy made a drawing of it ... '. Hardy's feeling for the traces of the past are strong here, despite his professional understanding of the need for perhaps drastic measures, and it was not merely the sentimental connotations of St Juliot that brought them to the fore. Nevertheless, Cornwall, though Off Wessex in (some versions of) the Hardyan cosmography, is certainly not the drearily banal North Wessex of *Jude*, but 'this vague romantic land of 'Lyonesse'' as he says on the same page.

While the Revd Swancourt is assiduously supervising the transmutation of his medieval church from near-ruin to modern restoration with the expert assistance of architect Knight, he expresses scorn – in a foretaste of one of the principal themes of *Tess* – for the dubious pedigree of his soon-to-be second wife, the widowed Mrs Troyton, and disdaining the Romantic fashion for folly-ruins places himself in the camp of the more Philistine Victorian modernisers: '... a pedigree that bears evidence of being rather a raked-up affair – done since the family got rich – people do these things now as they build ruins on maiden estates and cast antiques at Birmingham' (*A Pair of Blue Eyes* p.121). In the *Life* (p.147), Hardy places himself at odds with such a dismissive attitude (and further distancing himself from the character generally) when he declares that Romanticism will last 'as long as human nature exists'.

Hardy, the 'agnostic churchgoer' was inevitably disturbed in his later life by the excesses of church restoration. Noting (*Life* p.126) old church fittings dumped or re-used in builders' yards, he remarks, 'A comic business, church restoration'. Michael Millgate comments that Hardy's later membership of the Society for the Protection of Ancient Buildings was 'to make some restitution for those early acts of Church 'restoration' he grieved to remember in later years.'[23]

Hardy's 1895 Preface to *A Pair of Blue Eyes* loudly proclaims his sympathy for the SPAB for whom he acted in some capacity on sixteen buildings beginning with Wimborne Minster during his sojourn in that town, as revealed in a letter of October 20th 1881; the Preface begins:

> The following chapters were written when the craze for indiscriminate church-restoration had just reached the remotest nooks of western England, where the wild and tragic features of the coast had long combined in perfect harmony with the crude Gothic art of the ecclesiastical buildings scattered along it, throwing into extraordinary discord all attempts at newness there. To restore the grey carcases of a mediaevalism whose spirit had fled, seemed a not less incongruous act than to set about renovating the adjoining crags themselves. (p.389)

---

[23] Millgate, Career, p.122.

Moreover, like the prehistoric sites which Hardy knew so well in Wessex, the church graveyard in the novel had become even more indistinguishable from the landscape: 'The wild irregular enclosure was as much as ever an integral part of the old hill' (p.234). In a brief note in the *Life* (pp.93-94) about Tintern Abbey, another ecclesiastical ruin, Hardy the architect-son of a master mason gives a clue as to why he prefers the prehistoric archaeological remains which blend with the landscape to the more distinctly man-made remains of Classical or Medieval archaeology: 'But compare the age of the building with that of the marble hills from which it was drawn! ... '. He continues with a further more troubled reflection that shows the profound effect of Darwinian-geological ideas on this nineteenth century thinker: 'Here may be stated, in relation to the above words on the age of the hills, that this shortcoming of the most ancient architecture by comparison with geology was a consideration that frequently troubled Hardy's mind when measuring and drawing old Norman and other early buildings.' However, the graves at West Endelstow, such as that of young farmer Jethway, though emblems of mortality are, especially in a small community, also signs of human continuity – for tombs are built structures, whether Neolithic long barrows or Victorian slabs, and their occupants have living descendants.

At first glance, it seems that Hardy's Preface is contradicting the symbolic model of *Jude*, but it is original medieval Gothic that is to be restored, the outward expression of an outdated religious order (which Hardy feels is just what Victorian Gothic represents) – in other words, the crumbling architecture should be allowed to match the ruinous aspect of nature, dissolving back into the geology whence it came, and take its place in the long record of the past that Henry Knight sees so lividly recorded in the cliff strata. This seems the very antithesis of conservation, and one feels that he is over-egging the pudding here to make a point: perhaps a ruined church, not a non-existent one, is what is required for his purposes; but even so, the man's contradictions are exposed here by the dominance of his philosophical bias.

It is clear that without fairly radical work, such churches as St Juliot would not long have survived further neglect. The 'old tower of West Endelstow church had reached the last weeks of its existence' (p.162) and Hardy metaphorically represents the change of view in post-Darwin Victorian England – and not without some sadness, we feel – with his powerfully loaded comment that observers could climb the tower 'to enjoy for the last time the prospect seaward from the summit.' The historic shift may be inevitable, but it involves a wrench, a discontinuity that is innately disruptive when even 'the owls had forsaken this home of their forefathers'. The workers, 'six iconoclasts [a particularly astute choice of word] in white fustian', are slaves of modernism, for to them 'a cracked edifice was a species of Mumbo Jumbo'; Hardy's 'representative', Knight, is certainly not, however, for he is using his lodgings as a 'centre for antiquarian and geological excursions in the neighbourhood' (p.200). In a detail of such apparently incidental value is exposed an ambivalence about Victorian intellectual attitudes, for the newly developing sciences that were revealing the true extent of past time were in the process emphasising the relevance and value of the past, whereas the modernising, industrial tendency that could sweep away anything that stood in the way of a new railway line found a slightly different expression in the demolition of genuine medieval masonry in order to erect a fake, modern Gothic replacement to a different design. Though a fleeting comment, that reference to geology is telling, for it is on such an expedition that Knight is probably engaged when he becomes trapped on the cliff. In the midst of this perilous incident, pondering his own mortality, he recognises the geological features of what he is perforce staring at, what Andrew D. Radford calls ' ... a fan-like compression of an immensity of time.'[24]

Knight is therefore a paradoxical figure, occupied in the destruction of the ancient while pursuing an interest in it. He is thus a focus for some of the clashing, disturbing forces at work in the Victorian psyche, and in one of the most celebrated and noteworthy passages in all of Hardy's fiction, the young man might become their symbolic victim, in a moment rendered as dead as any of the multi-millennia-old fossilised creatures which confront him. Knight's serious interest in archaeology is confirmed in his travels, 'under colour of studying Continental antiquities' (p.348) (for his personal motive is the primary one and eventually he 'grew ... weary of these places'), during which 'he tried Rome [altered to the more specifically archaeological 'the Roman Forum' in later editions] ... the Plain of Marathon ... Thermopylae and Salamis ... Mars Hill [the Areopagus, as alluded to in 'In the British Museum']'. So Knight got much further than the Hardys on their continental tour: could this be Hardy hinting at an unfulfilled yearning to travel abroad again? - Perhaps not.

Ancient ruins provide an obvious commentary on the vanity of human wishes in Hardy's works, but, as I have noted of *The Mayor of Casterbridge* in particular, they also lend irony to immediate events and the characters' predicaments, as do the fossils for Henry Knight. In *The Hand of Ethelberta*, the eponymous heroine, for whom 'what was left in any shape from the past was her constant interest' (*The Hand of Ethelberta* p.235), notes that at Corvsgate Castle (Corfe Castle – Hardy calls it Coomb Castle in the original version in Penguin Classics) she might remind herself that 'the hints that perishing historical remnants afforded her of the attenuating effects of time even upon great struggles corrected the apparent scale of her own.'

The church tower, being the most badly degraded part of the building, provides *A Pair of Blue Eyes* with a continuing symbolic focus in the fact of its height. The tower represents past beauty, past certainties as well (for instance in its symbolic dominating view over the whole community and its witness to faith), but it can also stand for the future aspirations of the younger characters soon to be disappointed; again, Hardy integrates with real human sympathy the wider symbolic force of the ancient with the immediate and more transient concerns of his individual characters. Ironically, students of the limited surviving legacy of Anglo-Saxon churches (most, like all the Saxon cathedrals, were obliterated by Norman re-building) find that the tower is often the only substantial portion remaining since it was too solid and costly to be replaced – this phenomenon being evident even in such notable sites as Bede's monasteries at Jarrow and Monkwearmouth, and, ironically, in St Michael's, right in the centre of Oxford. West Endelstow's tower with its serious crack is a different case. There is no doubting the author's sub-text (even autobiographical self-mockery) in the clash of ideas between Reverend Swancourt, Elfride, and Knight in the following passage; Elfride's exclamation is worthy of the most outrageous satirist:

> A corner of the square mass swayed forward, sank, and vanished. A loud rumble followed, and a cloud of dust arose where all had previously been so clear.
>
> 'The church restorers have done it!' said Elfride. ...

---

[24] Radford, p.53.

> 'Poor old tower!' said Elfride [– expressing pain at the destruction, and Knight declares:] 'Yes, I am sorry for it ... It was an interesting piece of antiquity – a local record of local art.'
>
> (*A Pair of Blue Eyes* p.313)

The vicar, guardian of an ancient faith, speaks some of Hardy's wry humour in response: "Ah, but my dear sir, we shall have a new one,' expostulated Mr Swancourt; 'a splendid tower – designed by a first-rate London man – in the newest style of Gothic art, and full of Christian feeling. ... Oh yes. Not in the barbarous clumsy architecture of this neighbourhood; you see nothing so rough and pagan anywhere else in England." At the start of the twenty-first century, it is Swancourt's attitude to the ancient pile that seems old-fashioned and barbarous, a prejudiced taste akin to that which consigned prehistoric artefacts to the sidelines of the museums until late in Hardy's lifetime. The hybridity of styles that will result from the 'restoration' may exhibit unwelcome incongruity at the time of its completion, though for later generations it may, as with all of our cathedrals (except Salisbury which is England's sole example of medieval stylistic homogeneity), be an inherent source of charm. Hardy comments on this phenomenon in his remark in *The Hand of Ethelberta* that Enckworth Court's eighteenth-century re-building (Lychworth Court in the original version) 'had been planned with such a total disregard of association, that the very rudeness of the contrast gave an interest to the mass ...' (*The Hand of Ethelberta* p.295).

The details of Hardy's interest in the subject of preserving ancient buildings, together with a host of contemporary photographs and facsimiles of some of Hardy's letters and drawings and other material, form the subject of Claudius J.P. Beatty's fascinating book *Thomas Hardy: Conservation Architect*,[25] referred to in Chapter Five. Incidentally, as the *Life* tells us (p.419), Hardy remained a draughtsman, his last drawing being of Tintagel Castle – an archaeological site re-excavated at the end of the twentieth century, as well as an architectural one – to illustrate *The Queen of Cornwall*; Hardy had drawn an Early English altar at the site soon after his first fateful visit in 1870. Beatty's volume also reprints Hardy's address written for the SPAB in 1906, 'Memories of Church Restoration' in a variorum edition, correcting some errors in Orel's transcription of the piece. This material emphasises the mature Hardy's conservationist tendency, a notion underlined in his speech on accepting the Freedom of Dorchester from which I have already quoted.

Hardy's ambivalent nature, the forward-looking man of ideas who valued and was to an extent dominated by the past, is nowhere more clearly revealed than in his involvement with his own profession of architecture. The point is that for Hardy, conserving the traces of the human past (whether archaeological or historical) was no mere sentimentality or dilettantism, but an attempt to recognise and even celebrate the continuity of humanity and the existence, however insignificant, of the individual man or woman in the vast tracts of unrecorded and impersonal prehistory. Equally, to try to replicate the past is a falsehood or delusion, a denial of intellectual and moral progress.

---

[25] Claudius J.P. Beatty, *Thomas Hardy: Conservation Architect – His Work for the Society for the Protection of Ancient Buildings* (Dorchester: Dorset Natural History and Archaeological Society, 1995).

Bibliography

Thomas Hardy's works

Bjork, Lenart A., ed. *The Literary Notebooks of Thomas Hardy*. Gothenburg: Gothenburg UP, 1974.
Gibson, James, ed. *Thomas Hardy: The Complete Poems*. Rev. ed. Basingstoke: Palgrave, 2001.
Hardy, Thomas. *The Dynasts* and *The Queen of Cornwall*. London: Macmillan, 1931.
Hardy, Thomas. *Our Exploits at West Poley*. Oxford: OUP, 1952.
Ingham, Patricia, gen. ed. Thomas Hardy's novels. Penguin Classics Edition. London: Penguin Books. Individual volumes:
Desperate Remedies. Ed. Rimmer, Mary. 1998.
Under the Greenwood Tree. Ed.Wright, David. 1985.
A Pair of Blue Eyes. Ed. Dalziel, Pamela. 1998.
Far from the Madding Crowd. Ed. Blythe, Ronald. 1978.
The Hand of Ethelberta. Ed. Dolin, Tim. 1997.
The Return of the Native. Ed. Slade, Tony. 1999.
The Trumpet-Major. Ed. Ebbatson, Roger. 1987.
A Laodicean. Ed. Schad, John. 1997.
Two on a Tower. Ed. Shuttleworth, Sally. 1999.
The Mayor of Casterbridge. Ed. Seymour-Smith, Martin. 1978.
The Woodlanders. Ed. Gibson, James. 1986.
Tess of the d'Urbervilles. Ed. Skilton, David. 1985.
The Pursuit of the Well-Beloved and *The Well-Beloved*. Ed. Ingham, Patricia. 1997.
Jude the Obscure. Ed. Sisson, C.H. 1978.
Orel, Harold, ed. *Thomas Hardy's Personal Writings*. Wichita: Kansas UP, 1966.
Page, Norman, ed. *Thomas Hardy: The Complete Stories*. London: Dent, 1996.
Purdy R.L. and Millgate M., eds. *The Collected Letters of Thomas Hardy*. Oxford: OUP, 1978-1988.
Wain, John, ed. *Selected Shorter Poems of Thomas Hardy*. London: Macmillan, 1966.
Weber, Carl J. and Weber, Clara Carter. *Thomas Hardy's Correspondence at Max Gate: A Descriptive Check List*. Waterville, Maine: Colby College Press.
Wright, David, ed. *Thomas Hardy: Selected Poetry*. London: Penguin Books, 1978.

Thomas Hardy's life

Barber, D.F., ed. *Concerning Thomas Hardy*. London: Charles Skilton, 1968.

Beatty, Claudius J. *Thomas Hardy: Conservation Architect*. Dorchester: Dorset Natural History and Archaeological Society, 1995.
Blunden, Edmund. *Thomas Hardy*. London: Macmillan, 1951.
Draper, Jo. *Thomas Hardy: A Life in Pictures*. Wimborne: Dovecote Press, 1989.
Gittings, Robert. *Young Thomas Hardy*. London: Heinemann, 1975.
Gittings, Robert. *The Older Hardy*. London: Heinemann, 1978.
Greenslade, William, ed. *Thomas Hardy's 'Facts' Notebook: A Critical Edition*. Aldershot: Ashgate. 2004.
Hardy, Florence Emily. *The Life of Thomas Hardy*. London: Macmillan, 1962.
Millgate, Michael. *Thomas Hardy: A Biography*. Oxford: OUP, 1982.
Pinion, F.B. *Thomas Hardy: His Life and Friends*. London: Macmillan, 1992.
Pite, Ralph. *Thomas Hardy: The Guarded Life*. London: Pan Macmillan, 2006.
Seymour-Smith, Martin. *Hardy*. London: Bloomsbury, 1994.
Tomalin, Claire. *Thomas Hardy: The Time-Torn Man*. London: Viking, 2006.
Weber, Carl J. *Hardy of Wessex: His Life and Literary Career*. Rev. ed. New York: Columbia UP and London: Routledge & Kegan Paul, 1965. 1st ed. 1940.

THOMAS HARDY: COMMENTARY AND CRITICISM

Beer, Gillian. *Darwin's Plots: Evolutionary Narrative in Darwin, George Eliot and Nineteenth-Century Fiction*. London: Routledge and Kegan Paul, 1983.
Boumhela, Penny. *New Casebooks: Jude the Obscure*. London: Macmillan, 2000.
Clements, Patricia and Grindle, Juliet, eds. *The Poetry of Thomas Hardy*. London: Vision Press, 1980.
Cullen Brown, Joanna. *A Journey into Thomas Hardy's Poetry*. London: W.H. Allen, 1990.
Davie, Donald. *Thomas Hardy and British Poetry*. London: Routledge and Kegan Paul, 1973.
Davis, Philip. *Memory and Writing from Wordsworth to Lawrence*. Liverpool: Liverpool UP, 1983.
Dool, Josephine. 'Archaeology and Thomas Hardy'. Salisbury and South Wiltshire Museum. 9/12/1980.
Gatrell, Simon. *Thomas Hardy and the Proper Study of Mankind*. Charlottesville: UP of Virginia, 1993.
Gibson, James, ed. *Thomas Hardy: Interviews and Recollections*. London: Macmillan, 1999.
Gibson, James. *Thomas Hardy: A Literary Life*. London: Macmillan, 1996.
Hardy, Evelyn, *Thomas Hardy: A Critical Biography*. London: Hogarth Press, 1954.
Johnson, Trevor. *Literature in Perspective: Thomas Hardy*. London: Evans Bros, 1968.
Johnson, Lionel. *The Art of Thomas Hardy*. London: John Lane, 1895.
Kramer, Dale, ed. *Critical Approaches to the Fiction of Thomas Hardy*. London: Macmillan, 1979.
Mallett, Phillip V. and Draper, Ronald P., eds. *A Spacious Vision: Essays on Hardy*. Penzance: Patten Press, 1994.
Mallett, Phillip, ed. *The Achievement of Thomas Hardy*. London: Macmillan, 2000.
Millgate, Michael. *Thomas Hardy: His Career as a Novelist*. London: Macmillan, 1971.

Orel, Harold. 'Hardy and the Developing Science of Archaeology'. *Thomas Hardy Annual No.4*. Ed. Norman Page. London: Macmillan, 1986.
Page, Norman, ed. *Thomas Hardy: The Writer and His Background*. London: Bell and Hyman, 1980.
Paulin, Tom. *Thomas Hardy: The Poetry of Perception*. London: Macmillan, 1975.
Pinion, F. B. *A Hardy Companion*. London: Macmillan, 1968.
Radford, Andrew D. *Thomas Hardy and the Survivals of Time*. Aldershot: Ashgate, 2003.
Ray, Martin. *Thomas Hardy: A Textual Study of the Short Stories*. Aldershot: Ashgate, 1997.
Walbank, Christopher. *Authors in their Age: Thomas Hardy*. London: Blackie, 1979.
White, R.J., *Hardy and History*. Ed. James Gibson. London: Macmillan, 1974.
Widdowson, Peter. *Hardy in History: A Study in Literary Sociology*. London: Routledge, 1989.
Widdowson, Peter. *On Thomas Hardy: Late Essays and Earlier*. London: Macmillan, 1998.
Williams, Merryn. *A Preface to Thomas Hardy*. 2nd ed. London: Longman, 1993.
Wing, George. *Writers and Critics: Hardy*. London: Oliver and Boyd, 1963.
Woolf, Virginia. *The Common Reader*. Second series, 1928. London: The Hogarth Press, 1932.

Wessex locations; landscape and topography

Bradbury, Malcolm, gen. ed. *The Atlas of Literature*. London: De Agostini, 1996.
Brasnett, Hugh. *Thomas Hardy: A Pictorial Guide*. Ivychurch: John Waite, 1984.
Burke, John. *Musical Landscapes*. Exeter: Webb and Bower, 1983.
Cameron, Kenneth. *English Place-Names*. London: Batsford, 1961.
Campbell, James. *The Anglo-Saxons*. Oxford: Phaidon, 1982.
Cunliffe, Barry. *A Regional History of England: Wessex to AD 1000*. London: Longman, 1993.
Draper, Jo, ed. *Address by Lt-General A.H.L.F. Pitt-Rivers at the opening of the Dorset County Museum, 1884*. Dorchester: Dorset Natural History and Archaeological Society, 1984.
Draper, Jo. *Dorset: The Complete Guide*. Wimborne: Dovecote Press. Rev. ed. 1996.
Draper, Jo. *Thomas Hardy's England*. Introd. and ed. Fowles, John. London: Jonathan Cape, 1984.
Ekwall, Eilert. *The Concise Oxford Dictionary of English Place-Names*. Oxford: OUP, 1936.
Hawkins, Desmond. *Hardy's Wessex*. London: Macmillan, 1983.
Hoskins, W.G. *The Making of the English Landscape*. Ed. Christopher Taylor. Rev. ed. London: Hodder and Stoughton, 1988.
Hutchins, John. *The History and Antiquities of the County of Dorset*. Ed. William Shipp and James Whitworth Hodson. 3rd ed. Westminster, 1861.
Kay-Robinson, Denys. *Hardy's Wessex Reappraised*. Newton Abbott: David and Charles, 1972.
Kennedy, Michael. Notes. Adrian Boult, cond. Ralph Vaughan Williams. Symphonies 8 and 9. London Philharmonic. EMI, 1970.
Kennedy, Michael. Notes. Bernard Haitink, cond. Ralph Vaughan Williams. Symphonies 8 and 9. London philharmonic, 2001.
Lea, Herman. *Thomas Hardy's Wessex*. London: Macmillan, 1913.
Matthews, Colin. Notes. Gustav Holst. Orchestral Works. Compilation. EMI, 1988.
Moule, H.J. *Old Dorset: Chapters in the History of the County*. London: Cassell, 1893.
Pitfield, F.P. *Hardy's Wessex Locations*. Wincanton: Dorset Publishing Company, 1992.

Whitelock, Dorothy, rev. *Sweet's Anglo-Saxon Primer*. Oxford: OUP, 1967.
Whitelock, Dorothy. *The Pelican History of England: 2 – The Beginnings of English Society*. London: Penguin Books, 1952.
Winchcombe, Anna. *Hardy's Cottage*. London: The National Trust, 1994.
Wood, Michael. *In Search of the Dark Ages*. London: BBC, 1981.

Archaeology and the past

Bacon, Edward, ed. *The Great Archaeologists – and their discoveries as originally reported in the pages of The Illustrated London News*. London: Martin Secker and Warburg, 1976.
Barber, Robin. *Blue Guide Greece*. Sixth edition. London: A. and C. Black, 1995.
Bord, Janet and Colin. *A Guide to Ancient Sites in Britain*. London: Latimer New Dimensions, 1978.
Bowden, Mark. *Pitt Rivers* [sic]. Cambridge: CUP, 1991.
Brand, Vanessa, ed. *The Study of the Past in the Victorian Age*. Oxbow Monographs 73. Oxford: Oxbow, for The British Archaeological Association and The Royal Archaeological Institute, 1998.
Branigan, Keith. *Roman Britain: Life in an Imperial Province*. London: Reader's Digest Association, 1980.
Browne, Sir Thomas. *The Religio Medici and Other Writings*. Introd. Prof. C.H. Hurford. Everyman's Library no.92. London: Dent, 1906.
Charles-Pickard, Gilbert, ed. *Larousse Encyclopedia of Archaeology*. 2nd ed. London: Hamlyn, 1983.
Chippindale, Christopher. *Stonehenge Complete*. 2nd ed. London: Thames and Hudson, 1994.
Christie-Mallowan, Agatha. *Come, Tell Me How You Live*. London: Collins, 1946.
Clayton, Peter A. *A Companion to Roman Britain*. Oxford: Phaidon, 1980.
Daniel Glyn. *A Hundred Years of Archaeology*. London: Duckworth, 1950.
Daniel, Glyn. *A Short History of Archaeology*. London: Thames and Hudson, 1981.
Dool Josephine. 'Archaeology and Thomas Hardy'. Lecture, Salisbury and South Wiltshire Museum, 9/12/1980.
Dyer, James. *The Penguin Guide to Prehistoric England and Wales*. London: Penguin Books, 1982.
Fitton, J. Lesley. *The Discovery of the Greek Bronze Age*. London: British Museum Press, 1995.
Greene, Kevin. *Archaeology: An Introduction*. 3rd ed. London: Routledge, 1995.
Grinsell, Leslie V. *The Archaeology of Wessex*. London: Methuen, 1958.
Liddell and Scott. *Greek-English Lexicon*. 7th ed. London, 1897.
Macadam, Alta. *Blue Guide Florence*. 8th ed. London: A. and C. Black, 2001.
Macadam, Alta. *Blue Guide Rome*. 7th ed. London: A. and C. Black, 2000.
Macaulay, Rose and Beny, Roloff, photographer. *Pleasure of Ruins*. Rev. ed. London: Thames and Hudson, 1977.
MacGillivray, James Alexander. *Minotaur: Sir Arthur Evans and the Archaeology of the Minoan Myth*. 2000. London: Pimlico, 2001.
Muir, Richard and Welfare, Humphrey. *The National Trust Guide to Prehistoric and Roman Britain*. London: George Philip, 1983.

Newsome, David. *The Victorian World Picture*. London: John Murray, 1997.

Piggott, Stuart. *Ancient Britons and the Antiquarian Imagination*. London: Thames and Hudson, 1989.

Piggott, Stuart. 'The Early Bronze Age in Wessex'. 'Proceedings of The Prehistoric Society, no. 4'. London: The Prehistoric Society, 1938.

Pitt-Rivers, Lt-General A.H.L.F. *Address at the Opening of the Dorset County Museum*. Dorchester: Friary Press, 1984.

Pryor, Francis. 'The 'Seahenge' Phenomenon'. *Minerva*. September/October 2001. P46+.

Renfrew, Colin and Bahn, Paul. *Archaeology: Theories, Methods, and Practice*. 2nd ed. London: Thames and Hudson, 1996.

Salway, Peter. *Roman Britain*. Oxford: OUP, 1981.

Thomson, M. V. *General Pitt-Rivers*. Bradford-on-Avon: Moonraker, 1977.

Warner, Rex and Hurlimann, Martin, photographer. *Eternal Greece*. 2nd ed. London: Thames and Hudson, 1961.

Wheeler, Sir R.E. Mortimer. *Archaeology from the Earth*. 1954. London: Penguin Books, 1956.

Wheeler, Sir R.E. Mortimer. *Still Digging*. London: Michael Joseph, 1955.

Wheeler. Sir R.E. Mortimer. 'Reports of the Research Committee of the Society of Antiquaries of London. No. XII, Maiden Castle, Dorset.' London: Society of Antiquaries, 1943.

Wilson: Roger J.A. *A Guide to the Roman Remains in Britain*. 3rd ed. London: Constable, 1988.

Wood, Michael. *In Search of the Trojan War*. London: BBC, 1985.

Related modern fiction

Ackroyd, Peter. *First Light*. 1989. London: Penguin Books, 1993.

Fitzgerald, Penelope. *The Golden Child*. 1977. London: Flamingo, 1994.

Jacobson, Howard. *Peeping Tom*. 1984. London: Penguin Books, 1993.

Lively, Penelope. *Treasures of Time*. 1979. London: Penguin Books, 1986.

Murdoch, Iris. *The Philosopher's Pupil*. 1983. London: Penguin Books, 1984.

Sutcliff, Rosemary. *The Eagle of the Ninth*. Oxford: OUP, 1954.

Thorpe, Adam. *Ulverton*. 1992. London: Vintage-Random House, 1998.

Index of People and Places

Italics denote modern fictional names and places

Abbot's Cernel 96, 129-130
Abbot's Cernel, Giant's Hill 110
Abbs, Peter vi
Abel 30
Abelard 183
Achilles 16, 67
Ackroyd, Peter 2, 139, 152-153
Adam 107
Adam, Robert 18
Aegean 13, 34, 42
Aeschylus 104, 124-125
Albert (Prince) 67
Aldbrickham 199
Alexander the Great 2, 16, 149
Alexandria 135, 196
Alfred the Great 27-28, 30-34, 146
Alma-Tadema, Lawrence (Sir) 18, 53
America 54, 62
Anglebury 146
Aphrodite 133, 185
Ares 169
Argus 67
Aristotle 64
Arnold, Matthew 197
Artemis 107, 196
Ashtaroth 133
Asia Minor 16, 68
Aspasia 183
Athens vi, 115, 196
Athens, Acropolis 169-170
Athens, Areopagus 168-169, 204
Athens, Parthenon 149, 164, 170-171
Aubrey, John 21, 122-123
Auden, W. H. 158
Australia 93, 108
Avebury 21, 34, 37, 58

Avon (River) 29
Babylon 16, 149
Bacon, Edward 26
Badbury Rings 44-45, 81, 137
Bancroft, Squire (Sir) 58
Barham, Richard Harris 164
Barnes, William 13-15, 17, 30-31, 49, 58, 63, 109, 113, 124, 194
Barrie, J. M. 26, 58
Basingstoke 199
Bath 34, 178, 181,
Bathsheba 183
Beatty, Claudius 93, 205
Beer, Gillian 12, 16, 25, 117, 131, 150, 192
Bell, Moberley 58
Bencomb, Marcia 135
Bere Regis, St John's Church 100-101
Berkshire 28-29, 190-191
Bessel, Friedrich 140
Birmingham 202
Blackbarrow 144
Blackdon / Blagdon Hill 52, 136
Blandford Forum 180
Bliss, Howard 57
Blomfield, Arthur 77, 167, 189-190, 201
Blunden, Edmund 2, 5, 22, 58-60, 63, 193
Bord, Janet and Colin 80, 130
Borlase, William 3
Boucher de Perthe, Jacques 24
Boult, Adrian (Sir) 113
Bournemouth 69, 104, 144
Bowden, Mark 40
Bradbury, Malcolm 27, 30, 32
Bradley, A. G. 142
Brasnett, Hugh 137
Bridehead, Sue 192-194, 196-199

Bridport 81
Brighton Museum 50
Bristol Channel 29
Brittany 34
Brixham, Windmill Hill Cave 24
Brooks, Chris 92
Brown, 'Capability' 18
Browne, Thomas (Sir) 16-17, 23, 155
Brunel, Isambard Kingdom. 21
Budmouth 84, 132, 135, 149
Bulbarrow 105
Bunyan, John 125
Burke, John 46-47
Burton, Decimus 194
Buzzford 88
Byron 18, 23, 162, 171, 174
Caesar, Julius 65, 122, 184
Cain 30
Cambridge 188
Cambridge, Clare College 5
Camden, William 21, 46
Came Wood 56
Camelot 177
Cameron, Kenneth 29, 67
Canada 93
Cape (the) 136
Carchemish 5
Carinus 88
Carlyle, Thomas 110
Carter, Howard 15
Casterbridge 56, 62-72, 74-75, 79, 81, 83, 86-89, 146, 178
Casterbridge Museum 39, 43, 49, 200
Casterbridge, Bull Stake Square 66
Casterbridge, Cornmarket 66
Casterbridge, Durnover 68, 86, 184
Casterbridge, Jopp's Cottage 66
Casterbridge, Peter's Finger 70
Casterbridge, Priory Mill 66
Casterbridge, The King's Arms 66, 70
Casterbridge, The Ring 66, 73, 76, 80, 82-85, 179
Casterbridge, The Three Mariners 66, 70
Cerdic 162
Cerne Abbas 96, 129-130
Cerne Abbas Giant 109, 129
Cerne Abbas, Abbey Gate 130
Cerne Abbey 109
Chandler, Richard 18
Chaplin, Charlie 110
Charborough House 137
Charborough Park 137
Charborough Tower 137
Charles II 97

Charles-Pickard, Gilbert 16
Charley 155
Chaucer, Geoffrey 99, 164
Cheshire 69
Chester 86
Chichester Cathedral 102
Chickerel, Sol 144
Chippenham 21
Chippindale, Christopher 113, 116, 122-123
Chiron 67
Christie, Agatha (Christie-Mallowan) 2
Christminster 188-192, 195-196, 199-200
Church Ope 134
Church Ope, Rufus or Bow and Arrow Castle 131
Church Ope, St Andrew's Church 151
Clare, Angel 90, 93-94, 96, 98-100, 102-107, 111, 115-116, 118-122, 124-125
Clayton, Peter 80
Cleopatra 183
Clouds Hill near Moreton 4, 144
Cockerell, Sydney 3, 136, 157
Colliton House 88-89, 179
Colt Hoare, Richard (Sir) 22-23, 122
Commodus 130
Conquer Barrow 5, 52-53, 55-56, 78, 183, 185
Constable 106, 113
Constantine, Lady Viviette 181
Constantinople 135
Coomb/Corvsgate Castle 204
Cooper Willis, Irene 186
Copenhagen, Old Nordic Museum 19
Corker Marshall, Denton 115
Cornwall 28-29, 202
Cozens (Mr) 46
Cranborne Chase 40
Cranford 31
Crawford, O. G. S. 12
Creston 132
Crete 24, 42
Crick, Richard (the dairyman) 32, 108
Crickmay, George (of Weymouth) 160, 164, 190, 202
Cross-in-Hand (monolith) 112, 117
Cullen Brown, Joanna 159, 187
Cunliffe, Barry (Sir) 27, 29-30, 34, 71
Cunnington, Edward 22, 38, 45, 49-50, 54-55, 57
Cunnington, William 22-23, 122
Cybele 102
Danelaw 30
Daniel, Glyn 6, 12-13, 20, 22, 40, 45
Darby, Abraham 69
Dare, William 93, 170
Darwin, Charles 9, 24-25, 42, 65, 68, 92, 96, 183, 195, 203

Index

David (King) 183
Davie, Donald 152, 158-159, 163, 175, 186
Davis, Philip 63, 65, 84, 157-158, 161, 186-187
Dawkins, R 15
de la Lynd, Thomas 106
de Monmouth, Geoffrey 19
De Stancy, Charlotte 91
Demeter 107
Demetrius of Ephesus 133
D'Erlanger, Frederic 94
Derriman, Festus 102
Devil's Den, Clatford Bottom 37, 141-143
Devil's Door 141, 143
Devizes Museum 23
Devon 28
Diana 67
Diana Multimammia 76, 144, 185
Dickens, Charles 14
Dionysus 170, 197
Dole's Ash 108
Dollery (Mrs) 129
Dolman, Frederick 53
Donn, Arabella 184, 195
Dorchester vi, 2, 14, 23, 37, 39, 46, 50, 52, 56, 60, 62, 63, 66-72, 76-77, 79, 81-82, 83, 85, 87, 89, 95, 109, 144, 164, 166, 178, 189, 205
Dorchester (Dorset) County Museum 3, 8, 14, 21-22, 31, 39, 41, 52, 57, 61, 87-88, 179, 186, 194, 200
Dorchester, Maumbury Rings (henge and amphitheatre) 21, 39, 58-60, 63, 73-74, 82-85, 179
Dorchester, Poundbury Camp 21, 63, 73-74, 78-80
Dorchester, Shire-Hall Place 22
Dorset 22, 27-28, 31, 34, 45, 62, 68-70, 95, 110, 129, 132, 136, 162, 182, 190
Douglass, A. E. 131
Duddle Heath 144
Dunium 46-47
Dunster Castle, Somerset 93
Durbeyfield, Abraham 111, 139
Durbeyfield, Eliza Louise (Liza-Lou) 125
Durbeyfield, Jack (Tess's father) 25, 95-98, 100, 103
Durbeyfield, Joan (Tess's mother) 103
Durbeyfield, Tess 17, 90 94, 96-101, 103-111, 113, 115-116, 118, 120-125, 131, 146-147, 150, 167, 186
Dyer, James 34-35, 114-115, 124, 130, 142
East Anglia 30, 34
Eden 19, 107, 110
Edinburgh Castle 46
Edington 30
Egdon Heath 16, 19, 43, 56, 65, 71, 77, 104, 121, 126, 140, 144-152, 155, 185
Eggardon hillfort 179-180

Egypt vi
Elephanta (Temple) 189
Elgar, Edward 47
Elgin (Lord) 170
Eliot, George 31, 109
Eliot, T. S. 1, 15, 158, 195-196
Elizabeth II 83
Enckworth/Lychworth Court 205
En-nigaldi-Nannar 16
Etruria 174
Euphrates 5
Evans, Arthur 24, 36, 42
Evans, John 24, 42
Eve 107
Everdene, Bathsheba 181
Evershead 130
Exeter 69, 81, 180, 189
Fall, Damian 139
Farfrae, Donald 63, 65-66, 69-70, 72, 78-81, 86, 93, 108, 110
Fawley, Jude 98, 100, 166, 184, 189-190, 192-197, 199-201
Felkin, E. 8
Ffrangcon-Davies, Gwen 94
Fiesole (Faesulae) 173, 184
Fitton, J. Lesley 168
Fitzgerald, F. Scott 10
Fitzgerald, Penelope 2
Flintcomb-Ash 95, 105, 107-111, 118, 128
Flugelman, Barney 118
Fontover (Miss) 198
Fordington 60-61, 89, 184
Fordington Field 52, 55
Fordington Hill 55-56, 88
Fordington, St George's Church 88-89, 184
Frere, John 24
Freyja 133
Frome (River) 72, 144, 146
Frome Hill 185
Frome Valley 106, 144
Fuller, Roy 159
Gaskell, Elizabeth 31
Gatrell, Simon 72, 92, 98, 102, 105, 126, 140, 145, 192, 199
Germany 27, 46
Gibson, James 30, 32, 43, 52-53, 59, 136-138, 144
Gilmartin, Sophie 28, 62, 97, 102, 134, 192, 198
Glamorganshire 97
Gloucester 30
Gloucester Cathedral 165
Gloucestershire 29
Gordon, Alexander 20
Gosse, Edmund 191

Graves, Robert 158
Gray, Harold St George 58-59, 82
Graye, Ambrose 201
Graye, Owen 26, 201
Greece vi, 2, 7, 68, 91, 114, 121, 196
Greene, Graham 28
Greene, Kevin 19
Greenslade, William 3, 62
Greenwell, William 22
Greenwich, Royal Observatory 140
Grinsell, Leslie V. 34
Groby (Farmer) 108-109
Groby, Leicestershire 109
Guthrum 30
Hadrian (Emperor) 16-17, 53, 84, 88
Hadrian's Wall 20, 81, 181
Haitink, Bernard 113
Hambledon Hill 80, 82, 105
Hamilton, William (Sir) 18
Hampshire 28-29
Hands, Timothy 189
Hardy, Emma Lavinia (nee Gifford) (his wife) 45, 78, 158, 160-164, 171, 186-187, 189, 198
Hardy, Evelyn 3, 62-63
Hardy, Florence Emily (née Dugdale) (his wife) 2-3, 33, 52, 161, 186
Hardy, Jemima (his mother) 1, 15, 23, 160, 186
Hardy, John (his great grandfather) 15, 146, 164
Hardy, Mary (his paternal grandmother) 15, 146, 159, 190
Hardy, Thomas (Elizabethan) 95
Hardy, Thomas (his father) 68, 95, 107, 165, 188, 190
Hardy, Thomas (Sir) (Capt. Of HMS Victory) 15, 53, 95, 99, 101, 162
Harper, C. G. 33
Hartley, L. P. 126
Hawkes, Jacquetta 2, 114
Hawkins, Desmond 122, 180
Hazelbury Bryan 80
Heaney, Seamus 2, 158
Heath, F. R. And Sidney 60
Helena (of Troy) 183
Helith 130
Heloise 183
Henchard, Michael (Mayor) 63-72, 74-81, 83-88, 133, 144, 146, 161
Henchard, Susan (née Newson) (Henchard's wife) 69, 75, 78, 83-86, 88
Henderson, Thomas 140
Henniker (Mrs) 40, 84
Henry V 162
Henry VIII 20, 134, 152
Herculaneum 18

Hercules 130
Hertfordshire 95
Hicks, John 23, 164, 189-190
Higher Bockhampton 11, 14-15, 95, 150
High-Place Hall 88
High-Stoy Hill 128
Hill, Roland 13
Hogarth, D. G. 5
Holst, Gustav 47, 113, 144-145
Homer 36, 171, 197
Hood Monument, Butleigh, Somerset 137
Hope churchyard 134
Horatio (scholar-mentor) 57
Hoskins, W. G. 127, 150
Hoxne, Suffolk 24
Huett, Izz 108-109
Hughes, Ted 158
Hutchins, John 21-22, 45-46, 60, 68
Hutton, John 32
Huxley, T. H. 169
Hynes, Samuel 118
Icknield Street / Via Iceniana / Iknild Street 151, 194-195
India 93
Indies (the) 136
Ingham, Patricia 160-161
Ireland, John 46-47
Ironbridge (iron bridge over the Severn) 69
Isle of Slingers 132-133, 145, 148, 200
Italy vii, 18, 27, 39, 164, 171-172, 174-175, 196
Jacobson, Howard 118
Jael 183
James II 67, 88
James, Henry 62
Jarrow 204
Jerome 24
Jersey 95
Jerusalem 196
Johnson, Lionel 29
Johnson, Trevor 90
Joyce, James 15
Julian, Christopher 147, 168
Julian, Faith 168
Karnac, Thebes 87
Kay-Robinson, Denys 137, 142
Keats, John 18, 23, 47, 165, 169, 171-173, 197
Kegan Paul, Charles 31
Kennedy, Michael 113
Kenneri (Temple) 189
Kent 14, 29
Kepler, Johannes 24
King Duncan 65
King Lear 30, 65, 77, 121, 144

INDEX

King's Hintock 32
Kingsbere Church 101-103, 122, 167
Knight, Henry 25, 111, 168, 183, 189, 201-205
Knollsea 135
Knossos 24, 36
Lake District 109
Lambton, Lucinda vi
Lancashire 69
Laocoön 67
Larkin, Philip vi, 102, 158-159
Lawrence (Friar) 100-101
Lawrence, T. E. 4-5, 33, 53, 144, 158
Layard, Austen Henry 15
Lea, Herman vii, 33, 117, 137, 142, 148, 153, 185
Leghorn 172
Leland, John 20, 46, 132, 152
Lhwyd, Edward 21
Liddell, Henry 174
Little Father Time (Jude's child) 192, 199
Little Hintock 128-129, 131
Liveley, Penelope 2, 152
London 9, 24, 29, 36, 39, 86, 94-95, 106-107, 115, 133, 136, 142, 147, 150, 162, 168, 170, 180, 189, 198
London University 4, 25
London, British Museum 2, 4, 7, 15, 22, 24, 53, 91, 97, 102, 168-171, 173, 175, 197, 204
London, Charing Cross 70
London, Royal Hospital, Chelsea 7, 15
London, St Paul's Cathedral 133
London, the Athenaeum 22
London, Waterloo Station 95
London, Whitehall, Cenotaph 171
Long Meg and her Daughters, Cumbria 37
Lotis 106
Loveday, Miller 99
Lubbock, John (Sir) 24
Lulworth Cove 173
Luther, Martin 24
Lutyens, Edwin 171
Lyell, Charles 24
Macneices, Louis 27
Maiden Castle (Mai-Dun) 37-38, 43-49, 52, 56, 71, 73, 76, 78, 80, 82, 132
Mai-Dun 46-48, 58, 73, 78, 80
Mallowan, Max 2
Malta 93
Manston, Aeneas 132
Marathon 204
Mark Anthony 183
Marlborough Downs 141-142
Marlbury Downs 141
Marlott 103, 106, 111

Marygreen 190, 199
Marygreen Church 196, 198
Matthews, Colin 144
Max Gate 3-5, 22, 33, 39, 43, 51-53, 56, 74, 77-78, 81, 83, 94, 118, 123, 181-186, 188, 193
Melbury's homestead 131
Melchester 117, 199-200
Mellstock Hill 81, 145, 185
Mercia 190, 199
Mercury 45
Mereweather, John (Dean) 22
Middle East 4
Middlemarch 31, 109
Middleton Abbey 110
Midlands (the) 69, 70
Miele, Chris 93
Miller, Arthur 65
Millgate, Michael 5, 8, 12, 15, 20, 22, 28, 30-32, 49-50, 54, 61-62, 70, 84, 95, 106-107, 121, 125, 133, 135, 140, 149, 176, 188, 191, 202
Mills, Bill 143
Milne, James 3
Milton Abbas 109
Milton, John 110, 125, 197
Minerva 45, 67
Monet 128
Monkwearmouth 204
Moule, Henry (Revd) 56, 88, 184
Moule, Henry J. 39, 43, 45, 56-57, 194
Moule, Horace 15, 17-18, 43, 57, 192, 194
Mount Pleasant 52
Mountclere (young) 144
Muir, Richard 45, 72, 124
Murdoch, Iris 2
Mycenae 36, 114
Nabonidus 16
Naples 94
Naples, Bay of 172
Napoleon 129, 177
Nebuchadnezzar 16
Nennius 117
Neptune 61
Newsome, David 14, 26
Newson, Elizabeth-Jane 67, 78, 80, 83, 86, 88
Newson, Richard 70, 80
Newton, Isaac (Sir) 20
Nimrud 15
Nine Barrows (near Corfe Castle) 143
Nine Stones circle, Winterbourne Abbas 177, 180
Nine-Barrow Down 143
Nineveh 168
Norfolk 34
Normandy 97

North Wales 119
Nunsuch, Susan 148
Nuttlebury 80
Oak, Gabriel 71, 139, 150
Oedipus 65, 104, 149
Offa's Dyke 20
Old Melchester 168
Old Sarum 116, 168
Oldfield, E. 14
Orel, Harold 10-11, 23-24, 40, 42, 54, 56-60, 205
Othello 65
Ovid 67
Oxford 18, 31, 188, 190
Oxford, Jesus College 4
Oxford, Pitt Rivers' Museum 41
Oxford, Radcliffe Infirmary 190
Oxford, St Michael's Church 190, 204
Oxfordshire 29, 191, 199
Oxwell Hall 102
Paphos, Cyprus 185
Paris 128, 149
Paris (of Troy) 183
Parr, William 18
Paul (St) 168-169, 197
Paulin, Tom 26, 133, 159, 164, 173, 186-187, 189, 194
Pausanias 171
Pengelly, William 24
Pentney, Josephine (née Dool) 10-11, 42, 45, 52, 61
Percomb (barber) 128-129
Pericles 183
Perkins, T. (Revd) 3
Peter (St) 122
Peterson, Carla L. 196-197
Petherwin, Ethelberta 143-144, 146-147
Petra 5, 174
Petrie, Flinders 4, 39, 41-42, 170, 194
Pheidias 149, 170
Phillotson, Richard 192-193, 197
Pierston, Jocelyn 133-135
Piggott, Stuart 20, 34
Pinion, F. B. 67, 93
Pitfield, Fred 32-33, 137
Pitt-Rivers, Augustus Lane-Fox (General) 4, 15, 20-22, 38-42, 48-49, 52, 54, 56-59, 130, 140, 170, 194
Pompeii 18
Pope, Alexander 36
Port-Bredy 81
Portland, Isle of 132-135, 145, 176-177, 200
Postumus 88
Pouncy, W. 48
Pound, Ezra 158
Power, John 90-91

Power, Paula 90-91, 93
Preseli Mountains 114, 117
Prestwich, Joseph 24
Priapus 106
Priestley, J. B. 2, 114
Proctor, Richard, A.. 138
Pryor, Francis 12
Ptolemy, Claudius 46-47
Quiller-Couch, Arthur (Sir) 157
Radford, Andrew. D. 4-5, 21, 40, 49, 64, 66, 112-113, 117, 121, 132-133, 200, 204
Rainbarrow(s) 15, 38, 81, 94, 136, 144-146, 148-153, 155, 185-186, 192
Ramesses II 170, 173
Ray, Martin 32, 42, 48-51, 142
Reading 199
Reading Museum 2
Red King's Castle 134
Reece, Richard 81
Revett, Nicholas 18
Rider Haggard, H. 69
Ridgeway (Ridge-way) 80, 178, 189, 194
Rings-Hill (Weatherby Castle) near Milbourne St Andrew 137
Robin, Fanny 81, 102, 158
Robinson, Roger 13, 63, 65, 96, 104, 112, 149, 163, 184
Rogers, Samuel 172
Rome (Romae) 18, 72, 83, 134, 172-174, 181, 196, 204
Rome, Caligula's Palace, Palatine Hill 174
Rome, Colosseum (the) (Coliseum) 59-60, 83, 125, 172, 174
Rome, Pyramid of Cestius 137, 165, 171, 173
Said, Edward 192
Salamis 204
Salisbury 113, 116-117, 119, 199, 205
Salisbury Cathedral 112, 189, 200
Salisbury Museum 10
Salisbury Plain 22, 113-114, 119
Sandbourne 104-105, 146-147
Sandsfoot Castle 134
Sassoon, Siegfried 5, 53, 57, 158
Satchel, (Old) Andrey 129
Scandinavia 19
Schlesinger, John 56
Schliemann, Heinrich 3, 15-16, 25, 36, 54
Scott, George Gilbert 198
Scott, Robert 174
Seymour-Smith, Martin 82
Shaftesbury 192
Shaston 192
Shelley, Percy 18, 23, 165, 171-174, 187

INDEX

Sherborne Abbey 164, 166
Shorter, Clement King 48
Shottsford 110
Silbury Hill 21, 37
Silchester, Hants. 87-88
Sinai 5
Sisera 183
Smith, Stephen 83, 189, 202
Solomon's Temple 172
Somerset 28, 181
Somerset, George 91, 93, 201
Somme 24
Sophocles 104
Sorrow (baby) 117
South Africa 140
South, Marty 128
Spain 91
St Cleeve, Swithin 138-140, 150, 153, 181
St Juliot, Cornwall 160, 164, 190-191, 198-199, 202-203
St Pancras churchyard 78, 102, 190, 198
Stancy Castle 90, 93, 168
Stoke d'Urberville, Alec 91, 94, 96-99, 103-104, 111, 122, 130-131, 147, 167
Stoke-Barehills 199
Stoke-on-Trent 97
Stonehenge 1, 3-4, 21, 34, 36-37, 39, 57-58, 66, 78, 85, 90, 92, 94-96, 100-101, 104, 106-107, 111-125, 143, 152, 177, 180, 192, 194, 201
Stourton Tower 177
Struve, F. G. W. 140
Stuart, James 18
Stukeley, William 21, 23, 122-124, 142
Suffolk 24, 34
Sul 181
Surrey 29
Sussex 29, 62
Sutcliff, Rosemary 2
Sutton Hoo 143
Swanage 135
Swancourt, Christopher (Revd) 198, 202, 204-205
Swancourt, Elfride 204-205
Sweet, Blanche 94
Swinburne, Algernon 197-198
Syria 2
Tacitus 122
Talbothays Dairy 95, 103, 105-108, 110, 118, 122
Taylor, Christopher 127
Taylor, Richard H. 28, 62
Temple Sowerby, Cumbria 81
Templeman, Lucetta 70-71, 80-82, 84, 86, 88
Tennyson, Alfred (Lord) 14, 162
Thames 29, 191, 199

Thermopylae 204
Theseus 2
Thomas, Dylan 158
Thomas, Ronald Stuart 158
Thomsen, Christian 19
Thomson, M. W. 40
Thornycroft, Hamo (Sir) 33
Thorpe, Adam 2, 152
Tintagel 205
Tintern Abbey 203
Tivoli 175
Tomalin, Claire 3, 9
Tonbridge Priory, Kent 14
Trantridge 98, 103, 106
Trendle (conjuror) 19
Tringham (Parson) 19-20, 25, 94-98, 102-103
Troy 16, 36, 54
Troy, Francis (Frank) 181
Troyton, Charlotte (later Charlotte Swancourt) (Mrs) 202
Tull, Jethro 70
Turner, J. M. W. 94, 106, 113
Tutankhamun 15
Ur 15-16
Ussher (Archbishop) 24
Vale of Blakemoor / Blackmoor 105-106, 128
Vale of the Great Dairies 106
Vatican 175
Vaughan Williams, Ralph 113
Vaughan, W. 14
Venice 12, 172
Venus 133, 198
Vespasian 45, 48, 162
Vesuvius 19
Via Appia Antica 172
Vincy, Fred 109
Vindolanda, Northumberland 81
Virgil 197
Vye (Captain) (earlier Drew) 135, 149
Vye, Eustacia 93, 104, 149-150, 153, 155
Wain, John 157-158
Wainwright, Geoffrey 52
Wantage, Berkshire 190
Warborne 136
Wardour Old Castle 193-194
Wareham 146-147
Warne, Charles 22
Warner, Rex 171
Waterloo 15
Watling Street 82
Watt, James 69
Weber, Carl, J. 26, 57, 102, 168, 172
Webster, John 62

Wedgwood, Josiah 23
Weismann, August 96
WelbyPugin, Augustus 92
Welfare, Humphrey 45, 72, 124
Welland Park 137
Wellington (Duke of) 7
Wessex 1, 8, 10, 17-18, 21, 26-34, 36-37, 39-40, 43, 45, 47, 54, 57-58, 62, 66, 68, 70-71, 74-75, 80-81, 90, 106, 108-110, 115, 119, 126, 132, 136, 142, 150, 166, 171-172, 175-177, 180-181, 185, 190-193, 195-196, 199, 202-203
Wessex (Earl of) 32
Wessex, Countess of (Rhys-Jones, Sophie) 31
Wessex, Lower 28
Wessex, Mid- 28, 142
Wessex, North 28, 190-192, 199, 202
Wessex, Outer 28
Wessex, South 28, 132
Wessex, Upper 28
West Country 29, 114
West Endelstow 198, 203-204
West Kennet Long Barrow 75
West Poley (Mendip cave) 19
Wetherall, David 13
Weymouth 15, 21, 84, 132, 189
Wheeler, Mortimer (Sir) 4, 11, 16, 20, 25, 44-46, 54, 56, 60, 89, 132, 154
White, R. J. 7, 13, 15, 63, 106, 152
Whitelock, Dorothy 29
Whittle, Abel 30
Widdowson, Peter 14
Wildeve, Damon 104, 110, 149-150
Williams, Merryn 158
Wilson, Daniel 24
Wilson, R. J. A. 86
Wiltshire 180
Wimborne 21, 136
Wimborne Minster 166-167, 202
Winchester 31, 33, 124
Winckelmann, Johann 18
Windle, B. C. A. 33
Winfrith nuclear power station 144
Wing, George 28, 192
Winterbourne St Martin 46
Winterbourne, Giles 71, 102
Winton 165
Wintoncester 121, 124
Wood, Michael 30
Wood, Robert 18
Woolf, Virginia 15, 126
Woolley, Leonard 5, 15-16
Wordsworth, William 37, 102, 109, 119-121, 127, 158

Worsaae, Jens 19
Wright, David 157
Wright, Joseph (of Derby) 123
Wygmore (Abbot) 165
Yeobright, Clym 93, 98, 100, 132, 139, 150, 152-156
York 86, 181